LOVES, LIES, AND TEARS

Loves, Lies, and Tears

The Lives of America's First Ladies

Volume II

Ellen Wilson to Jacqueline Kennedy

1913–1963

Jacqueline Berger

ROSERITA BOOKS, INC.

Published by Roserita Books, Inc.

Books are available at special discounts when purchased in bulk for premiums and sales promotions, as well as for fundraising or educational uses. Special editions or book excerpts can be created to customer specifications. For details and further information contact:

Special Sales Director
Roserita Press
Roserita Books, Inc.
1534 N. Moorpark Rd., #228
Thousand Oaks, CA 91360-5129
Phone: (805) 497-8994
Email: firstladies.lady@verizon.net
www.FirstLadiesLady.com

For information or to book events contact the Special Sales Director, above.

A special thank-you to the Library of Congress for providing the photographs.

Library of Congress Control Number: 2010918373

Cataloging-in-Publication Data

Berger, Jacqueline
Loves, lies, and tears : the lives of America's first ladies, volume II :
Ellen Wilson to Jacqueline Kennedy 1913-1963
p. cm.
Includes biographical references and index
1. Presidents' spouses-United States-Biography. 2. Presidents' spouses-United States-History. 3. Presidents' spouses-United States-Social life and customs.
I. Title

E176.2 B47 973.099 v.2 2010918373

ISBN 978-0-9817041-1-1(v2)
ISBN 978-0-9817041-0-4(v1)

Cover design and interior layout by Lisa Hochstein
Copyediting by Catherine Viel

Printed in the United States of America

FIRST PRINTING: FEBRUARY 2011

10 9 8 7 6 5 4 3 2 1

Dedicated to my sister Lynda,
one of the most courageous women I know.
You inspire me to be a better person.

Contents

Part Four: Women of World War II

Part Five: Woman of Distinction

Acknowledgments

AS ANYONE WHO HAS EVER written a nonfiction book knows, countless hours of solitary writing, research, and contemplation go into its development. The process is lengthy, daunting, and literally takes years to achieve. At different times over this extensive period, I periodically found it necessary to hide in seclusion from all outside distractions. It can be a lonely, isolating, and painstaking progression. But that is not to say one does it alone. Quite the opposite; many people are involved in the evolution of a project this size and *only* because of *those* individuals is Volume II of *Loves, Lies, and Tears* a reality.

Words alone are inadequate to express my sincere gratitude for all of their assistance, support, and understanding. It has been a blessing to work with a team of extraordinarily talented women, all of whom share a high level of professionalism and a good deal of patience. I have been away from school for a long time and must admit this new English is akin to the new math. I don't understand either one very well. To that end, I want to thank my editor Catherine Viel for her impressive expertise, skill at stating things succinctly, incredible sense of humor, and never-ending endorsement. She has taught me a great deal and helped me overcome my fear of the Microsoft Word police.

My sincere appreciation to Lisa Hochstein for her wonderful cover design and creative input, and Angela Howard for her indexing skills. I would also like to acknowledge and apologize to Rita Rotenberg (may she rest in peace), whose name was inadvertently misspelled in the acknowledgements of Volume I, for graciously reading and rereading the original manuscript. Thank you also to Robyn Blachman for her eagle eye notations in Volume II.

To my children, Eric and Lauren Berger, Andrea and Rob Mettel, and my grandchildren Rachel, Jeremy, Jake, and Ryan, for their continual support and encouragement, I love you—always and forever.

For repeatedly putting my needs above her own, I once again extend my heartfelt gratitude to Barb Renee, my dear friend and associate. Her input and marketing expertise have been invaluable! To give of herself so graciously, for as long as she has, and receive only an occasional yogurt or even less frequent slice of pizza for compensation, she has truly been an angel from heaven.

Finally and most decidedly, I want to express my deepest indebtedness to my husband Bruce (even more so than for Volume I, because in the beginning we were both naïve as to the process and commitment involved in a project of this magnitude). However, after all of the pitfalls, obstacles, and consequences of Volume I, we moved forward with a clearer understanding of the numerous drawbacks and stumbling blocks involved in producing Volume II. Although his sacrifices increased measurably, his love and support never wavered. If not for his backing, *Love, Lies, and Tears, Volume II,* would still be an unrealized dream.

Last but certainly not least, I would again like to extend my deepest, heartfelt gratitude to the First Ladies of the United States, intrepid women who take on one of the most *difficult, unpaid* and sometimes *unappreciated* jobs in the world. I offer my sincere appreciation to the many historians and biographers who have shared their dedicated research and knowledge of these women. The list could go on for pages; however, here are just a few of the scholars whom I highly respect and whose writings I recommend: Carl Sferrazza Anthony, Betty Boyd Caroli, Bill Harris, Robert Watson, Edith Mayo, Dorothy and Carl Schneider, Blanche Wiesen Cook, Margaret Truman, Doris Kearns Goodwin, Michael Beschloss, and David McCullough.

A very special thank-you to each and every one of you.

Introduction

In Volume I of *Loves, Lies, and Tears* (Martha Washington to Helen Taft), I shared my motivation for writing this multibiography and the genesis of my fascination with America's First Ladies. My passion for this unique group of brave and notable women began in 1963 and has only increased over time. Their dignity, compassion, and strength are truly inspirational, and their hardships, predicaments, and personal tragedies provide enormously important life lessons.

To have attempted to distill the stories of all forty-plus First Ladies into one volume could have diminished their importance and impact. Instead, I elected to continue my journey with America's First Ladies here in Volume II and in the future Volume III, giving this remarkable sorority of women the consideration that is their due.

Here you will find stories of commonplace wives and mothers who during the course of their lives loved deeply, encountered deceit, and experienced heart-wrenching sadness. They were ordinary women with dissimilar backgrounds, diverse personalities, and varying financial and educational circumstances who lived extraordinary lives that included memorable tenures in the White House. That is the one common thread running through this group: they lived in what I like to refer to as a goldfish bowl made of magnifying glass. This common denominator means that the loves, lies, and tears of the First Ladies' lives will be scrutinized for generations to come.

When we left off in Volume I, the United States had battled, grown, and developed its way from a cluster of thirteen separate colonies to a world power, a feat enabled by the patriotic First Ladies who supported their brave presidential husbands. The accounts of the incredible women who helped shape an entire country with a new and experimental government—democracy—provide the backstory from which we launch into the present volume.

Volume II of *Loves, Lies, and Tears* (Ellen Wilson to Jacqueline Kennedy) covers the life stories of nine amazing women. As democracy and the United States face world conflict, Ellen Wilson is the initial First Lady to exercise her power. Then her White House death leaves her devastated presidential spouse to face World War I alone. Ellen's passing opens the door to the second Mrs. Wilson, Edith Galt, a woman with minimal formal education, who many believe ran the country in the aftermath of President Woodrow Wilson's debilitating stroke.

Following the First World War, Florence Harding, who began her adulthood as an unwed pregnant teenager, moves into the Executive Mansion. After years of enduring her husband's continual infidelity, the First Lady is suspected of killing the man generally acknowledged to be the country's most inept president, Warren G. Harding.

Vice President Calvin Coolidge, otherwise known as Silent Cal, succeeds to the presidency. Although his wife, the always smiling and congenial Grace Coolidge, is unsuccessful in teaching her taciturn husband polite social skills, she is exceptionally popular with the American public. Life deals a bitter blow less than a year into her tenure when the former teacher to the deaf endures the painful death of her sixteen-year-old son.

During the country's most devastating economic depression, a wealthy, intelligent, and charitable extrovert by the name of Lou Hoover occupies the presidential mansion. Her fascinating world travels (much aided by her astounding linguistic skills) are fully explored. The story of Lou's equally wealthy and well-traveled successor, Eleanor Roosevelt, is recounted in detail, as is Eleanor's early traumatic childhood, her sexuality, and her many achievements.

When Bess Truman reluctantly enters the White House, she is terrified her family secret will be exposed. She manages to keep her personal life private, including a later mastectomy, and today most people would feel only compassion for the shame she experienced.

By the time Mamie Eisenhower, the picture-perfect 1950s housewife, moves into the mansion, it has undergone a total reconstruction and overhaul. Despite ongoing rumors of presidential infidelity (even a television movie depicting the alleged affair), Mamie maintains that her five-star-general spouse was loyal to both his country and to her.

Volume II of *Loves, Lies, and Tears* ends with Jacqueline Kennedy, a young, sophisticated debutante who captures the world's curiosity and remains the target of ruthless paparazzi thirty years after her husband's assassination.

All these are true stories, even though some could be mistaken for the plot of a romantic novel. I invite you to open the doors of the White House with me and explore the compelling, moving, and illustrious lives of the women who occupied its storied rooms from 1913 to 1963.

For those who are familiar with the inspiring and sometimes tragic lives of the first twenty-seven women who served as First Ladies, can you identify just a handful of the women found in Volume I of *Loves, Lies, and Tears*?

> Which First Lady–elect was depicted in the newspapers as a whore and an adulterer, only to die two months before her husband's presidential inauguration?
>
> Which First Lady married the widowed sitting president who was thirty years her senior?
>
> Which First Lady pushed her reluctant husband into the presidency, only to suffer a stroke two months after becoming First Lady?

These and over a dozen more stories may be enjoyed in the pages of Volume I of *Loves, Lies, and Tears: Martha Washington to Helen Taft (1789–1913).*

A Chronology of America's First Ladies

VOLUME I
MARTHA WASHINGTON TO HELEN TAFT, 1789–1913

First Lady	Presidential Spouse	Tenure
1) Martha Washington	George Washington	1789–1797
2) Abigail Adams	John Adams	1797–1801
3) Martha Jefferson*	Thomas Jefferson	1801–1809
4) Dolley Madison	James Madison	1809–1817
5) Elizabeth Monroe	James Monroe	1817–1825
6) Louisa Adams	John Quincy Adams	1825–1829
7) Rachel Jackson*	Andrew Jackson	1825–1837
8) Hannah Van Buren*	Martin Van Buren	1837–1841
9) Anna Harrison*	William Henry Harrison	1841–1841
10) Letitia Tyler	John Tyler	1841–1842
Julia Tyler	John Tyler	1844–1845
11) Sarah Polk	James K. Polk	1845–1849
12) Margaret Taylor	Zachary Taylor	1849–1850
13) Abigail Fillmore	Millard Fillmore	1850–1853
14) Jane Pierce	Franklin Pierce	1853–1857
15) Harriet Lane (niece)	James Buchanan	1857–1861
16) Mary Todd Lincoln	Abraham Lincoln	1861–1865
17) Eliza Johnson	Andrew Johnson	1865–1869
18) Julia Grant	Ulysses S. Grant	1869–1877
19) Lucy Hayes	Rutherford B. Hayes	1877–1881
20) Lucretia Garfield	James Garfield	1881–1881
21) Ellen Arthur*	Chester Arthur	1881–1885
22) Frances Cleveland**	Grover Cleveland	1886–1889
23) Caroline Harrison	Benjamin Harrison	1889–1893
24) Frances Cleveland	Grover Cleveland	1893–1897
25) Ida McKinley	William McKinley	1897–1901
26) Edith Roosevelt	Theodore Roosevelt	1901–1909
27) Helen Taft	William Taft	1909–1913

* Five First Ladies never occupied the White House.

** Though President Cleveland's tenure began in 1885, he married Frances Cleveland the following year.

VOLUME II
ELLEN WILSON TO JACQUELINE KENNEDY, 1913–1963

First Lady	Presidential Spouse	Tenure
28) Ellen Wilson	Woodrow Wilson	1913–1914
Edith Wilson	Woodrow Wilson	1915–1921
29) Florence Harding	Warren Harding	1921–1923
30) Grace Coolidge	Calvin Coolidge	1923–1929
31) Lou Hoover	Herbert Hoover	1929–1933
32) Eleanor Roosevelt	Franklin D. Roosevelt	1933–1945
33) Bess Truman	Harry Truman	1945–1953
34) Mamie Eisenhower	Dwight D. Eisenhower	1953–1961
35) Jacqueline Kennedy	John F. Kennedy	1961–1963

VOLUME III
LADY BIRD JOHNSON TO LAURA BUSH, 1963–2009

First Lady	Presidential Spouse	Tenure
36) Lady Bird Johnson	Lyndon B. Johnson	1963–1969
37) Pat Nixon	Richard Nixon	1969–1974
38) Betty Ford	Gerald Ford	1974–1977
39) Rosalynn Carter	Jimmy Carter	1977–1981
40) Nancy Reagan	Ronald Reagan	1981–1989
41) Barbara Bush	George Herbert Bush	1989–1993
42) Hillary Clinton	William Clinton	1993–2001
43) Laura Bush	George W. Bush	2001–2009

PART ONE

WOMEN OF WORLD WAR I

INTRODUCTION

WARS HAVE EXISTED throughout the centuries and, despite the tragic devastation and destruction they cause, will likely continue forevermore. Conflicts waged on American soil include the American Revolution (1775–1783), the Indian Wars (1811–1890),* the War of 1812 (1812–1815), the Mexican-American War (1846–1848), the Civil War (1861–1865), the Spanish-American War (1898), and various whiskey, tax, and slave rebellions. By 1914, larger-scale hostilities had become far more global; with America now on the world stage, despite diligent efforts to maintain neutrality, the United States was facing its First World War, also known as the Great War.

World War I obliterated four empires (Austro-Hungarian, Ottoman, Russian, and German) and significantly changed the map of Europe. In addition to over nine million soldiers who lost their lives, millions of civilians died as well. After three hundred years, Europe no longer dominated the world.

For nearly a quarter of a millennium, America's commanders in chief have borne the burdens and anguish of war from the same house.† That exclusive residence became a kind of sorority home for America's First Ladies. It bonds a selective group of women in a way no other dwelling is capable of doing. The Chief Executive Mansion is the only home in America that, as long as the Union

* The Indian Wars were a series of wars between cultures dating back to the 1600s. Between 1811 and 1890, major conflicts included the Battle of Tippecanoe, the Black Hawk War, the Sioux Wars, three Seminole Wars, the Battle of Little Bighorn, and finally the Wounded Knee Massacre in 1890, which at last brought hostilities to a halt.

† George Washington is the only exception, as the White House was constructed after his tenure.

stands, is guaranteed to stand as well, sustaining its presidents and First Families in historical splendor.

When the United States entered World War I in 1917, the White House had already celebrated its one hundredth birthday and welcomed in a new century. Extensively reconstructed after the War of 1812, the Executive Mansion has been renovated, repaired, modernized, and redecorated repeatedly throughout its long history.

President John Adams went so far as to wish a prayer on the mansion. His words are engraved on a mantel in the State Dining Room:

> I pray heaven to bestow the best of blessings on this house and all that shall hereafter inhabit it. May none but honest and wise men ever rule under this roof.[1]

Considering the inevitability of war and its consequences, leadership, foresight, and education are all important attributes for the nation's Chief Executive. Up to this time, the Executive Mansion had been home to eighteen attorneys,* five military leaders,† a tailor, a teacher, and a writer,‡ along with their spouses and family members. How *wise* these men may have been is a debate for presidential historians. Nonetheless, many of them were considered exceedingly intelligent and although not all attended college,§ a handful were educated at some of the country's finest and most highly respected universities.

John Adams, his son John Q. Adams, and Theodore Roosevelt (who graduated magna cum laude) all graduated from Harvard.** Thomas Jefferson, James Monroe, and John Tyler graduated from the College of William and Mary. James Madison received his diploma from Princeton and William Taft graduated second in his class from Yale.††

* Adams, Jefferson, Madison, Monroe, J. Q. Adams, Van Buren, Tyler, Polk, Fillmore, Pierce, Buchanan, Lincoln, Hayes, Arthur, Cleveland, B. Harrison, McKinley, and Taft.

† Washington, Jackson, Wm. Harrison, Taylor, and Grant.

‡ A. Johnson, Garfield, and T. Roosevelt.

§ Washington, Jackson, Van Buren, Taylor, Fillmore, Lincoln, A. Johnson, Cleveland, and future president Truman did not attend college. In the twenty-first century, it is highly unlikely any individual will be elected to the presidency without a college degree.

** As did future presidents F. Roosevelt and Kennedy.

†† As did future presidents G. Bush Sr. and G.W. Bush Jr.

None of the above, however, had earned a Ph.D. in political science. That distinction goes to only one man, an individual initially believed to be a slow learner because he did not read until the age of nine.[2] This slow starter is America's only president who majored in history and government in college. Originally a professor, then president of Princeton University, he wrote his 333-page thesis on Congressional Government. It was published in 1884 and ran for fifteen editions. The author of that thesis was Woodrow Wilson, the country's twenty-eighth president and the Chief Executive who occupied the White House as the United States teetered on the brink of, became involved in, and helped end the War to End All Wars.

In August of 1914, Ellen Wilson, wife, mother, and Woodrow Wilson's devoted partner of twenty-nine years, was dying in the White House. Ellen was unaware that her passing would leave her devastated and lonely husband exceedingly vulnerable during one of the most crucial times in American history. Her final struggle was all the more difficult, not because a world war was pending, but because Congress had not yet passed a piece of legislation Ellen passionately supported. Having seen the squalor and unsanitary, substandard housing conditions that surrounded the nation's capitol, Ellen was the first presidential spouse to exercise the power of her position. She sponsored legislation (known as the Alley Bill) to improve the living conditions of impoverished blacks and Washington's most disadvantaged citizens.

President Wilson, like his early predecessor John Tyler, found living in the White House after his wife's death virtually unbearable. But the president once again found love and remarried, introducing Edith Galt Wilson to the history books. Many believed Edith, a woman with minimal formal education, earned the title of America's First Woman President.

The extraordinary stories of the two First Ladies who occupied the White House during World War I open Volume II of *Loves, Lies, and Tears*.

1

Advocate for the Impoverished

ELLEN WILSON

> I wonder how anyone who reaches middle age can bear it, if she can not feel, on looking back, that whatever mistakes she has made, she has on the whole lived for others and not herself.
>
> —Ellen Wilson

Born the eldest daughter of a Presbyterian minister and the granddaughter of two ministers (both maternal and paternal), Ellen Axson Wilson was affectionately referred to as "An Angel in the White House" by the staff of the Executive Mansion. Although she was a remarkably passionate and caring woman, with significant artistic ability, Ellen's brief tenure as First Lady was unfortunately overshadowed by other historical events.

#28A Ellen Axson Wilson

Born: May 15, 1860

Birthplace: Savannah, Georgia

Married: 1885 (Woodrow Wilson)

Children: 3

White House Years: 1913–1914

Died: August 6, 1914 (54 years old)

Fact: Third First Lady to pass away in the White House

AKA: An Angel in the White House; Elly-Lou

During her not-quite eighteen months in the White House, Ellen's achievements were remarkable. She was largely responsible for the creation and passing of the Alley Dwelling Bill, which had an enormous impact on the welfare of Washington's poorest citizens. She campaigned and lobbied Congress for this legislation to improve housing for poor and black slum dwellers after visiting their squalid living conditions in the capital city with the chairwoman of the National Civic Federation. Ellen took an interest in child labor laws and the treatment of the mentally ill; she was also responsible for improving sanitary conditions for hundreds of women working in federal government agencies.

When she redecorated the Executive Mansion, the First Lady put her purchasing power to good use, buying hand-woven products made by poor Southern women living in the Appalachian Mountains. Ellen purchased these goods from the Southern Industrial Educational Association, single-handedly creating an interest in and developing a market for these products.

Furthermore, during her tenure the White House experienced a historic renovation as well when the roof was raised to add five more bedrooms and two bathrooms on the third floor. (This renovation originated with an insightful suggestion to Ellen from her immediate predecessor, Helen Taft.) By installing a skylight in the White House attic, Ellen created a well-lit studio where she could continue her painting.

Ellen Louise, or Elly-Lou as she was known to her family, was the original Martha Stewart of her day. With her soft, southern Savannah drawl, gentle manner, and gracious hospitality, Ellen was a brilliant homemaker, from cooking delicious meals to decorating her surroundings both inside and out. She sewed beautiful clothing and designed a stained glass window for the president's home. (The inscription reads, "The human good is the activity of the soul in accordance with virtue."[1]) The First Lady also planned and oversaw the creation, elaborate layout, and landscape renovation of the White House Rose Garden. It remains today an elegant picturesque background setting behind the Oval Office. Perhaps her greatest coup was in the spring of 1913, when she presided over forty-one receptions with six hundred guests at each one. The First Lady was ably assisted by her cousin Belle Hagnar, whom Ellen hired as her social secretary.

It is an absolute wonder how Ellen had time to plan, within six months of one another, two of her three daughters' White House weddings.* (Her eldest daughter, Margaret, wanted to pursue a career and never married.) Middle daughter Jessie was engaged to Francis Bowes Sayre, a lawyer from the New York district attorney's office. In

* Margaret Woodrow Wilson (1886–1944), Jessie Woodrow Wilson [Sayre] (1887–1933), Eleanor (Nellie) Randolph Wilson [McAddo] (1889–1967).

a ceremony similar in size and scope to those for presidential daughters Nellie Grant and Alice Roosevelt, Jessie was married before five hundred guests in the grand East Room.

The wedding was planned for a Tuesday (because the couple met on a Tuesday) in the fall of 1913. It was an elaborate affair that almost did not occur. Before the ceremony, the groom went outdoors for a walk. When he returned to the Executive Mansion, Frank (as he was called) discovered he had neither a wedding invitation nor an admission ticket with him. The captain of the police guard was called in and it was quite some time before Frank could convince White House security that he was in fact the bridegroom!

When it came to maintaining anonymity, Mr. Sayre was not alone. On an earlier occasion two of the Wilson girls, Margaret and Eleanor, boarded a city tour bus posing as visiting sightseers. When they drove past the White House, Margaret managed to go unrecognized when she inquired, "Oh mister, can't we go in? I want to see where the Wilson girls sleep."[2] The irony was twofold, as both daughters closely resembled their father!

Around this same time, youngest daughter Eleanor fell madly in love with Secretary of the Treasury William McAdoo, twenty-six years her senior and a widowed grandfather with six children of his own. Eleanor, who would gain a stepdaughter her own age, had a small family wedding in the Blue Room.

Despite Ellen's compassionate and active concern for others, this exceptional, creative, and gifted woman, whose multiple talents ranged well beyond homemaking expertise, is frequently overlooked by history. Yet there was so much more to this "angel's" life.

Ellen had years of domestic as well as high-level hostessing experience before arriving in Washington. Prior to residing in the White House, she was hostess of the governor's mansion in New Jersey for two years while her husband was governor. That was the only political experience either she or Woodrow had before entering the White House (unless you count academic politics!). In less than two and a half years, Woodrow Wilson rose from private citizen who never held public office to president of the United States.

Woodrow (whose given name was Thomas Woodrow) was recruited for the presidency after eight years as president of Princeton University in New Jersey, where he had initially served as a professor. At Princeton, the Wilsons had an opportunity to get acquainted with former president Grover Cleveland and his wife Frances, who lived in the area. Compassionate in dealing with the presidential couple's pain, the Wilsons attended the Clevelands' eldest daughter's funeral when Baby Ruth passed away.*

Always the scholarly intellectual, Woodrow was attracted to government and history. He began to write historical and political texts as well as essays on American government; he ultimately published fourteen books. Ellen assisted her husband by researching material and later reviewing and reconstructing his political speeches. With the idea of going into public service, he obtained a law degree. However, finding the work of law boring and not as well-paying as he'd like, Woodrow elected to pursue an academic career, which intrigued him and provided a steady income.

Even though she was busy raising their three young daughters, Ellen oftentimes provided a home for other family members as well. Daughter Eleanor recalled miscellaneous relatives living with them during most of her years growing up. This is completely understandable once you know Ellen's background.

Ellen was tutored at home by her mother, Margaret Hoyt Axson, prior to attending and graduating from Rome Female College (which was really more of a glorified high school than a true college) in Georgia, at sixteen years old. Well-read and intelligent, after graduating from Rome College Ellen took postgraduate studies in German, French, political science, philosophy, and art.

Enjoying and possessing a particular talent in art, as a teenager, Ellen won a bronze medal for her freehand drawing. Her small crayon portraits were so good she was able to earn money by selling them. It was a time in her life when Ellen's father, Samuel Axson, described

* The unique and tragic story of Baby Ruth can be found in Volume I of *Loves, Lies, and Tears*.

her as "entirely too much inclined to have her own opinions."

A petite young woman (about five feet three inches tall), Ellen had coppery-bronze hair usually worn in a pompadour style, dark, deep-set eyes, and soft feminine features in a cherubic face. Warm-hearted and apparently without a jealous bone in her body, Ellen dreamt of pursuing her artistic talent. Those dreams were crushed, though, when Ellen's mother passed away shortly after giving birth to Ellen's youngest brother.

Close-knit and cohesive, the family all pitched in to help. Twenty-one-year-old Ellen took on the bulk of the family responsibilities, however, which included caring for her two younger siblings. Experiencing so much grief from the loss of his wife, Reverend Axson was ultimately said to have had a nervous breakdown. An additional drain on Ellen, both physically and emotionally, occurred when her father was committed to an insane asylum. Some believe he caused his own death there in 1884, two weeks after Ellen's twenty-fourth birthday. Ellen and her younger brothers then went to live with their paternal grandparents.

Ellen's grandparents talked with her about going off to achieve her dream of becoming a professional artist, using the small inheritance left by Reverend Axson. Oh, if life were only that simple. Prior to her father's passing, Ellen had already met a young attorney by the name of Woodrow Wilson. They were introduced in church when Wilson came to hear her father preach. Coincidentally, both of their fathers were Presbyterian ministers. Woodrow immediately fell head over heels in love with her and Ellen soon accepted his proposal of marriage; however, both understood a wedding would have to wait.

To begin with, Woodrow was not yet in a position to support a wife, and Ellen still felt a strong responsibility to stay with her brothers. After some time, Ellen's grandparents convinced her to enroll at the Art Student's League in New York City for professional training. On her way, Ellen stopped to meet Woodrow's parents in North Carolina before she established herself at the school.

In New York, Ellen studied painting and art. On Sundays, she went to the local city mission to teach African-American children. At the same time, Woodrow stayed in Savannah and worked hard at earning a living and saving money. The two were undeniably in love and corresponded regularly.

About a year later, Woodrow unexpectedly received an offer to teach at the Bryn Mawr College for women in Pennsylvania, at an annual salary of $1,500.*[3] Never particularly interested in teaching women solely, nonetheless, it was an opportunity to provide for a family and Woodrow accepted. At twenty-five, Ellen unhesitatingly gave up her dream and returned home to get married.

The bride designed her own wedding dress, and before her minister grandfather and Woodrow's father, the couple exchanged vows in the groom's parents' home. Four months later Ellen was pregnant with her first daughter. (She would have two more daughters within the next three years.) Now turning all of her ambition and attention toward her husband and his career, Ellen believed:

> It would not be a sacrifice to die for you [Woodrow]. How can it then be one to live for you?[4]

Woodrow told Ellen,

> My love for you released my real personality, and I can never express it perfectly in either act or word away from you and your immediate inspiration.[5]

Ellen, the consummate homemaker, kept a warm and welcoming home that was always open to family, well above and beyond Sunday evening meals. Several relatives lived in the Wilson home at various times, including Ellen's two brothers and a female cousin. Not only the heart and nucleus of the family, Ellen was also the stabilizing force in Woodrow's life. He grew exceedingly dependent on his spouse, the only person who could alleviate his periodic interludes of gloom.

While Ellen gave up what could have been a highly successful professional painting career for the sake of her spouse—she excelled

* Twenty-eight years later (1913), President Wilson's annual salary was $75,000 plus $25,000 for travel expenses.

at both portraiture and landscape painting—she never gave up painting itself. In fact, at age twenty-nine Ellen put on a one-woman show in New York and sold over twenty-five paintings. Throughout her entire adult life, she continued to paint and sell her work, donating the proceeds to charity.

The family moved from Pennsylvania to Connecticut so Woodrow could become a professor of history at Wesleyan University (and eventually at Princeton University*), and Ellen's life was happily structured around her husband and family. She homeschooled her daughters, including their religious lessons; made their clothes; and repeatedly opened her home to several relatives. In addition to being involved in charity work, Ellen engaged in an active social life with the university faculty. When Woodrow was elected president of Princeton, her duties escalated to include overseeing the chancellor's mansion and the extensive entertaining that accompanied Woodrow's position.

It has been said that Woodrow was the type of husband who required not only companionship but an audience. According to his daughter Eleanor, Wilson had a "delicious sense of fun and mischief." He enjoyed attractive, intelligent women and befriended several. Wilson treated women and men equally in friendship, seeing no difference between a male friend and a female friend. After Wilson's intensive correspondence with one woman (a certain Mrs. Peck) came to light, Ellen was compelled to express her view regarding her husband's various friendships with women. Without any apparent resentment Ellen simply stated,

> These women had the wit and charm [I] lacked and it was therefore really [my] duty to provide [Woodrow] with their friendship.[6]

It was during this same period of time in 1905 that Ellen experienced a heart-wrenching personal loss. Her brother Eddie, his wife, and their baby drowned. Their deaths brought Ellen considerable sorrow. One relative said of her, "She has a tragic capacity for suffering and being still about it."[7] Ellen later wrote,

* Woodrow had earned a Ph.D. in history and political science from Johns Hopkins University.

> I used to think that it didn't matter if you gave way if no one knew. Now I know that every time you let yourself go weakens you. I have not dared to give way a minute.[8]

Academic life led to the governor's mansion, which in turn led Ellen and Woodrow to the Executive Mansion. Throughout the entire journey, she maintained her own personal opinions, which did not always reflect those of her spouse. Although Ellen believed in women's suffrage, her husband did not, and Ellen made the decision to remain publicly silent on the topic. This discretion is very common among First Ladies, who are quick to discover how to carefully maneuver around emotion-laden political issues.

Once they reached the White House, the Wilsons immediately put their unique stamp on things. As an example of just how practical the new president was, Wilson canceled his inaugural ball because he believed it to be an unnecessary expense. Instead, the family dined alone in the state dining room and later watched a fireworks display from the White House windows.[9]

Admitting she was "naturally the most un-ambitious of women and life in the White House has no attractions for me," Ellen was still the first president's wife to exercise the power of her position. She advocated social change, with a passion to improve the quality of life for others.

Her fervor to improve housing conditions for poor and black families did not go unnoticed in political circles. Secretary of State William Jennings Bryan once spoke in support of the First Lady's efforts, saying,

> As crowded as my days are, I feel that if the wife of the president can find time out of her busy days to be here and work for this cause, I can too.[10]

Eleanor Roosevelt, the wife of the assistant secretary of the navy at that time, also took notice and filed away Ellen's example for future reference. Eleanor recognized the influence and force a First Lady can have, and years later after her husband became president she followed

Ellen's lead by advocating her own causes. Other future first ladies also followed Ellen's example of advocacy.

With her focus directed away from herself, Ellen was originally unaware of the seriousness of her physical condition, which deteriorated after she had a nasty fall in March 1914. She frequently felt tired and unwell, but assumed she was experiencing problems related to exhaustion.

By the summer of 1914, however, Ellen realized just how grave the state of her health was. She was diagnosed with Bright's disease; at that time, there was no cure for this fatal kidney ailment. As fate would have it, three months after daughter Eleanor's wedding and three days after the start of World War I, Ellen no longer had the strength to fight the debilitating illness.

Unaware of the war's imminence, Ellen told her husband, "I would go away more peacefully if my Alley Bill was passed by Congress."[11] Fighting his own despondence and despair, Woodrow had rarely left his wife's side. Meanwhile, the president immediately had his secretary deliver the First Lady's comment to Capitol Hill, and he doubtless added his support to the bill.

With compassion and genuine empathy for the First Family, the Senate rushed approval of the legislation's passing. Ellen received word that her Alley Bill had in fact passed approval, giving her some internal comfort. After learning of her triumph, true to her essence, she was thinking of her husband. Reportedly her final words before losing consciousness were spoken to the president's good friend and physician, Dr. Cary Grayson: "If I go away, promise me that you will take good care of my husband."[12]

When Ellen passed away at fifty-four years old (August 6, 1914), her husband and three daughters were at her side. Jessie, who married just nine months earlier, was pregnant with Ellen's first grandchild. The weeping president was said to have cried out, "Oh my God, what am I going to do?"[13] His anguish was evident and severe. Ellen, always a gracious Southern lady, was buried with her parents in Rome, Georgia.*

* Ellen Wilson was the third sitting president's wife to pass away in the White House. Letitia Tyler was the first (she died in 1842) and Caroline Harrison died in 1892. Both of their stories can be found in Volume I of *Loves, Lies, and Tears.*

After everything the First Lady accomplished both in and outside of the White House, sadly, she will eternally be eclipsed by her husband's second wife. Considering Ellen's lack of ego, I would suspect that just knowing her Alley Bill had passed Congress would be sufficient for her to rest in peace. Unfortunately, however, World War I intervened and the improvement of Washington's slums went unaddressed.

WHAT ELLEN TAUGHT ME

Ellen Axson Wilson, born in 1860 (the same year Georgia seceded from the Union), was very much a woman of her times and environment. Moreover, she was a lady who knew herself well and understood her personal needs. Despite her gifted and proficient artistic talent, Ellen unashamedly defined her very soul by the love she gave to and received from her husband.

Here is a very small sampling from Ellen's love letters to her spouse:

> I love you as my own soul. (1884)[14]
>
> I could not love anyone whom I did not admire and look up to and believe in wholly. (May 12, 1885)[15]
>
> You lavish upon me such delicious praise. Surely there was never such a lover before and even after all these years it seems almost too good to be true that you are my lover. All I can say in return is that I love you as you deserve to be loved—as much as you can possibly want to be loved. (August 27, 1902)[16]

Eleven years later, in 1913, Ellen again wrote to Woodrow:

> I idolize you—love you till it hurts.[17]
>
> I love you, my dear in every way you would wish to be loved—deeply, tenderly, devotedly, passionately.[18]

Woodrow's letters included these passages:

> It would be hard to say in what part of my life and character you have not been a supreme and beneficent influence. You are all-powerful in my development.[19]
>
> I have found [in you] what I need more than wealth or power or opportunity.[20]

With that said, Ellen also had solid feelings regarding women's potential. Never forsaking her abilities or well-defined persona, Ellen integrated her gifts into her personal world. Her lesson to me is best stated in her own words. Ellen believed no one should "rest on the laurels of another person. [Each] must grow to the limits of...[his or her] own spirit, mind and ability."[21]

2

First Woman Co-President

EDITH WILSON

Down inside me, I knew I could, and would, go to the end of the world with or for him [Woodrow Wilson].

—Edith Wilson

Edith Galt could hardly believe it. *How could this possibly happen?* she wondered. At any time she would have been embarrassed by her faux pas; on today of all days, though, she was particularly mortified. She was a meticulous dresser who wore designer creations, predominately from exclusive couturier Worth of Paris, and would never allow herself to be seen in muddy shoes.

#28B Edith Bolling Galt Wilson

Born: October 15, 1872

Birthplace: Wytheville, Virginia

Married: 1896 (Norman Galt; died)
1915 (Woodrow Wilson)

Children: None

White House Years: 1915–1921

Died: December 28, 1961 (89 years old)

Fact: Ninth generation direct descendant of Indian princess Pocahontas

AKA: America's First Woman President

But she found herself sporting exactly that footwear—on the second floor of the White House, no less! Of all the places in the world, on that one fateful afternoon in March of 1915, at that precise time, Edith found herself standing toe to toe with the president of the United States.

She'd been invited to tea at 1600 Pennsylvania Avenue, after a muddy walk in the park with her friend Helen Bones, the Chief Executive's cousin, who had been living in the Executive Mansion for some time. Helen had initially moved in to assist First Lady Ellen Wilson with her many responsibilities; however, after the First Lady's death, she stayed on to lend her presence and support to her very depressed presidential cousin, who was still in mourning.

Helen and Edith met and became friends some years before, and stayed close after Helen moved to the White House. They often drove to Rock Creek Park where they would go for walks, then end their visits back at Edith's Washington home for tea. This particular afternoon, Helen pleaded with Edith to come to the White House for tea instead, at least this one time.

"Oh, I couldn't do that," Edith replied, "my shoes are a sight, and I should be taken for a tramp."[1] Working to convince her proper, self-conscious friend that all would be well, Helen assured Edith that President Wilson was out golfing and absolutely no one, least of all the man himself, would see her shoes.

As fate would have it, returning home early from golf, the president and his good friend (and personal physician) Dr. Cary Grayson walked around the corner just as the two women stepped off the elevator. Dr. Grayson and Edith happened to know one another, and after Helen made a polite introduction to the president, Helen felt obligated to invite the gentlemen for tea.* Although very embarrassed, Edith naturally seconded the invitation. Delighted to accept, the president first excused himself to change out of his *muddy* golf shoes before joining them!

Shoes turned out to be a pleasant icebreaker, and since Edith was wearing a smart black suit, all was not lost in the fashion department. Wilson was immediately captivated with Mrs. Edith Galt, a forty-four-year-old widow. Although Edith turned down the president's dinner invitation for that evening, she did agree to come back. Soon thereafter, Edith was regularly dining in the White House and accompanying the president on automobile rides, a common pastime before the television was invented.

President Wilson had always enjoyed the company of witty women, particularly those who laughed at his jokes. Edith not only enjoyed the president's sense of humor, they both came from the South and shared many stories of common interest with one another.

Almost immediately the two were exchanging frequent letters (another common occurrence for the times, as writing was considered

* In fact it was Dr. Grayson who had introduced Edith to Helen. The doctor was courting and later married Alice Gertrude Gordon, a surrogate daughter to Edith.

the well-mannered form of courtship), hand-carried by a messenger. The president eventually had a phone installed in Edith's home with a direct line into the White House. They communicated freely and often, talking about everything in their lives, learning a great deal about each other in an exceedingly short time.

The president was intrigued to discover that this attentive, buxom woman, some five feet nine inches tall with very dark hair, a full round face, and violet-blue eyes, was a ninth-generation direct descendant of Pocahontas, the Indian princess. Furthermore, Edith was related to Martha Washington, Thomas Jefferson, and Letitia Tyler, either by blood or through marriage.*[2] The various connections were not nearly so surprising when the president learned that Edith's father, William Bolling, came from a very old and well-established Virginia family.

Sixteen years the president's junior, Edith confessed that older men had always been attracted to her. Norman Galt, her first husband, had been nine years her senior. Even though she was not in love with him, after a four-year courtship, Edith agreed to marry the gentleman. She described her marriage to a man with whom she shared a "close and delightful friendship" as a happy one.[3]

Edith's only child, a son, died very shortly after birth. Unable to have children after that, she spent her time enjoying the theater and opera, and traveled in luxury to Europe several times during her twelve-year marriage. Norman had inherited Galts, his family's one-hundred-year-old, well-known, and prosperous Washington silver and jewelry business, allowing the couple to live well. When he had passed away, seven years earlier, Norman had left the financially well-established company to his wife. Although not involved in the day-to-day workings, Edith administered the business until she eventually sold it to some longtime employees.

There was not much doubt that Edith was well off financially. She was the only woman in Washington in 1904 who owned and drove an elegant electric coupe around town. With glass windows and upholstered interior, the vehicle brought Edith some minor distinction.

* Three Virginians all linked to the White House, whose stories can be found in Volume I of *Loves, Lies, and Tears.*

Her prominence was ironic, because Washington was a political city and just about anyone of notoriety (positive or otherwise) was involved in politics. Not so with Edith. According to her own admission,

> [I had] little interest in whoever might be President of the United States. Permanent residents of Washington, who are not in politics, are likely to acquire that rather unusual state of mind.[4]

Edith had a sister-in-law who couldn't understand such a casual attitude toward politics and traveled a great distance just to watch the Democratic inauguration in 1913.* According to Edith,

> [I told my sister-in-law] I was going to stay quietly at home; that I had seen both McKinley's and [Theodore] Roosevelt's Inaugurations, and that they were all alike.[5]

On another occasion, this same sister-in-law managed to get an invitation, including one guest, to meet the president at the White House, "simply because she had worked for him during the campaign and was an ardent admirer." When she told Edith, "I will take you," Edith's indifferent answer was,

> I have lived in Washington seventeen years and never been inside the White House. Why should I bother a tired, busy man to shake hands with me?...Of course I will take you down [to the mansion], and ride round the block while you go in.[6]

Personally, I found that response astonishing! But apparently Edith did not possess even enough curiosity to see the inside of the Executive Mansion. In addition to never having expressed the slightest interest in political affairs, she had no knowledge of the subject...until she met Woodrow Wilson.

* Wilson was only the second Democrat in forty-two years to be elected president after the Civil War. Grover Cleveland was the first. Presidents Grant, Hayes, Garfield, Arthur, Benjamin Harrison, McKinley, Theodore Roosevelt, and Taft were all Republicans. (Democratic Vice President Andrew Johnson, who ran on the Republican ticket with President Abraham Lincoln, succeeded to the presidency; he was never elected.)

The president was smitten from the minute he met Edith, clad in her muddy shoes (which the White House staff had immediately rectified); his correspondence to her showed a passionate love affair. Within two months of meeting and merely nine months after his wife Ellen's death, the president proposed. Thunderstruck, Edith could only reply,

> Oh, you can't love me, for you don't really know me; and it is less than a year since your wife died.[7]

When they finally had a chance to be alone for the very first time, the two talked privately for over an hour. While the conversation was personal, history did record the president's brilliant and memorable response.

> Yes, I know...But, little girl [an absurd form of address!], in this place time is not measured by weeks, or months, or years, but by deep human experiences...and the period of time since Ellen's death was a lifetime of loneliness.[8]

In her book, *My Memoir,* Edith explained that if she needed to say yes or no immediately, the answer would have to be no. That being the case, as it would be impossible for the president to court Edith at her home, she would have to continue to see him around his schedule, in the company of others. As much as the president wanted to protect her, gossip was inevitable and the burden would be on her. They agreed that despite the public glare, they were entitled to continue their friendship.

Edith acknowledged that she was playing with fire, as she understood Wilson was not a man willing to wait very long. She admitted,

> Of course, there is a glamour around the man as President...and the flattering assurance he stresses that he needs the help I could give him in so many ways.[9]

Then again, Edith was sure she was right to give herself time to really know her own heart.

Over the next several months, the president discussed *everything* with Edith. They arranged their drives together, but only when Helen or Margaret (the president's unmarried daughter) could go with them, and limited sharing dinner or tea together in the White House to avoid stirring up more gossip. Their almost daily correspondence continued, however. Edith admitted to Wilson,

> Much as I enjoy your delicious love letters…I believe I enjoy even more the ones in which you tell me what you are working on…for then I feel I am sharing your work and being taken into partnership, as it were.[10]

She went on to write in her memoir,

> Together [we] read the latest dispatches sent from Washington, from Europe, from Mexico, from everywhere. The President would clarify each problem for me, and outline the way he planned to meet it.[11]

The president not only trusted Edith implicitly, he desperately needed her and was noticeably in love with her as well. By summer, Edith also knew she no longer had any doubts about her love for Woodrow. Her only remaining hesitation dealt with assuming all the responsibilities the White House brought with it.

Edith told Woodrow that if he were defeated for reelection that coming November, she would marry him. She also admitted to a certain amount of "stubborn pride" when it came to the outside world. Edith wanted it understood that "it was the man and not the president she loved and honored."[12]

In the midst of the president's personal emotional struggles, the War to End All Wars was destroying empires. The 1914 assassination of Archduke Franz Ferdinand, successor to the Austrian throne, was the beginning of several conflicts. In addition to those conflicts and disparities, far more complicated causes regarding militarism and democracy combined to ignite the Great War.

With World War I intensifying in Europe on top of all his other administrative obligations, duties, and responsibilities, the president wanted Edith by his side constantly. The best way he could accomplish that was to always include her in his daily state of affairs, communications and decisions: he had the most important state papers, briefings, and consultations sent to her daily. Edith wrote,

> In this way I followed day by day every phase of the mosaic which he was shaping into a pattern of statecraft, and we continued this partnership of thought and comradeship unbroken to the last day of his life.[13]

Edith was no longer simply a companion; she had accepted Wilson's marriage proposal and now, in addition to being his fiancée, she had ascended to become the president's confidant, consultant, and ultimately his guardian. Considering their vastly contrasting educational backgrounds, it was a high compliment to the woman he called "little girl." Wilson was a professor with a Ph.D. in political science, while Edith's education was rather informal and limited. She received some instruction from her father and paternal grandmother. Only occasionally did her family hire a tutor, and at fifteen, Edith attended Martha Washington College, a girls' finishing school, for one year. Then at seventeen, her formal education ended after one year at the fashionable Powell girls' school in Richmond, Virginia.

Though her father, William Bolling, was a lawyer and later a judge, Edith grew up seventh in a family of eleven children, which meant both the family's finances and living conditions were rather restricted. Mr. Bolling was a plantation and slave owner prior to the Civil War. As happened with so many other families, the Bollings' property was ravaged and pillaged beyond repair. Edith was born and raised, along with her numerous siblings and various impoverished relatives, in a small shabby house her paternal grandfather used as a Confederate hospital in rural Wytheville, Virginia.

Her Southern mother, Sally White Bolling, was a timid and gentle woman who deferred all decisions to her husband. She spent every waking moment caring for her large family and feeding countless visitors. In addition to all of her domestic responsibilities—cooking, cleaning, embroidering, and so on—Sally, along with Edith's paternal grandmother, "made nearly everything we all wore." Delighted to help her children with French or music, Sally was unable to assist them with arithmetic or algebra as she "never bothered with figures."[14] As was typical for the times, Edith was taught to idolize the men in her life, beginning with her father, whom she cherished. Woodrow would now feel Edith's worship.

The president confided in his son-in-law (and secretary of the treasury), William McAdoo, and his foreign affairs advisor, Colonel Edward House, about his clandestine engagement to the woman he was completely in love with. But the two men designed a strategy to sabotage Wilson's plans because they were convinced an engagement would hurt the president politically. In a nutshell, they schemed to embarrass the president out of marrying.

McAdoo told the Chief Executive that a certain Mrs. Peck threatened to expose "their romance" if the president married Edith. While Wilson was president of Princeton and still married to his first wife, he had shared what could have been construed as a romantic relationship with Mrs. Mary Hulbert Peck, a divorcée. In fact, the "relationship" consisted of warm, sensitive, and demonstrative letters, nothing more. Historians seem to agree that the two only participated in a rousing friendship. Furthermore, scholar Margaret Bassett contends that Ellen Wilson was always present during any of their encounters.[15]

Not willing to expose Edith to the inevitability of malicious, spiteful gossip, the president sent his good friend Dr. Grayson to explain the state of affairs to his sweetheart, and relieve Edith from their engagement. After sleeping on the news of this noble gesture, Edith made her decision.

> I will stand by you—not for duty, not for honor—but for love—trusting[,] protecting, comprehending love.[16]

With strong resolve, Edith would stand by her man and face the gossipy scandal.

The president was ebullient. Acting like a teenager in love, he would kick up his heels, clown around, and sing the popular tune "Oh, you beautiful doll! You great big beautiful doll!" The wedding, set to be held in Edith's home on December 18, 1915, was unanimously approved of by Wilson's three daughters before a formal announcement was made. As anticipated, some people criticized the widowed president for marrying so quickly. On the other hand, the engaged couple was also greeted by cheering crowds of supporters.

Ike Hoover, chief usher for the White House, was in charge of all the wedding details. It was a small, simple, and dignified ceremony, with approximately fifty close friends and relatives in attendance. Two ministers (Episcopalian for Edith and Presbyterian for Woodrow) were called on to perform the vows, and Edith's mother, Sally Bolling, gave away the bride (Judge Bolling had passed away sixteen years earlier).* In a black velvet gown, with a matching wide-brimmed black beaver hat, forty-four-year-old Edith Galt, the third woman to wed a sitting president, married fifty-nine-year-old Woodrow Wilson.†

Confirming the old adage that you can turn a corner and meet your fate, all three of these presidential marriages proved to be happy, with loving, devoted, and protective wives. Edith's social secretary, Edith Benham, complimented the couple a few years later when she noted in her diary,

> The more I am with the Wilsons, the more I am struck by their unrivaled home life. I have never dreamed such sweetness and love could be.[17]

The new First Lady had no intention of upsetting the existing White House applecart. She neither hired nor fired any staff, and completely arranged her schedule around her husband. Before long, Edith established herself as a guardian of sorts for him. When Edith determined that the Chief Executive needed more rest, she would often ask visitors to kindly return at another time. It quickly became

* Sally Bolling survived her new son-in-law by one year.

† Julia Gardiner Tyler was the first in 1844; Frances Folsom Cleveland was the second in1886. Both of their stories can be found in Volume I of *Loves, Lies, and Tears*.

apparent to all that, unless you had an appointment, the First Lady determined whether or not you could see the president.

As far as Edith was concerned, her primary role was to anticipate and provide for her husband's every need. In return, the president showered his bride with absolute desire and unmitigated love. Edith's essence of femininity was defined by her passion to be loved and needed, as well as her appearance and taste in clothing, but life outside the White House was viewed very differently by many American females. More and more women were seeking personal identity, fairness, and equality.

The women's suffrage movement was in full force, and supporters frequently picketed the White House, denouncing the president's chauvinistic attitude. The First Lady loathed suffragists, wished they would stop harassing her husband, and called them unladylike.

Ironically, over four decades earlier (the same year Edith was born), Susan B. Anthony and other feminists were arrested for trying to vote in the presidential election of 1872, which eventually paved the way for Edith to vote. At this time, the First Lady could perhaps protect her husband, but she was not yet able to cast a vote for him. It would be another five years before the Nineteenth Amendment to the Constitution was ratified, giving all women in the United States the right to vote, in August 1920.*

Other global and national stumbling blocks, together with further achievements, occurred the year Edith married. In New York, Alexander Graham Bell placed the first transcontinental telephone call to Thomas Watson in San Francisco, and Ford produced its one millionth car. After two steps forward in the suffragist realm the country took one step back when Margaret Sanger was jailed for supporting birth control after she published *Family Limitation*.

Meanwhile, a German U-boat (a type of submarine) torpedoed and sank the British ocean liner *Lusitania*, with 123 Americans aboard. With casualties now hitting home, more Americans began to support the United States entering the war. Holding on to neutrality with great restraint, President Wilson declared America had too much pride to fight.

* Jeanette Rankin was the first female member of Congress. She actually achieved the recognition in 1916, as her home state of Montana had ratified the amendment years earlier, before other states adopted the same philosophy.

> There is such a thing as a man being too proud to fight. There is such a thing as a nation being so right that it does not need to convince others by force that it is right.[18]

He also demanded an end to the attacks on passenger ships...which Germany complied with.

As the 1916 presidential election approached, the president's mind remained absorbed in the grave dangers imposed by the war. He recognized the adverse effects the nation would face during the last four months of his tenure if he were not reelected, for other countries would view U.S. foreign policy with uncertainty if Wilson were viewed as the rejected spokesman of the country.

To prevent this potential problem, the president intended to immediately resign if he lost his reelection campaign. (When the president and vice president are no longer capable or available to serve, the secretary of state [the country's third highest rank] temporarily assumes command.) Wilson's vice president had already agreed to resign, if and when the president did. Wilson now needed his secretary of state, Robert Lansing, to also consent to this plan. Two days before the election, the president wrote Lansing for permission to invite Wilson's presidential opponent to accept Lansing's position *if* Wilson lost the election. By temporarily accepting the position of secretary of state, the newly elected president would now succeed and officially be in charge, before his actual inauguration. The letter was written only as a courtesy, and would be moot if Wilson won.

But these preparations were unnecessary. With the slogan "He kept us out of the War!" President Wilson was elected to his second term, and both the vice president and secretary of state maintained their tenures as well. Five months later, after Germany attacked and sank three American merchant ships, the United States declared war against Germany and formally entered into World War I.

Like presidential wives before and after her, Edith did her part to support American troops. She passed out sandwiches and sewed clothing for the Red Cross. All White House entertaining was suspended, and Edith spent time naming and christening ships that were going into battle.

The White House observed meatless Mondays and wheatless Tuesdays, joining the sacrifices of all American households. The First Lady purchased no new clothing, and when gasless Sundays were initiated, the couple's pleasure drives also came to an end. In what would now be seen as an ecologically smart move, sheep became the mansion's new form of lawnmowers, and their wool was sold to benefit the Salvation Army.

Above everything else, Edith continued to make her husband a priority. She monitored his sleeping, exercise, and interruptions to his schedule, in addition to ensuring that he engaged in vital recreation. Even when the president went to play golf (the First Lady occasionally played as well), she would accompany her husband and work on mail in the car.

Edith was equally involved in her husband's daily work. There was nothing too classified or confidential for the president to discuss with his wife; she was aware of every element of the armistice negotiations. As he typed his correspondence, she would read his notes to him. Most telling, Edith was the only individual other than the president who could decode high security messages between him and his foreign affairs advisor.

Early in 1918, the president outlined his famous Fourteen Points for world peace as well as an agreement to develop the League of Nations. When the Versailles peace conference convened in Europe at the end of that same year, the president was determined to personally attend. There was no question about it: when Wilson sailed to France, the First Lady would be at his side.

Edith sat in on many of her husband's sixteen-to-eighteen-hour meetings during the prolonged peace conference. The six months of stressful, taxing arguments and negotiations took its damaging toll on the president. Finally, at the end of June 1919, a peace treaty was completed. Returning to the United States on the SS *George Washington,* both Edith and Dr. Grayson were concerned for the president's health. Edith looked forward to some rest and relaxation back at home, unaware of the equally grueling and punishing battle the president would face with the U.S. Senate.

Even with the president's emotional and eloquent persuasiveness, the debate to approve the Treaty of Versailles was a battle he could never win with his government's legislature. Convinced he could rally the American people to force the treaty and the League of Nations through the Senate, the president decided to take his case directly to the public.

Wilson had been experiencing devastating and blinding headaches; even in light of his deteriorating health, Edith could not dissuade her husband from taking his crusade directly to the people. Intensely mindful that he sent American troops into war to die, the president said,

> I feel it is my duty, and my own health is not to be considered when the future peace and security of the world are at stake. I promised our soldiers, when I asked them to take up arms, that it was a war to end wars; and if I do not do all in my power to put the Treaty in effect, I will be a slacker and never able to look those boys in the eye. I must go.[19]

The approval of the League of Nations—his concept for world peace—was the core heartbeat sustaining the Chief Executive.

Living in a railroad car, traveling from city to city making daily passionate appeals for his position while still attending endless meetings and official conferences, the president soldiered on until his body could fight no more. Twenty-two days and forty speeches later, on September 19, 1919, the president called out to his wife at 11:30 that night. Edith documented the following:

> I realized that we were facing something terrible. That night was the longest and most heartbreaking of my life. Nothing the Doctor could do gave relief.[20]

She went on to say:

> The dear face opposite me was drawn and lined; and as I sat there watching the dawn break slowly I felt that life would never be the same; that some thing had broken inside me; and from that hour on I would have to wear a mask—not only to the public but to the

> one I loved best in the world; for he must never know how ill he was, and I must carry on.[21]

It was imperative the trip be suspended. Dr. Grayson explained to the president that any other action could bring disastrous, even fatal consequences. Still the president replied, "No, no, no. I must keep on." It was the First Lady who finally convinced her husband that the fight was over and so was the tour. Edith wrote, "[It was] the hardest task that has fallen to my lot."[22] The presidential train then sped nonstop back to Washington, D.C., but the damage had already begun.

Days after returning to the White House, the president's condition had not improved. Then one night, Edith found her unconscious husband on the bathroom floor, blind in one eye, his speech distorted and half his face drawn downward. Without notifying the White House staff, Edith immediately contacted Dr. Grayson at his home; he came without delay. The president had suffered a stroke that paralyzed the entire left side of his body. When Wilson regained consciousness, he was able to convey his thoughts along with his fears. He wanted no one to know of his health condition, as he was convinced the League of Nations would never get approved if the politicians and public knew of his circumstances. Edith immediately cut off everyone: all White House staff, personnel, cabinet members, even the vice president, were denied access to her husband.

The only individuals permitted in the personal family quarters were various specialists and nurses attending to the president. According to Edith, Dr. Francis Dercum, Dr. Sterling Ruffin, and Admiral E. R. Stitt of the Naval Medical Corps indicated the president's brain was "as clear as ever" and there was "every reason to think recovery possible" —*if* the president were free from all "disturbing problems." One doctor went on to say, "[The president's] nerves are crying out for rest." Rest being the operative word—undisturbed, anxiety-free, and peaceful rest.[23]

Dr. Grayson, too, was confident that the president had maintained his mental capacity; however, he feared if the president were removed from office, he would have nothing further to live for. The only battle Wilson cared about, and his greatest incentive to recover, was to get his League of Nations approved.

Edith put her husband's health above the country:

> Woodrow Wilson was first my beloved husband whose life I was trying to save...after that he was the President of the United States.[24]

The First Lady made a conscious decision to save her spouse. That meant keeping the president in office and allowing his body to mend.

> So began my stewardship. I studied every paper, sent from the different Secretaries or Senators, and tried to digest and present in tabloid form the things that, despite my vigilance, had to go to the President.[25]

For weeks on end, Dr. Grayson gave deliberately vague statements to the press regarding the president's condition. The First Lady continued to insist that any matter requiring the president's attention had to go through her. She prevented all access to her husband; the items she deemed less important were put aside for later consideration.

Irrefutably, Edith had an awareness and perception of her husband's political positions and points of view. Therefore, after discussing the most important situations with her spouse, Edith was confident she could convey his opinions accurately.

Since no one was allowed to see or speak to the president, Washington gossip soon concluded the Chief Executive was mentally incompetent. Some believed the First Lady had overwhelming ambition to act as commander in chief and unilaterally appointed herself such. Many alleged she was the country's First Woman President.

Edith vehemently denied those claims.

> I, myself, never made a single decision regarding the disposition of public affairs. The only decision that was mine was what was important and what was not, and the very important decision of when to present matters to my husband.[26]

Given Edith's personality, nature, and past behavior, I disagree with her critics' assertion of power hunger. It is only rational to believe Edith *never* intended to take charge of the country, and certainly had no desire to do so. Considering the Wilsons' relationship and how the couple operated together, regardless of some critics' opinions, it appears to me that Edith's only reasonable goal was to protect her husband and preserve his life.

Yet it is impossible to ever know exactly which, or how much, information the First Lady chose to communicate to the president, or if the First Lady was in fact running the country for a brief period of time. In actuality, no other official government leader saw or spoke to the president during a six-week period in 1919. Another reality was, many items were put on hold for future attention or given to the appropriate executive department heads to deal with.

Today, many physicians say it would have been impossible for the president's mental ability *not* to have been adversely affected in some form—for at least a short time anyway. The bottom line was that a woman with minimal formal education who had only recently become schooled in political affairs was doing her very best to assist her newly handicapped husband in governing the country.

As if the president's stroke were not enough, he also developed a serious complication. There was a blockage from his bladder on which his specialists wanted to operate immediately, telling Edith it could be fatal. Dr. Grayson, on the other hand, was convinced the president would not survive surgery. Trusting Dr. Grayson's opinion regarding her husband's chances for survival, the First Lady refused the operation. Thankfully, the blockage cleared naturally.

As time went on, so did the debate over the Versailles Treaty. Without the president's forceful analysis and favorable pleas, defenders of the treaty in its totality were backed into a corner. Some of the opposition agreed to approve the treaty, but only with modification. When a good friend of the president's pleaded with Edith to have her husband accept the treaty with compromises, arguing "half a loaf is better than no bread," Edith agreed.

In desperation Edith went to her husband and begged him to accept the modifications, "For [her] sake." The president replied,

> Little girl, don't you desert me; that I cannot stand. Can't you see that I have no moral right to accept any change in a paper I have signed without giving to every other signatory, even the Germans, the right to do the same thing? It is not *I* that will not accept; it is the Nation's honour that is at stake. Better a thousand times to go down fighting than to dip your colours to dishonourable compromise.[27]

Feeling more esteem and reverence for her husband than Edith ever thought possible, she never again faltered with any of Wilson's decisions.

In the end, the Senate rejected the Versailles Treaty. Upon hearing the news, the president sat silent for a few moments. After sacrificing his own health and then learning of his defeat, one cannot possibly imagine the sorrowful agony the president and the First Lady must have felt. Still lying in his sickbed, experiencing pounding headaches and unable to move his left arm or leg, the president responded:

> All the more reason I must get well and try again to bring this country to a sense of its great opportunity and greater responsibility.[28]

Not long thereafter, the Senate demanded a face-to-face meeting with the president to determine his competency. Edith orchestrated the meeting; it was decided two senators, one Democratic and the other Republican, could meet and talk with the president.

Propping her husband upright and confident his paralyzed arm and leg were well covered, while his right hand remained free for easy movement, the First Lady sat in on the discussion and took notes. Edith's presence had long since become routine and her notes made certain the gathering would be reported accurately.

Republican senator Albert Fall, a harsh critic of the president, entered the room and immediately told the Chief Executive, "Well, Mr. President, we have all been praying for you." To which the president replied, "Which way, Senator?"[29] After some shared laughter, the meeting happily ended in a triumph for Edith, and things returned back to politics as usual.

The First Lady continued to screen visitors, but other obligations also took her attention. By the summer of 1920, she reluctantly agreed to have her portrait painted. "On hot, busy days I would put on a black velvet evening gown and sit by the hour," Edith recorded. Meanwhile, the president felt well enough to again preside over cabinet meetings. At his doctor's insistence, the president's workload was kept to a minimum; still unable to walk, he was assisted by a wheelchair.

In December, Wilson was the second president to receive the Nobel Prize for Peace.* On behalf of the president, the American minister to Norway acknowledged the prize and its 150,000 kroner (approximately $29,100) gift.

With the end of her tenure less than a year away, Edith carried on just as she had at the beginning of it. Everything in her life revolved around the needs and comfort of her husband. They continued to enjoy leisurely afternoon motor rides, spend hours sitting outside on the South Portico, and watch a great many movies.

Looking ahead to life outside the White House, the couple frequently talked about various cities they considered living in. A few that ranked the highest were Baltimore, Boston, and New York. In the end they decided to stay in Washington for two main reasons: the president planned to write a book on government, and the Library of Congress afforded the facilities he needed; and it had been Edith's primary residence before marrying her husband.

Wilson performed his last presidential task on March 4, 1921. He accompanied his successor, Warren Harding, to the Capitol; however, he did not stay for the inauguration. The Wilsons moved into a comfortable three-story, five-bedroom, five-bathroom home on S Street, where Edith immediately had an elevator installed.

The former president hoped he could practice law, but he soon discovered all of the many cases offered to him "touched in some way the government structure." Honorable to his core, Wilson believed his former official position might unfairly influence decisions in his clients' favor. After Wilson turned down a case with a $500,000 retainer, Edith urged him to end his law partnership with his most recent former secretary of state, Bainbridge Colby.

* Theodore Roosevelt was the first in 1906.

Sadly, his book on government was never written either. Typing, with only the use of his right hand, proved too tedious, and meanwhile the former president's physical health continued to deteriorate. Edith hired her brother Randolph as a secretary to censor all mail or news stories that could upset Wilson; this was in addition to the full-time nursing care he received.

The next few years flew by with Edith trying to distract her frustrated and depressed husband with every form of enjoyment she could think of. After only a brief marriage, which presumably felt more like an eternity, Edith was widowed again: former President Wilson died in his sleep at the age of sixty-eight on February 3, 1924.

Another chapter ended in Edith's life. After a year of mourning, all future chapters were predictably devoted to her husband's legacy. During her long second widowhood, in addition to diverting herself with travel, friends, and the theater, Edith attended public events as a symbol of her husband. She also traveled to Europe several times on occasions that honored her husband's vision of a League of Nations.

The Woodrow Wilson Foundation and Woodrow Wilson School of Public and International Affairs at Princeton were important to her. Edith maintained full script control for a film biography in 1944 entitled *Wilson*, and worked hard to establish her husband's birthplace as a national shrine. In addition, she held the literary rights to all of her husband's papers.*

More familiar now with politics, Edith knew who the presidential candidates were and even campaigned for Franklin D. Roosevelt in 1933. Fifteen years after her husband's passing, she wrote *My Memoir*, which she chose to end with her husband's death.

Furthermore, Edith developed a warm friendship with future First Ladies Grace Coolidge, Bess Truman, and Eleanor Roosevelt (whom she sat next to when President Franklin Roosevelt delivered his declaration of war to Congress in 1941, whereby the United States entered into World War II). She also attended John F. Kennedy's inauguration in 1961 and later that same year witnessed President Kennedy's formation of a memorial to her late husband.

* This was before presidential papers were seen as public documents.

On December 28, 1961, one day before what would have been Woodrow's 105th birthday, Edith's heart failed. Nearly thirty-eight years after her husband's death, Edith died at the age of eighty-nine and was buried in Washington National Cathedral, as was Woodrow Wilson.

WHAT EDITH TAUGHT ME

All of her sorority sisters experienced far more years with their spouses, either before and/or after living in the White House. Edith Galt Wilson was married a mere eight years to her presidential husband; still, in a lifetime that spanned nearly nine decades, Edith's calling was defined by those few years.

During a concise, yet significantly distressing and demanding period of time in history, the country's Chief Executive was in desperate need of a partner. Woodrow Wilson probably said it best:

> She [Edith] seemed to come into my life...like a special gift from Heaven...a sweet companion who will soon make me forget the intolerable loneliness and isolation.[30]

We now know Edith was far more than a companion! While her husband's authority and responsibility was to *all* of the people in the United States, Edith exerted her enormous power for the benefit of only one man. It would have been easy to allow political adversaries to come in and remove her husband from office. Particularly in the very early days of his stroke, I believe it would have been fairly easy to build a case of incompetency against the ill president. But in Edith's mind, doing so meant the guaranteed demise of her husband.

Determined and confident, Edith taught me to never understate one's own power and how important it is as well as to not be dissuaded by intimidation. When you allow others to intimidate you, you turn your strength and authority over to them.

PART TWO

WOMEN OF THE ROARING TWENTIES

INTRODUCTION

When President Wilson left the White House in 1921, the country had survived the horror of its first world war and most Americans were looking ahead, eager to put death and destruction behind them. One shameful exception was the Ku Klux Klan, which promoted white supremacy and sought to control politics in many Southern communities, often by violent means.

Since prior to the Civil War, women had been fighting for political equality. With the ratification of women's suffrage, refocused feminists proposed the Equal Rights Amendment to prohibit sex discrimination against women. A new age was dawning; it would become known as the Roaring Twenties or the Jazz Age. In 1922, KDKA, the first commercial radio station, began broadcasting in Pittsburg, Pennsylvania. Other stations rapidly followed and the popularity of jazz grew equally fast. Louis Armstrong, one of the greatest jazz musicians of all times, emerged on the scene in the early 1920s.

The popular syncopated music became associated with sophistication and decadence. Women cut their hair short and their skirts even shorter, showing lower legs all the way to the knee! Knickers (loose-fitting short pants gathered at the knee) and raccoon coats were the height of men's fashion, and both sexes shimmied doing the kicky Charleston dance.

Art Deco was the design style of the era; the Chrysler Building in New York City, completed in 1930, is a classic example of Art Deco architecture. Prior to the construction of the Empire State Building in 1931, the Chrysler Building was the tallest building in the world.[1]

Entrepreneurs produced homemade alcohol, otherwise known as bathtub gin, by the bucket loads. In the hopes of improving daily life and lowering crime, Congress passed the Eighteenth Amendment to the Constitution making the manufacture of alcohol as well as its sale and transportation illegal. Creating just the opposite effect, crime increased.

Illegal bars called speakeasies provided drinks for those who craved liquor, while gangsters smuggled in the intoxicating beverage and profited from its distribution. Al Capone, murderer and one of the best-known gangsters of all time, earned upwards of one hundred million dollars a year in alcohol sales and other illegal ventures. As a point of reference, the United States' population in the mid-1920s was approximately one hundred twenty-two million, with citizens' annual income averaging less than sixteen hundred dollars.

Vaudeville was becoming an entertainment of the past, while Hollywood exploded with talent. Favorite actors of the day were Rudolph Valentino (the Don Juan of his time), Mary Pickford (America's Sweetheart), and comedian Charlie Chaplin. In 1923, Cecil B. DeMille released his original silent film *The Ten Commandments.* It was universally successful and for decades, he was encouraged to make another version. (It was over thirty years later, 1956, before DeMille produced his second adaptation of *The Ten Commandments.* Since then, the lengthy film [nearly three hours and forty minutes] has gone on to become one of the most viewed movies of all time.) Soon, sound and dialog were introduced into the movies, making them talking pictures, and Al Jolson, known as the World's Greatest Entertainer, starred in *The Jazz Singer,* the first feature-length movie originally presented as a talkie.

In the world of pop culture, a popular book by F. Scott Fitzgerald, *The Great Gatsby,* highlighted what some described as the self-indulgence of the post–World War I age. *The New Yorker* magazine debuted and Mickey Mouse was a favorite cartoon character. *Winnie the Pooh* by A. A. Milne was a beloved children's book, while Wrigley's chewing gum began a new trend.

By the middle of the decade, prosperity was widespread as mass production made technology affordable to the middle class. With the development of the assembly line, Henry Ford's company was manufacturing nine to ten thousand automobiles per day. He then introduced his five-dollar workday (generous pay for the time), which might have helped Ford employees to purchase one of his Model Ts at the reduced price of only $240.

Well-known people during this period included sports hero Babe Ruth, the professional ball player who hit sixty home runs in one season, Albert Einstein, the great scientist, and Harry Houdini, the illustrious magician. And let's not forget Annie Oakley and her amazing sharpshooting skills. In 1927, it took Charles Lindbergh over thirty-three hours to fly nonstop across the Atlantic. On the fifth anniversary of Lindberg's historic Atlantic flight, Amelia Earhart became the first woman to fly solo across the Atlantic. With improved technology, she made the trip in just under fifteen hours. In addition to receiving the National Geographic Society gold medal, Earhart was awarded the Distinguished Flying Cross as a civilian aviator.

Regarding the two First Ladies who resided in the White House during the Roaring Twenties, one ruled the roost, while the other was dissuaded from having so much as an opinion of her own.

Florence Harding, nicknamed the Duchess, was a strong, willful woman with no interest in becoming a mother, yet she found herself pregnant and unmarried at nineteen. She was a very talented pianist, and a determined, ambitious woman who developed into a successful businesswoman. Due to Florence's efforts, her second husband found himself hosting his regular poker games in the Executive Mansion while she served her presidential spouse and his cronies liquor during Prohibition.

Her successor, Grace Coolidge, was a teacher to the deaf, yet she could not train her habitually uncommunicative and withdrawn husband to speak. A loving mother and avid baseball fan, she never learned to drive an automobile because her husband forbade it. A happy and fun-loving woman, Grace was content to relinquish all authority to her spouse.

Other than being very popular First Ladies, the two women had only one thing in common—both had a parent who adamantly disapproved of their spouse. Their distinctively different stories follow.

3

The Duchess

FLORENCE HARDING

I've always worked...I may wear out, but I shall never rust out.

—FLORENCE HARDING

BORN IN 1860 JUST NINE MONTHS before the start of the Civil War, Florence Kling came out of the womb fighting and never stopped. Her entire existence was one long battle, and although she did win a skirmish here and there, she still lost the overall war. Florence's greatest desire, which she sought all her life, was to be loved and wanted by the men in her life. Sadly, she never achieved that one goal; her ambition and strong drive to make something of her life had to sustain her when her menfolk did not.

#29 Florence Kling De Wolfe Harding

Born: August 15, 1860

Birthplace: Marion, Ohio

Married: 1880 (Henry De Wolfe; divorced)
1891 (Warren Harding)

Children: 1 (with De Wolfe)

White House Years: 1921–1923

Died: November 21, 1924 (64 years old)

Fact: Abandoned by first husband; consulted an astrologer

AKA: The Duchess

Her woes began with her oppressive and dictatorial father, who was overtly disappointed his first-born was not a son. Florence went on to elope with her alcoholic first husband, who later abandoned her and left her penniless and homeless. She did eventually marry a man she genuinely loved, but he was soon engaged in repeated long-term affairs. Only four years into the marriage, he fathered a baby girl with their neighbor; after nearly twenty-eight years of marriage he had yet another daughter with one of his other mistresses.

Her unhappy love life did not affect Florence's ability to get things done out in the world. She was a suffragist who supported educational, economic, and political equality for women, and was adept at making her voice heard. A good businesswoman, Florence was highly conversant in political affairs, and in her day she was an enormously popular First Lady who supported World War I veterans and advocated for animal rights. Alas, even though all that was certainly true, she will be eternally remembered as the woman who *may* have poisoned the most incompetent and inept man ever to occupy the Oval Office.

The life of Florence Kling De Wolfe Harding is a tale of struggle, rejection, manipulation, and yearning...and it ended in scandal and rumors. Her intriguing story imparts a simple and pragmatic message, which offers a fundamental reality that merits awareness. Love cannot always fix undesirable behaviors—sometimes you need to face the truth and walk away.

Amos Kling was a successful business owner and ultimately a powerful banker in Marion, Ohio, during the late 1800s. Considered one of the wealthiest men in the area, Amos dominated his family and demanded respect and obedience from his three children as well as from his meek, depressed wife, Louisa Bouton Kling. Louisa was an invalid who died at the age of fifty-eight. Incredibly little is known of her life or her relationship with her daughter. Florence's only commentary on her mother was to say, "Mother had ill health for so many years that she was glad to defer to father's opinion."[1] In actuality, Amos's opinion was the only thing that mattered in the Kling household and he was candidly angry his first child was a girl; as a result, Flossie (as they called Florence) always managed to disappoint or displease her father.

Often described as tyrannical and emotionally abusive, Amos treated his only daughter exactly the same way he treated her two brothers when they came along. On the constructive side, Florence was given business training along with her high school education, piano lessons, and music conservatory schooling. On the damaging side, Florence was humiliated and physically hurt when her father whipped her with a cherry tree switch for every perceived failure to adhere to his suffocating demands and restrictions.

Growing up in a mansion that boasted horse stables and extensive acreage, Florence developed an early compassion for animals and was an accomplished horsewoman who reportedly hated automobiles. Later in life, her presidential husband went so far as to say of Florence,

> [Their car] was the only thing we ever owned that she did not have a desire to run.[2]

Florence, like her father, was independent and determined, which naturally led to many conflicts between them. Fortunately, they were in accord on Florence's playing the piano. Here, she was driven to exceed even Amos' harsh regimen for her practice: legend contends that Florence practiced so long one day her fingers actually bled. Originally intent on becoming a concert pianist, she later recalled, "I spent seven hours a day at the piano for over three years."[3]

In order to polish off her schooling, at age seventeen Florence became a boarding student at the Cincinnati Conservatory of Music, where courses included social refinement, fashion, and languages. She was not allowed to finish school, though, as she was called home, most likely to care for her ill mother. Once more sharing living space with her father, a defiant Florence became indomitable in her opposition to him.

Staying out late at the Merry-Roll-Round skating rink with young men her father disapproved of, missing her curfew, and betting on horse races all contributed to loud father-daughter clashes. The rebellious teenager and the controlling parent would regularly butt heads, which included protracted screaming brawls. (Unlike the average parent who would worry about their adolescent's safety when he or she doesn't come home by curfew, Amos was known for locking his children out of the house overnight, forcing them to fend for themselves till morning.) Predictably, young Florence was headed for disaster with few options open to her.

Living under her father's roof was becoming intolerable for Florence. But in the late 1800s, young women simply did not leave their parents' home, unless of course they were away at school or got married. School was no longer feasible for Florence, but one sure way of getting married was available to her; she just needed to get herself with child.

In 1880, not yet out of her teens and three months pregnant, Florence eloped with Henry (aka Petey) De Wolfe, a budding alcoholic. Said to have gotten pregnant "to gain her freedom from her father," Florence pointed out, "Vice often comes in at the door of necessity, not at the door of inclination."[4] Neither the De Wolfe nor the Kling families approved of the union (and Henry questioned whether he was the baby's father), yet the immature lovers seemed eager to humiliate their parents and elected to set up house together.

Amos responded predictably to the young rebels' perceived marriage by immediately cutting off all contact with his daughter. Though Florence and De Wolfe lived together as husband and wife, several historians believe that the couple was never legally married as there is no evidence of a marriage certificate.*

Just two years later, three days before Christmas, Henry left Florence and her young son Marshall in a "small furnished room" with no food and no money.† Even though Florence had been abandoned with a child to support all by herself, Amos refused to give his daughter any assistance. After breaking into an empty home and spending the night on the cold floor with her son, Florence sought the help of a girlfriend. Her friend's father gave Florence shelter, and a short time later, with the assistance of a borrowed piano, Florence began giving lessons at fifty cents an hour in an effort to feed her little boy.

A couple more years would pass under these uncertain circumstances before Florence would file for marital separation. When she did so, Amos sent her a message. He still had no intention of helping his daughter out; however, he did make a proposition that would indirectly benefit Florence monetarily if not emotionally. Amos would for all intents and purposes "adopt" Marshall, raise him as his son,

* Though Ohio no longer recognizes common-law marriage, if a couple cohabited in the 1800s with the intent of marriage (obviously demonstrated by the birth of a child) there was no time requirement to establish a common-law marriage.

† Marshall Eugene De Wolfe (1880–1915)

give him the Kling name, and relieve her of all financial responsibilities and burdens for Marshall's care. Her acceptance would mean the relinquishment of her son. Even though Florence never had an overwhelming desire to be a mother, I would like to think that it was a difficult decision for her to make.

Perhaps she truly believed (or convinced herself) it was a better option for Marshall. After all, there was no question that Amos could offer her child far more fiscal security than Florence could ever hope to provide. She may have talked with her little one about the opportunities they would still have to spend outings, holidays, and the occasional overnight visit together...at least one would hope such a discussion took place.

In the end, Florence buried her emotional scars of rejection and gave up her four-year-old son to the one man she felt compelled to run away from, surrendering her child to the domineering father she could not and would not live with herself. In doing so, Florence forfeited her son's happiness and well-being in favor of her own. The psychological effect on Marshall was predictably devastating, as borne out by his later alcoholism, habitual gambling, and inability to hold a job.

Years later, looking back and reflecting on her first marriage, Florence would only say,

> That short unhappy period of my life is dead and buried. It was a great mistake. It was my own private affair and my mistake. I did all that was possible to correct it and obliterate it.[5]

With no going back, Florence was ready to make a new and better life for herself. Now free and unencumbered, she proclaimed,

> No man, father, brother, lover or husband, can ruin my life, I claim the right to live the life the good Lord gave me, myself.[6]

Convinced she had to do everything herself (and confident she could), Florence seized her self-reliance. She supported herself with a tenacity to achieve more; she also returned to socializing at the local skating rink. Noted in her diary:

> I have no desire to sit before a desolate fireplace, gazing at the dead embers of an unfortunate past.[7]

Somewhat tall at five feet seven inches, with large hands and feet, Florence was considered more masculine in appearance than feminine. Her oval face sported a cleft chin, strong jaw, thin mouth, and nearsighted blue eyes; like former presidents Woodrow Wilson and Teddy Roosevelt, Florence wore pince-nez eyeglasses. Her hair was wavy, brown before it turned a gray-silver color at a fairly young age. Florence was high-strung and domineering, usually speaking with an abrupt tone of voice. Inwardly, the divorced, now-childless mother remained insecure and highly suspicious, often taking offense at the slightest provocation.

As Florence's youth began to gradually slip away, the nation steadily moved ahead. According to the 1890 census, there were nearly sixty-three million people living in the United States at that time. The states of Idaho (the forty-third) and Wyoming (the forty-forth) were admitted to the Union, while an act of Congress created the Sequoia and Yosemite national parks. In other parts of the country, New York initiated the first electric chair execution, and the first black female dentist, Dr. Ida Gray, established her private practice in Cincinnati.

In contrast, Marion, Ohio, remained a very small, narrow-minded Caucasian town, where gossip ran in abundance. Yet even with her checkered and curiosity-provoking past, Florence continued to live, work, and party freely there.

It is not known if Florence had many or few male callers. What has been recorded was Florence's infatuation with Warren Harding from the first moment she laid eyes on him. Warren played the cornet at the Merry-Roll-Round rink and was the owner/editor of the struggling four-page *Marion Star* newspaper. It soon became obvious to everyone in the gossip mill that it was Florence who brazenly and insistently chased the dark-haired young man, five years her junior, who was an older brother of one of her piano students.

Warren was considered good-looking, genial, and virile, so Florence had a great deal of competition when it came to getting his attention (plus, he already had a steady girlfriend). Young and charming, Warren was a man-about-town who enjoyed poker, gambling, and liquor. He also had a voracious sexual appetite, an attribute even his father acknowledged:

> Warren, it's a good thing you wasn't born a gal…because you'd be in the family way all the time. You can't say no.[8]

Once again, Amos objected strenuously to his daughter's choice in men and was frankly enraged. Not only did he believe Warren would never amount to anything, rumors of "Negro blood" in Warren's family followed him his entire life. Amos was adamant in his judgment and wanted to hear nothing about the relationship. Seeing Warren on the street, Amos called him a derogatory racial name. Another time, he went so far as to threaten to kill Warren if he married Florence.

Despite her father's vehement disapproval and the local female competition, Florence pursued Warren with a determination both stronger and more powerful than the two men's combined opposition or resistance. She succeeded, and plans for the wedding went forward. Amos crafted every possible obstacle imaginable, including investing heavily in the *Republican Transcript*, a rival newspaper, with the objective of putting the *Star* out of business and bankrupting his future son-in-law. As trustee of the Epworth Methodist Church, Amos prevented the ceremony from occurring there. But he couldn't prevent the wedding, although he refused to attend it.

Florence's will to get her own way carried the day, and the couple was married in their home in July 1891. Known to consult with astrologers and clairvoyants, Florence insisted that the ceremony begin precisely at 8:00 P.M. and end no later than 8:30 P.M. If the service was not finished by then, it was to stop at 8:30 and not recommence until 9:00. The thirty-year-old bride firmly believed,

> You can never count on anything in this world, but you can always count on the stars—they never fail you.[9]

In defiance of her husband, Louisa Kling reportedly snuck in the back entrance, silently observed the wedding service, and departed immediately thereafter. She left before hearing her daughter proclaim that she would now make her new husband "president." Nor would Louisa see Florence live in the White House. She passed away just two years after the wedding.

Amos completely washed his hands of his recalcitrant daughter, cutting off all contact for the next seven years. An additional eight years would pass before Amos would again visit Florence in her home. Unwavering during this long period of estrangement, Florence noted:

> The very lessons my father had drilled into me of careful thought, self-reliance, self determination, gave me strength to use my own judgment despite his objections.[10]

Not long after marrying, Warren checked into the Kellogg Battle Creek Sanitarium for his second stay—he had suffered his first nervous breakdown at just twenty-four years of age, and the neighborhood buzz had it that his wife's constant nagging drove him there again less than two years later. During his absence, the paper's business manager quit, and Florence went down to the *Star* to help out temporarily. She worked full time for the next fourteen years. In due course, she took complete charge of the newspaper and proved to be a good manager.

Warren had purchased the then-irregularly published newspaper with two friends for three hundred dollars. After that he borrowed heavily to buy his partners out, putting the paper into even greater debt. It was Florence who turned the newspaper into a profitable business and began publishing it daily (with eight pages—twelve on Sunday), earning the respect of her employees, whom she called "her boys." She increased circulation and would "sell" papers to her newsboys for a penny apiece, who in turn sold them for two cents.

With her customary nonconformity, Florence hired the first female reporter to work on any Ohio newspaper. In support of women's equality, declaring "I don't like badges," Florence also chose not to wear a wedding ring. Regarding her preference for business over domesticity, she affirmed, "I'd rather go hungry than broil a steak or boil potatoes. I love business."[11]

Nonetheless, Florence believed managing a home was as important as managing a company. Once Warren was back on the job editing the *Star* (he was in the Sanitarium for several weeks), Florence would leave work an hour ahead of her husband, ride her bike home to put dinner out, and then occasionally return to the office after dinner. She still held the traditional opinion that "every wife owes such service to her husband and to her home."[12]

The Hardings' marriage, like the majority of marriages that endure thirty-two years, was undeniably a partnership. Florence genuinely loved her husband, and Warren enormously respected his wife's judgment. There was no question he admired her drive and intelligence, or that he relied wholeheartedly on his spouse. Certainly they needed one another.

However, their personal partnership never seemed to reach the level of emotional (and certainly not physical) intimacy desired in most marriages. It was obvious that Warren had put up a wall between them physically and it was also evident from the start that he was not a faithful husband, nor would he ever be.

Only four years into the marriage, he fathered a daughter with a childhood friend of Florence's, Susan McWilliams Hodder. The baby, Marion Louise, was named after the town she was conceived in. This was the mid 1890s, and the situation was considered so shameful and scandalous that Mrs. Hodder, who was already estranged from her husband, moved out of state with her daughter and never returned. While Warren contributed monetary support for the child during her early years, he never had a relationship with what the townspeople referred to as "Warren's bastard daughter."

Betrayed once again by a man in her life, Florence somehow overcame her devastation. She later noted, "I have become a better wife for all the difficulties I have been through."[13] With every personally humiliating and crushing setback, Florence grew more domineering and professionally ambitious.

The same year Marion Louise was born, 1895, Warren held his first political office as Marion County auditor. Influenced and persuaded by his wife, it was not long before Warren went on to the state senate and later lieutenant governorship of Ohio. Florence managed his campaign, soon discovering she battled more than her husband's political challengers. Amos Kling was doing everything in his power to ruin his son-in-law's candidacy. Warren's victory was a double win for Florence, for she triumphed in a decisive and public way against her father.

Not long thereafter, two things became utterly apparent: Florence thoroughly enjoyed being a political wife, and she accompanied her husband *everywhere*. Her motivation came partially from the gratification of her newfound status and partly because she refused to let Warren out of her sight. Recalling his infidelity, she emphasized,

> There is no devotion like a husband's provided he is far enough out of his wife's sight to do as he pleases.[14]

With Warren's greater visibility and national recognition, Florence's role as watchdog over her spouse's promiscuity became more and more time consuming. It took a near-death experience from nephritis (a kidney inflammation) in 1905 to prevent Florence from keeping an eye on her unfaithful husband. Her recovery from surgery included five months of hospital bed rest.

During his wife's recuperation, Warren began an affair with her purported best friend and neighbor, Mrs. Carrie Phillips (Carrie and Jim Phillips often vacationed with the Hardings). As soon as physically possible, Florence resumed her role of constantly traveling with her spouse; now, however, Warren did not need to travel far for his trysts. The old expression "with friends like that, who needs enemies" appeared to be a fitting commentary on the women in Florence's circle.

A number of years would pass before Warren and Carrie's affair became known. Not only was Warren skillful at keeping his love affair under the radar, several other dramatic distractions took place in Florence's life during this period. To begin with, her son Marshall, now twenty-seven years old, married the daughter of Marion's Democratic mayor and made Florence the grandmother of a little girl. Marshall was also diagnosed with tuberculosis and was told he needed to relocate to a dry climate in order to survive. He then moved his family to Colorado.

Marshall was not the only Kling to marry during that period. At seventy-four, Amos Kling married a very young widow and had a change of heart regarding his daughter. Apparently Florence's thirty-five-year-old stepmother (nearly eleven years her junior) convinced Amos to at last make peace with his daughter. That meant Amos would have to acknowledge Warren as well. Although it took additional time to complete this reconciliation—if you can call it that—Amos did finally concede, "My daughter married a nigger, but he's a smart nigger."[15]

On the political front, although Warren lost a bid to become Ohio governor, powerful Republican Party boss Harry Daugherty befriended Harding, believing he would make a dandy (and submissive) president. Florence naturally agreed and saw herself akin to sitting First Lady Helen Taft.* After all, they shared a number of obvious similarities.

Both women were ambitious, studied music in Ohio, taught piano, established professional working partnerships with their spouses, and were completely comfortable in the business arena. They also held greater political aspirations than those of their spouses and were the driving forces behind their passive husbands. I suspect that after Florence met Helen in 1911, at the Taft's twenty-fifth wedding anniversary celebration held at the White House, she believed she was equally capable of filling the mansion's hostess duties.

That same summer, Florence discovered her husband's longstanding affair, and knowledge of Warren's betrayal nearly ended the Harding marriage. It is reasonable to theorize, in fact, that such an outcome was exactly Carrie's intention, since she mailed a love letter to the Harding residence. Carrie was willing to divorce her spouse and fought hard to convince Warren to do the same. Eventually, she gave Harding an ultimatum: divorce Florence or Carrie would move to Germany.

Warren continued to profess his love for Carrie (some believe she was the love of Harding's life), but he would never divorce Florence. Warren recognized his wife's implicit loyalty to him, weighing heavily in addition to her fierce desire to protect him and her ability to manage his business affairs. He would join Carrie in marriage, but *only* if Florence died first. Carrie moved to Germany and within a few weeks, the love letters between Warren and his mistress resumed. But this time, Carrie mailed hers to the *Star*.

* Helen Taft's story may be found in Volume I of *Loves, Lies, and Tears*.

The betrayal by her best friend was nearly as devastating to Florence as Warren's infidelity. She noted in her diary,

> There is no enemy so bitter, as the friend who's been trifled with...It seems to me that to be friendless is the worst condition next to being in want, that a woman could be reduced to.[16]

Florence confronted her husband and seriously considered divorce. She recorded,

> Most of the pain in this world is located in the hearts of women. Many women are forced into mute acceptance of disloyalty, faithlessness and humiliation because this is, after all, "a man's world."[17]

However, by now, the perfectly matched duo needed one another more than ever before. Warren had become Florence's career and her identity, and both Hardings were looking ahead to the U.S. Senate. Rationalizing things, Florence wrote,

> Why stick stubbornly to decisions made in the heat of anger? It is only big souls who can see there must be a change of their minds in cooler moments.[18]

Nonetheless, the marriage had been eternally wounded. While Warren's *trust* in his wife's loyalty to him never wavered, her permanent *mistrust* of him (and for that matter all other individuals) was now cast in stone. Their partnership would continue with only a platonic fondness for one another.

In the fall of 1913, Warren reported to his sister that Florence had suffered a serious kidney attack, provoked by her faulty heart:

> Florence has been in bed for nine weeks with a bad heart [causing her current kidney illness] and nervous breakdown. She is in bad shape.[19]

Sustained stress was known to inflame kidney ailments, and

although Florence struggled to maintain serenity, the men in her life were not much help.

Warren's affair with Carrie was still going on. In addition to their salacious love letters, they shared at least one clandestine meeting in Montreal and another in New York. Meanwhile, Marshall had become a full-blown alcoholic and suffered under mounting debts; he continuously harassed his mother for money. During this same period, Amos Kling lay bedridden with a long serious illness of kidney disease.

Amos died that October, leaving his daughter some real estate and $35,000—a hefty sum in 1913. Marshall appealed to his mother for his share of the inheritance; he was still living in Colorado and struggling with health and financial problems, plus a new baby boy to take care of as well.

The following year brought more illness and heartache as well as anticipation of a new stage of life for the Hardings. Up until then, senators had been chosen by state legislatures. The enactment of the Seventeenth Amendment now allowed the direct election of United States senators. With the backing of Florence and Republican heavyweight Harry Daugherty, it would not be long before the Hardings were moving to Washington.

Marshall learned of his stepfather's political victory, but before Harding attended his first senate session, Marshall Kling died of advanced tuberculosis, aggravated by alcoholism. He was thirty-four years old. Before Marshall's wife and small children returned to live in Marion, Florence made a trip to Colorado for the purpose of paying her son's debts and seeing to his final arrangements. Although it was clear that Florence was cleaning up the loose ends of Marshall's distressing and troublesome life, it was also apparent that she was not yet ready to let her son go. She kept an urn with Marshall's ashes in her living room; eleven months would pass before Florence chose to bury those ashes and turn her attention forward.

If during that period Florence had any fantasy about savoring her newfound status as a senator's wife, it was soon squelched. War broke out in Germany and (possibly a worse catastrophe for Florence) Carrie Phillips returned to Marion. In addition to orchestrating multiple rendezvous and penning love poems, Warren also bought his mistress a Cadillac (at her strong urging), using funds from a discreet personal account.[20]

It is unlikely that Florence ever knew about the Cadillac. What is reasonable to believe is that she was more than ready to move on with her life and leave the town of Marion and its memories behind her. The vibrant city of Washington, coupled with Warren's new position in the Senate, may have been a welcome change, but sadly, nothing was different about the couple themselves. Each one picked up conducting their life right where they had left off.

As before, Florence wanted and needed to be in the middle of her husband's career. She participated in the long-held tradition of making social calls, but Florence Harding was nothing like former First Ladies Dolley Madison or Julia Grant. Nor was she young and captivating, like Julia Tyler or Frances Cleveland, when she arrived in the cliquish political city. A bit dowdy, socially ill at ease, and perpetually mistrusting, Florence was described by one senator's wife as "Courageous, ruthless and shrewd."

Primarily ignored by her new peers, Florence said of her initial Washington induction,

> I wonder if anyone ever anticipated the coldness, the aloofness that one meets here at first, [more than] in any other city of the world. It is indescribable.[21]

Needless to say, Florence did not make many friends, with the exception of multimillionaire Evalyn Walsh McLean,* a much younger Washington socialite who drank, smoked, took morphine, and flirted with men (regardless of their marital status). Evalyn was married to Ned McLean, chief of the *Washington Post*. Through that friendship, Florence was introduced to several prominent individuals.

Florence went to Washington intending to work hard—motivated by ambition for both Warren and herself—and indeed she did. She rarely missed a Senate debate, learned the inner workings of

* Evalyn McLean was the last private owner of the Hope Diamond, which is now on display in the Smithsonian Institution.

Washington, and was compulsive about advising and managing her husband. According to historian Bill Harris, it was common knowledge that Warren deliberately met with important people in his home, as opposed to his office, just so "his wife could take charge of the discussions, without staffers around to overrule her ideas."[22] The Duchess (as Warren always called her) remained indispensable to her husband.

Florence was essential to Warren's career, but his proclivity toward involvement with other women never diminished. In addition to several more casual encounters, Warren began a protracted affair with Nan Britton. Nan was a young woman from Marion who at sixteen had developed a schoolgirl infatuation for Harding when he was still editor of the *Star*. Now living in New York and a mature woman—all of twenty years old—she wrote the fifty-one-year-old senator a letter inquiring if he could assist her with employment. The following week, Harding and Nan were sharing a room at the Manhattan Hotel.[23]

How Warren found time to accomplish any Senate business is a mystery in itself. His love letters to Carrie continued unabated and he now wrote Nan ardent correspondence on blue Senate stationary and saw her almost weekly in New York. Unstoppable in his amorous pursuits, Harding was also involved romantically at this time with staff worker Grace Cross, a beautiful, married blond.* In addition to being the newest recipient of Harding's reckless notes, Grace was paid from his own funds, a common occurrence when all government-paid positions were already filled.

Meanwhile, World War I was raging and Warren's backers began to seriously consider him for the presidency. He told a state colleague,

> I think you know me quite as well as anybody in Ohio, and you know that I am unsuited to the higher position if it were possible for me to attain it, and you know that I am truthful when I say that I do not desire it and most sincerely wish to escape the responsibilities that a candidacy alone would bring.[24]

* A truly astonishing number of other women were connected with Warren Harding. Stories of alleged illegitimate children, abortions, and sexual encounters are bountiful. Rosa Cecelia Hoyle, Augusta Cole, and Ruby Evelyn Randall are named most frequently.

Then again, the final decision was not his. Initially Florence was decidedly opposed to it, although many were not convinced of her sincerity. Those that were, believed she was being protective of Warren, wanting to downplay his many escapades, something she sensed would be a hopeless task should he win the presidency. A Kansas City reporter quoted Florence as saying,

> I do not intend to permit him [Harding] to run. Because of the condition of his health it would bring a tragedy to us both.[25]

Harding's handlers were steadfast with their urging, but reportedly it was only after seeing an astrologer named Madame Marcia that Florence changed her mind. Then and only then did Warren toss his hat into the presidential arena. "Senator and Mrs. Harding will make the best president we have ever had" became the insider's motto.[26]

Before the Republican National Convention even took place, Harding's reprehensible and immoral behavior caught up with him. Giving up her fantasy of ever marrying Warren, Carrie Phillips told her husband about the long-standing affair. Like a clichéd scorned woman, she then demanded a large sum of cash or else she would publish Harding's love letters from the past fifteen years.

Warren wanted to pull out of the race, yet responded in his typical manner. When the going got tough, go to Florence, and she had a better plan. The Hardings were now married for twenty-eight years and Warren had been involved with Carrie for over half that time. The couple had long ago "struck a compact" when it came to "Carrie, adultery, their marriage, and political ambitions."[27]

If the blackmail wasn't paid, Florence believed that Warren would not only lose the potential presidency but his Senate seat as well. She would not consent to his withdrawal; instead, she proposed that they accede to Carrie's demands, but only after Warren received the Republican nomination. At that time, he would be in a position to divert campaign funds for the payoff.

In a rather lengthy letter, Warren attempted to appease Carrie. In small part the letter reads:

> I have been thinking very intently, very solemnly about our interview and all you said...I could not make myself believe that you would threaten me...I have some good qualities. I never betrayed a public trust...frankly I was heart-broken over your revealment... No lies were told. We felt the same sense of family obligations. Your proposal to destroy me, and yourself in doing so, will only add to the ill we have already done. I can't secure you the larger competence you have frequently mentioned...I will pay you $5,000 per year, in March each year, so long as I am in that public service...I wish it might be more, but one can only do that which is in his power...So much depends on your decision. I [am] nearly ill with the worry involved, but still hope...Mrs. H. has not mentioned your name in years. She has no part in seeking to annoy you. We have blundered. We will not talk about the blame. I accept my full share of it...I give you the most tribute that a man can. There was no cheating.[28]

Apparently Carrie felt Harding's offer of five thousand dollars per year, for as long as he held public office, was too little and too late, as she did not consent. Inevitably, Warren's other affairs began to emerge. Party leader Harry Daugherty wanted to bury his candidate's scandals once and for all. Personally soliciting money from wealthy supporters, Harry raised the extortion funds himself. A number of former lovers were reportedly paid off with small amounts of cash, although others were denied anything. Harry's final offer to Carrie was $25,000 and a promise of $2,000 every month Harding was in office. (The Republican National Committee also sent Carrie and her husband on a conveniently timed, expenses-paid vacation abroad.)*

She accepted and apparently relinquished "enough" of the damaging evidence to satisfy Harding's handlers. I say only enough, because in the late 1950s Carrie gave more of Harding's letters to author Francis Russell, with the stipulation that they remain secret until after Carrie died. When she passed away in 1960, her daughter Isabel

* Carrie Fulton Phillips is the only known person to have successfully blackmailed a major political party.

Phillips Mathee and Harding's nephews became entangled in a legal battle for custody of those still unpublished letters. Joining forces, the nephews received an injunction which prevented Russell's use of the correspondence in his 1968 biography on Harding entitled *The Shadow of Blooming Grove.* The book contains blank pages where the letters would have been quoted. The courts ultimately sealed the material until the one hundredth anniversary of Harding's death.*

The affair that remained a well-kept secret for years to come was that of Nan Britton, the young woman who supposedly maintained her devoted love for Harding until her death. Historians seem to agree that Florence was unaware of this specific extramarital liaison. Warren now had a particular reason to keep it that way. In 1919, Nan told Warren she was pregnant with his child, who was conceived in his Senate office during one of her Washington visits. Warren suggested an "operation" and later an adoption after the baby girl, Elizabeth Ann, was born. Nan refused both options. Warren reportedly set Nan up in a New Jersey house and continued to supply her with funds when she eventually moved to Chicago. Years later Nan wrote,

> It secretly amused him [Harding] to realize...that the scandal in which Mrs. [Phillips's] name and his were linked...was for us the greatest source of protection...Democrats who were "slinging mud"...were not looking for [me].[29]

Meantime, the campaign went into full swing. No presidential spouse had ever played such a significant or pivotal role in a campaign as Florence Harding did. Speaking to all the various feminist groups, Florence confirmed she was a suffragist, although she had not marched with them. She was of the opinion that:

> There are certain times and places wherein women must be militant to obtain their proper degree of justice and right.[30]

* The Ohio Historical Society is in possession of the material, which cannot be made public until 2023.

The Nineteenth Amendment to the Constitution guaranteed suffrage for women; this being their first opportunity to vote, Florence courted them heavily.

Her decades-long connection to the newspaper business also gave Florence compassion and support for the media. *The New York Times* confirmed that Mrs. Harding was the only candidate's wife who came more than halfway to meet newspaper reporters. As much as she disliked having her photo taken, she agreed to photographic sessions and developed a degree of closeness with the journalists. Florence would often say,

> Come on, boys. I always take a frightful picture and I hate this. But I know you've got to do it.[31]

When it came to endorsements, Florence added celebrities to the list. Both Hardings were devoted moviegoers, and top entertainers like Al Jolson, Douglas Fairbanks, Mary Pickford, and Lillian Gish showed their support by going to Marion. As historians Dorothy and Carl Schneider described it, "She [Florence] lobbied unashamedly, the only woman among approximately five hundred men doing the same thing." Her role in the campaign was unequivocally a vital one; Warren acknowledged he "couldn't have swung it but for the Duchess."

Once completing the initial front-porch campaign (similar to ones Caroline Harrison and Ida McKinley had participated in), Florence accompanied her husband on his whistle-stop train promotion. Florence could always be found standing beside her husband on the observation deck. It didn't matter if there were other important personages standing beside Harding: he always introduced his wife to the crowd first. Florence was a bona fide audience pleaser everywhere they went.

As the first presidential spouse ever to vote, Florence not only saw her husband elected president in 1920, Harding won the landslide election by the greatest percentage (60 percent) of popular votes to date.* Florence commented to a friend,

* President Lyndon Johnson won the highest ever popular vote (61 percent) in 1964.

> You and I both know if Warren had been defeated I would have been the most miserable woman in the world this morning instead of being the happiest. I am a regular fraud to say that I am scared out of my happiness by the responsibility, even as great as that responsibility is, for I am not.[32]

As it was for her predecessor Helen Taft, inauguration day was more of a triumph for Florence than for her husband. It has been repeatedly said that Florence whispered every word of the presidential oath while her husband said it aloud. The new First Lady understood the immense responsibility the White House brought with it. Upon entering the Executive Mansion, Florence turned to her husband and said,

> Well, Warren Harding, I have got you the presidency, now what are you going to do with it?[33]

The new president recognized he was "a man of limited talents" and replied, "May God help me, for I need it."[34]

When it came to her personal agenda, living in the White House did not change Florence's priorities. First, keep as watchful an eye as possible on her morally challenged husband; second, continue to direct his career; and third, accomplish whatever she set out to do.

The first order of business was her husband's cabinet. Having total confidence in her shrewd political insight, the president immediately put his wife in charge of screening potential candidates. While Florence did seem to have a keen judgment of people, she also had a keen misjudgment when it came to recognizing good character (or lack thereof).

Harding declared he wanted only the best, most qualified individuals for the job. However, he had a number of favors to repay and liked to surround himself with friends and poker cronies. To complicate things further, Florence had maintained a little red book of individuals who had either supported or snubbed her over the years. All these things factored into the decision-making process, and all contributed to the disastrous makeup of this important group of insiders. In the end, Harding's cabinet proved to be a major factor in the downfall of his administration.

Meantime, the First Lady actively supported several causes. World War I veterans were her greatest passion; while still a senator's wife, Florence worked tirelessly on their behalf. In addition to hospital visits with "her boys" (veterans were now included with her newsboys), she accompanied veterans on arranged outings, assisted war workers in locating housing, and fed soldiers at the Red Cross. As First Lady, she continued the hospital visits, remembered her boys' birthdays, and offered any man walking in uniform a ride in her chauffeured automobile. Due to her influence, countless individual problems dealing with the bureaucracy in the Department of Veterans Affairs were resolved.

When it came to women's issues, the First Lady was the preeminent standard-bearer:

> I have such great faith in the women of America, that I think it is through them that order will come about after the chaotic condition into which our country was thrust as a result of the war.[35]

She supported the League of Women Voters and the National Woman's Party. The First Lady was the only Republican board member for Sunshine House, a facility dedicated to helping unfortunate and needy working women. Florence assisted directly or focused attention where she saw a need, whether it was launching the first federal reformatory for female prisoners or helping establish a free clinic for pregnant women. She supported women aviators by flying in a hydroplane piloted by a woman, and invited African-American and Roman Catholic women's organizations to the White House. Supporting higher educational opportunities for women was also crucial to her and she encouraged *all* women to learn financial management.

The First Lady not only held informal press conferences for female reporters, she once again opened the White House to the public. It had been nearly three years since the mansion had been closed due to the war and former President Wilson's illness. Believing no one should need a ticket to visit her (in the past, individuals required such from their congressman), the First Lady personally guided tours of the Executive Mansion and willingly posed for photographs when she was out walking her dog, Laddie Boy.

A lifelong animal lover, Florence embraced animal rights causes with gusto. She was associated with the Animal Rescue League and the American Society for the Prevention of Cruelty to Animals (ASPCA). She proclaimed,

> Cruelty begets cruelty; hardness toward animals is certain to breed hardness toward our fellow men.[36]

Refusing to attend rodeos or Wild West shows, which she viewed as painful to animals, she instead endorsed a White House women's tennis match and cheered all women's participation in sports.

In a relatively short time, the First Lady was enormously popular with the American public. Always visible and accessible to both the public and the press, she was praised for her warm and outgoing civic personality. Despite her bouts of suspicion and insecurity among Washington's elite, the First Lady genuinely liked people and was often described as folksy. Florence freely acknowledged that she loved all the hoopla associated with her position as spouse of the country's highest ranking politician.

Naturally, she also had her critics. Defensive, mean-spirited, and vengeful were also adjectives used to describe Florence. Early on, she developed an aversion toward Vice President Calvin Coolidge, and she was jealous of his universally liked wife, Grace. When Florence learned Senator John Henderson's widow, Mary, offered their home, which was dubbed a castle, as a permanent official residence for the vice president, the First Lady's reaction was perhaps not surprising:

> Not a bit of it. Do you think that I am going to have those Coolidges living in a house like that? A hotel apartment is plenty good enough for them.[37]

In the end, the appropriation bill did not pass Congress.

Then there were those who labeled Florence dowdy, with a poor upbringing, and those who denounced her extravagant entertaining.

In addition to the customary formal receptions and state dinners, scores of White House evenings consisted of official entertaining with scheduled guests. The First Lady was also famous for her garden parties, which she held in honor of World War I veterans.

Florence appeared excitable, bustling, and sometimes angrily resentful (particularly with her husband, whom she called *Wurr'n* in a high-pitched voice), and although she was involved in every aspect of her husband's administration, she could not be in charge of everything or everyone. Frequently the president would say, "I'll have to check with the Duchess" or "You better ask the Duchess." Acting as if she were a cabinet member herself, all other cabinet members consulted with her regularly. The National First Ladies' Library website goes so far as to say, "She [Mrs. Harding] worried incessantly about Harding's grasp of events and had the Cabinet report to her." Surprisingly, she received little criticism compared to her predecessor, Edith Wilson, regarding her apparent control over the White House. Perhaps Edith helped pave the way for the Duchess's rule.

The responsibilities and sense of duty the presidency gives rise to apparently had no profound impact on Warren Harding. His nonchalant manner when running the *Star* simply carried over to his management of the White House and the United States government. Simply put, he depended heavily on others—predominately his wife and then his cabinet.

The president's active social life continued without a hitch. He enjoyed afternoon golf games and poker, and, of course, his extracurricular sport. When Nan came to Washington she continued her affair with Harding; the two were known to carry on their lovemaking in a closet. Alice Roosevelt Longworth's husband Nick was a close friend of Harding's, and the former "Princess Alice" offered yet another one of her classic retorts.

> [Harding] put the White House closets to a whole new range of uses.[38] [He] was not a bad man. He was just a slob.*[39]

* Many humorous stories of President Theodore Roosevelt's daughter Alice can be found in Volume I of *Loves, Lies, and Tears.*

During his occupancy in the Executive Mansion, Harding's regular poker games were legendary. What applied to the official dry receptions held downstairs evidently did not apply to the private quarters of the White House. In the face of Prohibition, and a constitutional amendment prohibiting the "manufacture, sale or transportation of intoxicating liquors," the First Lady acted as bartender of the well-stocked bar available to the president's poker buddies.

To date, only two presidential wives had been older than Florence when their husbands were elected president. At sixty-five, Anna Harrison remains the eldest. Too ill to travel to Washington, Anna never acted as hostess during her husband's incredibly brief term. Abigail Fillmore, sixty-two and in delicate health, was quite content to delegate several of her social responsibilities to her young daughter.*

Florence, at sixty, wasn't about to bow to those precedents, and indeed appeared to go out of her way to give a youthful and energetic impression. Though it might seem ludicrous, it was as if she was in competition with the likes of Frances Cleveland or Dolley Madison, two youthful, highly admired, enthusiastic, and stylish former hostesses. Some snidely said Florence tried to cover her wrinkles by wearing her trademark black velvet neckband or high necklines with lacy collars. She rouged her cheeks to create a rosy color and wore her hair firmly waved and tightly set in place. According to one newsman,

> In appearance she was a little too mechanically marcelled, too shiningly rouged and lipsticked, too trimly tailored.[40]

Another described her simply as over coiffed, over roughed, and over dressed.

Compared to former First Ladies Caroline Harrison and Eliza Johnson, both doting grandmothers whose grandchildren lived with them, the First Lady never spoke of her deceased son's children, nor did they ever visit the White House. Most of the country did not even know of their existence.

The public was also unaware of the First Lady's acute kidney illness

* Future First Lady Barbara Bush was sixty-four when her husband was inaugurated in 1989.

(nephritis). Despite her recurring ailments, Florence was continuously on the go, at all times a willing, eager participant in her life. She presented a healthy façade, so naturally it was a shock when Florence collapsed in early September of 1922—yet in truth, it was not a surprise. "This isn't going to be a short illness, I've gone through these before," confirmed her husband. In addition to kidney failure, the First Lady also suffered from what used to be called a weak heart. This particular nephritis attack was categorically life-threatening, and Florence came as close to death as one can, yet still survive.

Whether an incident at the White House the previous month had anything to do with Florence's grave illness is unknown. Then again, I don't believe in coincidences. In the midst of all his governmental pressures, the president had arranged an August tryst with Nan. No sooner had Miss Britton been delivered to the president's office by Secret Service Agent Walter Ferguson than one of Florence's in-house spies notified her of a woman's presence in the Oval Office.

Within minutes, Florence arrived and requested entrance. Agent Ferguson replied that the door was secured by Secret Service regulations, which prevented *her* entrance as well. Furious, she demanded the door be opened—again she was denied. Fergy, as he was known, was dutifully loyal to the president. He knew of Nan's child and intercepted Nan's letters for Harding. He also made it possible for the president to secretly dabble in the stock market, using an account in Ferguson's name.

Determined to see her husband, Florence went around the corner and once more angrily demanded access through an aide's office. After fumbling for a moment, the aide opened the rear door to Warren's office. By this time, Agent Ferguson had taken care of matters.

> I showed the girl the way out and told her to find my car and wait for me...As soon as I thought it was safe, I went to the car and took the girl to a hotel.[41]

If the First Lady confronted her husband about this episode, the conversation itself, and when it happened, remains a mystery. Nevertheless, it is fair to say that Florence still felt deep anger and resentment toward her husband's continuous betrayals. Her distress, in fact, was no secret, and her suffering surely negatively impacted her subsequent serious illness. It was noted in her physician's diary at the end of August, "Mrs. H very ill."

When, on September 7, 1922, the White House announced cancellation of the First Lady's appearances, it was the president who requested "honest public disclosure." A medical bulletin was then released.

> It is admitted that her [Mrs. Harding's] life hangs in the balance. Hope has not been abandoned by any means, but it is realized that the physicians in attendance are battling against tremendous odds.[42]

Florence Harding's biographer, Carl Sferrazza Anthony, provides an outstanding account of the occurrence. He describes how the American people, in a national vigil, showed their mutual love and collectively prayed for the gravely ill First Lady. Over one hundred seventy thousand members of the Disabled American Veterans, plus Veterans of Foreign Wars, Seventh-Day Adventists, various Christian churches counting some four million members, and synagogues, all joined in group prayers. Individuals of all faiths, young, old, black and white, united. African-American jazz societies, the Girl Scouts and Boy Scouts, Camp Fire Girls, and newspaper boy leagues, as well as the third Women's Conference on the League of Nations meeting in Switzerland, participated in this unprecedented avalanche of support. Silent standing prayers were even conducted at movie houses, theaters, and vaudeville performances.

Over the previous thirty years, the country had experienced other First Ladies on the brink of death—Ellen Wilson, Ida McKinley, and Caroline Harrison. All three were respected and admired by the nation's citizens. Florence Harding, however, possessed an additional appealing quality, described best by a *Washington Star* reporter.

> No former mistress of the White House ever lived in such close personal touch to the American people. Mrs. Harding had a big

> conception of what the people of the United States wanted to know about the White House and the people who live in it, and she used every method to let them know.[43]

Two of the First Lady's doctors said surgery was the only chance she had of survival. Her right kidney was twisted, which not only caused severe pain but made it impossible to expel urine. Unrelieved, bodily toxins in the blood system would cause fatal poisoning. The only physician opposed to surgery was Dr. Charles Sawyer (aka Doc), the Hardings' family doctor from Marion, who had treated Florence for years and whom she had complete confidence in. Doc Sawyer played a vital part in maintaining the Hardings' health; he temporarily moved to Washington and even traveled with the presidential couple during their White House years.

Doc was convinced Florence's weak heart would never survive the strain of surgery, even though it appeared to be the only way to treat her kidney disease. Refusing to give in, Doc had a conversation with Evalyn McLean, the only other individual Florence agreed to see besides her husband and medical team. Doc was unyielding.

> I have pulled this woman through many and many a time. I know her constitution. I know what she can stand and I know she cannot stand another operation.[44]

Wrapped in heavy blankets and hot towels, the First Lady's only hope of survival was to continually perspire and sweat the poisonous liquid out of her system through her pores. Things were going to get worse; the president found himself pacing from room to room. Florence began to slip in and out of consciousness. After yet another consultation between the doctors, a unanimous decision could still not be reached. Doc remained opposed to surgery, and during one lucid period, the decision was "left entirely to Mrs. Harding," who also opposed it.[45]

As family, friends, the press, and the public maintained an all-night vigil, the First Lady's fever rose to 105 degrees. "She was so sick it was impossible for her to carry on a conversation," reported Dr. Charles

Mayo. The opium she received for pain was ineffective. Purportedly Doc muttered, "Her last chapter is being written."[46]

Above all else, Florence believed Warren needed her. It was only afterward that the First Lady was able to verbalize her experience.

> I realized I was dying, which I was determined not to do...I knew that I was losing consciousness and...if I did lose consciousness, I would die. I must live. I must live.[47]

Dr. Joel Boone, who strongly favored surgery, wrote,

> She began to drain spontaneously from the kidneys voluminously...I have never experienced such a positively definite exhibition of mind over matter as eventuated in Mrs. Harding's case...[S]he demonstrated that, when death was on the threshold for her, she kept herself from dying truly by pure willpower.[48]

Florence continued to experience discomfort, yet gradually improved. It was mid-October before she was able to sit upright and December before the doctors felt confident the First Lady would in fact survive. Six months would pass before Florence felt well enough to resume her duties.

If her near-death experience taught her anything, it was that:

> The one thing that counts when you are down in the Valley of the Shadows is: What have you done for human beings...for those you love? Reading, material things, collections or hobbies all count for naught.[49]

Protecting her husband from himself as well as others, and continually spurring him on to bigger and greater accomplishments, remained Florence's primary objectives. Now, like a dog chewing on a meaty prime rib bone, Florence held on to Warren tighter than ever before. Not surprisingly, the manner in which she attempted to achieve her lofty and admirable aspirations did not, nor would it ever, achieve her goals.

Incessantly dominating, mandating, and badgering her husband to work harder, play less, or always remain within her eyesight, only contributed to Warren's desire to pull further away from his wife. He once petulantly remarked to her friend, "Evalyn, I'll get even with her if it's the last act of my life. Damn her soul!"[50]

During Florence's convalescence, the president was no longer willing to risk being caught in his office with his pants, literally or figuratively, down. Instead, he was seen visiting women at the home of Evalyn McLean, of all people. Evalyn's husband Ned and Harding had become bonded playmates.* In addition to golf, bridge, drinking, and smoking, the two cohorts shared an inclination for chorus girls and prostitutes. Evalyn knew her husband had mistresses over the years, and she also knew both her husband and Warren Harding used her home to meet their respective lovers. Evalyn certainly participated in her own vices of whisky, tobacco, and drugs, but heaven only knows why she would betray Florence and permit Warren's hurtful and callous behavior in her own home.

Still, as difficult and trying as 1922 was, 1923 proved to be even more grueling for the First Lady. Only two weeks into the New Year, the president was severely afflicted with a violent and debilitating virus. Warren was bedridden for weeks and severely ill for months after that. And yet the health issues both Hardings were recuperating from were merely the tip of a disturbing and devastatingly destructive iceberg.

Leaks and rumors were just beginning to surface regarding several scandals about illegal activities involving various members of the president's cabinet. Harding's poker buddies and several other individuals (collectively known as the Ohio Gang, operating out of a home on K Street in Washington) were involved in the corruption and thievery that scandalized the Harding administration. Blackmail, bribery, and payoffs were the distressing behaviors most often attributed to this group.

* Harry Daugherty, now Attorney General in Harding's cabinet, made Ned McLean an agent of the Bureau of Investigation. His annual salary may have been only one dollar, but compensation comes in various lucrative forms. As an agent of the government, McLean's legal access to all kinds of information and business documents proved invaluable.

The most famous scandal was that of the Teapot Dome oil leases, which involved the Attorney General (Harry Daugherty, who survived two hung juries) and the Secretary of the Interior (Albert Fall, who was later convicted and sent to prison).* Secretary Fall secretly and improperly leased large government naval oil reserves (at Teapot Dome, Wyoming, and Elk Hills, California) to private oil companies in exchange for approximately $400,000 in cash and gifts and no-interest loans. The oil companies were owned by millionaire oilmen Harry Sinclair and Edward Doheny.

Though the president and First Lady received no personal benefit or financial gain, the illegal actions of several government officials (which ultimately resulted in short prison sentences for some and heavy financial fines for others) contributed to the administration's corruption. Other charges levied against high-ranking officials included conspiracy to defraud the government, contempt of Congress, and jury tampering. In the end, the president's reputation was irreversibly ruined.

How many of his friends' illicit activities were discovered by the president—and when—is rather murky. Considerably clearer is the fact that Harding was handpicked for his job because he was a man the political bosses believed they could control. Furthermore, the president's strong dependency on others, coupled with his casual business attitude and naivety regarding character and trustworthiness, proved to be literally a deadly combination for him.

Preoccupied with planning a previously cancelled business trip to Alaska and the West Coast, both the president and First Lady were incensed at and tormented by the treachery coming to light within their administration. An investigation of the Veterans Bureau for "waste, extravagance, irregularities and mismanagement" directly affected the compassion Florence held for "her boys." She insisted then-director Charlie Forbes be fired and later acknowledged that she and the president "never recovered from the Forbes betrayal."†

* Jess Smith, a personal aide to Daugherty, committed suicide after destroying papers.

† Forbes was convicted of fraud/bribery charges and sentenced to two years in prison. Charles Cramer, an aide to Forbes, committed suicide. Thomas Miller, head of the Office of Alien Property, was also convicted of accepting bribes.

Harding was quoted as saying, "I am heartsick about it." As more and more of the corruption was revealed, the president grew increasingly distraught. At one point he could be heard shouting,

> My God, this is a hell of a job! I have no trouble with my enemies, but my damn friends, my God-damned friends...they're the ones that keep me walking the floor nights![51]

The president's doctors were concerned for his health, for he was severely fatigued physically and mentally. They advised Harding against going on the extended two-month, fifteen-thousand-mile Alaskan trip. It was to cover fifteen states with over seventy major speeches as well as dozens of parades, dinners, receptions and train whistle-stops. Even so, the president insisted he had "promises to keep." He also admitted,

> I cannot yield to one-tenth of the demands that are now being made upon me in connection with this trip. The grade is too steep. I need rest, but at the same time I want to see my country and its people.[52]

Moreover, the First Lady was very eager for the trip. Harding would be the first president to visit Alaska, and as Florence wrote to an aunt, "Out west they don't know they have a President, and I am anxious to have them see Mr. Harding."

As if the president's political problems were not enough, Florence had recurring sorrow from open wounds tugging at her heart. Thanks to Alice Roosevelt Longworth, Florence learned of Evalyn's disloyalty pertaining to Warren's unrelenting infidelity. We can only imagine Florence was wounded to the quick by this double betrayal and the mental anguish would surely destroy her physically. She needed to stay busy, distract herself from worry, and focus on more pleasant activities. The president's two-month planned Western trip would include encounters with an admiring public; therefore, the First Lady chose to divert all her attention into her public relations expertise and the upcoming tour.

Five weeks into the trip, after visiting Alaska and arriving in Vancouver, British Columbia, the president became ill. Once again, competing physicians disagreed with one another's diagnosis. Doc, an older and homeopathic physician, believed the president was suffering from indigestion and shellfish poisoning. (Evidently others on board ship had also become ill, presumably from eating tainted crabmeat.) Dr. Boone, younger and more modernly trained, believed the president had a serious heart condition, which was further weakened by the strong purgatives Doc prescribed to rid Harding's system of poisons.

When the president's temperature spiked, the First Lady cancelled the balance of the trip and her husband was transferred to the Palace Hotel in downtown San Francisco. Within days, the president died. His final words were, "That's good. Go on; read some more." The First Lady was reading a flattering profile of him written in the *Saturday Evening Post.* Florence continued to read until Harding appeared to have fallen asleep. The First Lady quietly walked out of the room when nurse Ruth Powderly entered.

Reports of the president's death were contradictory. One said, "Mrs. Powderly noticed the president's face twitch, his mouth drop open and his head roll lifelessly to one side."[53] The doctors concluded Harding had suffered a stroke. Pneumonia, ptomaine poisoning, purgatives which led to heart failure, a blood clot on the brain, and a heart attack were other sources to which his demise was attributed. Stories from several individuals, all involved in the president's inner circle, had discrepancies in them. Whether it was cardiac arrest or a cerebral hemorrhage that killed President Harding will never be known definitively.

Florence Harding, like First Lady Margaret Taylor before her, refused an autopsy. Another similarity to her predecessor's circumstances: rumors began circulating that the First Lady had poisoned her husband.* It was widely speculated that she killed Harding either to protect him from the allegations that would soon destroy his

* When President Zachary Taylor died unexpectedly in 1850, First Lady Margaret Taylor was also rumored to have poisoned her husband. Those rumors were passed down in history, until the president's body was exhumed 141 years later and the stories were scientifically proven false. Margaret Taylor's interesting life history can be found in Volume I of *Loves, Lies, and Tears.*

administration and presidency or because of his continuing unfaithfulness, or perhaps both.

Gaston Means, a private detective, bootlegger, and extortionist, who once worked for the FBI during the Harding administration, went so far as to accuse the First Lady of murdering her husband with the assistance of her good friend Doc. Means chronicled his suspicions in the book *Strange Death of President Harding*.

Plots or conspiracy theories involving various members of the Harding cabinet were also whispered about. Only two things appear to be generally agreed upon. First, Warren Harding died on August 2, 1923; second, some information was in fact covered up. Most researchers wound up concluding there was a misdiagnosis of the president's heart problems which, improperly treated, led to his death. Various physicians had identified Harding's cardiac condition, and every physician involved had some responsibility for the proper care of the president. Therefore, they also had reasons to conceal information.

Many, including a respected judge, believed the doctors' collective incompetence caused Harding's death, and negligence was the basis for the cover-up. Judge A. A. Hoehling wrote in part,

> Certainly confusing to me since the testimony doesn't seem to point to a dying man, or one with advanced arterial sclerosis...I am certain there was no foul play concerned with Harding's death—I am equally convinced there was "covering up" during those last 7 days of what was really happening to the President, and I know why.[54]

Rumors often begin when individuals are left with unanswered questions, or their expectations of how another person should act in a particular circumstance are not fulfilled. The First Lady's stoic behavior and lack of public tears did nothing to allay the gossip surrounding her. She maintained her unsentimental iron will throughout the entire ordeal. What the country did *not* know was that Madam Marcia had predicted that Harding would die while still in office (along with other prophecies that proved accurate). The prediction occurred before Harding had even won the election.

Florence's belief in the stars eliminated any element of surprise and enabled her to greet the inevitable with the stoic acceptance the public saw as cold-hearted. (Which raises the unanswered question, why did she allow Warren to run?) In addition, it was Doc who, prior to moving back to his home in Marion, convinced Florence not to approve an autopsy, as he believed it to be a "very disgusting thing."

Understanding the importance of a state funeral, the First Lady had the president's body returned to the White House. It was there she spent private time talking aloud to her husband; the staff, along with her sometimes-friend Evalyn, heard her say, "No one can hurt you now Warren." Florence then confided in Evalyn, "Now that it is all over, I think it was all for the best."[55]

Just as devoted to Harding after his death as before, Florence was committed to preserving his memory—as seen through her eyes. Instructing her staff to start a fire in the fireplace, Florence immediately began to burn the couple's private papers, beginning with the contents of a locked safe. She moved on to the Oval Office and ordered that all executive papers be boxed up and delivered directly to her. After reading and scrutinizing every piece of paper, she fueled the fireplace with documents for five solid days and nights. When Florence realized there were still over a half dozen jam-packed wooden crates, ten feet tall, remaining, she ordered them sent to Evalyn's estate.

After the president's burial in Marion, Ohio, Florence returned to Washington, D.C. She stayed at Evalyn's home; any question of disloyalty between the two women appeared to have been made moot by Harding's demise, and they resumed their friendship or at least dealt together with equanimity. They removed all presidential papers from the remaining wooden crates, destroying anything which Florence perceived could harm her husband or his administration. (Harry Daugherty managed to confiscate the president's remaining love letters.) Florence went so far as to request that all personal letters from the president to friends, family, and associates be returned to her for a presidential collection. Almost everyone complied.

Needless to say, considerable gaps exist in the history of Harding's tenure. Unlike Martha Washington who only burned private letters,

Florence was not protecting her privacy, but rather attempting to influence public perception of her husband's reputation. Additionally, she destroyed all her own personal correspondence and early records as well.

Florence could no more control Warren's life and reputation than she could anyone else's. Fortunately for her, she did not live long enough to learn of the Nan Britton humiliation or what it would do to her husband's prominence. In 1927, Nan not only revealed her six-year sexual affair with Harding, she also declared that the former president was the father of her daughter, Elizabeth Ann. Recorded in great detail in her bestseller *The President's Daughter*, Nan describes how her child was conceived in Harding's senate office in 1919.

Allegedly, Nan only wrote the book when Harding's relatives refused to acknowledge and help support her daughter. She said Warren accepted responsibility, paid child support, and promised to always help her monetarily. Now in financial need—and in support of other unwed mothers—Nan told her story to the world.*

Other stories were just beginning to leak out during the short fifteen months Florence survived her husband. Hearings delving into the corruption inside the Harding administration began. During that brief period, in addition to protecting her husband, Florence appeared to be shedding her prior life. She gave away her beloved dog Laddie along with much of her clothing and moved into the Willard Hotel. She spent time arranging the creation of the Harding Memorial Association and looked forward to taking a trip to Europe, which unfortunately never transpired due to her poor health.

The state of Florence's health had always been fragile, but now that she was declining Doc insisted she return to Marion and live in his sanatorium there. Florence did not want to go; she preferred living in Washington and never wanted to return to the now buried memories of Ohio. But Doc was adamant and would not take no for an answer. The former First Lady moved home and spent her remaining months

* Nan Britton married and lived well into her nineties. Daughter Elizabeth Ann Blaesing confirmed publicly that her mother told her Harding was in fact her biological father. Elizabeth Ann died in 2005. According to her son, Thomas Blaesing, his mother "was not interested in seeking DNA evidence confirming paternity" (http://en.wikipedia.org/wiki/Elizabeth_Ann_Blaesing).

in Marion, isolated and lonely, with no close friends nearby. When Doc Sawyer died unexpectedly in September 1924, Florence was devastated. She wrote a cousin, "My world was going to bits."[56]

Florence stayed informed on current events and visited Warren's tomb regularly. Never forgetting "her boys," she attended a veterans' parade in October. For an unknown reason (perhaps out of respect), Florence chose to stand in the drenching rain rather than remain in her vehicle. It was her last public appearance. On November 21, 1924, Florence died at the age of sixty-four and was laid to rest beside her husband.

First Ladies are often committed to memory accompanied by just one salient fact from their life. Abigail Adams, for instance, is known for her views on independence; Dolley Madison saved George Washington's famous portrait; and Lucy Hayes served lemonade in the White House. However, like Florence Harding, there is a great deal more to these ladies, and they should not be remembered or defined by a single catch phrase.

Sadly, some will only pair Florence's memory with the possible poisoning of her husband. In reality she was a dedicated and loyal spouse, and deeply in love with Warren. She was also ambitious and successful in a man's world, and always remained devoted to "all her boys" with the possible exception of her own son (with whom she shared a tangled, sad, and ultimately loss-filled relationship). She showed an interest in and was genuinely kind to newsboys and hard-hitting reporters alike. Even journalist Samuel Hopkins Adams, a critic of Florence, called her:

> A woman of firm principle, of clear purpose, and of essentially decent standards, possessed of a high heart, a shrewd brain, and a rigid will.[57]

Known for her compassion for veterans and consideration for the public in general and women's rights in particular, Florence was also expert in public relations, although she did not manage the White House or its staff as successfully as she might have wished. Given the nature and agenda of her husband's administration, perhaps no one could have managed it.

WHAT FLORENCE TAUGHT ME

Part of Florence Kling De Wolfe Harding's misfortune was to be born decades ahead of her time. Growing up with a submissive and depressed mother of generations ago was very different than what most women in Western cultures experience today. Nowadays, with women being encouraged and accepted in multiple ways, Florence would have a better opportunity to escape the philosophy drilled into and sanctioned by women of her era. She recorded,

> My life has been a series of tragedies and while I have never allowed myself to bend to the heartbreaking sorrows that have fallen me, I feel that much of my unhappiness was in the blood and I have never been able to lay down this birthright.[58]

Not bending or breaking from sorrows can be admirable; then again, Florence represented a lesson even more worthwhile to me. I learned from this strong but flawed woman's example what *not* to do. Instead of choosing friends and committed relationships based on charm or appeal, it's prudent to pick your companions based on the individual's principles, morality, and character. It is unwise to trust and rely upon someone who is dishonest, disrespectful, or shameless. Associate with good and honorable men and women, and then deal with them in kind. Had Florence been privy to the lesson her life represents to me, what a different tale it could have been.

4

Teacher to the Deaf, Not the Mute

GRACE COOLIDGE

> There was a sense of detachment. This was I, and yet not I...This was the wife of the President and she took precedence over me; my personal likes and dislikes must be subordinated to the consideration of those things which were required of her.
>
> —GRACE COOLIDGE

GRACE COOLIDGE, THE WOMAN WHO immediately succeeded Florence Harding in the White House, was Florence's total opposite. Grace described herself as "This was I, and yet not I" when she lived in the Executive Mansion. Conversely, Florence grew up in a mansion and was always herself, whether she slept in the White House or on the floor of a vacant home.

#30 Grace Goodhue Coolidge

Born: January 3, 1879

Birthplace: Burlington, Vermont

Married: 1905 (Calvin Coolidge)

Children: 2

White House Years: 1923–1929

Died: July 8, 1957 (78 years old)

Fact: Teacher to the deaf

AKA: National Hugger

Florence was often referred to as domineering and politically ambitious. She loved business, was assertive with a hands-on style, and was in the forefront for women's rights. Grace, on the other hand, was dominated and submissive with a passive manner; did not follow politics; and would have made the perfect choice for the cover of *Home Domesticity*. Moreover, Grace, unlike her predecessor, endorsed no causes.

Their upbringing was equally different. Florence was raised like her male siblings, and her father, opposed to her marriage, refused to attend the wedding. Grace was an only child—the center of her parents' attention—and although her mother objected to Grace's choice of husband, Grace was married in her parents' home, with both attending (her mother, we assume, reluctantly). Additionally, Grace was one of the founders of her college's chapter of the Pi Beta Phi sorority, while Florence never belonged to a sorority, or even attended college.

Even when it came to grieving, the two women were at opposite ends of the spectrum. Florence buried a son the country knew nothing about, whereas Grace mourned her son's death in view of the entire nation. One thing they did have in common: they were enormously popular. Even there they differed, however: Florence had her critics, but was still popular. Grace enjoyed universal approbation and was rarely, if ever, criticized.

After all the scandals, extramarital sex, and unlawful activities going on during the Harding administration, the Coolidge administration may sound rather tame. The most attractive aspect of the Coolidges' habitation in the White House was in fact Grace Coolidge herself. Appropriately named, Grace was a delightful woman, with a warm and vivacious personality, spontaneous nature, and gregarious temperament.

It is a little ironic that Grace Coolidge would directly follow Florence Harding as First Lady, considering the disparate life lessons each one's behavior taught me.

Grace's mother, Lemira Goodhue, was opposed to her twenty-six-year-old daughter's wedding in 1905. She always believed the thirty-three-year-old lawyer courting her only child was not good enough for Grace. Even years later, while her daughter was residing in the White House, Lemira thought her son-in-law had only achieved his prominence because of Grace. Andrew Goodhue, Grace's father, was a mechanical engineer who gave all indications that he approved of his daughter's intended.

It was difficult to grow fond of John Calvin Coolidge, Grace's other, not necessarily better, half. Calvin Coolidge was often described as sour faced, dour, and boorish. Alice Roosevelt Longworth said frankly that he "looks as though he's been weaned on a pickle."[1] Had Coolidge made the slightest attempt to converse with people (which he never did), his dry sense of humor would no doubt have helped offset his sober façade.

Like his fiancée, Calvin had deep-seated ethics; he was extremely close to his relatives and believed strongly in family. The Goodhues were a close-knit family as well, and Lemira eventually agreed to have the couple married in her Burlington, Vermont, home. The wedding took place on October 4, 1905, the day before the Wright Brothers' dramatic and remarkably long flight of twenty-four and a half miles, which took only thirty-eight minutes.

The bride had been living independently in Northampton, Massachusetts, for several years, teaching at the Clarke School for the Deaf. Working with the deaf was a lifelong passion of Grace's which began when she was a child of four and her father sustained a serious injury while chopping wood. In addition to damaging an eye, Mr. Goodhue broke several bones in his face, including his nose and jaw. During her father's recovery, which required total peace and quiet, little Grace was sent to live with family friends (the Yale family) in Northampton. Mrs. Yale was the principal of Clark School and introduced Grace to the world of the hearing-impaired.

Before beginning her teaching career, Grace graduated from the University of Vermont with a bachelor's degree in philosophy. Grace had always been a good student, and although not many women attended universities in the late 1800s and early 1900s, it had always been her intention to continue with her education. She spent the year after high school graduation at home, performing special exercises, a kind of physical therapy, to offset her scoliosis (curvature of the spine). During that year Grace had the good fortune to take lessons in piano, voice, and elocution, all of which she pursued in addition to her church activities.

Upon entering the coed college, Grace's intelligence and charming personality made her a popular student. It was at the University of Vermont that Grace and a girlfriend founded their female fraternity—what eventually became known as a sorority, it was the first national college fraternity for women in the United States. Many years later, Grace would become the Eastern regional president of Pi Beta Phi. The friendships she formed at school were maintained her entire life.

Soon after graduation, Grace applied to and was accepted at the Clarke School's training and teaching class. Grace resided in the school's dormitory and as fate would have it, while standing outside one day, she looked across the street to a sight she would never forget. Visible through an uncurtained window, wearing only long johns and a hat, a man stood shaving. Apparently he could hear her laughing from all the way across the street.

Feeling the need to explain himself, the long-john-clad cowboy requested an introduction to the spirited young woman. As he explained when they met, his unmanageable hair interfered with his morning ritual...hence the hat. Thus began a remarkable partnership that took this unlikely couple through triumphs and tragedies alike. As in the case of Jane and Franklin Pierce, the attraction of opposite types proved to be a powerful and binding ingredient in their relationship.

The ambitious though atypical politician was immediately captivated by Grace's warmth and engaging personality. She appeared to be attracted to his offbeat sense of humor—not surprising, since her own wit was often described as impish. With nothing in common except hailing from Vermont, the couple still made a perfect match. Coolidge was shy, somewhat moody, habitually uncommunicative, cautious, at times sarcastic, and pigeonholed as a controlling male chauvinist. But he also loved and valued the one woman who understood him better than anyone else in the world.

That exceptional woman was exuberant, unfailingly pleasant, sociable, impulsive, always gracious, and accustomed to accepting directives from people she respected. Many years later, Grace acknowledged her and Calvin's contrasts and characterized her marriage as encompassing two people with "vastly different temperaments and tastes."[2] Coolidge stated the "plain facts" when he wrote in his autobiography,

> We thought we were made for each other. For almost a quarter of a century [at the time of his writing] she has borne with my infirmities, and I have rejoiced in her graces.[3]

Calvin pursued the remarkably compliant teacher, whose curly black hair and gray-green eyes mesmerized him, with a passion never shown before or since. She was petite and ladylike at five feet four inches tall, nicely complementing his medium height of about five feet nine.

With total determination and a glimpse into their future, Calvin, who *literally never* asked his wife's opinion, made a bold announcement one day: "I'm going to be married to you."[4] After a short courtship they were married in the fall of 1905 and settled into a relationship lifestyle that remained steadfast for their entire union. It was the epitome of a traditional marriage, which at that time meant there was only one head of the household—the man. Coolidge took it further than most people would have dared and made *all* the decisions, including the when, where, and how of things, while Grace cheerfully and unquestioningly followed his lead.

One peculiarity that many a wife would not have tolerated arose immediately: Grace did not always know if or when her husband expected her to accompany him on his various political commitments. This meant that Grace needed to always be prepared and ready to follow Calvin out the door. At times she was properly dressed with hat in hand, only to discover she would not be attending a particular event. Unable to break her husband of this inconsiderate habit, Grace chose to make a game of it and take pleasure in the surprise of not knowing the outcome. This fit well with her resilient and optimistic attitude; she once remarked, "I have never outgrown my childish enjoyment of the unexpected."[5]

Some freedoms other women might have taken for granted were outright prohibited to Grace. Because her husband forbade it, Grace never learned to drive an automobile. Nor was she allowed to ride horses, dance in public, wear culottes, or have her hair bobbed (a fashionable hairstyle of the day). Not surprisingly, Grace resigned from teaching as soon as they were married, since Calvin would be the sole financial support of the family. Grace's role was to be a well-dressed, charming homemaker and loving mother to their children when they arrived.

Although she enjoyed socializing and staying out late, Grace would leave functions with her husband at an unfashionably early hour because he insisted on observing his 10:00 P.M. bedtime. His simple expression, "Better not," was the only thing Grace needed to hear to be deterred from any activity. This arrangement apparently suited them both; Grace would later say,

> I have such faith in Mr. Coolidge's judgment that if he told me I would die tomorrow morning at ten o'clock, I would believe him.[6]

One story frequently repeated over the years pertains, strangely enough, to Calvin's socks. It seems fifty-two pairs were in need of mending, and he handed them over to his new bride all at once. When Grace inquired if he had married her in order to get his socks darned, he responded, "No, but I find it mighty handy."[7]

Eleven months into their marriage Grace gave birth to their first son,* whom they named John in honor of his paternal grandfather. John Sr. adored his daughter-in-law and remained exceptionally close to her, his son, and his grandchildren. Calvin Jr. followed John less than two years later. Like so many other political wives, Grace often found herself being a single parent while her husband worked his way through various political offices. He was a mayor, a member of the Massachusetts House of Representatives, a member of the Massachusetts state senate, lieutenant governor, and finally governor of Massachusetts. Calvin never discussed politics with his wife, nor did he consult with her regarding any of his career decisions.

Home and children would forever remain the center of her life. It was Grace who taught her sons how to play baseball (it was said she could throw a ball better than the average man), a sport she adored and followed till the end of her life. She delighted in laying out and operating miniature train tracks, building a playhouse, or turning a wooden box with roller skate wheels into a sports car.

Grace had discovered her domain, which happened to be an area Calvin was inept at and more than willing to have her take over. When it came to their sons, Grace earned her husband's total respect. Regarding any situation involving her children, she commented, "I marvel at the father's confidence in my ability to cope with the problem."[8]

* John Coolidge (1906–2000), Calvin Coolidge Jr. (1908–1924).

The family lived simply and frugally (some might call their lifestyle miserly), even after it was no longer necessary. Somehow, Grace always managed to stay within her husband's very tight budget. A good example of Calvin's thriftiness became apparent when a local hotel went out of business. For years to come, all of the Coolidges' linens and silverware were stamped Norwood Hotel! They used a party telephone line (whereby multiple Ma Bell customers were all connected to the same line and could freely eavesdrop on one another), and for years lived in a two-family home at 21 Massasoit Street, Northampton, Massachusetts, which Calvin proudly furnished himself. "When it was ready Mrs. Coolidge and I walked over to it."[9] Rent on the home started at twenty-eight dollars a month and had risen to forty by 1919, when Coolidge was governor. He said of this simple, cozy house, "When we could have had a more pretentious home we still clung to it."[10]

Coolidge's government salary was never grand; he would often have to supplement it with income from his law practice, or borrow funds from his family. Mindful that his elected position was always tenuous, and wanting to make independent political decisions with no need to pacify those who might fund him, Coolidge remained economically prudent (many called him penny-pinching and cheap) his entire life. The Coolidges did not own an automobile (and Calvin apparently didn't believe in using taxis), so they took the train or public transportation to social and political events.

Oddly enough, Coolidge had one exception to his thriftiness. His only exclusion applied to Grace's wardrobe. He frequently encouraged his wife to buy expensive clothing and often shopped both for and with her. He enjoyed picking out her many hats and never liked seeing her in the same gown twice. Known for her fashionable style, Grace was particularly fond of red and made the color popular long before anyone ever heard the name Nancy Reagan.

Grace enjoyed the simplicity of her life. She loved to play the piano and read, and was a talented and vigorous knitter. In addition to maintaining her home, taking care of her children, and participating in church activities, Grace continued to maintain contacts and friendships with her sorority sisters, including attending Pi Beta Phi conventions. It was a complete surprise to Grace when her husband accepted the vice presidential nomination in 1920 under Warren Harding; predictably, Coolidge never discussed it with her. While Grace had been contentedly lost in the periphery of her husband's career, life was about to change.

Grace had remained in Northampton during the earlier years of their marriage, while her husband either stayed in Boston or commuted the one-hundred-plus miles to take care of his business and political commitments there. However, the vice presidential appointment necessitated Grace's moving to Washington with her husband. The boys, now twelve and fourteen, were sent off to boarding school in Pennsylvania. Shortly after her arrival, Grace noticed an uncharacteristic change in her painfully shy husband. Dinner parties were suddenly in abundance, and Calvin accepted any and all invitations extended to him. When Grace inquired what had changed, he replied laconically, "Gotta eat somewhere."

As an inexperienced hostess now living in a city that obligated one to entertain, Grace was fortunate to have several things in her favor. To begin with, she genuinely enjoyed people and cared about their welfare. Grace was wholeheartedly unpretentious, and she soon became the lucky recipient of guidance from other Washington socialites. She also had the useful knack of remembering names and faces, an invaluable asset in a Washington wife. Just like in college, Grace was popular the moment she hit town. She quickly became known as "one of her husband's greatest assets"; it has been said that "never a single disparaging remark" was heard about her. Looking forward to launching her Washington social life, Grace commented,

> We haven't entertained much. We never could afford it, but I'm sure I shall enjoy it.[11]

Congress had earlier turned down a bill that would provide a residence for the vice president, and purchasing a home in Washington was out of the question. Consequently, on her husband's new $12,000 annual salary, Grace made their home in a small suite at the Willard Hotel, which cost $8 a day. Quite a step up from when Calvin paid

55¢ per day for his two-room law office, twenty years earlier. At that time he had just accepted the position of city solicitor at $600 a year, believing it would make him a better lawyer.

The Willard Hotel continued to be their home for the next two and a half years. Grace presided over informal meetings with senate wives and continued to charm all of Washington with her geniality. Even Alice Roosevelt Longworth, who never minced words about anyone, said,

> She had simplicity and charm...[Grace] was always absolutely natural and unimpressed by it all.[12]

The couple continued to spend part of their summers with Calvin's father on his farm in Plymouth, Vermont. It was in Colonel Coolidge's Vermont home that the couple was woken up after midnight to receive distressing news. President Harding had unexpectedly passed away.

After dispatching a telegram to Mrs. Harding, Coolidge began to examine a copy of the Constitution, reviewing its stipulations and requirements for his succession to the presidency. Colonel Coolidge happened to be a notary public, which meant that requirement was covered. At 2:47 A.M. on August 3, 1923, in the sitting room of his home, the Colonel administered the presidential oath of office to his son by the light of a kerosene lamp. It was the only time in history that a president was sworn into office by his father. Three witnesses observed the historical event in addition to Grace, who reportedly cried. Without any further delay, the new president immediately returned to bed.

It was nearly three weeks before the new First Family moved into the White House, as the departing First Lady feverishly worked on gathering all her papers. The country welcomed Grace with open arms. She had no personal agenda, a sense of humor, and a wonderful ability to make people feel comfortable.

Life was good, and the country seemed to be recovering from all of the havoc, corruption, and scandal of the Harding administration. It was the Roaring Twenties, with great jazz music, wonderful talking films, and a First Lady who could laugh at herself as well as her husband.

Humor was a necessity when it came to living with Coolidge. Shortly after moving into the White House, Grace requested,

> Calvin, I wish you would have your Secret Service men give me your engagements. [The president replied,] Grace, we don't give that out promiscuously.[13]

Calvin also supervised much of the White House. He determined the guest list and seating charts for their entertaining, chose the menus, and forever had his nose in the kitchen and pantry.

The First Lady accepted this all in stride—besides, it gave her more free time to receive delegations and groups of individuals during most of her afternoons. Grace loved to see movies and attend symphonies, and was also a frequent theatergoer. She always chose to sit in the fifth row, orchestra section, as opposed to the reserved box seats the president and his family would typically occupy.

More and more the public began to understand how the president earned his nickname Silent Cal. Coolidge had always been a man of few words, but many never truly understood *just how few*. Thankfully the First Lady was an extraordinary conversationalist, and, like Dolley Madison, she was able to smooth over her husband's verbal shortcomings.

The stories regarding Silent Cal are legendary; when asked if all of them were true, Grace responded, "The best of them are."[14] Even before the couple married, when you would think a courting gentleman would go out of his way to be cordial, Calvin was…well, always Calvin.

Grace recalled one time when he escorted her to a college friend's home so the two could meet. "Not one word did he utter and when, at last, he could bear it no longer, he arose and said simply, with one of his best smiles, 'We'll be going now.'" Upon leaving, her friend whispered, "My land, Grace, I'd be afraid of him!" Grace was reportedly annoyed that Calvin had appeared bored and unfriendly. When she confronted her fiancé and told him what her friend had said, Calvin's only response was, "She'll find I'm human."[15]

Things never changed. A classic encounter occurred at the White House. At a dinner party one evening, a woman repeatedly tried to engage the president in conversation. Having no success, she finally explained to him that she had made a bet with friends that she could make him say more than two words. With that the president replied, "You lose."

Coolidge was aware of his reputation and defended his taciturn demeanor.

> I have noticed that nothing I *never* said ever did me any harm...Four-fifths of all our troubles would disappear, if we would only sit down and keep still.[16]

Ishbel Ross, then a reporter for the *New York Herald Tribune*, described Coolidge as "silent in a period of verbosity." The famous joke at the time was, "If Grace could teach the deaf to speak, why didn't she teach Cal?" Then again, when Cal did speak, he could be abrupt and mocking, so perhaps his reticence benefited his presidential reputation.

Luckily for him, Grace understood her husband's humor and form of teasing. She never claimed to be a good cook; in fact, Grace candidly admitted, "I could cook a little but, I must confess, I was never a great success at this," thus making her efforts at baking an easy target for Calvin's mockery.[17] One time Coolidge intentionally dropped a biscuit on the floor and stamped his foot to emphasize the thud. Another time he asked a friend,

> Don't you think the road commissioner would be willing to pay my wife something for her recipe for pie crust?[18]

Yet she never doubted or underestimated the depth of his devotion to her. Calvin worshiped Grace and she knew it. Their interplay was all in fun—Grace was good at bantering, and Calvin appreciated his wife's quick wit. She would mimic Calvin's expressions and copy his nasal twanged voice with devastating accuracy. Grace would even make kindhearted jokes at her husband's expense, knowing it would barely cause a ripple in his unflappable temperament.

When a reporter questioned her about their early romance, she deadpanned, "Have you ever met my husband?"[19] On another occasion, after spending an evening entertaining two female houseguests in typical Silent Cal style, the president inquired of Grace at breakfast, "And where are my two fair ladies?" Still in their rooms, "exhausted by your conversation of last evening," the First Lady responded.[20]

Throughout their marriage, Grace possessed enough vivacity and warmth to offset her husband's aloofness. In addition to her playfulness with humans, she also loved animals (as did the president, probably because they didn't talk), and enjoyed lighthearted humor with them as well.

She had calling cards engraved for Prudence Prim and Rob Roy, two beautiful white collies, and would leave their cards alongside her own when calling on personal friends. The First Lady kept a cageful of canaries in addition to several dogs, and then there was Rebecca the raccoon. Americans were well acquainted with Rebecca, who frequently posed for pictures with the First Lady. Not quite the variety of pets as in the Roosevelt White House, but then again, Teddy Roosevelt could have opened a zoo.

Whereas Grace's love of animals was well known, people did not generally know that she smoked (she only did it out of public view). She was also an avid walker and was said to walk five to six miles a day. One such outing caused the president a horrific scare.

On vacation in South Dakota, Grace was walking in the hills with her Secret Service agent. When she did not return in time for lunch, the president became frantic, for in addition to his well-known insistence that his wife always be properly dressed, he demanded punctuality. By the time Grace arrived two hours late, Coolidge was convinced something terrible had happened. When Grace explained that they had gotten lost, the president immediately fired the agent, who was then transferred to another detail.

Predictably, it was rumored that the president was jealous. True to form, Grace managed to find humor rather than humiliation in that theory. But the First Lady did not approve of her husband firing the agent, and remained friends with her former protector and his family for years to follow.

It seems only one thing could take away Grace's perennial smile, and that would involve a tragedy. Like most tragedies, it was not only unexpected and dreadful, it was life-changing. It happened during an election year; the president was the odds-on favorite to win the coveted position in his own right, the boys were home from school, and life felt serene for the First Family.

Their serenity was shattered one summer day—incongruously enough, it happened on the White House tennis court. Calvin Jr. was playing a match and sustained a blister on his foot that soon became seriously infected. Hospitalization could do little for Calvin; the physicians at Walter Reed were helpless to cure the young man. Antibiotics had not yet been invented and the blood poisoning running through Calvin's system was not only deadly, it was excruciatingly painful to endure.

His distraught, impotent parents could only watch their son suffer while praying that the infection would cure itself. Out of his mind with the pain and fever, young Calvin begged his mother and father for some kind of relief, and the president himself was said to be in and out of delirium. Sixteen-year-old Calvin Jr. died on July 7, 1924, leaving his entire family devastated.

It will never be known how Calvin Jr. might have eventually distinguished himself. Once when he was referred to as the first boy of the land, Calvin replied in part,

> I think you are mistaken...I have done nothing. It is my father who is President. Rather the first boy of the land would be some boy who had distinguished himself through his own actions.[21]

An emotional service was held in the East Room of the White House, and the promising young man's body went home to Vermont for burial. Afterward, in honor of Calvin's memory, a tree from Plymouth was planted where it could easily be seen on the White House grounds. There is no right or wrong way to grieve, and everyone must mourn in their own way. However, a First Lady (and president, for that matter) is forced to grieve in view of an entire nation. There could be no greater test of personal fortitude.

Unlike Mary Todd Lincoln, who remained secluded, cried continuously, and was unable to bear witness to her son's burial, Grace, with tremendous strength and dignity, returned to her full work schedule just two weeks after burying her son.

President Coolidge, like his predecessor Teddy Roosevelt, never appeared to recover from his son's death. Today, Coolidge would probably be diagnosed with severe clinical depression. He not only slept eleven hours every night, he would rarely go into his office before 10:00 A.M., would leave no later than 5:00 P.M., and took daily naps. Judging by his autobiography, the president somehow blamed himself for his son's misfortune.

> We do not know what might have happened to him under other circumstances, but if I had not been President he would not have raised a blister on his toe...I do not know why such a price was exacted for occupying the White House.[22]

Coolidge won the 1924 presidential election, but his heart was no longer in it. He said simply,

> When he [Calvin Jr.] went, the power and the glory of the Presidency went with him.[23]

Time may or *may not* heal; nevertheless, it will always continue to move on.

> Sustained by the great outpouring of sympathy from all over the nation, my wife and I bowed to the Supreme Will and with such courage as we had, went on in the discharge of our duties.[24]

Within two years, death would once again weigh heavy on their hearts. Colonel Coolidge died in his Vermont home at eighty-one years old, creating additional sorrow for the First Family. Coolidge was aware that his father was "passing his last days," and tried to bring the elderly gentleman to Washington. The Colonel, however, preferred to remain in his home. Although he rushed to be with his beloved father, a sad and distressed son poignantly recalled, "He sank to rest while I was on my way. It cost a great deal to be President."[25]

Through it all, the Coolidges' public responsibility and profound pride for their country never wavered. In 1926, the White House joyously celebrated the country's 150th anniversary of independence. Inconceivable to the founding fathers, that same year American naval personnel were reportedly the first in the world to fly over the North Pole. What took eight months to traverse by dogsled took only fifteen hours and fifty-one minutes by plane.[26]

On the aviation front, the following year, aviator hero Charles Lindbergh made his historic solo flight across the Atlantic. Afterward, Lindbergh was a guest at the White House as was the remarkable Helen Keller. Grace had the pleasure of communicating with and befriending Ms. Keller, the first deaf-blind person to earn a bachelor of arts degree. The First Lady's love of baseball stayed strong, and she closely followed Babe Ruth's record-breaking baseball achievements.

Forever unchanged by her prominence, the First Lady continued to make some of her own dresses (in addition to the lavish gowns her husband purchased for her), crocheted a coverlet for the Lincoln Bedroom, and stayed involved with her volunteer work. Once when she was stopped by a woman who commented that she resembled the First Lady, Grace responded, "Sometimes I am."[27]

Although she refused (or was forbidden) to give interviews, one time when the First Lady felt forced into giving a speech, she used only sign language. Grace remained a popular First Lady and was known to hug so many children she earned the nickname National Hugger. Author and philosopher Will Rogers, whose eclectic career included stints as a cowboy, movie and Broadway star, syndicated newspaper columnist, and radio commentator, dubbed Grace Public Female Favorite Number One.

In 1928 the president's now famous "I do not choose to run" announcement was heard by the press and public before Grace knew anything about it. No surprise there—Coolidge remained true to form until his last breath. When Grace learned of her husband's decision not to seek reelection, she simply acquiesced.

> I'm rather proud of the fact that after nearly a quarter of a century of marriage my husband feels free to make his decisions without

consulting me or giving me advance information concerning them.[28]

Frankly, the First Lady was happy about the decision. Not only had she been concerned about her husband's health, the plain truth was that neither of them had sought all the public attention and scrutiny. Years later, Grace professed, "When I reflect upon my Washington career I wonder how I ever faced it."[29]

For two individuals who never desired the spotlight, the First Couple was photographed a great deal. The First Lady was always smiling, and while the president could barely force a grin for the camera, he was usually willing to autograph his picture. Once a visiting congressman requested a current photo of Coolidge, who responded, "I don't know what you want another for. I'm using the same face."[30]

In the official oil portrait of the First Lady (such a portrait is now customary for all First Ladies), she wears her favorite color red and is accompanied by her beloved Rob Roy. The portrait, which cost three thousand dollars, was a gift from her friends in Pi Beta Phi. Thirteen hundred current and past sorority sisters were present when the painting was unveiled in the East Room of the White House.

The First Lady proudly had her gold fraternity pin included in the painting. The now famous red evening dress was donated to the Smithsonian Institution. Years later Grace would give her original fraternity pin to them as well, to be attached to the gown.

Other portraits were also painted of the First Lady. Her son John felt that one particular portrait showed his mother in an uncharacteristically solemn mood. When he inquired why, the artist explained, "Because I once saw in your mother's face a look of resignation."[31]

Grace certainly looked forward to retirement. When the time came to leave the capital city, she returned to her original little house in Northampton, Massachusetts, as planned. Just six months after leaving the White House, a delighted Grace would welcome a daughter-in-law into the family. John married Florence Trumbull, who was not unfamiliar with politics, as her father was the governor of Connecticut.

As is so often the case, though, low times followed the high. One month after her son's wedding, Grace's mother passed away. (Andrew

Goodhue, Grace's father, had died six years earlier.) Although expected, the death of her mother naturally saddened Grace, and another cause for sorrow—a nationwide one—occurred a week later with the unprecedented stock market crash of October 1929, which precipitated the Great Depression. The former occupants of the White House were no doubt glad to be out of the public spotlight during such tumultuous times.

Living in the White House never changed or transformed the Coolidges personally; however, it did make it impossible to return unscathed to their formerly quiet and tranquil lives. The couple lost all anonymity. Automobiles filled with sightseers and tourists on foot paraded by the house, hoping to see the former president sitting on his front porch (Coolidge's favorite pastime). The activity caused so much congestion and turmoil the Coolidges ultimately elected to leave town and purchase an estate, The Beeches, on eight acres of land just outside of Northampton.

Good Housekeeping magazine named Grace one of America's twelve greatest women, citing her dedication to family and home. Smith College, followed by Grace's alma mater, the University of Vermont, awarded her honorary degrees. Grace remained a sparkling "Public Female Favorite" even after she was no longer in the public spotlight. Despite the sorrow and upheavals of her past, especially losing her son, Grace remained steadfastly upbeat; several years passed in relative harmony at The Beeches.

That serenity ended, though, when Calvin died suddenly from a heart attack in 1933, just two days after Grace's birthday. She was overwhelmed and vulnerable:

> I am just a lost soul. Nobody is going to believe how I miss being told what to do. My father always told me what I had to do. Then Calvin told me what I had to do.[32]

She had just turned fifty-four, and in the ensuing years Grace would at last realize that she *could* find her own way.

Widowhood lasted nearly as long as her twenty-seven-year marriage. Understandably, the former First Lady remained very close to her son, daughter-in-law, and two grandchildren; she also created a meaningful, busy life filled with several other activities. Her support of the deaf never waned, and she was in fact president of the Clarke School board from 1935 to 1952. Community service work included the Eagle Scouts as well as Christmas Seal campaigns.

Hiking and swimming kept Grace in good physical shape, and she kept her mind exercised by reading all the best sellers of the day. She traveled to Europe with a female friend (involving a ten-country tour) and frequented her beloved baseball stadiums. Grace supported her team, the acclaimed Boston Red Sox, followed the various leagues, and attended games whenever possible, once even in the rain.

The president of the American Baseball League always sent the former First Lady tickets for the World Series. When the difficulties of travel and her increasing age made it impossible for her to attend those games, "an amazing arrangement of flowers" would arrive on opening day. Grace confessed,

> I am not smart enough to follow the clues in "who dun its" but have no trouble in following the play by play descriptions of the baseball games as the commentators bring them to us over the radio.[33]

In 1939, Grace turned sixty and was blessed with her second granddaughter. She was a loving and participatory grandmother but after raising boys, it may have felt a little like being a fish out of water because Grace commented,

> Surely sixty should be the "Age of Wisdom" but I often think that the older I grow the less wise I am.[34]

Finally out from under her husband's restrictions, Grace occasionally gave interviews, wrote articles for various magazines, and published poetry. One poem written on the fifth anniversary of her son's passing was eventually published in *Good Housekeeping*. Grace felt the poem wrote itself and was poetic in thought, as opposed to form.

You, my son,
Have shown me God.
Your kiss upon my cheek
Has made me feel the gentle touch
Of Him who leads us on.
The memory of your smile, when young,
Reveals His face,
As mellowing years come on apace.
And when you went before,
You left the Gates of Heaven ajar
That I might glimpse,
Approaching from afar,
The glories of His Grace.
Hold, Son, my hand,
Guide me along the path,
That, coming,
I may stumble not,
Nor roam,
Nor fail to show the way
Which leads us—Home.

After deciding to sell The Beeches, the large estate she had shared with her spouse, Grace had a smaller home built where she first lived in Northampton, on Massasoit Street. In keeping with her philanthropic character, she eventually lent it to the Navy's Women in Voluntary Emergency Service (WAVES) personnel.

Offering up her home and moving into a friend's house in the interim was only the beginning of Grace's active support during World War II. Strong feelings had uncovered a voice and she spoke out in favor of early United States intervention. Moreover, she remained an involved advocate of the war. In addition to lending out her home, she raised funds for the war's child refugees, entertained soldiers, assisted the Red Cross, and supported war bond drives. Grace acted as a private citizen and avoided publicity, shying away from misuse of her name.

Always gracious and unpretentious, with natural dignity and a sincere caring for people, it's no wonder Grace Goodhue Coolidge was adored by nearly everyone and had no known adversaries. Everett Sanders, a secretary to the former president, stirred up irrepressible rumors of marriage to the widow of his former boss. Grace managed to avoid direct communication with inquiring reporters and was said to have "carefully weighed the question" before declining Sanders' proposal.

Newspapers provided Grace with her primary source of information. (Another thirteen years would pass before Grace owned her first television.) She remained informed and followed the national news and politics from behind the scenes. Regardless of which party was in office, political prejudice did not exist for Grace. Liked by and very friendly with subsequent First Ladies Lou Hoover and Eleanor Roosevelt, Grace cared about people more than she did about politics, analogous again to Dolley Madison.

With great empathy Grace wrote a compassionate letter to Mrs. Elizabeth Truman when Bess found herself living in the undesirable spotlight of the Executive Mansion. Both women preferred a private and anonymous life, yet both found themselves in the center of public attention when Presidents Warren Harding and Franklin Roosevelt died while in office.

Mamie Eisenhower once wrote to Grace describing how the White House looked twenty-four years after her departure and giving Grace an open invitation to visit her former residence at any time. Like some of her White House compatriots, though, Grace never returned to the mansion.

Every year on the anniversary of Calvin Jr.'s death, his older brother John would remember him and send his mother flowers. "I am blessed among mothers and beyond my deserving in having so devoted and thoughtful a son," Grace wrote in her thank-you note to John, on July 7, 1955.[35] After all, while people eventually stop acknowledging a tragedy, a mother never, ever forgets the date her heart was crushed.

One night in the summer of 1957, just after returning home to his family from a visit with his seventy-eight-year-old mother, John was called back to his mother's home. Grace passed away from heart disease, some say on July 8. John, however, as well as others, believed that Grace died before midnight, on July 7, 1957.

According to Grace's biographer, Ishbel Ross, it was her desire to be cremated. There is, however, a very simple and plain matching headstone (with the exception of the presidential seal) next to her husband's and son's markers at the Plymouth Notch Cemetery in Plymouth, Vermont. Grace also bequeathed a piece of history to posterity: her husband's birthplace (Colonel Coolidge's former home), along with all of its contents, was gifted to the state of Vermont so that future generations could visit the sitting room where Calvin Coolidge was sworn in as president in 1923.

WHAT GRACE TAUGHT ME

Unassuming and unaffected, Grace Goodhue Coolidge remained down-to-earth and affable to everyone she met. More than that, it was her willingness to see another person's point of view which so beautifully impressed me.

Prior to marriage, when Grace wanted her fiancé to make a good impression with her friends, she could justifiably have been furious when Calvin remained stoic and uncommunicative. Instead she sought to understand his behavior. Listening to him describe his feelings, Grace discovered that Calvin did not like being put on display. In spite of that, he still went with her, was dressed immaculately, and according to her, "made every possible preparation to present an appearance which would do me honor."[36]

Initially, Grace may have believed she could train her husband, admitting, "I thought I would get him to enjoy life and have fun but he was not very easy to instruct in that way," yet she intuitively comprehended that people are in fact...simply different.[37] An individual's behavior can appear strange or even peculiar, yet that does not make them awful or somehow not human. Calvin had confidence that people would eventually discover he was, indeed, "human."

While some labeled her solely as a dominated wife, Grace saw it differently. She acknowledged:

> During the time that my husband held a responsible and exacting office [which was literally from the beginning of their marriage] I made it my business to be on hand in case I could do any little thing to ease the burden. I guess I spoiled him and I know I got myself into the habit of making no plans for myself until I had made sure that he wouldn't need me.[38]

Calvin's communication habits were not going to change, but understanding his feelings and point of view, Grace learned to lovingly accept him for who he was. She chose to take pleasure in being uninformed and enjoy the unexpected when it came to dealing with Calvin's quirk of keeping her in the dark about even the most important of issues. With humor and exquisite tact, Grace loved and accepted her taciturn husband for just *who* and *how* he was. In doing so, she earned his devoted affection and elegantly educated me in the art of respecting personality differences.

PART THREE

WOMEN OF THE GREAT DEPRESSION

INTRODUCTION

It is an undeniable truth that every president ponders his legacy upon leaving the White House. How will history judge his decisions and actions (or lack thereof)? Silent Cal, the man of few words, is famous for saying,

> Four-fifths of all our troubles in this life would disappear if we would only sit down and keep still.[1]

When Calvin Coolidge left the presidency in 1929, prosperity was widespread. He commented,

> If I had permitted my failures, or what seemed to me at the time a lack of success, to discourage me I cannot see any way in which I would ever have made progress.[2]

While the early 1920s were known as the Jazz Age, many believed that the mid-1920s were the Golden Twenties. It was a period of great advancement in both urban and commercial venues. The automobile provided accessibility and promoted growth throughout the entire American economy. The construction of roads and highways created a market for service stations, motels, and a wide variety of new businesses. Suburbs sprang up as people no longer needed to rely on public transportation to get to work, resulting in an unprecedented housing boom.

The assembly line and mass production reduced the cost of consumer goods, which increased purchases and in turn a demand for labor. More people could now afford small appliances such as pop-up toasters and hairdryers, while homemakers relished the convenience offered by refrigerators and vacuum cleaners. Manufacturers increased advertising to broaden their markets nationally, consequently generating an assortment of new jobs.

Radio debuted as the first mass broadcasting medium and during this period, known as the Golden Age of Radio, programming was as varied as TV programming is today. Amos 'n' Andy, a nightly serial, and Rudy Vallée's Fleischmann Hour, a musical variety program, both debuted on NBC radio.

While the beginning and middle of the decade roared with music, laughter, and success, the end of the decade crashed with deafening silence, despair, and poverty. The conclusion of the Coolidge administration was the end of another era, as well as the prosperity experienced after World War I.

The Dow Jones Industrial Average had seen a five-year run of increased value, and the New York Stock Exchange had grown into the largest stock market in the world. Prosperity and success had fueled the stock market. As shares of stock continued to rise in value, more and more people began to invest. Furthermore, the speculative Dow Jones boom encouraged investors to increase their investments, and a significant number of people even borrowed money, to the tune of over eight and a half billion dollars, to purchase more stock.

One of the most devastating stock market crashes in American history began on Thursday, October 24, 1929. Five short days later, on October 29, 1929, the day now known as Black Tuesday, the enormous stock losses caused widespread panic and launched a dismal period in American and world history whose effects lingered for decades. The broad scope and sheer size of what became known as the Great Depression were overwhelming. Those negatively affected included nearly the entire nation, with consequences spreading to Europe and then encompassing the rest of the world.

As stock values began to collapse, record numbers of shares—nearly thirteen million—were traded. By Black Tuesday, the total loss of stock value for the previous five days equaled close to thirty billion dollars. (Keep in mind those losses were at 1929 values. Today that figure would be over *three hundred billion dollars.*) This massive sale of stock contributed significantly to the longest and most catastrophic economic collapse in history. In July of 1932, the Dow had plummeted to its lowest level of the twentieth century. Over twenty years would pass (November 1954) before the market returned to pre-1929 levels.

The cause of America's Great Depression is an ongoing debate that continues to this day. Some historians believe the stock market crash was the instigating event, while some economists disagree, pointing to other factors. Regardless, the results of the downward slide in the market were devastating and enormously damaging to the entire country.

When the bottom fell out, thousands of investors were ruined, completely shattered, as everything was lost. Contrary to common folklore, people were not jumping out of windows, but suicides did occur. The decline in stock prices caused business closures, bankruptcies, and a massive number of laid-off workers. Banks and financial institutions closed, forced into insolvency because of their large stock-based portfolios. Of the twenty-five thousand banks in the country, eleven thousand had failed by 1933.

As citizens decreased their spending levels nationwide, demand for products shrank; production declined, and more and more people found themselves unemployed. With 25 to 30 percent of the workforce cut, mass unemployment rose as high as fifteen million people.

Now jobless, homeless, and penniless, many families without food turned to the government for assistance. Just as the Civil War affected (in one way or another) every citizen who survived it, nearly every person who lived through the Great Depression experienced some form of deep-seated apprehension about money over their entire life.

Ironically, the two First Ladies who resided in the White House during this horrific time were both very well-off financially. The first, Lou Hoover, married a self-made millionaire. The second, Eleanor Roosevelt, came from a wealthy family and married a distant cousin with considerable wealth of his own.

Both women had great compassion and empathy for the entire nation and all those who suffered. Each in her own way did what she could to assist hundreds of thousands of people around the world, and contributed to the betterment of humanity. Their benevolent caring and selfless giving restore one's faith in humanity.

5

Humanitarian Linguist

LOU HOOVER

I am a lucky woman to have had my life's trail alongside the paths of three such men and boys.

—Lou Hoover, in a letter to her husband and sons

Our life's trail begins as a mystery and is influenced by scores of unpredictable and changing factors. Just a few variables include the period of history in which we are born, the various individuals we meet along the way, and the timing of events in our life, as well as personal interests. Other influences are the opportunities afforded us, and, more importantly, the opportunities we *create* for ourselves. One thing is sure, the trail is never a straight course; it is often diverted and seldom known to us in our early lives.

> **#31 Lou Henry Hoover**
>
> **Born**: March 29, 1874
>
> **Birthplace**: Waterloo, Iowa
>
> **Married**: 1899 (Herbert Clark Hoover)
>
> **Children**: 2
>
> **White House Years**: 1929 –1933
>
> **Died**: January 7, 1944 (69 years old)
>
> **Fact**: First female Geology major to graduate from Stanford University; spoke 5 languages fluently
>
> **AKA**: The Original Girl Scout

I trust Lou Henry had no idea, certainly not in her youth, that her life's trail would wend across the entire globe several times over. At different periods in her life, her primary residence was located in Monterey, California; Tientsin, China; London, England; and the Waldorf-Astoria Hotel in New York. This amazingly well-traveled woman also lived in or repeatedly visited Australia, the British Isles, Burma, Egypt, France, India, Japan, Korea, New Zealand, and Russia.

Just a hundred miles away from where she was born in Waterloo, Iowa, lived a young boy five months her junior. It would be twenty years before the two youngsters would meet; however, after their paths crossed, Lou's life took a completely new and capricious direction. Eventually she became proficient in five languages (English, Latin, German, Spanish, and Chinese); grew into an international hostess; and helped feed, as well as clothe, millions of war refugees. Her personal interests, the people she met, and world events all contributed to Lou's fascinating life journey that began on March 29, 1874.

Parts of the country in the early 1870s were still very much the Wild West, with Jesse James and his gang robbing passenger trains throughout Iowa, Missouri, and Kentucky. Meanwhile, a young girl—with a boy's name—who loved to climb trees, hike in the hills, and camp under the stars was discovering the great outdoors.

Lou's father, Charles Henry (whom she adored), was a bank manager and avid outdoorsman. Henry had initially hoped his first child would be a boy (hence her name...I assume); however, Lou had no problem accompanying her father on his nature adventures.* She genuinely loved the natural world around her and enjoyed participating in all of Henry's rough-and-ready outdoor activities like hiking, hunting, and mountaineering.

When she was not camping, Lou organized baseball games, played basketball, rode horses both sidesaddle and bareback, was an expert ice-skater, perfected her archery, and liked to sled. Lou wasn't exactly a "play with dolls or pretend dress up" young girl, so it should be no surprise that her childhood pet was a horned toad. An only child until she was eight years old, Lou's reaction when her parents brought home her only sibling, a baby sister named Jean, has not been recorded for posterity. Judging by their adult relationship, it appears the sisters got along fine throughout their lives.

Their mother, Florence Henry, was said to have had health problems related to breathing. By the time Lou was eleven, the family had moved from Iowa to California in hopes that the more clement weather

* Some biographies suggest that Lou Henry's birth name was either Louella or Louise. However, the majority of First Lady historians and both the National First Ladies' Library and the Herbert Hoover Presidential Library all agree that Lou was in fact her given birth name.

would improve Florence's health. Presumably it did help as the Henrys stayed in the sunshine state. Initially living in the Los Angeles area, the family ultimately settled down in Monterey. Henry became a partner in a bank, while Florence, a former school teacher, taught her daughters how to sew and maintain a home. Lou was proficient in her studies, which included geography, history, and Latin. In keeping with her tomboy ways she also excelled at her many athletic endeavors.

After high school graduation, young Lou transferred to the California State Normal Schools system, choosing the school that boasted "the best gymnasium west of the Mississippi."[1] The Normal Schools were teaching colleges with various campus locations (the name "Normal" came from the college's established teaching standard—the "norm"). Lou enrolled initially at the Southern California campus and later transferred to San Jose. The campus sites she attended eventually became California State University and San Jose State University. Over time, additional campuses were added, including the school that later became the University of California, Los Angeles. After graduating with a degree in teaching, nineteen-year-old Lou Henry taught school and also worked in her father's bank—a fulfilling and active life for an energetic young woman in pre-1900 California.

But there was more in store for Lou. At a geology lecture given by a professor from Stanford University in Palo Alto, Lou found her passion. Wasting no time, she applied and was accepted for admission to Stanford as its first and only female geology major. Her enthusiasm for geology would bring another passion into her life, a human one this time: she met fellow Iowa-born geology enthusiast Herbert Hoover while both attended Stanford.

A senior when they met, Bert (as she called him) had only one year to get to know the intelligent and unusual young lady who shared his love of rocks and minerals. A shy man, Hoover was nonetheless attracted to the adventurous and outgoing brown-haired young woman. Although at five feet eight inches tall Lou was healthy and fit, she appeared heavy due to her large womanly frame. It is nearly impossible to find pictures of Lou openly grinning, most likely because of the gap between her front teeth (which did not detract at all from the sparkle in her blue-gray eyes).

Immediately after graduation, Hoover accepted a mining engineer position in California; he was based in the Sierra Nevada. Soon after that, he was hired by an engineering firm to explore mines in Australia. Bert and Lou exchanged letters for the next four years while she continued her studies. In 1898, Lou was not only the first woman at Stanford to receive a bachelor's degree in geology, she was the first woman in the United States to receive a college degree in scientific earth studies.* Accolades aside, Lou soon discovered geology was still a man's world and no one wanted to hire a female geologist.

Later in 1898 Lou received a telegram that launched her on the first of many journeys across the world. Hoover wired exciting news: he had accepted a consultant position for an English firm in China, at a much higher salary than his current job in Australia. (According to First Lady historian Betty Boyd Caroli, Hoover's Australian annual salary was forty thousand American dollars. His cable to Lou did not reveal exactly how much his new salary would be.) The message also contained a marriage proposal. Lou immediately accepted by return cablegram.

As with Julia and Ulysses Grant, neither time nor distance could lessen the intense feelings Herbert and Lou had for one another; even though Herbert had not seen his twenty-four-year-old sweetheart for several years, his love was steadfast, as was hers. Herbert arrived back in California with just enough time to marry Lou before they took off for China.

Oddly enough, the Episcopalian bride and Quaker groom were married by a Roman Catholic priest. It seems the city of Monterey did not have a minister in either one of their faiths. Years earlier, when Lou first moved to California, she lived in a Quaker community and was very familiar with their teachings, having often attended services with her Quaker girlfriends. Ultimately she converted to her husband's faith.

Immediately after their whirlwind wedding on the afternoon of February 10, 1899, which took place in the Henrys' Monterey home, Lou and Herbert boarded the train for San Francisco where they

* Times were definitely changing, albeit very slowly. In 1877, a female student from Boston University was the first woman to earn a Ph.D. Two years later, the first woman was admitted to practice before the U.S. Supreme Court. Then in 1881, seventeen women who had challenged society's standards and earned college degrees founded the American Association of University Women.

would catch a ship for China the very next day. Once there, Lou lost no time immersing herself in her new home and adopted culture. She learned to speak and write Chinese and also developed an appreciation for Chinese porcelain, eventually accumulating a large and valuable Ming Dynasty collection. Moving to foreign locations for her husband's work was just one way Lou evinced the team spirit of her marriage to the future president.

In a manner very similar to that of Sarah and James Polk, the Hoovers' common background and dovetailing interests proved to be enormously useful for the couple. Lou traveled with her husband and not only understood his work but could catalog it for him as well. She declared forthrightly, "I majored in geology in college but have majored in Herbert Hoover ever since."[2]

During the Hoovers' stay in China, the Boxer Rebellion began.* The Boxers invaded the Chinese capital of Beijing and killed 230 foreigners. The Hoovers were living in a foreign compound in Tientsin (known today as Tianjin), approximately sixty miles from Beijing. For safety purposes Herbert instructed his wife, household servants, and staff of employees to leave the city.

Although his entire staff heeded Hoover's warning, Lou remained behind with her husband and helped to fortify their compound. They barricaded themselves along with other foreigners in homes along the edge of the city, bags of grain and sugar serving as makeshift defenses. Hoover's extensive knowledge of the local terrain proved to be an exceptionally useful tool. During the height of battle, he guided U.S. Marines around the city of Tianjin. Russian soldiers who were also trapped in the city (along with some eight hundred other Americans and Europeans) helped fight the Boxers and protect the compound.

During the attack, which lasted over a month, it was inevitable that some houses were destroyed and some people wounded. Lou was one of the first to volunteer her assistance, leaving the relative shelter of her home to feed and care for those in need. Food and other supplies

* Chinese rebels, known as Boxers, disapproved of the various foreign influences that came to China during the country's early modernization. Although the Chinese emperor approved of the foreign developers, the Boxers rebelled against them and wanted the "foreign devils" either killed or run out of the country.

dwindled daily. Her only form of transportation down the dangerous streets within the compound was by bicycle. On one occasion Lou was nearly shot, but thankfully the bullet only struck her bicycle tire. On another evening, a shell burst through a window in the Hoovers' home and exploded against the front door; no one was injured, but the situation was harrowing in the extreme. Lou soon learned to use a pistol, further demonstrating her courage and resolve. Surely her childhood as an active, adventurous girl contributed to her resourcefulness during this extremely dangerous period of her life.

In August of 1900 an international relief force from eight countries finally arrived and the rebels retreated. Having had enough of the turmoil, Lou and her husband moved to London, where Herbert became a partner in the engineering firm of Bewick, Moreing & Co., the company that had originally hired him to go to China.

For the next thirteen years London remained Lou's home base while she continued to act as her husband's geological assistant and travel the world with him on business. At various times they lived in different exotic locations, but they always returned to their English retreat. During her stays in London, Lou gave birth to two sons.* Each boy began traveling with his mother at just five weeks of age. Purportedly the eldest, Herbert Jr., had crossed the globe twice before his first birthday.

The mining industry was developing and expanding, and Hoover was in the middle of it. Years later, reflecting back on how and when he earned his massive fortune, Hoover called that period of time "the golden age of mining." As Hoover became internationally known, the family wealth increased considerably, and it is fair to say that some people considered Herbert and Lou snobbishly rich. But bear in mind that this fortune came through the Hoovers' own efforts: Herbert was orphaned by the age of ten, as both his parents died in their mid-thirties without leaving any fortune behind. He was often referred to as a self-made *multi*millionaire, and Herbert's rag-to-riches story underscores the benefits of education and diligent work. It should also be noted that Lou worked alongside her husband and assisted him in *all* of his many ventures, so she was hardly the idle, pampered society wife.

* Herbert Clark Hoover Jr. (1903–1969), Allan Henry Hoover (1907–1993).

One five-year project involved the translation into English of a sixteenth-century Latin manual on minerals and mining. The most highly regarded encyclopedia on mining and metallurgy available at that time, the manual had been translated from Latin to German but was still difficult to understand, and, of course, incomprehensible unless one read those languages. Using the original Latin and German material, Lou drew on her multilingual expertise to translate the 673-page tome into English while Hoover performed experiments and updated the diagrams as well as parts of the text.

Agricola's 1556 volume *De Re Metallica* was published in 1912 in English (as translated by the Hoovers). It is still in print and considered a valuable resource in the field. In addition to their scholarly contributions, the Hoovers were generous and principled individuals: they published some three thousand copies at their own expense, and then, instead of selling them, gave away countless books to mining students and experts in the field. For their selfless and tireless efforts, they earned the Distinguished Contributions to the Literature of Mining award from the Mining & Metallurgical Society of America.

An unforeseeable twist in events temporarily derailed Hoover's plans for starting his own mining consulting firm. As he was preparing to leave Bewick, Moreing & Co., he discovered that a senior partner in the firm had embezzled hundreds of thousands of dollars in company funds. Hoover and other officers in the firm risked their own personal fortunes and agreed to cover the losses. (He believed so strongly in a high ethical standard that he incorporated a chapter addressing a mining engineer's moral obligation in his book, *Principles of Mining.**)

Hoover then designed a financial repayment plan for the culpable partner. During the period of time it took for the man to repay his debt, Lou assisted the partner's wife and family by providing a living allowance from her own personal funds. When the debt was at last paid back to Bewick, Moreing & Co., Hoover was finally able to start his own engineering consulting company in 1908. With offices in San Francisco and New York as well as Europe, the Great Engineer, as he

* Hoover published sixteen books between 1909 and 1963. *The Memoirs of Herbert Hoover,* which was counted as only one book, actually consisted of three volumes.

was known, consulted for governments and companies throughout the world.

Although they were still based in London, Herbert and Lou always intended to return to California and make a home in Palo Alto. Lou made sure that in addition to visiting places like Siam and Siberia, she took the boys on camping and fishing vacations in the United States. She also believed an American education was important for her sons; therefore, establishing residences on both continents soon became appropriate.

In order to place the boys (eight and twelve years old) permanently in California schools, Lou and her sons sailed to America on the SS *Lusitania* and settled the boys in Palo Alto. Herbert Jr. and Allan remained in boarding school in California until they graduated and went on to college, traveling to be with their parents for holidays and summers in the intervening years. In 1915, eight short months after Lou and her boys' trip across the Atlantic, the *Lusitania* was torpedoed by a German submarine and sank, killing nearly 1,200 of the 1,959 people aboard.

World War I had already begun in Europe and President Wilson turned to the one individual he knew could and would be of great service. Hoover was named head of the Belgian Relief Commission and became responsible for supplying thousands of Belgians with food, shelter, and clothing. Lou returned to England to once again aid and support her husband, this time in war relief efforts. As in the past, Lou worked right alongside her spouse and led a campaign to help Belgian women devastated by the war.

By now Lou had established social and philanthropic relationships on both sides of the Atlantic. During her previous sojourns in London, she became president of the American Women's Club, a service organization that raised money to help feed and house the poor. It also provided scholarships for students who could not otherwise afford school. According to different accounts, anywhere from seventy thousand to one hundred twenty thousand Americans were stranded in Europe. While Hoover assisted these families financially, both with personal funds and through establishing credit for the families, Lou assisted the women and children with locating relatives back home, finding places to live, and collecting clothing for them.

In order to fully contribute, Lou needed to sail across the Atlantic several times. In America she raised funds for necessary overseas supplies. In London, she worked with the Society of American Women's War Relief and American Women's Hospital in Belgium. With the onset of German occupation, Belgium was in particular need of assistance, and Lou Hoover gave generously of her time and talents to help the Belgian people. Years later, after the war ended, the king and queen of Belgium came to the United States to bestow one of Belgium's highest awards, the Cross of Chevalier, on Lou, in honor of her unstinting service to their country.[3]

When the war intensified and Europe became an increasingly dangerous place to be, the Hoovers were forced to return to the United States, relocating to Washington, D.C., in 1917. They were home only a short time before the country entered World War I and President Wilson again turned to Hoover for assistance, appointing him U.S. Food Administrator. Lou encouraged and supported the American policy of not eating meat or wheat on designated days, offering special recipes omitting those items to newspapers and magazines.

To aid the thousands of women seeking employment in the capital city, Lou once again not only gave generously of her personal funds, she founded yet another guild. The Food Administration Club was set up to help these women with obtaining food and shelter. Needless to say, her home was always open and welcomed American servicemen and women.

Additionally, Lou began her lifelong commitment to the Girl Scouts of the United States of America, a girls-only organization designed to build character, develop self-worth, and encourage social conscience. She initially served as a local troop leader and eventually became national president of the organization.

Responsibility, independence, and athleticism were character traits that Lou encouraged and worked hard to foster in girls. These personal attributes were ingrained in Lou her whole life; as she said:

> I was a Scout years ago, before the movement started, when my father took me fishing, camping and hunting...here is what I always wanted other girls to have.[4]

As vice president of the National Amateur Athletic Federation (NAAF), Lou continued to advance the athletic opportunities available to women by organizing a women's division of the NAAF.

When the war ended, Lou and her husband continued to approach their relationship and their various projects as a team, and a very effective one it was. While Lou remained in the States to raise funds for the country's latest cause, Hoover returned to Europe as director of the American Relief Administration. According to historian William DeGregorio, during 1919 and 1920 "some thirty-four million tons of American food, clothing, and supplies valued at $5.2 billion" were provided to the war needy.[5] At one benefit dinner alone, Lou raised three million dollars.

Talk had already begun to surface that Hoover was considered a potential presidential candidate. Instead, he was appointed Secretary of Commerce under the Harding and Coolidge administrations. Lou continued all of her charitable work, and still found time to design the plans and begin construction of their long-anticipated dream home in Palo Alto, on the campus of Stanford University. Both Hoover sons would graduate from their parents' alma mater and go on to receive degrees from Harvard Business School. In 1925 Herbert Jr. (who incidentally had worn a hearing aid since childhood for his partial deafness) got married and started a family.

Nineteen twenty-eight brought both joy and sadness for Lou. That June, Hoover unanimously won the Republican nomination for president on the first ballot. The following month, Lou's beloved widowed father died without ever knowing the triumphant outcome of that election (her mother had passed away seven years earlier). Hoover won by over six million votes, and Chief Justice William Howard Taft administered the same oath of office to Hoover that he himself had accepted twenty years earlier.* Lou Hoover was about to become one of the most educated, experienced, and confidently competent First Ladies ever to reside in the White House.

* William Howard Taft, the nation's twenty-seventh president, went on to become the chief justice of the U.S. Supreme Court. John Quincy Adams, the nation's sixth president, went on to serve seventeen years in Congress before he died in the Speaker's Room of the House of Representatives, five months before his eighty-first birthday.

While many of her predecessors were overwhelmed by their change in status, Lou took the move to the White House easily in stride, for it was not that much of a change from the last several decades of her life. Already comfortable with Washington social life, Lou was undeniably cosmopolitan and a proven international hostess. In addition to speaking several languages, she had studied many cultures and had extensive experience living in and traveling to many parts of the world.

Conveniently, the new First Lady was accustomed to running large households and supervising numerous staff members and servants. She was entirely comfortable giving orders, had frequently and lavishly entertained hundreds of influential people, and moreover shared in every aspect of her husband's professional, business, and political careers. Respected for her many accomplishments, Lou had established strong connections with hundreds of friends and fellow volunteers on projects of great, often worldwide, significance. Minimal transition was required for Lou to immediately step into Grace Coolidge's shoes.

There was also every reason to think the new First Lady would be as popular as her predecessor. The economy was going well and Lou had achieved success in her other venues. Another move guaranteed to make Hoover a popular president: he chose not to take a salary. (According to the Hoover archives, his presidential salary was banked and given entirely to charity.) The archives continue:

> From the day Hoover organized the Belgian Relief in 1914, until his death fifty years later, he never accepted for his private use any payment for public service. Hoover believed that "Being a politician is a poor profession. Being a public servant is a noble one."[6]

With dedicated public servants like the Hoovers, what more could the country want from the First Family? Only time would answer that question; however, anyone who eagerly anticipated the typical honeymoon period was soon and sorely disappointed. The Hoovers did not have even a year to enjoy their new position before the crash of the economy would throw the nation into unprecedented turmoil.

But not knowing what was in store, Lou simply continued her charitable habit of using personal wealth to fund, promote, and support projects or matters of importance to her. She paid for an increased White House staff as well as a number of additional private secretaries for both herself and her husband. However, though Lou was generous and kind, *popular* was not a word used by employees when describing their feelings for the First Lady. All of her charity work aside, the staff found Lou difficult to work for. Ava Long, a White House employee, probably said it best.

> Finer people never lived. But the President and Mrs. Hoover rarely broke through the barrier between those who serve and those who are served.[7]

Sixty years had passed since the era of Julia Grant's expensive and extensive multicourse entertaining, but presidential hospitality was about to be brought to new levels of excess. Lou was familiar with and utterly unfazed by habitual and constant entertaining, the likes of which had never before been experienced by the White House staff.

Although Lou preferred to keep things somewhat casual in nature, visitors still came in unprecedented numbers, and dinners with as many as seven courses were common. Not only did the First Lady hold daily (sometimes twice daily) afternoon teas in the Green Room, large numbers of guests joined the family for breakfast, lunch, and dinner, day after relentless day. The White House housekeeper was quoted as saying, "Company, company, company, often arrived on short notice." The First Lady's exhausted social secretary, Mary Randolph, referred to the White House as "the Big Top with plenty of side-shows and lots of ballyhoo." She also said, "Every meal was a party, with parties in between, and between the parties every day Lou received women's organizations."[8]

As if the comings and goings of invited guests were not enough, there was a ten-month period when Lou's daughter-in-law and two grandchildren moved into the Executive Mansion. During this time, eldest son Herbert Jr. was in North Carolina, where he received treatment for tuberculosis.

To say that the Hoovers liked company at mealtimes would be a monumental understatement. White House Chief Usher Ike Hoover—

no relation—reported that the presidential couple enjoyed less than a dozen meals by themselves during their entire tenure (excepting wedding anniversaries, which they celebrated alone).

Lou had one incomprehensible quirk: she was concerned that someone might confuse Ike Hoover with her husband and insisted that the entire staff always refer to Ike using his title of chief usher. This was despite repeated assurances that *everyone always* referred to the Chief Executive as either the President or Mr. President. Referring to the president by his last name had *never* nor would *ever* happen in the White House itself. Nevertheless, Lou still had her doubts.

Furthermore, servants were *not* to be heard or seen. Staff was so well trained on this point it was not uncommon for maids to jump behind walls, hide in closets, duck behind plants, and be heard speaking only in whispers. During dinner parties, signals were used to convey the First Lady's instructions, and if waiters were noticed at all, it was only because of their formal attire. Butler Alonzo Fields (who later served as chief butler and then maitre d'hotel) reports in his book, *My 21 Years In The White House*,

> After each service I took my position and stood at attention. Above all, I could show no interest in the conversation. To smile at some joking remark, overheard by chance, would mean the last time I would go into the dining room.[9]

Lou had said her new residence was "as bleak as a New England barn."[10] In addition to the continuous revolving door of guests, Ike Hoover reported on the upheaval of the inanimate objects in the Hoovers' purview:

> Two days after Mrs. Hoover's arrival all furniture, rugs, pictures and everything were ordered moved. The transformation was startling.[11]

In reference to the mansion's private quarters, Ike noted:

> Never was the place so changed, so torn up, so twisted around... Three months after this [Hoover] Administration had been in ex-

> istence, there was not a room on the entire second floor that had not been completely altered, and not one of them was finished.[12]

The First Lady also began a project to restore the Lincoln Study. Locating as much original furniture as possible, she again paid for many items personally. Cost never appeared to be a consideration for Lou: she wanted the best, whether it was in furnishings, art, or food. She used thousands of dollars of personal funds to purchase many items that ultimately became government property.

Oddly enough, although perfection was crucial to the First Lady, she was indifferent to her clothing. (A remnant of her tomboy past, perhaps?) She stood tall and carried herself gracefully, now with a full head of gray hair, but her attire was dreary and unbecoming. Except when decked out in exquisite evening gowns, she was often described as dowdy.

Something very important to Lou was providing her husband with a retreat. Somewhere he could relax and go fishing. After discovering an ideal location in the Blue Ridge Mountains of Virginia, she oversaw the construction of one large family cabin and a dozen smaller guest cabins. Camp Rapidan, which was as comprehensive as the White House, was referred to as a small village. Over time, hundreds of individuals visited and spent time at the camp with the First Family. Never having lost her childhood delight in being outdoors, Lou was able once more to indulge in favorite activities like riding horses, hiking, and trout fishing.

When the First Lady learned there was no local school for the children residing in the area, she and her husband built the President's Community School. They then hired a teacher and provided a small apartment for the teacher's use, all at their own expense.

There was no doubt: Lou was indeed her own woman. She even insisted on driving her own car around Washington. Although her husband was a connoisseur of wine, she believed no one was above the law. Prohibition was still in effect, and unlike the Hardings (it was common knowledge they regularly served alcohol to their guests), Lou insisted her husband discard his substantial wine collection. Ouch! Considering the Hoovers' desire for and insistence on having only the finest of everything, not to mention their ability to afford anything, we can only imagine what once existed in that wine cellar. The *Woman's Home Companion* said of the First Lady's style, "She does not keep the rules, but mixes the great and the near-great with the obscure and the near obscure."[13]

Lou encouraged women to pursue careers as well as marriage. This philosophy went hand in hand with her belief that women should be independent and responsible, characteristics she encouraged in young women she met during her travels around the country. Lou was in a unique position to further her championship of women's independence and self-reliance. It is believed Lou's influence was behind Hoover's executive order to amend Civil Service Rule VII to require nominations "without regard to sex." The president went so far as to name seven women to positions that required Senate approval.

Supporting women in all respects was a priority for Lou. However, since she preferred the theater to movies, we don't know if the First Lady was interested in the inaugural Academy of Motion Picture Arts and Sciences' presentation of the Oscars to actors (both male and female), which occurred early in 1929. We do know that Lou devoted her full attention to the White House conference on the country's economic decline later that same year.

The great stock market crash of 1929 occurred some eight months into Lou's tenure as First Lady.* The chance for her to establish a productive and admirable legacy was destroyed forever: history was writing its own story, and no amount of intellect, compassion, or generosity on her part was going to be noticed or acknowledged.

The Great Depression (the United States' most damaging and horrific financial decline in its history) impacted the entire country and devastated millions of individuals and families. Both the president and the First Lady believed strongly in volunteerism, and boldly encouraged all Americans to follow their lead with charitable endeavors. Lou, the first First Lady to give regular radio broadcasts, even pleaded for Girl Scouts across the country to provide aid and service,

* Inauguration Day was originally held on March 3. In order to speed up the changeover time between administrations, in 1933 Inauguration Day was moved up to its current date of January 20.

in keeping with their altruistic tenets. She was certain that, "If everybody helped, there would be plenty of food and clothing for all."[14]

> My plea is that our most important duty is to find when, how, and where people need help.[15]

No one could possibly question that Lou's strong sense of duty to serve others was anything but genuine; she had demonstrated this characteristic repeatedly and persistently. Her position under these circumstances, however, was more idealistic than realistic. Predictably, the First Lady was asked for and gave financial assistance. Letters from all over the country flooded into the White House. Lou was forced to hire yet another private secretary to handle the deluge of pleas for help. In line with her well-established orders regarding privacy for herself and the president, the First Lady insisted on strict confidentially, giving only anonymously to individuals, the Red Cross, and other charitable organizations.

As willing and ready as she was to help those in need or distress, Lou was equally *un*willing and reluctant to share any details of her personal life. Both the president and First Lady demanded an exceedingly high level of privacy. In fact the president rarely spoke to White House employees. The First Couple's nonpublic life was *strictly* off limits to both the press and their own staff. The two were even known to converse in Chinese, ensuring that no one, not even their closest aides, would be privy to certain conversations. Years later, Hoover confirmed his wife's "deep resentment of the intrusion of the press and public into our family life."[16]

When it came to sharing information with the newspapers and other media, the First Lady was quite gun-shy. She had already experienced a storm of negative press from many Southern legislatures and newspapers, which was unleashed when she invited the wife of African-American congressman Oscar DePrist to a White House tea.

The last time a black individual (Booker T. Washington) was invited to the Executive Mansion, in 1901, race riots broke out in the South. The First Lady's strong morals precluded discrimination, however, and trumped any anxiety she might have felt. The result was that Mrs. DePriest was graciously welcomed into the president's home. The *Mobile Alabama Press* called it "an arrogant insult" to the nation.

Some people did, unfortunately, condemn the First Lady, while others praised her courage and leadership in facing down discrimination. The president was not lucky enough to garner even mixed reviews. Hoover was vilified because of the ongoing catastrophic financial ravagement of the Depression, even though he certainly could not be held personally accountable for the disaster. The president believed that businessmen and larger corporations would nurture the economy back to health, which was in keeping with his conviction that government should not intervene in such instances. His faith was not borne out; unemployment still doubled to twelve million in 1931, and countless families were left homeless when their breadwinners were unable to scrape together rent or mortgage payments. Shantytowns and Hoovervilles were synonymous with destitute living conditions.

On a more positive note, the following year was historic for American women. The first female was elected to the Senate (others had been appointed), and Amelia Earhart was the first woman to complete a solo transatlantic flight. Pleased about this multidimensional progress for women, the First Lady now strongly encouraged them to exercise their newfound right to vote. She asserted,

> Bad men are elected by good women who stay at home from the polls on Election Day.[17]

After repeated (and futile) declarations that prosperity was just around the corner, the president finally gave $2 billion of government aid to farmers, bankers, and bankrupt businesses. Sadly, it was insufficient, and ultimately immaterial in terms of redeeming Hoover in the public eye. Franklin D. Roosevelt won the 1932 presidential election by over seven million popular votes and 89 percent of the electoral vote. Lou was bitterly disappointed by her husband's defeat and especially resented the lack of confidence shown in the electoral vote.

In her mind, there was not a soul that deserved more credit for helping others than the man with whom she had worked side by side over the past thirty-three years. No one had labored harder or longer than her husband to serve the needs of the country; Hoover, in fact, consistently worked sixteen-to-eighteen-hour days. Understandably, the First Lady remained unshakeable when it came to believing in her husband's commitment and capabilities.

Lou resided in the Executive Mansion during an exceptionally troubled and worrisome period, similar to that of Mary Todd Lincoln. The disastrous state of the country during their tenures overshadowed the accomplishments of these women, and neither received credit or acknowledgement for the many positive aspects of their stints as First Ladies.

After leaving the White House, Lou Hoover lived and conducted her final eleven years in exactly the same fashion as her life up till that point. She resided in her Palo Alto home but maintained a second residence—a large suite in the Tower at the Waldorf-Astoria Hotel in New York. Each home supported a full staff of servants and secretaries to assist Lou and Herbert with their ongoing charitable efforts. Herbert Jr., who refused to cash in on his name, was now the father of three and a respected mining engineer, inventor, and diplomat in his own right. Younger brother Allan, who married four years after his parents left the White House, also fathered three children and became a wealthy California rancher prior to promoting his father's legacy later in life.

Lou remained national president of the Girl Scouts and continued to support aid organizations such as the Red Cross. She supported the arts, including the Friends of Music at Stanford, which sponsored various concert series, the ballet, opera, lectures, and musical instruction.

Her organizational skills were also directed at preserving her husband's birthplace in West Branch, Iowa. A library, museum, and the Hoover Society were all established to honor her spouse and his legacy. Today the complex includes an eighty-one acre park, the Hoover Presidential Library, and the former president's and First Lady's gravesites.

Lou's humanitarian efforts did not stop there. With her husband, she put together a two-hundred-thousand-volume Hoover Library at Stanford University, and also donated Camp Rapidan and the surrounding 164 acres to the Shenandoah National Park. Her dedication to war relief efforts would also surface once more: Lou lived to see yet another world war devastate Europe and other parts of the globe. As chair of the Western Women's Committee, she organized a clothing drive for millions of war refugees, distributed through the Salvation Army. Again she and her husband worked hard in support of people all over Europe.

After spending what was to be her final afternoon enjoying a concert, the sixty-nine-year-old former First Lady suffered an acute heart attack and died on January 7, 1944. (Her namesake and youngest grandchild had just turned a year old.) One of Lou's final wishes was to donate the dream home she had personally designed to Stanford University as a permanent residence for all future university presidents. Fifteen hundred individuals attended her funeral, including two hundred representatives from the Girl Scouts.

After Lou's passing, to his great surprise her husband found dozens and dozens of uncashed checks in her personal effects. The checks were from individuals attempting to repay loans given to them over the years by the First Lady. This was money she had graciously gifted, with no intention of ever attempting to collect on the debt.

Lou was originally buried in Palo Alto, but her remains were reunited with her husband's in Iowa after the former president died twenty years later, in 1964, at the age of ninety.

At the time of his death, thirty-one years had passed since Hoover left the White House. Two of those years (1947 through 1949, during the Truman administration) were spent as chairman of the Commission on Organization of the Executive Branch of the government, otherwise known as the Hoover Commission. Of the 273 recommendations made by the commission to streamline government, about three-fourths were adopted. Then later, during Hoover's second commission (1953 through 1955, during the Eisenhower administration), 314 additional recommendations were submitted, and of those, two-thirds were adopted.

Today Hoover is one of, if not the most, honored presidents in American history. He received over a hundred miscellaneous honors, more than seventy medals and awards, over twenty-five honorary degrees from foreign universities, and fifty-plus honorary degrees from American universities. Additionally, the Colorado River's Hoover Dam, originally known as Boulder Dam or Boulder Canyon Dam (situated on the border between Arizona and Nevada), was renamed in honor of the thirty-first president. After twenty-five years of disagreement over water allocations, then–Secretary of Commerce Herbert Hoover negotiated an agreement between six states (Arizona, California, Nevada, New Mexico, Utah, and Wyoming) to make the dam a reality.

In 1964, on the one hundredth anniversary of Columbia University's School of Engineering, Herbert Hoover and Thomas Edison were named the two greatest engineers in United States history.[18] As an engineer, statesman, and dedicated humanitarian, Hoover's contributions cannot be overlooked. Yet when Hoover died at the age of ninety, befitting his Quaker faith, a simple funeral without eulogies was conducted.

WHAT LOU TAUGHT ME

Lou Henry Hoover's exciting life of travel, adventure, and fortune has far deeper meaning than simply sightseeing or experiencing other cultures. Her life was centered on volunteerism, certainly not because she wanted to be recognized for it, but because she sincerely wanted to make things better, if only in a small way. She strongly believed,

> The ambition to do, to accomplish, irrespective of its measure in money or fame, is what should be inculcated. The desire to make the things that are better—in a little way with what is at hand—in a big way, if the opportunity comes.[19]

Lou taught me the importance and value of volunteering; certainly, if more people helped, fewer would be in need.

However, the cavalier way she sometimes dealt with people she deemed "serving class" showed me another, less admirable, side of Lou Hoover. Her hierarchical viewpoint serves as an uncomfortable reminder that labeling people, and only seeing the label—*staff member, worker, subordinate, housekeeper*—benefits no one. Lou's avid need for complete privacy was understandable; nevertheless, an individual has the inherent right to be seen and recognized as a human being before all else. Lou's unfortunate habit of treating those who worked for her simply as "staff" rather than as an individual named Joan or Richard (or Ike Hoover) reminds me to be vigilant in acknowledging all individuals as people rather than positions.

6

Devoted Business Partner

ANNA ELEANOR ROOSEVELT

> You gain strength, experience and confidence by every experience where you really stop to look fear in the face. You must do the thing you cannot do.
>
> —Eleanor Roosevelt

During some of America's greatest historical crises, the United States was fortunate to have unique and notable women who refused to hide behind their fears. Martha Washington, Abigail Adams, and Dolley Madison stood as pillars of support during the desperate times of the Revolution. Later, when the Civil War threatened the country's very existence, First Ladies Lucretia Garfield, Lucy Hayes, Julia Grant, and Mary Todd Lincoln sublimated their private fears in order to sustain and champion their courageous husbands.

#32 Anna Eleanor Roosevelt Roosevelt

Born: October 11, 1884

Birthplace: New York, New York

Married: 1905 (Franklin Delano Roosevelt)

Children: 6

White House Years: 1933–1945

Died: November 7, 1962 (78 years old)

Fact: First Lady for 12 years; wrote newspaper column "My Day"

AKA: First Lady to the World

Throughout the Great Depression, it was Lou Hoover who gave generously of her talents and finances to help those in need, followed by Eleanor Roosevelt, who wrote the above quote. Do not believe for one minute that these brave heroines did not have their own intense anxiety—because they did! But they refused to allow fear to weaken them, and managed to gain the strength necessary to move forward and succeed.

In Eleanor Roosevelt's case, her fears and insecurities began at a very young age. Orphaned before her tenth birthday, Eleanor was a product of the Victorian era and struggled through her insecurities to break out of the stereotypical boundaries for women. She was born Anna Eleanor Roosevelt on October 11, 1884, the year Grover Cleveland won his first nonconsecutive presidential bid.*

That same year, France constructed the Statue of Liberty and presented it to America as a universal symbol of freedom and democracy. Very apropos, as Eleanor herself was to become an enduring symbol of freedom and democracy to the entire world.

It seems everyone had a strong opinion about Eleanor Roosevelt, a woman whose life was steeped in great controversy, both personal and political. People's comments about her ran the gamut:

> Her very presence lit up the room...She was the ugliest woman I ever saw...Her voice could shatter glass; and she was so unbearably righteous...She changed my life, just by caring.[1]

Four future First Ladies praised her, even though they did not always agree with her political bias. In 1964, Lady Bird Johnson said of her:

> Courage sustained by compassion—that was the watchword of her entire career.[2]

On the centennial of Eleanor's birth in 1984, Nancy Reagan remarked,

> [She was] a truly great American lady who always seemed to be larger than life to me...[Although] I didn't agree with everything she did, you couldn't help but be a fan. Whether you were a Republican or Democrat didn't make any difference.[3]

In 1987 Betty Ford admitted,

* Frances Cleveland, the country's youngest First Lady (and the only one to be married in the White House), served as the twenty-second and twenty-fourth First Ladies. See Volume I of *Loves, Lies, and Tears* for her romantic and exciting soar into history.

> Eleanor Roosevelt was another important role model for me. I admired her ability to speak out in support of her beliefs, although I didn't always agree with the causes she championed.[4]

And fifty years after Eleanor moved out of the White House, Hillary Clinton said in 1995,

> I am often challenged, as I ask myself, am I even living up to one small percentage of the example she set, because it was ground breaking. There will never be another woman who did what she did.[5]

The woman who became a powerful political advocate was a passive, dependent child who grew into an assertive, independent, and bold adult. Considering her childhood and the domination she endured throughout her early adulthood, Eleanor's accomplishments are truly inspirational.

Unlike European nobility, which dates back several centuries, American aristocracy traces its roots to the seventeen hundreds, when the lives of elite American families of the highest social class were centered in New York City. Names like Alsops, Astor, Vanderbilt, McAllister, and Livingston were part of the distinguished upper echelon of New York society known as the "Knickerbockers."*

On the Knickerbocker Society's original list of prominent persons were Mrs. Mary Livingston Ludlow Hall (Eleanor's maternal grandmother) and Mary's stunningly beautiful daughter Anna Livingston Hall (Eleanor's mother). It was said that poet Robert Browning "asked merely to gaze upon her" as Anna sat having her portrait painted.[6] It was an era when a woman's attractiveness and personal appearance

* Washington Irving, the American author and essayist of the early nineteenth century, best known for his short stories "Rip Van Winkle" and "The Legend of Sleepy Hollow," had a hand in establishing the Knickerbocker name. In 1809, Irving, using the pseudonym Diedrich Knickerbocker, published a satire titled *A History of New York*. It lampooned New York culture and politics in a style akin to *Mad* magazine.

meant everything, overshadowing her education and personality.

The significance of beauty was so ingrained in Eleanor's psyche that years later it still took priority over all other particulars. In volume one of her three-volume autobiography, *This Is My Story*, Eleanor began with, "My mother was one of the most beautiful women I have ever seen."* Attractiveness, stature, and prominence were attributes the Hall family had in abundance; however, education and intelligence were not important when taking the measure of a woman.

Mary Hall took great pride in the fact that one of her relatives signed the Declaration of Independence, and another became the first governor of New York. Her husband, Valentine G. Hall (Eleanor's maternal grandfather), came from great wealth and had considerable real estate holdings in the most valuable New York City neighborhoods.

At nineteen, Anna Hall married the charming and handsome twenty-three-year-old Elliott Roosevelt of the Oyster Bay (New York) Roosevelts. A hard-working and intelligent clan, the Roosevelt family tree dates back to the mid-sixteen hundreds. Pioneers and explorers who hailed originally from Holland, they eventually found their way to New Amsterdam (later called New York) and fought for freedom during the American Revolution. Roosevelt descendants numbered over fifty families by the eighteen hundreds. As farmers, merchants, bankers, businessmen, lawyers, and real estate financiers, the Roosevelts amassed large fortunes. They settled and remained predominately in the Oyster Bay and Hyde Park regions of New York.

Elliott's father, Theodore Roosevelt Sr. (Eleanor's paternal grandfather), was a noted New York City philanthropist. He made his fortune in the family plate glass importing business and helped found the New York City Children's Aid Society and the New York Children's Orthopedic Hospital, as well as the Metropolitan Museum of Art and the American Museum of Natural History.† Theodore Roosevelt Jr.,

* Eleanor Roosevelt's autobiographies are *This Is My Story*, *This I Remember*, and *On My Own*. *The Autobiography of Eleanor Roosevelt* is an abridged version of her three-volume series, with the addition of three subsequent years.

† In 1860, Theodore Roosevelt Sr. had intended to run for the presidency, but was forced to drop his plans when he contracted tuberculosis.

Elliott's older brother (Eleanor's uncle), went on to become the twenty-sixth president of the United States.*

Anna and Elliott's marriage began idyllically and was reported in the *New York Times* on December 2, 1883, as "one of the most brilliant weddings of the season."[7] Ten months later, Anna Eleanor (always known as Eleanor), their only daughter and the eldest of their three children, arrived to great anticipation. Unfortunately, things began to unravel rather quickly for the young couple shortly thereafter. Elliott, a bored and unambitious man of means, was continually in search of excitement. His quest frequently took him away from home and family. On weekdays he would drink for hours at his favorite Knickerbocker Club; weekends were spent hunting with the hounds or playing polo, while months were consumed traveling around the world, hunting large game.

While he was away, Elliott made a point of writing frequent letters to Eleanor, and he doted on her when he was home. In turn Eleanor adored her father, romanticized his lifestyle, and developed something like hero worship for him. In truth, she also felt abandoned—physically and emotionally—every time he left.

Perhaps things would have been somewhat easier on Eleanor had her mother been more demonstrative toward her. However, Anna did not have the emotional wherewithal to compensate for or counterbalance her daughter's feelings of inadequacy. Simply put, Anna could not relate to the daughter who shared her given name but was nothing like herself. Like her husband, Anna enjoyed parties, and she organized numerous charity balls for popular causes of the day. She was also the founder and creative director of the Amateur Comedy Club of New York.

* The Roosevelt lineage is rather long and perplexing and many of the family members' lives cross over with one another. An example would be Laura Delano (the younger sister of Sara Delano [Roosevelt]—a woman who would play an enormously large part in Eleanor's life). Laura Delano invited her sister Sara to an engagement party Laura hosted for her friend Anna Hall (and future husband Elliott Roosevelt). A few years earlier, in 1880, Sara Delano (twenty-six years old) married James Roosevelt (a fifty-two-year-old widower) of the Hyde Park Roosevelts. Sara and James grew close to Elliott Roosevelt (a distant cousin) whom they subsequently asked to be godfather to their only child, Franklin Delano Roosevelt. If you are not yet totally confused with the various Roosevelt relations, let me just add that Eleanor Roosevelt's great-great-great-great-grandfather and Franklin Delano Roosevelt's great-great-great-grandfather were brothers, making Eleanor and Franklin fifth cousins.

Truly her mother's opposite, Eleanor was a shy and solemn child who openly admitted, "I never smiled," a statement supported by pictures of Eleanor in her youth. Eleanor's somberness frankly irritated Anna. When speaking to visitors, Anna described her daughter as a "funny" (strange) child—"so old fashioned."[8] To Eleanor's humiliation, her mother nicknamed her "Granny," which made her want "to sink through the floor in shame."

Although Eleanor had lovely blue eyes and long, thick blond hair, she also had protruding teeth. Compared to her dashing and likable father and strikingly attractive mother, Eleanor was rather plain and considered the ugly duckling of the family. Actually, her mother told her as much when Anna instructed Eleanor, "You have no looks, so see to it that you have manners."[9]

When Eleanor was five her mother gave birth to her younger brother Elliott Jr. Two years later (1891) she delivered another son whom they named Gracie Hall (after a relative), and called him Hall. But disappointment, abandonment, and alcohol were soon to shatter the privileged legacy Eleanor and her brothers were born into. Her father was subject to sudden explosions of jealousy, and then wallowed in self-pity. It did not take long before Elliott's behavior became even more erratic; he would disappear for days at a time only to return more depressed and remorseful than ever. Anna begged her husband to give up drinking and drugs (he was also taking morphine and laudanum), but to no avail.

As if things were not already stressful enough, Katy Mann, a servant employed by Anna, also delivered a son around the time of Hall's birth and claimed that Elliott was the child's father. Originally, Elliott maintained that he was not; however, after a period of time he admitted he "could be" but did not remember.* Foolish as that sounds, Elliott was telling the truth about his memory. He had experienced seizures in the past and more recently blackouts from his heavy drinking. The "most brilliant wedding" proved to be a marital nightmare for Anna.

* Katy Mann requested ten thousand dollars for support, and Elliott's brother Theodore believed it would be better for Elliott to pay than have his reputation publicly disgraced in court. Apparently they reached a settlement; however, Katy reportedly never received any money. Attorneys allegedly stole the trust funds designated for Katy's son, Elliott Roosevelt Mann.

She felt lonely and neglected, while Elliott felt repentant and spoke of suicide. Then on August 18, 1891, the *New York Herald* reported:

> Elliott Roosevelt Demented by Excesses. Wrecked by Liquor and Folly, he is now confined in an asylum for the insane near Paris.[10]

Publicly shamed and now a mother of three young children, Anna emotionally withdrew even more. She had continually supported her husband and made every possible excuse for his behavior, but now she just wanted her life to move on. Except Anna was neither a widow nor a divorcée, and her circumstances were disheartening at best. The entire family suffered. Eleanor missed her father more than ever and described her mother's behavior toward her as cold and distant.

> I was always disgracing my mother. I felt a curious barrier between myself and these three [referring to her mother and younger siblings].[11]

Up until that time, a French governess had tutored Eleanor daily at home in reading and writing. However, her mother soon sent Eleanor away to a convent school to try and protect her during this latest ordeal. She remembers being miserable at the convent and was an adult before she could acknowledge, "I now realize I was a great trial to my mother."[12] Sadly, her circumstances would not improve for some time.

In November of 1892, Anna underwent an unidentified operation and shortly thereafter contracted diphtheria. She did not want to see her husband, and her mother, Mary Hall, was determined to honor those wishes. Only twenty-nine, the beautiful New York socialite died on December 7, 1892.* Sent to live with their widowed Grandmother Hall, in Tivoli, New York, were eight-year-old Eleanor and her two brothers.

Anna's death did not have much meaning for young Eleanor, other than buoying her hopes that she could spend more time with her father—hopes which were brutally dashed. Depressed that he had

* Ironically, forty-nine years to the day later, another tragedy would heavily influence Eleanor's life.

been unable to see his wife before her death, Elliott was now living at the Keeley Center for the treatment of alcoholism in Dwight, Illinois, some nine hundred miles away. Grandmother Hall continued to stay in written contact with her son-in-law, but she was unwilling to allow him to see his children alone.

Though his visits to Tivoli were sporadic, Elliott continued to write his daughter frequently and Eleanor read and reread her father's letters of support, instruction, and encouragement. Along with urging her to study hard at her lessons, he also told her, "Oh, my dear companionable little Daughter, you will come to Father and what jolly games we will have together."[13] Eleanor noted,

> With my father I was perfectly happy...He was the center of my world.[14]

> Above all, I loved the way he treated me. He called me "Little Nell" (after the Little Nell in Dickens's Old Curiosity Shop)…I only knew it was a term of affection, and I never doubted that I stood first in his heart.[15]

Looking back at that period in her life, Eleanor remembered,

> They [her family members, governesses, and maids] always tried to talk to me, and I wished to be left alone to live in a dream world in which I was the heroine and my father the hero. Into this world I retired as soon as I went to bed and as soon as I woke in the morning.[16]

She went on to say that her mother's death was,

> A tragedy of utter defeat for him [Elliott]. No hope now of ever wiping out the sorrowful years he had brought upon my mother...He had no wife, no children, no hope![17]

Trust funds were established to provide his children with a monthly income of $625, and Elliott assured their grandmother he would send additional money if needed.* Then in May of 1893, a brief five months after Anna's passing, Elliott Jr., not yet four, died from diphtheria. Not surprisingly, Elliott's concerns were for his daughter.

> My own little Nell—We bury little Ellie tomorrow up at Tivoli by Mother's side. He is happy in Heaven with her now so you must not grieve or sorrow.
>
> I cannot write more because I am not feeling very well and my heart is too full. But I wished you to know you were never out of my thoughts and prayers for one instant all the time. With abiding and most tender devotion and Love I am always, Your affectionate Father.[18]

Later that same year, according to Eleanor's biographer Blanche Cook, Elliott moved back to New York and shared an apartment with his mistress, who was identified only as a certain Mrs. Evans. Father and daughter still continued to exchange letters and one in particular stands out.

> *August 13, 1894*
>
> What must you think of your Father who has not written in so long...I have after all been very busy, quite ill, at intervals not able to move from my bed for days...I hope my little girl is well...Kiss Baby Brudie for me and *never forget* I love you.[19]

The very next evening, Elliott died suddenly at the age of thirty-four. Weeks earlier, he had returned to drinking heavily and was again using stimulants. After running up and down the stairs repeatedly at a punishing pace, Elliott jumped out of a second story window. He survived the fall, but later that night suffered a seizure and died. Upon learning of her father's death, a numb Eleanor's only comment was, "I

* Using the Consumer Price Index "relative values measurement," $625 in 1892 would be equivalent to approximately $15,200 in 2009 (www.measuringworth.com/uscompare).

did want to see father once more."[20] Mary Hall did not allow ten-year-old Eleanor to attend her father's funeral.

To outsiders, Grandmother Hall appeared harsh and rather strict—and, indeed, she was. Mary insisted on punctuality and was a disciplinarian with high standards. As she had done with her own four daughters (Mary also had two sons), Grandmother Hall forced Eleanor to take long walks up and down a road alongside the Hudson River near their home. Behind the girls' shoulders and hooked at their elbows was a long stick, which made this marathon task even more difficult. The exercise was designed to ensure that the girls grew into proper society "ladies" demonstrating excellent posture. Even worse, when Mary became convinced that Eleanor suffered from curvature of the spine, she had her granddaughter wear a corrective steel brace for nearly a year.

The fact is that Mary's experiences consisted only of high society behavior and she was a very sheltered and dominated wife while her husband, Valentine Hall, lived. She was ill prepared to manage a household with so many emotional and physical demands. Her husband always made all of the family decisions. He literally treated Mary like one of the children and exercised complete control over every aspect of her life. Valentine not only refused to discuss their family finances, he either accompanied his wife on shopping trips or had designer clothes sent to their home for his wife to try on.

When Mary was widowed at thirty-seven, with six children to raise, she turned to her eldest child, seventeen-year-old Anna, for assistance. Anna managed the family budget but had little success with her unruly younger brothers, both of whom developed serious drinking problems. After Anna's passing, Mary struggled to cope with her challenging sons and young grandchildren. As one cousin recalled of Mary,

> She seemed beaten [down] as though life was more than she could bear.[21]

I think it is fair to say that Mary tried to protect her grandchildren, albeit with an iron hand, and provide them with every possible opportunity. Eleanor loved languages and studied both French and German. She was introduced to poetry and good literature and attended opera, theater, and dance performances. Tutored in music, Eleanor also received piano and ballet lessons, a surprising treat. The only other students in her weekly ballet class had plans to perform on the stage. Mary, however, was far more concerned that her tall granddaughter not appear "awkward." It was apparent that, at this point, Mary's grandchildren were the focus of her life. Eleanor recalled,

> My grandmother's life had a considerable effect on me, for even when I was young I determined, that I would never be dependent upon my children by allowing all my interests to center in them.[22]

It is curious, however, why Mary did not have Eleanor's teeth fixed. Per her critical cousin Alice Roosevelt Longworth, also known as Princess Alice when her father Teddy Roosevelt was president,

> It's true that her [Eleanor's] chin went in a bit, which wouldn't have been so noticeable if only her hateful grandmother had fixed her teeth.[23]

Nevertheless, given the structure and sense of belonging that had been missing from her life, Eleanor no longer felt neglected. Additionally, she had doting aunts and uncles who genuinely cared about her well-being and provided Eleanor with love and attention. They taught her to jump horses, play tennis, ride a bike, and participate in any sport she enjoyed. Most important, they encouraged the child in her to have fun.

At fifteen, Eleanor was sent abroad to attend Allenswood Academy, a French-speaking private girls' school located outside London. Having had a French governess and private French lessons proved very beneficial! Anna had always wanted her daughter to go to a European boarding school, and her aunts were optimistic that the new environment would help Eleanor get over her painful shyness. Women were still denied access to higher education in 1899; Allenswood, well known for taking women's education seriously, created an environment that encouraged its students to think independently and believe in their own intellectual talents.

The school emphasized cultural history, literature, composition, the arts, and foreign languages. Besides doing well in German, Eleanor learned to speak and read Italian, and she became thoroughly fluent in French. Eager to learn, she studied diligently and maintained an enthusiasm and interest in all her work, including algebra, piano, and composition.

Far from being a mere finishing school for young affluent women, Allenswood stressed rigorous analysis, critical thinking, independence, friendship, and forthright behavior. Classes *and* exercise were mandatory; literally every hour of the day was accounted for, with no idle moments. There was time for lessons, time to practice; time for research, time to exercise, time to study...and after the jam-packed day, students had fifteen minutes to dress for the nightly formal dinners. Many evenings were spent reading, listening to poems and stories that were read aloud, or attending leadership classes. Discipline became a primary force in Eleanor's life.

The headmistress, Marie Souvestre, was a bold feminist with strong liberal political convictions who recognized Eleanor's capabilities and cultivated her talents. Mademoiselle Souvestre was equally comfortable in the world of politics and high culture. She encouraged her students to be compassionate and have clarity of vision. She was far more than simply a teacher. In addition to being an intellectual influence for Eleanor, who became Souvestre's protégé, she was also a mentor, therapist, friend, and role model. During the three years Eleanor spent at Allenswood, summer vacations and Christmas holidays were spent traveling in Europe with Marie Souvestre. They visited not only the magnificent sights in Paris, Marseilles, the Mediterranean coast, Pisa, Florence, Rome, Alassio, Germany, Switzerland, and Austria, but the poverty and squalor as well. Part of the adventure was to discover the joy of travel, gain understanding for the needs of others, and develop self-reliance. It was Eleanor's responsibility to make the arrangements, check train schedules, and buy the tickets. Slowly but surely, she acquired self-assurance.

> I really marvel now at myself—confidence and independence, for I was totally without fear in this new phase of my life.[24]

During the first eight years of Eleanor's childhood, her mother's disapproval heavily overshadowed the advantages available to her. Then she was placed in the care of a harsh and unsympathetic grandmother. Prior to her father's death just two years after she moved in with Grandmother Hall, Eleanor acknowledged,

> Attention and admiration were the things throughout all my childhood which I wanted, because I was made to feel so conscious of the fact that nothing about me would attract attention or would bring me admiration![25]

Fortunately, her Allenswood experience proved differently; they were the brightest and happiest years of Eleanor's adolescence, perhaps her life. Acknowledged for her achievements, she learned to express her thoughts and inner feelings, excelled at various tasks, and made profound friendships. (Until the day she died, Eleanor kept a picture of Marie Souvestre on her desk.) The awkward young duckling was stretching her wings and began to gracefully embrace living in her somewhat gangly six-foot frame. It was now Eleanor's deepest desire to extend her education for a fourth year, and then join the school's faculty.

However, it was 1902, Eleanor was eighteen years old, and Grandmother Hall insisted Eleanor return home to make her debut in New York society. The dreadful ordeal made Eleanor uncomfortable and self-conscious. She would never become a notable belle as her mother and aunts had been, nor did she enjoy the social activities and demands required of her position. She was taller than most of the young men and found the gaps between dances torture.

> By no stretch of the imagination could I fool myself into thinking that I was a popular debutante.[26]

> I knew I was the first girl in my mother's family who was not a belle, and...I was deeply ashamed.[27]

Nonetheless, given her notable pedigree, her name automatically appeared on everyone's invitation lists, and a few eligible young men courted her.

Meanwhile, she maintained a correspondence with her adored mentor, and after her social debut, which consisted of a series of parties and balls, Eleanor returned her attention to Mademoiselle Souvestre's advice:

> Give some of your energy, but not all, to worldly pleasures...bear in mind that there are more quiet and enviable joys than to be among the most sought-after women at a ball.[28]

There existed a wide range of social issues that attracted Eleanor's attention. First, however, she took over the duty of running Grandmother Hall's home. At fifty-nine, Mary Hall was by no means an old woman, yet one could not help but notice how worn out she was. Her home, described as "a very unpleasant place," looked as though it were "semi barricaded." No light entered through the pulled-down shades, and doors between rooms were perpetually closed. It was obvious to outsiders that Mary was an unhappy woman, but Eleanor characterized her grandmother's life as unfulfilled and incomplete.

> Her willingness to be subservient to her children isolated her, and it might have been far better, for her boys at least, had she insisted on bringing more discipline into their lives simply by having a life of her own.[29]

Eleanor also assumed the major responsibility for her younger brother Hall. When the time came, Eleanor made sure Hall got settled at Groton, a college preparatory boarding school in Massachusetts.* In addition, she went to visit her brother for a weekend at the end of

* Several other Roosevelts were Groton graduates, including Franklin D. Roosevelt.

every term, and wrote him letters almost daily for the next several years. She wanted him to know that someone cared about and loved him. Eleanor maintained a parental role in Hall's life until his premature death in 1941 of alcoholism—obviously a family shortcoming—which had to evoke painful memories of her father's demise. Hall was fifty years old.

Assisting family was natural to Eleanor, as she deliberately and literally committed her life to the service of others. She joined the Junior League (a fundraising organization for the less fortunate) and quickly became their leader. As a volunteer for a settlement house (which provided educational and recreational opportunities for poor immigrants on Manhattan's Lower East Side), Eleanor taught calisthenics and dance to young girls. She became a member of the Women's Trade Union League (dedicated to banning child labor) and the Consumers' League (which sought to improve the working conditions of garment workers and department store clerks). Years later she acknowledged, "I think I came to feel that the underdog was always the one to be championed."[30]

Eleanor found her work far more rewarding than all the "dinners and dances I was struggling through in formal society each night."[31] In addition to volunteering, she made time to take classes in sociology and political economy. Like her Uncle Teddy, who read relentlessly (sometimes an entire book a day), Eleanor was an avid reader. She always regretted the loss of a college education, as her formal instruction ended when she left Allenswood.

During this period, a family friend introduced Eleanor to artists and writers in the Greenwich Village section of New York. Then, during the summer, she spent time in Washington with Aunt Bye (Anna Roosevelt Cowles, Theodore Roosevelt's older sister), who was well acquainted with the political world. Christened "the little White House," Bye's home was a favorite gathering spot during her brother's presidency. In addition to important political figures, Bye introduced her niece to influential young women such as Cissy Patterson, the future owner and publisher of the Washington *Times-Herald*, and Catherine Adams, granddaughter of Louisa Adams (America's sixth First Lady) and great-granddaughter of Abigail Adams (America's second First Lady). Eleanor rapidly earned a reputation for being sophisticated and interesting.

One admirer in particular was impressed with her intellect and compassion. An undergraduate at Harvard, Franklin Roosevelt was a distant cousin of hers and godson to Eleanor's parents. She had not seen Franklin since her early teens, when the family gathered at Aunt Corinne Roosevelt's holiday party several years earlier. Now young adults, their paths would cross multiple times at various political, social, and family gatherings. They had an easy friendship, shared common interests, and made one another laugh.

In December of 1902 (during Uncle Teddy's administration), they spent New Year's Eve together at the White House and Franklin noted in his diary, "Sat near Eleanor...very interesting day."[32] They had already begun a regular correspondence and at the end of January 1903, Eleanor attended Franklin's twenty-first birthday dinner. Their fleeting encounters developed into a secret romance, which Franklin chose to keep hidden from his overbearing and domineering widowed mother, Sara.*

Over the years, rumors persisted that Franklin breast-fed until the age of three and even older. Just prior to his ninth birthday, in a letter to his father Franklin wrote, "Mama left this morning and I am going to take my bath alone."[33] It is not surprising that Sara Delano Roosevelt, who never felt Eleanor was good enough for her son, would play a central role in the young couple's life.

It was curious to some, why Eleanor would be so attracted to a man many people referred to as a prissy, spoiled mama's boy. He was also flirtatious and what might be termed overly sociable. Described as "pretty" as opposed to "handsome," it was not his good looks or his gallantry toward his family that made him attractive to Eleanor. Irrefutably, Franklin never stood up to his mother, nor would he defend the woman he reportedly loved. He simply refused to "get in the middle," as he would say, of the two women. Surely there was a physical chemistry between the distant cousins, but more important were the common goals and intellectual connection the two shared. Franklin

* Franklin's father James was a widower (with a twenty-six-year-old son, James "Rosy" Roosevelt) when he married twenty-six-year-old Sara Delano [Roosevelt] (who became Franklin's mother). Franklin was eighteen when his father died.

respected Eleanor's judgment and admired her compassion, while she appreciated his attentiveness toward her and his leadership abilities.

From the moment Sara learned of her son's interest in marriage, she worked hard to intervene and separate the couple. She believed they were too young, and her unfavorable feelings toward Eleanor were well known. No amount of effort would ever change her critical and disapproving opinion. Considering the unhealthy stranglehold Sara had over her only child, any woman would have found herself in competition for Franklin's time and affection; understandably, however, Eleanor took Sara's harsh and critical scorn personally.

Ironically, Eleanor initially held warm feelings toward the woman she referred to as Cousin Sally, predominately due to Sara's early fondness for Elliott Roosevelt prior to his passing. For many years to come, even long after her marriage, Eleanor worked in vain to gain Franklin's mother's love and acceptance. A letter Eleanor wrote to her "Dearest Cousin Sally" expressed her deepest yearnings.

> *December 2, 1903*
>
> I know just how you feel and how hard it must be, but I do so want you to learn to love me a little. You must know that I will always try to do what you wish for I have grown to love you very dearly during the past summer. It is impossible for me to tell you how I feel toward Franklin, I can only say that my one great wish is always to prove worthy of him.
>
> With much love, always devotedly,
>
> Eleanor.[34]

During Christmas of 1903, Eleanor accepted Franklin's marriage proposal and Sara insisted the couple keep their engagement secret for a minimum of one year. She then immediately arranged to take Franklin away on a six-week Caribbean cruise, in hopes that his feelings for his clandestine fiancée would diminish. During his absence, Eleanor wrote Franklin lengthy letters (sometimes five or ten pages) daily. Those familiar with Eleanor's White House years may not recognize the timid and self-doubting teenager.

> I miss you [Franklin] so much dear, it really frightens me to see how dependent I am growing and how the whole world turns for me around one person.[35]

When mother and son returned home, Sara imposed on her friendship with the U.S. ambassador to the Court of Saint James. She asked him to take Franklin to London as his secretary, but to her great disappointment, the ambassador refused her request. When Franklin graduated from Harvard in June of 1904, both Sara and Eleanor were proudly in attendance. Sara then rented a house on Madison Avenue in New York, so she could live with her son when he enrolled in Columbia Law School.

In October, on Eleanor's twentieth birthday, Franklin surprised her with an engagement ring from Tiffany's.

> You could not have found a ring I would have liked better. I love it so I know I shall find it hard to keep from wearing it![36]

After almost a year of compulsory silence, Eleanor was anxious to announce her engagement. She was deeply in love with Franklin, or so she believed. Excerpts from various writings included,

> I love you dearest and I hope that I shall always prove worthy of the love which you have given me. I have never known before what it was to be absolutely happy.[37]

> Though I only wrote last night...I miss you every moment & that you are never out of my thoughts dear one. Oh! so happy & I love you so dearly.[38]

> I miss you dreadfully and feel very lonely, but please don't think it is because I am alone, having other people wouldn't do any good for I just want you![39]

Looking back, Eleanor acknowledged,

> I know now that it was years later before I understood what being in love or what loving really meant. I had high standards of what a wife and mother should be and not the faintest notion of what it meant to be either.[40]

Meanwhile, she filled her letters to Franklin with loving support and encouragement for his interests, activities, and goals. She offered advice and championed his achievements. Her guidance, which she gave freely, was always directed at Franklin's success, his accomplishments, and his leadership, never her own. It was a theme well cultivated in their relationship and one which would continue throughout their journey to the White House.

While Eleanor bolstered Franklin's self-image, and continually reassured his self-worth, she repeatedly disparaged her own. Away from Marie Souvestre's guidance and inspiration, Eleanor's recurring lack of self-confidence and insecurities went far beyond her physical appearance.

> Why do you read over my old letters dearest, they really are not worth it—but you write nice letters and I love them and mine are often very dull I fear.[41]

Deep-rooted self-deprecation would forever remain Eleanor's nemesis. Regardless of everything she accomplished, she saw herself as unimportant, minimally skilled, and untalented. Years later, Eleanor taught school for a while but on reflection said, "I feel sure I was a very poor teacher." Even after twelve years in the White House and countless personal successes, she remained humble in the extreme. During a tour to promote the United Nations, as Eleanor arrived at an airport she commented, "Oh, look! Somebody significant must be flying in."[42] The airport had rolled out a red carpet and young children were ready to greet the former First Lady with flowers.

Her role in life (to encourage, support, promote, and advance others) was already well established. Over time, Eleanor would expand her knowledge and indeed grow, but in her mind never beyond a secondary position.

The couple's engagement was finally announced on December 1, 1904. "Town Topics," a column in the local newspaper, noted,

> [Eleanor was] attractive...unusually tall and fair with a charming grace of manner that has made her a favorite since her debut.[43]

Even on her wedding day, when all brides deserve to be the center of attention, Eleanor was the lesser, inferior attraction. President Roosevelt and First Lady Edith Roosevelt offered Eleanor a White House wedding, but she preferred to get married in her godmother's New York home. Uncle Teddy would escort the bride down the aisle; therefore, the president's schedule would supersede any of the couple's marital plans. President Roosevelt wanted to make a few speeches and attend the Saint Patrick's Day Parade in New York on March 17, 1905, so that determined the couple's wedding date.

Not exactly the best of plans, because not only were Fifth and Madison Avenues both blocked off for the parade, but all of the extra police protection for the president created massive disruption and interference. Things were so congested, several guests arrived only after the ceremony ended (the ceremony itself could barely be heard above loud parade noise and singing). Afterward, "the great majority" of guests immediately followed "Uncle Theodore." As Eleanor recalled,

> Guests were far more interested in the thought of being able to see and listen to the President.[44]

Cousin Alice Roosevelt, one of Eleanor's six bridesmaids, confirmed,

> Father [Teddy Roosevelt] always wanted to be the bride at every wedding and the corpse at every funeral.[45]

March 17 was significant for other reasons as well. It would have been Anna Hall Roosevelt's forty-second birthday. Wearing her grandmother's wedding dress and her mother's long wedding train and lace veil, surely Eleanor had thoughts of her beautiful mother and dearly departed father on that auspicious occasion. Moreover, although she received a one-word congratulatory telegram ("Bonheur," or happiness) from her ailing mentor and good friend Marie Souvestre, just two days later Souvestre died of cancer.

As soon as Franklin's law school finals were finished, the couple went on a three-month European honeymoon. Among other locations, they visited London, Paris, Rome, Florence, Venice, the Dolomites, Saint-Moritz, and cities in Scotland and Germany. In addition to doing some whirlwind shopping, Eleanor came home carrying a very special package: she was pregnant with their first child. In their absence, Sara had rented a house for them just a few blocks from her own home. However, even more intrusive, Sara took it upon herself to furnish it and hired the servants.

So began Eleanor's marriage, which set the structure of her life for many years to come. Her struggle to find a personal identity would be a lengthy and arduous process. Lest we forget, at twenty, Eleanor was barely out of her teens. Her primary focus was on championing the underdog, fighting for their rights and their needs. Now newly married, she was unaware that she herself was in fact the underdog. Coming from privilege (at least in the sense of financial security) and marrying into even greater wealth and social standing, Eleanor was determined to be worthy of her circumstances, which meant being the ideal wife and daughter-in-law. After all, her generation predominantly expressed themselves in the stereotypical belief that "a woman's place is in the home."

The country had barely embarked into the twentieth century. To put the era in perspective, just ten years earlier (1895), a serum to fight the bubonic plague (an infection that attacked the lymph nodes and killed many millions of people) was discovered, yet a vaccine to fight polio, a contagious and historically devastating disease that caused muscle paralysis and even death, was not discovered until the mid-1950s.

Only five years had passed since work first began on the New York subway in 1900. At that time, the census bureau estimated seventy-five million people were living in the United States. Life expectancy was only forty-eight years for men and fifty-one for women. Although some 15.5 million children were attending public schools, only one in ten stayed beyond the age of fourteen.

In 1901, the famous painter Pablo Picasso began his "blue period" (whereby his somber paintings were rendered only in various shades of blue), and an inventor by the name of King C. Gillette invented a safety razor with disposable blades. Educator, author, and political leader Booker T. Washington published his autobiography *Up From Slavery* (still available today), while J. P. Morgan formed U.S. Steel Corporation, the first billion-dollar corporation in the world.

By 1902, a travel time record was broken when an express passenger train—the Twentieth Century Limited—traveled from New York to Chicago in only twenty hours. On the other side of the country, the first motion picture theater opened in Los Angeles. The following year the longest film to date, *The Great Train Robbery*, lasted twelve minutes (now there is an evening of entertainment) and you could travel across the American continent by automobile in fifty-two days! Regarding pop culture, baseball offered its first World Series or post-season play, and five cents bought you a box of eight Crayola crayons.

The United States hosted the Olympic Games for the first time in St. Louis, Missouri (1904), and work had scarcely begun on the Panama Canal. It is almost inconceivable today, but that same year a New York policeman arrested a woman for smoking a cigarette in public.[46] Within the previous decade, medicine and technology had achieved much progress, but there was still a great deal further to go in the areas of social reform and women's rights.

Living within the constraints Eleanor had to deal with, she did her very best to be the model homemaker. Taking a back seat to literally everyone else in her family, Eleanor placed her husband's and mother-in-law's desires and happiness above her own. The relationship between the two women forever proved to be a difficult one, with continuous feelings of frustration, anger, and resentment on Eleanor's part followed by short periods of an armed truce. Regardless of what Eleanor did, she could never fully please Sara. Consequently, the loving mother-daughter relationship Eleanor craved never transpired.

Before the children were born, Sara convinced Eleanor that hired nurses knew more about taking care of an infant than she did. In the beginning, that was true. Like so many other young and inexperienced first-time mothers, Eleanor was clueless when it came to babies—she never even played with dolls. Nevertheless, the reality was that no one bothered to teach her the fundamentals and in fact everyone sabotaged her efforts. In time, Eleanor adjusted to her circumstances and while nurses cared for her children, she had plenty of time to read, knit, and study languages.

After the birth of her daughter Anna in 1906, Eleanor went on to have five sons.* Her first son James (named after Franklin's father) arrived less than eighteen months later. Then in March of 1909, she gave birth to Franklin, who sadly died at seven months from influenza. Devastated, Eleanor blamed herself. Intentional or not, one month after Franklin's death, Eleanor was again pregnant. Elliott, her third son, arrived in 1910. Four children in five years would be challenging enough, but four babies and a meddling mother-in-law like Sara Roosevelt would push anyone to the breaking point. It is truly remarkable how much time passed before Eleanor would reach hers.

When Sara determined that the growing family needed more space, she had a twin six-story townhouse built next to her own with slide-away partitions and connecting doors. At any time, on any floor, Sara would walk in uninvited and take over, which she did regularly. Eleanor recorded, "One never knew when she [Sara] would appear day or night."[47] If Sara didn't like the furniture arrangement, she would simply move things. If she disagreed with Eleanor's parenting, she told the children something different and then announced that they did not have to listen to their mother. (Sara repeatedly told her grandchildren, "I was your real mother, Eleanor merely bore you.")[48]

In an effort to please her husband and win over her appalling mother-in-law, Eleanor cowered under Sara's powerful and daunting control. She was subservient and acquiescent, but just being agreeable with Sara was insufficient. You needed to think like her and share her narrow-minded cultural opinions. To avoid disagreements and

* Anna Eleanor Roosevelt [Dall, Boettiger, Halsted] (1906–1975); James Roosevelt (1907–1991); Franklin Roosevelt (1909–1909); Elliott Roosevelt (1910–1990); Franklin Delano Roosevelt (1914–1988); John Aspinwall Roosevelt (1916–1981).

stressful situations, Eleanor found herself either silent or mimicking Sara's opinions and suppressing her personal, opposing point of view.

> I was not developing any individual taste or initiative. I was simply absorbing the personalities of those about me and letting their tastes and interests dominate me.[49]

She was often depressed, had little energy, and did not participate in activities outside the home. Since Sara pretty well managed her home life, Eleanor lost her sense of purpose and ambition. Looking back, she remembers there was always someone "to decide everything for me."

Unlike the average middle-class family, who if they were lucky owned one home, Eleanor had the advantage of access to two other residences. The family frequently stayed at the Roosevelt Hyde Park estate, but yet again it was Sara's home and Eleanor was merely a guest. The one place she truly enjoyed was a cottage (as they called it, actually it consisted of eighteen bedrooms) on Campobello Island in New Brunswick, Canada.*[50] That too Sara purchased for her children, not far from her own cottage on the island.

Feelings of anger or hurt consumed Eleanor to the point of total withdrawal. She would utterly clam up, say nothing, and exude only coldness, to such an extent it was said, "Once Eleanor Roosevelt decided to ice you out you could be frozen to death."[51] Sara tapped in to all of Eleanor's insecurities, and reinforced her feelings of inadequacy as a wife and mother. The death of her son Frank and the hormonal changes she experienced during and after Elliott's birth brought Eleanor unbelievable despair. For years, she had swallowed her voice, masked her feelings, and fought against her core being. She was literally eating herself up inside.

In order to feel any personal value, Eleanor needed to be productive and assist others. The high society life she was born into and now living in was never comfortable for her. In a letter she wrote to Franklin during the summer of 1904, Eleanor confessed,

* On occasion, between the children, their tutors, servants, and guests, all eighteen bedrooms were occupied.

> I'm afraid I wasn't born to be a high life lady, dear, so you'll just have to be content with a simple existence, unless you teach me how to change.[52]

The truth is Eleanor never changed. She wanted her independence and a home of her own, not one run by a powerful matriarch. She was now at the end of her rope; Franklin came home one night to find his wife crying nonstop.

Both Eleanor and Franklin received money from separate trust funds. In all probability, the income was sufficient to support their family, albeit not in the lifestyle Franklin had become accustomed to living. The majority of their financial support came from Sara, and as the saying goes, whoever has the money has the power. Apparently, Franklin's comfort and enjoyment won out over his wife's unhappiness, or presumably the couple would have moved. Although he did not receive much satisfaction from his job at a law firm, Franklin benefited from his social life outside the home. There were late night poker games at the Knickerbocker Club and dinners at the Harvard Club. Meetings and luncheons occurred with interesting and prominent people.

Then very unexpectedly, a group of influential Reformed Democrats approached Franklin regarding the New York State Senate seat. With their support and financial backing, he agreed to take on his first political campaign. Eleanor, enthusiastic and supportive, was anxious to know every detail of her husband's new venture. For the previous three decades, this particular district (Dutchess County) had been Republican run and dominated, which made Franklin's victory in 1910 all the more triumphant. It was a new beginning in many aspects, and Eleanor was thrilled. At twenty-six, she was embarking on a new direction in her marriage and her life.

To begin with, she was exceptionally proud of her husband, and this was an opportunity to be involved with issues of importance to her. The Hall family was never supportive of Eleanor's social work, as they felt it was demeaning to a woman of her stature. (Then after she had children, Sara Roosevelt was so afraid of diseases and other unsavory ailments that Eleanor could come in contact with during her ghetto visits she put a stop to her daughter-in-law's direct work with the poor altogether.) Not the least of Eleanor's delight was the fact that Franklin's victory meant moving to Albany, the state capital, some one hundred fifty miles away.

> I wanted to be independent. I was beginning to realize that something within me craved to be an individual.[53]

This time the Roosevelts chose the home they would live in, and Eleanor would finally be the master of her domain. She hired new servants and an English governess for the children. Management of her family was at last her own, and in addition, Eleanor could be productive once more and useful to those she loved. Her productivity and the success of others were continual themes in her letters to Franklin (who was often known by his initials, FDR), dating back to his college years.

> My own dearest boy, I cannot tell you how glad I am you got on the Class committee for I know how much it means to you and I always want you to succeed. I hope so much that someday I will be more of a help to you.[54]

Now a political wife, Eleanor had another opportunity (the first was during her time at Allenswood) to discover her own personage. Politics added a new dimension to their lives and both husband and wife saw one another in a new light. Albany rejuvenated the Roosevelt marriage and bonded their love into a unique partnership.

> It was a wife's duty to be interested in whatever interested her husband, whether it was politics, books, or a particular dish for dinner.[55]

The time she had spent with her political family members in Washington gave Eleanor some insight into the world of politics. In actuality, she was deeply interested in political affairs and Franklin admired her intelligence, respected her opinion, and trusted her advice.

Her natural warmth and genuine depth of caring ingratiated Eleanor to people in all walks of life—those who were political and those who were not. She made it her business to meet and talk with everyone and involved herself in every aspect of the political game. Like other successful political wives before her (Dolley Madison, Louisa Adams, Sarah Polk, and Grace Coolidge, for instance), Eleanor won praise from her husband's critics. She had the exceptional ability to build bridges and make alliances with both opponents and rivals.

Eleanor was an adept listener. In addition to regularly attending Senate and Assembly debates, she spoke with her husband's colleagues and their wives as well as his constituents and adversaries.

> I found that almost everyone had something interesting to contribute to my education.[56]

Shedding her high society trappings, Eleanor would now attend and host gatherings of a different nature, where issues were discussed, debates were encouraged, and friendships were forged.

When FDR came out in favor of suffrage, Eleanor said,

> [I was] somewhat shocked, as I had never given the question serious thought. [I] took it for granted that men were superior creatures and still knew more about politics than women. [Then] I realized that if my husband were a suffragist I probably must be too.[57]

Separated frequently during this period on account of various family commitments and political obligations, the couple exchanged daily letters and their relationship seemed to strengthen as well as deepen. Franklin wrote his wife in 1912,

> I do wish you were here—it is hard enough to be away from the chicks [children], but with you away from me I feel too very much alone and lost. I hereby solemnly declare that I *refuse* to go away the next time without you...I can't tell you how I long to see you again.[58]

The dawn of Eleanor and Franklin Roosevelt's political partnership had begun. Regardless of any future problems or tragedies the couple would endure, their political collaboration forever remained intact.

Their first (political versus personal) trial occurred rather quickly thereafter. Former president Theodore Roosevelt, who in 1908 had firmly stated he would not run for another presidential term, had to swallow those words. (He later said he meant another *consecutive* presidential term.) His good friend and handpicked successor William Howard Taft had begun retreating from the reform platform Roosevelt strongly supported. Since the Republican Party would endorse Taft, Roosevelt began his Bull Moose movement to back a third-party candidate.

The presidential election of 1912 was dubbed "The Big Three," not because of the candidates themselves but rather due to their allegiances to the leading college football powers at that time. Those running for office consisted of former president Theodore Roosevelt, also known as TR (Bull Moose ticket and Harvard class of 1880), sitting president William Howard Taft (Republican ticket and Yale class of 1878), and future president Woodrow Wilson (Democratic ticket and Princeton class of 1879).

Roosevelt's Progressive Party platform encompassed all of the ideals Eleanor stood for: the guarantee of decent housing; protection for women workers and an end to child labor; and a national system of accident, old-age, and unemployment insurance. The platform affirmed and TR assured "without qualification or equivocation,"

> No people can justly claim to be a true democracy which denies political rights on the account of sex.[59]

Franklin Roosevelt believed the Bull Moose movement was "dead in the water," and became New York's leading supporter of Woodrow Wilson, a southerner who incidentally did not support suffrage or desegregation. Eleanor quietly stood by her husband, although in a letter to one of her closest friends she wrote,

> I wish Franklin could be fighting now for Uncle Ted, for I feel he is in the Party of the Future.[60]

Woodrow Wilson won the 1912 presidential election and offered Franklin a position in his cabinet as assistant secretary of the Navy—ironically the same position TR held in 1897. On his eighth wedding anniversary (March 17, 1913), Franklin took his new official oath of office. Politics has been and always will be a down and dirty profession. The trick is to learn the art of compromise; also, the real pros do not take anything in the world of politics personally. Without apparent irony or rancor, on March 18, 1913, TR wrote FDR,

> It is interesting to see that you are in another place, which I myself once held. [TR was also once a member of the New York State Assembly.] I am sure you will enjoy yourself to the full...and that you will do capital work.*[61]

At twenty-eight and thirty-one years old, respectively, the Roosevelts moved to Washington, D.C., and rented Aunt Bye's popular political-gathering residence. (Bye had since moved to Connecticut.) It was not long before the young couple became entrenched in the center of Washington politics. Quickly becoming the seasoned political wife, Eleanor made the daily, tiresome, traditional calls on all wives whose husbands were associated with politics, a custom dating back to the beginning of the Union. Whether congressional, cabinet, or Supreme Court spouses, Eleanor met every one of them, maintained a detailed calling journal, and reported everything to her husband.

During those early Washington years, in the course of the obligatory formal dinners she attended as well as hosted on most nights, Eleanor won praise for her brilliant conversational skills and her linguistic abilities, which came in handy when she translated for foreign guests at diplomatic dinners. She also found time over those first few

* A few years later, TR would once again respect FDR's political position. Obviously, TR and Woodrow Wilson (whom he called a skunk in the White House) were not on the same team. In 1915, TR fervently opposed Wilson's resistance to entering World War I. When TR came to Washington to meet with President Wilson, he wrote Eleanor, "I am very anxious to see you and Franklin, whenever the chance offers; but I do not want to compromise Franklin by being with him just at this time. I wish you would tell him that from all quarters I hear praise of the admirable work he has done for the Navy, under very difficult conditions. With love, Your affectionate Uncle." (*Eleanor Roosevelt, Volume I 1884-1933*, 214.)

political years to give birth to two more sons (the second Franklin Jr. in 1914 and John in 1916). An active, thinking, and participatory spouse—now a true marital partner in every sense—Eleanor was developing personal pride, as she was discovering she no longer needed to be intimidated by or fearful of others. Although there were still occasional clashes and disagreements with her mother-in-law, she was learning to handle those situations better as well.

In addition to being a supportive and dedicated wife, Eleanor efficiently managed a large home with a variety of servants and five children. But a hidden ailment plagued her. Her high energy level and numerous commitments camouflaged the debilitating migraine headaches she regularly suffered through.

> I could never say in the morning, I have a headache and cannot do thus and so. I could not be a burden and add any care to a man [Franklin] who had plenty of official things to do.[62]

Prior to the country's involvement in World War I, Franklin recognized the necessity for a strong navy and singlehandedly worked toward establishing one. (Even Franklin's boss, Josephus Daniels, disagreed with him at the time. It was 1916 before Roosevelt would convince Daniels otherwise.) Meanwhile, Secretary of State William Jennings Bryan resigned to lead a peace crusade, and the Woman's Peace Party and the American Union Against Militarism were organized. Yet even as President Wilson's reelection campaign slogan boasted, "He kept us out of war," his administration was preparing for battle.

When the United States entered World War I in 1917, Eleanor turned her attention and boundless vitality to Red Cross efforts and organizing military canteens. She made sandwiches and coffee alongside other volunteers at Washington's Union Station for those coming from and going to war. She knitted for and visited hospitalized sailors, and raised funds for a badly needed recreational and physical therapy center for wounded soldiers. Now, because there was a need outside her personal satisfaction (always a motivating factor), Eleanor learned to drive an automobile, something she had readily given up on a number of years earlier during her insecurity phase when her husband discouraged the idea. As the outside world changed, so did Eleanor's personal world.

Between her responsibilities at home (her children were now between the ages of one and eleven), her numerous community commitments (she worked past midnight most evenings), and her husband's political life, the couple's social interests varied considerably. At thirty-five, Franklin enjoyed the company of his Harvard college pals and spent time at the Army, Navy, and Racquet clubs. He could relax at stag dinners, enjoy a poker game, or play a round of golf.

Leading up to the war, Franklin began to spend less and less time with Eleanor and the children during their sojourns at Campobello Island and now even less time at home. Tensions ran high between the couple and arguments erupted more frequently. During this somewhat fractured time in their lives, Eleanor caused herself and her spouse an enormous embarrassment. It seems housewives across the country were signing pledge cards to save on food and reduce waste during the war. The Food Administration wanted a model for large households and Eleanor agreed to give the *New York Times* an interview.

> The food-saving program adopted at the home of Franklin D. Roosevelt...Mrs. Roosevelt does the food buying and listed seven family members with ten servants. Each servant has signed a pledge card, and there are daily conferences. The cooks see that there is no food wasted, the laundress is sparing in her use of soap, each servant has a watchful eye for evidence of shortcomings on the part of the others...only two courses for lunch, and three for dinner. Meat is served but once daily, and all "left overs" are utilized....Everybody eats fish at least once a week. Making the ten servants help me do my savings has not only been possible but highly profitable, said Mrs. Roosevelt today.[63]

Franklin immediately wrote his wife saying,

> I am proud to be the husband of the Originator, Discoverer and Inventor of the New Household Economy for Millionaires! Please

> have a photo taken showing the family, the ten cooperating servants, the scraps saved from the table...I will have it published in the *Sunday Times*.[64]

Eleanor was mortified and never again referred publicly to even the existence of her household staff.

> I do think it was horrid of that woman [reporter] to use my name in that way...So much is not true and yet some of it I did say. I never will be caught again that's sure and I'd like to crawl away for shame.[65]

True, Eleanor brought that specific shame upon herself, but another form of embarrassment and humiliation was hiding in the shadows. During Eleanor's many trips to Campobello with the children, or when she worked day and night on her various war projects while the children were visiting their grandmother Sara in Hyde Park, Franklin was off somewhere else doing other business—some professional, some recreational. Now, reminiscent of Eleanor's father, Franklin was away from home frequently and it was common for her to spend weeks at home alone with the children. Feelings of abandonment tweaked internally, but Eleanor fought against repeating her mother's cold, withdrawn, and judgmental response.

In 1918, a deadly flu epidemic swept through the country. Eleanor's entire household was infected and every child was soon bedridden. Franklin was at sea (returning from England on business relevant to the close of World War I) when he and numerous other crewmembers and officers became incapacitated. By the time he returned home, FDR had double pneumonia. It was a trying and worrisome time for Eleanor. Unfortunately, things would get worse before they became tolerable again.

During this time, Eleanor found a packet of love letters her social secretary of four years, Lucy Mercer, had sent to Franklin. Forced to face the reality everyone else in Washington already knew, Eleanor could no longer live in denial. She had seen and sensed it for some time, as Franklin had done a poor job of hiding his emotions or the romance. Maliciously, Cousin Alice participated in the gossip and even invited FDR and Lucy to her famous Washington dinner parties. Mockingly, Alice said, "Franklin deserved a good time. He was married to Eleanor." The comment was not surprising considering it came from a woman who proudly displayed a needlepoint pillow on her sofa stating, "If you haven't got anything nice to say about anybody, come sit next to me."[66]

Genuinely heartbroken and wounded to the core, Eleanor was publicly humiliated and tried desperately to understand. Her husband not only betrayed her privately, he dishonored her openly in the presence of others. Eleanor loved Franklin intensely, but every childhood fear and insecure emotion resurfaced, and it would take years to regain her footing. If her husband no longer wanted her, Eleanor could not bear to stay. She offered Franklin his freedom, yet she never herself asked for a divorce. Regardless of her own feelings, Eleanor would never destroy Franklin's political career, which a divorce would clearly damage.

Whether Franklin seriously considered a divorce or not we will never know, because his mother absolutely forbade it! The thought horrified Sara and she threatened to cut him off financially if he left his wife and children. Aside from divorce being a public scandal and ending Franklin's career, his lifestyle was at stake; most importantly, there were five young children involved. Reportedly, Roosevelt was the love of Lucy Mercer's life, but that love came at too high a price.

Instead, they negotiated an armistice and Franklin agreed to never see Lucy again...a promise he did not keep. (Although Lucy married Wintie Rutherford in 1920—a wealthy widower with five children, and they had one daughter together—she and Franklin maintained contact throughout the years.) According to Margaret Truman, presidential daughter and author on the First Ladies, Roosevelt was "banned from Eleanor's bedroom forever."[67] Nobody knows if that is precisely accurate, but there is no question the Roosevelts' marriage was forever changed and at *some* point their affection for one another became strictly platonic. (The couple maintained separate bedrooms wherever they were domiciled, and Eleanor had her own cottage on the family's Hyde Park estate.) Years later, J. B. West, then assistant to the White House chief usher, said of the Roosevelts,

> We never saw them in the same room alone together. They had the most separate relationship I have ever seen between man and wife. And the most equal.[68]

However, immediately after the affair was uncovered, both partners worked hard at rediscovering the joy they had once shared. Eleanor would accompany her husband to parties and they left together as a couple. Franklin brought home thoughtful gifts for his wife and spent more time with the children. They talked more openly with one another, they collaborated, they had conflicts, they renegotiated, and they talked some more.

Throughout 1919, the couple would experience many ups and downs, and Eleanor spent a good deal of time in self-reflection and contemplation. Photographs of her during that time show her looking both forlorn and very thin. Her letters reflect her inability to keep food down, and her teeth appeared to have suffered from frequent vomiting. Grandmother Hall died that year and Eleanor looked long and hard at her grandmother's life, in addition to her own. She wondered if her grandmother, as well as Hall's six children, would have benefited had Mary Hall cultivated a life of her own, outside the home.

The next few years were taxing to say the least and presumably, the mutual respect and admiration the Roosevelts shared diminished somewhat, but it did not vanish altogether. Feeling out of control, Eleanor needed to take charge of her life. She wanted to be needed and helpful, yet she felt lonely and inadequate. In order to reclaim her personal value she needed to find a serious project to which she could contribute.

> For ten years I was always just getting over having a baby or about to have one, and so my occupations were considerably restricted.[69]

It may sound like a cliché but it was true: unmistakably one door in her life had closed, but a new one was about to open. That was encouraging, because Eleanor was determined to embark on a new life. She had concluded that what she lacked was,

> The sense of being really needed and wanted which gives us the greatest satisfaction and creates the most lasting bond.[70]

After Eleanor attended the First International Congress of Working Women, she supported their efforts to improve working conditions. She met other intelligent, dedicated, and supportive women who felt as passionate about politics and the Progressive Movement as she did. These included Margaret Dreier Robins, who opened the International Congress; Ester Everett Lape, one of the founders of the League of Women Voters; and Elizabeth Read, an accomplished lawyer who became Eleanor's personal attorney and financial adviser. Eleanor also championed the organization of women into unions and backed the Women's Trade Union League, the International Ladies' Garment Workers' Union, and unions for teachers, waitresses, telephone operators, and shoe workers. In addition, for over a decade she remained steadfast in her backing of the League of Nations because according to her, it was "the only way that we can prevent war."

Keep in mind that women were still a few months shy of winning the right to vote (Congress ratified the Nineteenth Amendment to the Constitution—women's suffrage—in August 1920). Yet Eleanor pronounced herself a dedicated Democrat because,

> The Republicans are, —well I believe they are more conservative, you know, and we can't be too conservative and accomplish things.[71]

Meantime she did not accompany Franklin to the Democratic convention in June of 1920 (nor was she invited), because she did not yet have a role in the political process. During the long convention, it took forty-four ballots to elect James M. Cox, governor of Ohio, as their compromise candidate. Nominated unanimously as his vice presidential running mate was Franklin Delano Roosevelt.

In the midst of her own personal pain and turmoil, Eleanor supported, encouraged, and stood by Franklin during the ugly politicking of 1920. To substantiate that politics has not changed much over the years, Eleanor wrote at the time,

> I feel rather sad about politics...there are so many who are out for themselves and not for the good of the country in both parties and conditions are so unsettled that we need a really fine leader.[72]

Franklin wanted his wife to accompany him on his campaign train. He needed her solidarity and asked her to keep a record of all the various happenings. Together they forged a new alliance, one of loyalty, reliability, and trustworthiness. Roosevelt had other assistants and advisers, but none whom he turned to more frequently than this highly gifted, intelligent, and dutiful partner.

Publicly the Roosevelt family was united; privately, however, the extended family loyalty had died when Uncle Teddy passed away the previous year. TR's widow and former Republican First Lady, Edith Roosevelt, said, "Franklin is nine-tenths mush and one-tenth Eleanor."[73] During this time, Louis Howe, FDR's chief senior assistant, advisor, and longtime activist, recognized Eleanor's unique talents and befriended her independently of his friendship with FDR. He included her in every aspect of Roosevelt's political career and was interested in her opinions. They discussed wide-ranging subjects and collaborated on a variety of projects. Howe became one of Eleanor's deepest and dearest friends. He encouraged, advised, and defended her, genuinely caring about her well-being. She trusted, respected, and grew to love him.

The Democrats lost the White House in 1920; however, Eleanor personally benefited from the loss. She gained a new level of confidence and esteem, while at the same time she came to terms with her playboy spouse and their marriage. She could now joke about Franklin's flirtatious mannerisms and the groups of adoring women surrounding him. Marguerite LeHand, known as Missy, became her husband's new secretary and full-time companion. She was efficient, valuable, and dedicated to FDR and his work. Whether at Hyde Park, New York, Warm Springs, Georgia, or the White House, Missy maintained her own residence. Freedom, balance, and equality became the new foundation for the Roosevelt marriage.

Still very young at thirty-eight, Franklin returned to New York and created a new law firm with two friends (Emmet, Marvin, and Roosevelt). He participated in various business speculations—some successful, some not—and waited for another political opportunity to make his mark. His thirty-six-year-old wife, who occasionally referred to herself as a prude or puritan, recognized the importance of eliminating labels and determined, "The life you live is your own." Eleanor had an insatiable appetite for life and discovered she enjoyed being around people. Now, unlike her youth when she preferred to be alone with her fantasies, Eleanor collected people and friends like someone else might collect stamps. In addition, she was ready to expand the sphere of her life and serious about carving out her own niche in public service and national affairs.

She became an active board member of the New York League of Women Voters and soon found herself at the nucleus of the women's political movement. Ironically, the independent, non-high-society life Eleanor chose for herself was not available to her daughter. The voice and opinions she expressed in the world outside would not prevail over her mother-in-law's staunch and formidable opposition. Even though her daughter Anna objected to and loathed the thought of being a debutante, at fifteen her grooming had already begun for her coming-out party. In three years she would be forced to suffer the same angst Eleanor had to endure at eighteen. Nor was the college education that Eleanor had craved offered to Anna. Furthermore, against Eleanor's objection, her sons all attended Groton (just as their father had) when they reached the age of twelve. Sara demanded as much.

On the twenty-seventh anniversary of her father's death (August 14, 1921), Eleanor wrote Franklin's half brother Rosy a disturbing letter. In it, she described how Franklin had suddenly taken ill at their Campobello home. The following evening, he experienced so much pain in his back and limbs that she insisted he see a doctor. By the next day, Franklin had lost all ability to move his legs. As his condition worsened, he went in and out of delirium due to intermittent high fevers. Louis Howe was there to help Eleanor turn and bathe Franklin; however, they still did not have a diagnosis.

It had been three weeks and Eleanor would not leave her husband's side. She slept on a couch in his bedroom and watched as her husband lost control over his vital functions. In addition to feeding, bathing, and shaving Franklin and massaging his legs, Eleanor gave her husband enemas and administered catheters, something one of her children's nurses instructed her on how to do. It was an extraordinarily frightening and distressful time. The couple's relationship strengthened, as each one tried to reassure the other. Franklin tenderly expressed his earnest admiration and deepest appreciation to his valiant wife. There were kindhearted moments and even some occasional laughter.

A Boston specialist diagnosed his condition as polio, an infantile paralysis with no known cure. Resolute in their decision to remain optimistic and cheerful, the Roosevelts faced the terrifying unknown together. Mindful of Franklin's political career, Howe had the presence of mind to keep his hero's physical condition out of the press and shrouded in secrecy. As soon as he was ferried to the New Brunswick mainland, they arranged for a private train to transport Franklin from Campobello to a hospital in New York City, where he convalesced for four months. Only there was no improvement in his condition. Upon his release home, the couple's battle had just begun.

Eleanor hired a live-in nurse (to whom she gave her personal bedroom) in addition to a daytime nurse, and Louis Howe moved in full time as well. With the family and existing staff, some twenty people were now part of the Roosevelts' household. Howe spent his days at Franklin's law office managing his business affairs. During this period, Eleanor slept on a twin bed in one of the boys' rooms.

Eleanor described the winter of 1921 as "the most trying winter in my entire life."[74] It was impossible to protect her children from the situation, yet Eleanor wanted to minimize its enormity. Her five- and seven-year-old sons wanted a father to physically play with, and Anna was—well, she was a hormonal teenager! In addition to being confrontational and defiant toward her mother, Anna had a rather unpleasant demeanor. Add to that eleven- and fourteen-year-old sons, plus an overbearing and imperious mother-in-law, and it was only a matter of time before anyone—even Eleanor Roosevelt—broke down.

At every turn, Sara was interfering and fighting against Eleanor's goals and hard work. To begin with, Eleanor believed it was imperative to keep Franklin motivated and interested in public life. She wanted him to get better, stronger, and back into the game. Sara, on the other hand, wanted her son to live at Hyde Park, a coddled and indulged invalid. There was no compromise position between the women. To embrace a different point of view is one thing, but when you manipulate your grandchildren and take advantage of their rebellious attitudes so they will side with you and battle their mother, that's crossing the line, which Sara had no problem doing.

In April of 1922, Eleanor reached her limit and snapped. Inconsolable, she sobbed for hours. Her children had never seen their mother that way and it was overwhelming, not to mention frightening for them. Even her dear friend Howe tried to comfort her, with no success. The night wore on as Eleanor descended further and further into hopelessness. Eventually she pulled herself together and when she did, Eleanor knew she had to reinvent herself once again. On the positive side, she became closer to her children. They had a glimpse into her despair and developed compassion for her and the situation. Gradually, Eleanor began to confide in her daughter and take her to the theater and plays. In an effort to fill the void her husband's paralysis created, she went camping, hiking, sailing, and swimming with her boys, activities their father once enjoyed with his sons. She noted,

> I would have to become a good deal more companionable and more of an all-around person than I had ever been before.[75]

In order to achieve her objective, Eleanor recognized she needed training. She took swimming lessons because she was terrified of going into the water. When it came to everyday food preparation, Eleanor felt dependent. (She had made thousands of sandwiches, but there was always someone else to prepare full meals.) To demystify the kitchen, she took cooking classes. It was never her intent to become a gourmet cook, nor did she; however, when Eleanor designed a menu and prepared a complete five-course dinner, she gained personal pride. It happened to be the one and only time she ever did that, but she learned that she could. To be more efficient in other areas, she also enrolled in a secretarial course and learned how to type and take shorthand, which proved invaluable for years to come.

Learning to balance her life, Eleanor found satisfaction and purpose. Her duty to service, both private and public, was her life's journey. Now with her husband at his most vulnerable, more than ever, Eleanor worked hard at keeping her spouse and his political career buoyant. This is not to say that Eleanor did not have her own political interests, because clearly she did.

The sheer number of issues and causes Eleanor participated in is staggering. It is inconceivable to me that any individual could possibly possess the amount of stamina and fortitude that Eleanor Roosevelt exhibited. Her interest in and involvement with civil liberties, inequality, racial justice, and world peace were boundless. Some of the progressive reform issues she felt passionate about included better working conditions, a minimum wage, equal pay for equal work, an eight-hour workday, maternity protection, and the end of child labor. She fought for the appointment of women to state and federal employment boards, better education, the eradication of poverty, the prevention of lynching, and a national health-care program.

At the League of Women Voters, she chaired the Legislation Committee and did in-depth research on pending congressional bills. Every week, Eleanor studied the *Congressional Record,* spoke with members of Congress, outlined the status of bills, and met with League officers to discuss the information. Additionally, she wrote the League's regular newsletter. Eleanor joined the League in 1920 and was a board member for the New York State branch for eight years.

For thirteen years, beginning in 1922, Eleanor held various positions for the Women's Division of the New York State Democratic Committee. In addition to her campaigning throughout the entire state for candidate Alfred Smith, she was also the editor and columnist for their monthly newsletter.* That same year she joined the Women's Trade Union League and remained a member for thirty-three years.

For one year (1923), she helped to organize and chair a committee for the World Peace Movement. Their objective was to award $100,000

* Smith won the 1924 gubernatorial race, becoming an ally of Eleanor's. By the way, Smith's opponent was Theodore Roosevelt Jr., Eleanor's first cousin.

for the best plan that would ensure eventual world peace. Her role was establishing a bipartisan jury selection for the 22,000 entries.*

As if that were not enough, Eleanor joined the Women's City Club and eventually served on the board of directors as vice president. Their objective was to educate women on current political issues; Eleanor was a member for four years. From 1924 to 1928, Eleanor was literally the club's voice as she did radio broadcasts to help keep women informed. It's no wonder that, according to Mary Ann Glendor (a Harvard Law professor), Franklin would include in his prayers, "Oh Lord, please make Eleanor tired."[76]

While Eleanor was keeping the Roosevelt name familiar and active, Franklin worked on his disability. Work consisted of painful exercise and very warm water treatments to relax his muscles and provide some relief from the severe pain. The common belief (or hope) was that with treatment the paralysis would subside. In addition to the warm waters off the coast of Florida, where Franklin purchased a houseboat and enjoyed some deep sea fishing with friends, he also sought treatment at a summer resort in Warm Springs, Georgia. The natural buoyant mineral springs provided eighty-eight-degree water temperature where Franklin could perform swimming exercises.

Over the next two decades, Roosevelt was a frequent visitor at Warm Springs. Though he found no miracle cure, he did receive some relief. In addition to a private home Franklin had built for himself, he began constructing a comprehensive rehabilitation center in 1927 to treat others with polio.† The existing rundown buildings at Warm Springs were in need of much repair, but Franklin saw promise and potential. He purchased the complex for $195,000 from his friend and philanthropist George Peabody. He was determined to do everything possible to help himself and others from being, in his words, "helpless."

Missy LeHand remained devoted to her boss and resumed her

* Charles Levermore, founding president of Adelphi College, won the Bok Peace Prize with his proposal of immediate United States cooperation with the World Court, which was created under the League of Nations.

† Today the Roosevelt Warm Springs Institute for Rehabilitation remains true to its original mission to "empower individuals with disabilities to achieve personal independence."

secretarial duties as soon as Franklin returned to his various business dealings. She accompanied him (as did Franklin's valet) everywhere and even acted as his hostess when Eleanor was unavailable, which was often. It was obvious to everyone when Missy began to take over more of the domestic responsibilities at Warm Springs, yet she and Eleanor were friendly and it did give Eleanor more time to pursue her personal interests.

Even as the Roosevelts drifted further apart in their individual spheres, their commitment to protect one another grew stronger. Their unique marriage remained bonded by their mutual respect and genuine devotion, even though they did not share marital intimacy or passion. The reality was, they had entirely different groups of friends, and the party environment of free-flowing rum that Franklin enjoyed, Eleanor loathed. More frequently separate than together, the couple exchanged regular correspondence, which reflected professional esteem and tenderness. Eleanor wrote letters virtually every day (a habit she had long established and continued with several close friends), and all of her letters to her husband began with "Dearest Honey" (or something equally affectionate) and ended with "Ever lovingly."

Their correspondence shared daily details of their lives, and though Eleanor frequently told Franklin how "dreadfully missed" he was, neither made significant time for the other. They always knew each other's whereabouts, as well as whom they were with, and did not have a need for secrets. Some say Eleanor maintained a "don't ask, don't tell" philosophy, and perhaps she did. The main point was that Franklin and Eleanor needed one another, they wanted one another, and in fact, they still had each other. Their family rituals included Thanksgiving at Warm Springs, Christmas at Hyde Park, and their wedding anniversary off the coast of Florida. Only now, their individual groups of friends were also included. Over the years as their friendships increased, so did their gatherings. People from all walks of life, all religions, all lifestyles, married couples as well as singles, both political and nonpolitical, joined their family.

It was during this time, when Franklin was picnicking with Eleanor and two of her dear friends, Nancy Cook and Nancy's lifelong partner Marion Dickerman, that they discovered a beautiful area of land on his Hyde Park estate about two miles from Springwood, Sara's large residence. Franklin had purchased the extensive surrounding acreage (some eleven hundred acres) years earlier, and he now suggested that the three women build a year-round retreat cottage for themselves on his land. (Eleanor, Marion, and Nancy were like the Three Musketeers—practically inseparable whenever they were all in New York). Marion, thirty-five, and Nancy, forty-one (whom Franklin affectionately called "the girls"), had been graduate students at Syracuse University, both were suffragettes, and both were very politically active. They shared Eleanor's dedication to education and progressive reform. Furthermore, they had political loyalty and a sincere friendship with Franklin, whom they found charming.

Roosevelt gave the women a life interest in several acres of land. The beautiful location had a stream, which acted somewhat as a moat. In 1925, they erected a bridge over the water and built a Dutch Colonial house and stone cottage on the property. Eleanor had a barrier constructed which functioned as a dam, turning the stream into a private swimming pool for Franklin and their invited guests. Val-Kill (Dutch for "stream") was the only home Eleanor considered her own and she said of it,

> Val-Kill is where I used to find myself and grow. At Val-Kill I emerged as an individual.[77]

After its construction, whenever Eleanor went to Hyde Park, she stayed at Val-Kill (eliciting her mother-in-law's disapproval), and was only in attendance at the large estate when other guests or dignitaries were present. Not surprisingly, Sara disliked Eleanor's friends and took every opportunity to express her disdain for them. Many years later, after Franklin's death, Eleanor made Val-Kill her permanent home (though she also maintained an apartment in New York). It was there she did much of her writing, and entertained world leaders and political figures in addition to engaging in her delegate work for the United Nations.*

* Today, Val-Kill is the only National Historic Site dedicated to a First Lady. It is maintained by the National Park Service, which provides tours for the general public.

A skilled artisan, Nancy Cook made most of the home's furniture (which bore the initials E.M.N.) in her own factory. Eleanor in turn embroidered towels and linens with their initials, E.M.N., and guests would frequently give them gifts of crystal or pewter also engraved with the same initials. Eleanor shared a deep personal relationship with her friends Marion and Nancy as well as with Caroline O'Day, a wealthy suffragist and pacifist who devoted her entire life to the Progressive Movement and social reform after her husband died. In addition to their abiding friendship, the four women were also business associates in multiple joint ventures under the name Val-Kill Partnership.

Nancy presided over Val-Kill Industries, a small furniture factory making reproduction pieces of her furniture for commercial use. The small business turned into a four-story factory, employing many of the unemployed workers in the rural area of Hyde Park. The partnership then purchased the Todhunter School for Girls in New York City. At the time, Marion Dickerman was the school's vice principal, and when she learned Winifred Todhunter, an Oxford University graduate, was considering returning to England and selling the school, she suggested the women buy it.

After becoming a part owner, Eleanor taught American history, American literature, and English. Incorporating what she learned from Marie Souvestre, Eleanor included an exercise curriculum and took her students on field trips. Locations would be various tenements or the New York Children's Court. Her objective was to show her students real New York problems and what the government did to address the issue. Regarding her history exams, a typical question would be:

> Give your reasons for or against allowing women to actively participate in the control of the government, politics and office through the vote, as well as your reasons for or against women holding office in the government.[78]

Thinking independently and encouraging juniors and seniors to do the same, Eleanor held a current events class called "Happenings." Additionally, the partnership published the *Women's Democratic News*, which predictably Eleanor edited.

In 1928, Eleanor once again campaigned for Democrat Alfred Smith for the presidency. This time, she coordinated all of the various activities performed by other women volunteers. A Democratic Party loyalist, she had grown into an informed political advocate of her own. The *New York Times Magazine* recognized Eleanor's increasing political clout and in their April issue featured a lead article on her influence. She had learned to play the game of politics, and although she did not have equal power (keep in mind that women just won the right to vote eight years earlier), she had earned equal representation.

Al Smith wanted FDR to succeed him as New York's governor, but unlike Eleanor, Louis Howe was very much against the idea and advised Franklin to wait. On Howe's counsel, Franklin avoided taking Smith's phone calls, but Eleanor knew he would take hers, so while out campaigning for Smith one afternoon she phoned her husband. After Roosevelt got on the phone, she said politely, "Hello, Dear," then something along the lines of, "I know you'll do what you feel is necessary"—and then handed the phone to Smith as she raced out the door, in typical Eleanor fashion, to make another campaign speech.

Smith's phone call was successful, as Franklin agreed to go back out on the campaign trail. Though Roosevelt needed and used a wheelchair to get around in private, he learned how to lean in and with sheer strength and assistance thrust his hip forward in order to walk for short distances. Howe had done such a good job of minimizing FDR's disability that people were unaware of Franklin's full handicap. It was doubtful the public would vote for a physically impaired candidate, but with clever maneuvering and stage-managing his public appearances, Franklin could keep people's attention on his policies as opposed to his mobility. Standing erect, balancing on a cane, no one could see the seven-pound steel braces strapped on each leg supporting him. With the assistance of an aide, Franklin would then manage a few shuffles to a podium where he could again balance himself.

When Roosevelt won the New York governorship in 1928, as New York's First Lady, Eleanor had to redefine herself once again. Her eldest child Anna was now married, and her youngest child John was off at Groton. Reexamining her role, Eleanor told her son James,

> She knew that [FDR] had wanted her to become active in politics primarily to keep his case in the public eye and that he would expect her to move into the shadows if he moved into the limelight.[79]

It was difficult after all Eleanor had done to establish herself politically to now abandon the stature she had earned; however, she gave up her position at the Democratic Women's Committee (DWC). Teaching was something else entirely and Eleanor was reluctant to resign. Not only had she made a commitment, but also she loved her work at the school. In response to a question posed by *Good Housekeeping* magazine, "How would [she] define a modern wife's job?" Eleanor responded, "It is essential [for a wife] to develop her own interests, to carry on a stimulating life of her own."

Eleanor's schedule would soon become more complex than ever. The most enjoyable and inspiring part of her life was teaching, which would require a weekly commute (between Albany and New York City) for her to continue. To perform her First Lady duties to the state of New York, she would spend Mondays, Tuesdays, and Wednesdays in the state-provided governor's mansion in Albany. Then every Wednesday afternoon Eleanor would board a train for New York City, taking the opportunity to grade papers or prepare lessons. When her classes at Todhunter ended on Friday, she spent her weekends entertaining business associates, colleagues, and supporters at her New York City residence until it was time to catch the train back to Albany.

Additionally, she continued to broadcast her "Women in Politics" series on NBC radio for the Women's City Club, and edited the *Democratic News* without credit. It was a delicate balancing act to keep her interests and priorities connected and parallel with those of her spouse. Because it was difficult for FDR to travel, Eleanor became her husband's eyes and ears. When required by either Franklin's immobility or his schedule, Eleanor substituted for the governor at political meetings and conferences. She had an opportunity to meet with the most progressive governors, senators, and state officials, including their wives. Building strong political alliances and creating bipartisan friendships became the cornerstone of Eleanor's career.

She also did considerable fundraising for the National Democratic Women's Activities Committee and successfully lobbied for the appointment of Frances Perkins as state Secretary of Labor. Because Eleanor felt it was important, she championed the appointment of individuals who had the courage to disagree with FDR and those who candidly opposed him.

It came as a surprise to some (only those who didn't know Eleanor) when the First Lady of the State refused limousine service. Besides that, she politely declined a chauffeur (other than for official ceremonies). She had worked hard to earn her independence and she intended to keep it. When FDR heard that his "Missus" (his favorite nickname for her) would be driving her own car, Franklin insisted she have a bodyguard. (Whenever Eleanor's mind was made up, FDR would say, "Well, what can I do? She's my Missus.")

Assigned to protect her was thirty-two-year-old Earl Miller, an athlete and Navy middleweight boxing champion. Twelve years her junior, Earl was good looking, with an athletic physique and charm to match. As her official escort and daily companion, Earl could affectionately tease the woman he called the "Lady." Reluctant at first, Eleanor soon discovered they talked easily with one another and shared laughter. Earl too was orphaned and in his case homeless at twelve. Through their shared pain, the two developed a special bond.

Miller saw Eleanor for the woman she was—intelligent and warm—moreover, he was devoted to her interests, happiness, and safety. Genuinely concerned for Eleanor's well-being, Earl bought her a trained watchdog and taught her how to shoot a gun. Encouraging her athletic interests, he coached her tennis game, gave her riding lessons, and instructed Eleanor on how to dive, something oddly important to her. While her sons laughed at her belly-flops and made fun of Eleanor's form, Earl encouraged her, defended her, and watched over her. Additionally, he gave her a mare named Dot, who Eleanor enjoyed riding daily at Hyde Park. The two shared an endearing, protective relationship that would last until Eleanor's death over thirty years later.

It has been highly speculated the two shared a romantic relationship; characteristically, Eleanor wrote Miller a massive amount of letters. Reportedly those letters contained considerable "warmth and affection," which I do not doubt for one minute (although no letters have survived). Much of Eleanor's correspondence to the people she cared for most in life included affection, warmth, and tenderness.

Always a gentleman, Miller remained discreet and protective of his friendship with the "Lady." There is no question they shared a profound and trusting relationship. The level of that tenderness or where it might have led remains private between Eleanor and her bodyguard. What is clear is that the Roosevelt marriage was complicated and entangled, with no easy definition or characterization.

For the record, Miller was married and divorced three times. His second marriage (to Ruth Taylor Bellinger) took place at the Roosevelt Hyde Park estate (September 1932) and collapsed almost immediately thereafter. Ironically, in the midst of planning Miller's wedding, two of Eleanor's children were in the throes of failing marriages: Anna (who was matron of honor) and her brother Elliott (who was Miller's best man) were simultaneously discussing divorce in their respective marriages.*

Ruth's parents arranged an annulment on the grounds that she "was under 17 when married and did not have their consent."[80] Miller was thirty-five and admitted he was not in love with Ruth, but had hoped the marriage would quash the rumors about him and Eleanor. His efforts were futile as Miller confirmed, "But I was never successful in killing the gossip."[81] In 1941, Miller got married for the third time (to Simone von Haven) and Eleanor was godmother to their two children, Earl Jr. and Anna Eleanor. Simone was granted a divorce in 1947, based on a packet of "endearing" letters Earl had received. Purportedly, the letters were from Eleanor and the court had them sealed. It's believed the letters were independently purchased and destroyed. Whoever the letters were from, none have ever surfaced.

If it is possible to muddy the Roosevelt waters even more, it was also common knowledge that Earl and Missy LeHand had an affair during Roosevelt's governorship. As late as 1972, Miller told a friend,

* It seems all five of the Roosevelt children were unlucky in marriage and all were divorced more than once. Between them, they had a total of nineteen marriages, fifteen divorces, and twenty-nine children.

> I admired Missy very much & was attracted to her by her devotion to family as I was. Missy & I spent our free time together whenever we were with the family & both the "Boss" [FDR] & Lady encouraged. I suppose that could be misconstrued also.[82]

Just ten months after Roosevelt's gubernatorial inauguration in 1929, the country experienced Black Tuesday, also known as the most devastating stock market crash in the history of the United States. Eleanor's initial response was to encourage women to face the business future courageously.

> There is no reason why we should not have a female Henry Ford. I am hopeful for women in industry.[83]

Used as an example was Val-Kill Industries, which had grown from six employees to thirty. Managed and owned entirely by women, "they weathered the Wall Street crash...without having to lay off one workman."[84]

Meanwhile, Eleanor campaigned for unionization to secure jobs for working women and stressed their need to educate themselves for gainful employment. This was in direct opposition to the belief that women should not compete with men for jobs. She publicly supported strike efforts and the need for better living conditions, a wage scale, and imaginative ways to end unemployment.

> It is nice to hand out milk and bread. It gives you a comfortable feeling inside. But fundamentally you are not relieving the...reasons why we have to have this charity. We are not only a part of the government, but we are the government, and on each one of us devolves the responsibility of trying to help solve these economic problems.[85]

Many of FDR's advisers resented Eleanor's influence, and she was criticized for her liberal positions. Sam Rosenman, Franklin's attorney, speechwriter, and former state assemblyman, was one of many who sought to "get the pants off Eleanor and on to Franklin."[86]

By 1930, sixty branches of New York City's Bank closed and thirteen hundred other banks soon followed. Although Eleanor never challenged her husband in public, the Roosevelts were not always of the same opinion, particularly on political timing regarding civil rights and the World Court. However, privately, she encouraged Roosevelt to institute emergency programs, giving food to the needy and jobs to the unemployed. As one of the first governors to do so, Roosevelt gained national exposure and countrywide enthusiasm for the 1932 election.

Twelve years earlier, when Franklin was assistant secretary of the Navy, he had only praise for Herbert Hoover, then chairman of the European Relief Council.

> [Hoover] is certainly a wonder and I wish we could make him President of the United States. There could not be a better one.[87]

However, feeding Europeans in the wake of World War I was dramatically different from feeding Americans the following decade. Roosevelt's opinion of Hoover and the federal government's response to the Great Depression was now anything but favorable and FDR wanted his opposition heard loud and clear.

The political arena is perplexing and unpredictable at best. You can have the strongest supporter and greatest ally in one campaign only to be locked in a vicious fight against the same person the next time around. It is a business of backdoor deals and under-the-table handshakes. One-time allies Al Smith and Franklin Roosevelt were now involved in a bitter rivalry for the 1932 Democratic presidential nomination. There were several opponents in the race, but the Smith-Roosevelt opposition divided the convention.

Both Louis Howe, the Roosevelts' staunchest advisor and longtime assistant, and Eleanor found themselves outsiders looking in. Franklin was now more interested in listening to his other advisors; he never so much as consulted his wife on anything related to the campaign. (Eleanor had to have been hurt!) Living in the governor's mansion was one thing, but living in the White House was something entirely different, and the Roosevelts' political partnership was about to face another difficult trial.

The Democratic convention, held in Chicago, was deadlocked. Though Roosevelt held the lead, the New York delegation remained split. Al Smith was second and Jack Garner third, holding on to critical votes from Texas and California. Joseph Kennedy (father of future president John F. Kennedy) was a well-known power broker and Roosevelt supporter. Kennedy needed the backing of newspaper magnate William Randolph Hearst; knowing he loathed Newton D. Baker, Kennedy phoned Hearst and told him the convention's choice would be either Baker or Roosevelt. Hearst agreed to back Roosevelt on two conditions: he name Jack Garner as his vice presidential running mate and *never* support the League of Nations or the World Court.

Howe talked with Roosevelt who in turn phoned Hearst. To Eleanor's disgust, FDR agreed and the deal was sealed. For the previous ten years, Eleanor had been an ardent supporter of the League, and Franklin's willingness to sacrifice principles nauseated her. On the other hand, he believed politics required some pragmatic decisions. In short succession, Garner released his delegates, California supported Roosevelt, and the convention erupted into "Happy Days Are Here Again." Shortly thereafter, Franklin told Agnes Brown Leach, a good friend of Eleanor's, that his wife "hasn't spoken to me for three days."[88]

Once he was selected, FDR became the first presidential candidate to accept his party's nomination in person. (Previously, candidates were notified and responded by mail.*) On July 2, 1932, FDR chartered a ten-passenger tri-motor airplane and flew from the governor's mansion in Albany to Chicago, to tell the convention delegates, "I pledge you, I pledge myself, to a new deal for the American people."[89]

To reassure voters that polio would not be a deterrent for him, Roosevelt undertook a strenuous campaign traveling around the country. His uniquely designed automobile was equipped with hand controls, which added to his mobility and distracted attention away from his paralyzed legs. During speeches given from a podium, FDR appeared to be standing when in fact he could lean or practically sit

* In 1848, Whig candidate Zachary Taylor was unaware of his party's nomination because of his personal policy to refuse "postage due" correspondence. At that time, the post office delivered "collect letters" which could be sent without prepaid postage, requiring payment from the recipient. This story (and why Margaret Taylor prayed feverishly for her husband's presidential defeat) is located in Volume I of *Loves, Lies, and Tears*.

on a tall stool concealed from public view. However, to avoid making the laborious trip to a platform, he often spoke from the rear seat of an open touring car.

Forced to a peripheral role on the sidelines, Eleanor was horrified at the prospect of becoming First Lady. She would have to give up so much of her life—things she cherished like her independence, teaching at Todhunter, and weekends with friends, not to mention her own political work. There were renewed rumors of divorce. Marion Dickerman said of her friend,

> [Eleanor] could not bear to become First Lady!...being a prisoner of the White House...forced onto a narrow treadmill of formal receptions, dedications, teas, and official dinners...She won't do it!...She'll run away with Earl Miller.[90]

Nevertheless, the sanctity of the Roosevelt marriage would not be broken.

At that time, Lorena Hickok (known simply as Hick) was the only woman in the group of political writers for the Associated Press. In her dealings with New York State politics she had covered Governor Roosevelt, but interviewed the state's First Lady only once during her four years in the governor's mansion. She recalled Eleanor was reticent and very guarded.

> I wanted very much to know Mrs. Roosevelt. But she always held me at arm's length—and her arms were very long.[91]

The Associated Press then reassigned Hickok to cover Eleanor on a regular basis. Out of courtesy, Hick went to Eleanor's office to explain that she would now have to follow Eleanor everywhere. Less than thrilled, Eleanor responded,

> I'm afraid that you won't have much to write about. I'll not be doing anything very interesting. I do realize that it's your job, of course, and you may go with me whenever I do anything publicly.[92]

Truly, there was no story suitable for print. Whatever Eleanor's personal feelings were, she maintained her poise and self-control. During her husband's presidential campaign, only sporadically was Eleanor invited to participate. Like the pro she was, she never refused to speak or travel when asked, and the public always responded favorably to her sincerity and integrity. It was the story behind the story that preoccupied Eleanor. She never wanted her husband to be president; moreover, she did not want to be First Lady!

Assuming he won, Franklin had determined that his bodyguard, Gus Gennerich, would accompany him to Washington, but Earl Miller would not. Up until that point, Earl and Eleanor were inseparable. Whether Franklin intentionally wanted to deprive Eleanor of the friendship or if Miller even wanted to relocate to Washington, we do not know. Either way, it would be yet another devastating blow for Eleanor. Once again, events in her life seemed totally out of her control, leaving Eleanor depressed for some time.

As the election grew closer, so did the friendship between Eleanor and the female reporter assigned to shadow her. Over time, Eleanor grew to trust Hick and discovered she could share information that would remain private.*

Finally there was a story (beyond Eleanor's remarkable energy and endurance) which Hick could report. Former First Lady Edith Roosevelt began receiving congratulatory notes regarding "her son Franklin's nomination." An understandable mistake, when you consider the sheer number of Roosevelt men. However, not only was Franklin "not her son," she wanted people to know she was a Republican supporting President Hoover.

Mrs. Teddy Roosevelt was an extraordinarily popular First Lady and one of the most private individuals you would ever meet. This made her 1932 appearance at the Republican Convention in Madison Square Garden even more surprising. Unbeknownst to the enormous crowd, the seventy-one-year-old widow, dressed entirely in black, had come to introduce Herbert Hoover to the thousands upon thousands

* As with all of Eleanor's intimate friendships, she began writing daily letters to Lorena Hickok which began in 1932 and ended only with Eleanor's death.

of delegates in attendance. The moment Edith stepped on the rostrum, to her amazement the cheering crowd erupted into deafening applause that went on endlessly. Her appearance actually eclipsed President Hoover. When Hick told Eleanor of her aunt's overt antagonism to FDR's candidacy, Eleanor's only response was a calm and quiet, "How very interesting."

On the evening before the election, Eleanor accompanied her husband to one final rally that did not end until just before midnight. Without hesitation, in the pouring rain, she got into her car, accompanied by Hick, and drove to New York (approximately one and a half hours away) to teach her morning classes. After school, Eleanor returned to Hyde Park and voted. That evening she graciously hosted a buffet dinner for family and friends before going over to the Biltmore Hotel for a large campaign party. According to Hick and as Eleanor later confirmed,

> Through it all, she [Eleanor] kept smiling, but once she looked directly at me. She shook her head, ever so slightly, and the expression in her eyes was miserable.[93]

> I did not want my husband to be president…it was pure selfishness on my part, and I never mentioned my feelings on the subject to him.[94]

Franklin made his pledge to a new deal for the American people, and now the balance of Eleanor's life rested in their hands. Roosevelt disguised his disability so well, it is impossible to say whether the public would have knowingly voted for a handicapped individual in 1932. However, unaware of the full truth, both the public and eighty-nine percent of the Electoral College overwhelmingly elected FDR the country's thirty-second president.

To some extent, his victory was Eleanor's loss, at least in regard to her various positions and commitments. As a governor's wife, she could still manage her individual vocations. But as First Lady–elect she resigned her teaching position at the Todhunter School and curtailed her contributions to the Democratic National Committee, the

League of Women Voters, the Non-Partisan Legislative Committee, and the Women's Trade Union League.

Clearly, Eleanor was reluctant to become First Lady. She openly admitted,

> For myself I was deeply troubled. As I saw it, this meant the end of any personal life of my own. I cannot say that I was pleased at the prospect. The turmoil in my heart and mind was rather great.[95]

> I never wanted to be the president's wife, and don't want it now. There isn't going to be any First Lady. There will just be plain, ordinary Mrs. Roosevelt. And that's all.[96]

Both the public and the press were at odds over how professionally active a First Lady should be. Criticism and jokes about Eleanor were plentiful. She was frequently portrayed with unflattering cartoon characteristics in national newspapers and magazines, including regular appearances in the *Harvard Lampoon*. Aware of the criticism, Eleanor said, "I'll just have to go on being myself, as much as I can. I dare say I shall be criticized, whatever I do."[97] On a more positive note, her friend Hick wrote,

> The prospective mistress of the White House thinks people are going to get used to her ways, even though she does edit Babies—Just Babies, wears $10 dresses, and drives her own car.[98]

In January 1933, former Republican president Calvin Coolidge passed away and Eleanor attended his funeral with her son James. Her presence was unexpected; however, out of respect to her former sorority sister Eleanor wanted to support Grace Coolidge, who appeared touched by the thoughtful gesture. Crossing the political divide, the women thereafter shared a pleasant friendship.

As her husband's inaugural drew closer, Eleanor's autonomy was dwindling away. Nevertheless, she did draw the line when it came to Secret Service protection. She was of the firm belief that,

> Nobody is going to hurt me. I'm not important enough.[99] If any Secret Service man shows up and starts following me around, I'll send him right straight back where he came from.[100]

Eleanor maintained her staunch position even after an incident on February 15 of that year. Just three weeks shy of FDR's inauguration, an unemployed Italian immigrant bricklayer attempted to assassinate the president-elect. Roosevelt was in Miami at a crowded political rally when six shots rang out.

After having accompanied Eleanor on one of her many speeches, Hick had just returned to her Associated Press office when she heard the news. She immediately rushed to Eleanor's New York City residence and found her friend, "sitting on the foot of her husband's bed—her face drawn and pale."[101] Louis Howe was standing nearby, frantically trying to get a call through to Miami. As Eleanor looked up, she said quietly, "This is what it's like to be in public life, Hick."[102] Thankfully, Franklin was uninjured; however, five others were wounded and the mayor of Chicago, Anton Cermak, later died.* The following day Hick observed how quickly her friend bounced back after a near tragedy.

> [Eleanor] was calm and relaxed as she talked. [She stated] That's apt to happen to any man in public life. He must always face the possibility, and so must his family. But it's best not to think about it any more than you have to. One cannot live in fear.[103]

Ironically, just a few weeks earlier Hick, Eleanor, her son Elliott, and Howe were having lunch when the subject of assassination had come up. As Hick recalled, she and Howe found themselves engulfed in laughter as mother and son conversed. If someone started shooting at her husband, Eleanor said,

> I'd step in front of him, of course. [Eleanor]
>
> That would be just dandy, then you'd both get shot. [Elliot]

* Giuseppe Zangara was expeditiously electrocuted on March 20, 1933, at the Florida State Prison.

> Oh, but I have a secret weapon. I have this oversized fountain pen... [given to me by the Secret Service] and it shoots out tear gas.
>
> Can't you just picture the scene? The guns will be blazing away at Pa, and Mummy will be fishing things out of her handbag, throwing them right and left, saying: It's here—I *know* it's here. I saw it only this morning. While Pa will be saying patiently: You'd better hurry, dear![104]

Inaugurated the following month, Roosevelt acknowledged the strong support of the Electoral College and for the first time ever invited the 531 electors to his inaugural at the Capitol. Like her predecessor, Lou Hoover, Eleanor was well equipped to step into the First Ladyship—running a large mansion with numerous servants and all the related trappings—however, she had far less confidence in her abilities.

Insecurities aside, unlike any of her predecessors, just plain Mrs. Roosevelt managed to revolutionize the role of First Lady. Only two days after assuming her new position, Eleanor held her first routine get-together with women reporters. (She remains the only First Lady ever to have done so.) She asked for the reporters' cooperation in helping her inform the public of White House activities and national policies.

The journalists were very appreciative for two good reasons. First, it helped them maintain employment during the Depression, and second, because it was exclusive to women, it gave them an opportunity to scoop their male counterparts. When newspaper editors realized that the First Lady wanted to focus on serious problems and breaking news, more papers began to hire women. Some reporters cautioned Eleanor to speak off the record, but she defended her position, knowing some statements would,

> Cause unfavorable comment in some quarters...[but] I am making these statements on purpose to arouse controversy and thereby get the topics talked about.[105]

With every new administration, there is always an adjustment period. No two families have the same needs or habits. The Roosevelts had long ago developed a distinct and separate circle of personal and political allies, which only added to the complexity of the transition. White House usher Mr. J. B. West confirmed,

> The mansion was always full of people...the President's people, and then there was Mrs. Roosevelt's people.[106] [And] contrary to published reports, Eleanor Roosevelt never *walked* anywhere. She ran.[107]

In addition to the Executive Mansion being the private residence of the First Family, on any given day it is also the workplace for dozens of employees, staff, and workmen, as well as a tourist attraction. The new First Lady had respect for protocol, but she also wanted life in the White House to be "a little less formal." Besides, for a woman on the run, some of the established codes of behavior simply took too long. For instance, whenever the First Lady wanted to leave the upstairs private residence, it was customary for an usher to escort her into the elevator and operate it for her. Once inside, he would ring a specific bell notifying the staff and Secret Service of her location. It was not long before the staff discovered Mrs. Roosevelt racing around the entire mansion without a bell ever ringing. After several futile attempts to rein her in, the staff had no choice but to accept the fact that the First Lady would operate the elevator at her own convenience and show up anywhere at any time.

Even more surprising to the staff was Eleanor's rather casual approach in greeting guests. Protocol stated that guests be escorted into the Red Room and once everyone had gathered, the First Lady is formally announced. One can only imagine the staff's reaction the first time Eleanor ran to the front door of the White House to meet visitors!

One piece of etiquette Hick learned the hard way. Attending an event with the First Lady and the vice president's wife, Mrs. Ettie Garner, Hick and Mrs. Garner happened to be standing closer to a door while Eleanor was a few feet behind them. To get out of the way Hick walked through the doorway, but suddenly a Secret Service man jumped in front of her and pushed her back. Unbeknownst to her, nobody except the president is supposed to precede the First Lady through a doorway. After Hick regained her composure, she looked around to find the two women laughing.

Originally unclear of her role and direction, Eleanor moved into the White House depressed; yet, she proved once again that constructive activity (particularly helping others) is most beneficial, and having cherished friends with whom you can confide is priceless. In 1933 she wrote,

> I never talked to anyone. That was why it all ate into my soul...In other words, I was a morbid idiot for many years! Only in the last ten years or so have I made friends to whom I have talked.[108]

During this time, Hick gave Eleanor a sapphire ring surrounded by diamond chips, which she treasured and wore for the remainder of her life.

Hick was wholeheartedly loyal and dedicated to Eleanor's well-being and happiness. In turn, Eleanor respected Hick's opinion and sought her advice. With the help of her dear friend, Eleanor was able to carve out a more meaningful life than purely attending dedications and ceremonial teas. It was Hick who initially suggested Eleanor meet with reporters and establish a good working relationship. Later, after receiving dozens upon dozens of letters from Eleanor describing her everyday happenings, Hick had the idea that the public would be equally interested in the First Lady's experiences. Indeed, the letters to Hick proved to be the forerunner of "My Day," a newspaper column Eleanor would later write.

It was a distressing and demanding time. Eleanor's busy life included family, public events, and social obligations. Her close relationships with people (including Hick, Earl Miller, and later Joseph Lash) may have had their difficulties and heartaches, yet they were warm, devoted, and caring friendships that only ended with Eleanor's death.

Just five months into her tenure, Eleanor began penning a monthly column for *Women's Home Companion* magazine called "I Want You to Write to Me." It was an open invitation whereby people asked Mrs. Roosevelt for her opinion or advice on personal and political questions. She never shied away from conflicting points of view and encouraged the public to share their opposing opinions, needs, and observations. Not surprisingly, the response was overwhelming—the first five months alone, three hundred thousand people wrote her—and she donated her one thousand dollar monthly fee to various charities. To avoid the appearance of partisanship, after a two-year run, when campaigning began for those seeking election, the magazine ended the column.

The first year of Eleanor's tenure was an unmanageable and worrisome time for the majority of Americans. Eighty-five thousand businesses had failed and 25 percent of the workforce (over thirteen million Americans) was unemployed. A number of cities, including Chicago and New York, began to default on their payrolls. According to the Federal Reserve Board, one week before FDR's inauguration, a quarter of a billion dollars in gold had poured out of the system.[109]

President Roosevelt had introduced a number of major changes, government regulations, and massive public works projects to stimulate a recovery. Some were successful while others were not, and unemployment remained high. The Federal Deposit Insurance Corporation, created in June of 1933 to reestablish confidence, now insured bank deposits up to $2,500.*

During this time, Eleanor helped boost her husband's New Deal programs. She went on firsthand, fact-finding missions for the president and visited schools, factories, miners, farmers, and administrators all across the country. Eleanor was a trained observer and had a great capacity to identify with people. Millions of citizens needed hope and Eleanor was the perfect First Lady who could give it to them. Those who initially believed she was only seeking publicity quickly changed their minds. Eleanor was the real deal; she listened intently, understood people's needs, reported accurately, and then poked, prodded, and persisted until something was done.

At Eleanor's urging, for the first time a president's cabinet included a woman. Frances Perkins, a labor reformer and political activist who worked with the First Lady in New York, became Secretary of Labor. As Eleanor grew more confident, she reached out further and further. I believe Margaret Truman said it best: "The mere catalog of her activities

* As of 2010, funds are insured up to $250,000.

would fatigue a squadron of Olympic athletes."[110] During her first year in the White House, the *New York Times* wrote 320 stories on Eleanor. Future First Lady Jackie Kennedy is the only one who surpassed that number, although that was mainly because the public and media were so enamored of her, not necessarily because of her accomplishments.[111]

At the end of the year, the Twenty-First Amendment to the Constitution repealed Prohibition. Having seen the destruction alcohol can cause families, Eleanor originally supported the Eighteenth Amendment, restricting the manufacture and transportation of alcohol. But now, far more concerned with civil liberties, she believed the Fourteenth Amendment (defining and protecting citizenship) and the Fifteenth Amendment (ensuring voting rights) were far more critical issues to enforce. African Americans, women, young people, and world peace led Eleanor's list of crusades.

By 1935, Eleanor added yet another vocation to her already impressive résumé.* She was in demand as a pubic speaker and gave approximately fourteen hundred speeches (all written herself—no speechwriters) throughout her tenure as First Lady. When she signed a contract with the W. Colston Leigh Bureau (Leigh Bureau, Ltd.) to do two lecture circuit tours a year, she began taking voice lessons with a professional vocal coach. She resigned from the bureau six years later, after approximately seven hundred paid lectures.[112]

In December of that same year, Eleanor wrote her first newspaper column. Consistently for six days a week (the only exception being four days after her husband's death) and lasting until 1962, "My Day" appeared in approximately sixty syndicated newspapers. For four years, she also wrote a series of monthly columns, "Mrs. Roosevelt's Page," for the *Democratic Digest.* When she believed a topic required a more in-depth assessment (civil rights, for example), Eleanor expressed herself in lengthy magazine articles. Her editorials appeared in over 142 different publications.

In addition to print media, Eleanor used the airwaves to share her perspective. In 1937, she signed a contract with NBC Radio to do mul-

* A prolific author, Eleanor wrote eighteen books, which does not include those she coauthored or the innumerable newspaper columns, magazine articles, speeches, lectures, and letters she wrote.

tiple broadcasts on various subjects. The first year she did thirteen of them and by 1940, the number had increased to twenty-six recordings of fifteen minutes each. In her spare time, Eleanor chaired national conferences and addressed national conventions on social reform, all the while continuing to be her husband's eyes and ears.

Appalled at racism, Eleanor did everything in her power to fight social injustice. When the Daughters of the American Revolution refused to allow black singer Marian Anderson to perform in the DAR's Constitution Hall, Eleanor arranged for her to sing at the Lincoln Memorial and had her perform at the White House. On another occasion, she demonstrated true courage in the heart of segregated Alabama. While attending the Southern Conference on Human Welfare in Birmingham, whites and blacks were required to sit apart from one another. In protest, Eleanor straddled her chair over the dividing aisle and sat between them. As she said so eloquently, "Action creates its own courage." As a board member for the National Association for the Advancement of Colored People (NAACP), Eleanor worked diligently for an anti-lynching bill.

Equally concerned for the nation's youth, who saw no hope in the devastated job market, she pushed for youth programs that would service public and nonprofit organizations. She became involved in the American Student Union and the American Youth Congress.

It is true that Eleanor was away from the White House a great deal of the time, but when she was in residence, she performed her hostess duties with charm and grace. The Executive Mansion remained a very busy household with several full-time residents. Missy LeHand, FDR's personal secretary for twenty-one years, had a private two-room apartment on the third floor.* Journalist and historian Joseph Lash, executive secretary for the American Student Union, was one of Eleanor's closest confidantes and a devoted friend for twenty-three years.† Later, when

* Missy was welcomed as a member of the Roosevelt family. In 1941, she suffered a major stroke and remained an invalid until her death in 1944.

† Lash wrote several books and in 1971 won the Pulitzer Prize for *Eleanor and Franklin*. As with Eleanor's friendship with Earl Miller, there was speculation that Lash and the First Lady were having an affair. Twenty-five years Eleanor's junior, Lash met his second wife through the First Lady and said of the rumors, "There wasn't any such relationship. It's an absurd accusation." www.nytimes.com/1987/08/23/obituaries/joseph-p-lash-is-dead-reporter-and-biographer.html?pagewanted=2.

Hick left her job at the Associated Press and began working for the Democratic National Committee in 1941, she too had her own small room on the second floor of the White House.

Mr. West confirmed that the First Lady "collected people" like her "husband collected books." The tomes covered every inch of space on the White House shelves and "overflowed into stacks and stacks on the third floor."[113] Eleanor's "collection" fared a bit better: the mansion could accommodate twenty-one overnight visitors and it was a constant game of musical chairs. Informal meals often depended on who might be around on any given day. The five Roosevelt children were all married during their father's administration (a couple of them more than once), and between spouses, grandchildren, other relatives, colleagues, assistants, and friends, the Roosevelts seldom dined alone.

Cuisine in the White House, unlike today, was by no means considered five-star quality, in fact just the opposite. It is fair to say the housekeeper in charge of meals, Henrietta Nesbitt, was not one to receive compliments on her repetitive, tasteless menus. Actually, one of the better meals Eleanor made herself. Well known for her scrambled eggs, the First Lady served them in a large silver chafing dish set directly on the dining room table. The staff often referred to it as "scrambled eggs with brains," because the main course was always conversation.

Eleanor made no apologies for her lack of interest in cuisine. To those who knew her well, it went hand in hand with her unaffected, self-effacing, down-to-earth attitude. She rode buses, ate on the run at drugstore lunch counters, bought apples from men on the street, and was annoyed when hotels gave her the presidential suite, because "one room would have served her purpose."[114] As Bess Furman so accurately reported, "Washington has never seen the likes of Eleanor Roosevelt!"[115]

In September of 1939, Germany invaded Poland and later Russia, causing Britain and France to declare war on Germany. It was the start of World War II. The United States proclaimed neutrality, as it had done at the beginning of World War I. The following year Eleanor wrote *The Moral Basis of Democracy*, while Franklin pondered his future. In over 140 years, no other president had challenged the two-term tradition.

Not everyone in the Democratic Party establishment agreed with Roosevelt's New Deal policies. Many urged Vice President John Garner, who himself opposed many of Roosevelt's programs, to seek the nomination, which he did. Roosevelt finally announced that he would run for an unprecedented third term and after easily winning re-nomination, he dropped Garner from the ticket in favor of Henry Wallace.

It was a very unpopular decision, and as delegates threatened to revolt, Roosevelt dug in his heels. It was the second day of the three-day Democratic National Convention of 1940, and things were rapidly spinning out of control with delegates loudly rebelling against FDR's vice presidential candidate. Frances Perkins told the president, "This thing is going to blow up."[116] He suggested she phone Eleanor and urge her to fly to the convention immediately. Eleanor in turn phoned her husband and asked his opinion. "Well, would you like to go?" FDR asked. "No," Eleanor responded, "I wouldn't *like* to go!...Do you really want me to go?" His simple reply of "Perhaps it would be a good idea," caused Eleanor to interpret the request as something she had to do.[117]

When she arrived at the convention, pandemonium had broken loose. The noise was deafening and you could not even hear your own voice. No other First Lady had ever addressed a political convention and Eleanor still had no idea of the considerable influence she had garnered. She no sooner stepped onto the podium than mayhem in the convention hall ceased. Impromptu and without notes, she said,

> This is no ordinary time, no time for weighing anything except what we can best do for the country as a whole. No man can carry this situation alone...responsibility is only carried by a united people...You cannot treat it as you would an ordinary nomination in an ordinary time. You will have to rise above considerations, which are narrow and partisan.[118]

When the going got tough Franklin once again turned to his most ardent supporter and strongest ally, his partner of thirty-five years. Yet again, Eleanor came through supremely for him. The convention floor went wild with enthusiasm and as Eleanor headed back to New York, the delegates confirmed the Roosevelt-Wallace ticket. One headline read, "Mrs. Roosevelt stills the Tumult of 50,000."[119] For years, Eleanor had struggled to find her own role; it appeared that she had finally discovered it in smoke-filled rooms, with hard-drinking politicians.

That October, one month prior to the presidential election, all men between the ages of twenty-one and thirty-five were required to register with local draft boards. Roosevelt won reelection with both the popular and nearly eighty-five percent of the electoral votes. He incorporated in his 1941 State of the Union address, four fundamental freedoms that people "*everywhere* in the world" ought to enjoy: freedom of speech and expression, freedom of religion, freedom from want, and freedom from fear.[120]

The First Lady's editorials were equally as popular and the *Ladies Home Journal* contacted Eleanor regarding a new monthly column. "If You Ask Me" ran for nearly nine years. *Journal* editors reviewed the mail and chose about ten questions a month for her to answer. Since she was now earning twenty-five hundred dollars a month from her *Journal* contract alone, critical newspaper editorials were appearing regarding the First Lady's "undignified commercial ventures."* Still, Eleanor maintained that the large donations to charity were far more important than her popularity. A few years later, she would write yet another column for *McCall's* magazine that would run for thirteen years.

Eleanor courageously followed her principles regardless of where they led and was willing to take an unpopular stand. When asked why she did so many controversial things the First Lady responded,

> I have access to the president. And if you don't use that access to do things that need to be done in this country, need to be done for people, I would be sorely remiss and irresponsible.[121]

Today, historians call Eleanor the self-appointed conscience of the Roosevelt administration. Looking back, Eleanor confirmed,

* Using the Consumer Price Index "relative values measurement," $2,500 in 1941 is equivalent to approximately $36,000 in 2009 (www.measuringworth.com/uscompare). This amount did not take into consideration all of her other lucrative speaking and writing commitments.

> [It was] hard to remember that I was not just Eleanor Roosevelt, but the wife of the President. I think the personage is an accident and I only like the part of life in which I am a person.[122]

Over twenty years had passed since World War I ended and in conjunction with her position on civil rights, Eleanor had worked hard to promote world peace. However, Adolf Hitler, the chancellor of Germany, and Benito Mussolini, prime minister of Italy, forced her to abandon her pacifism. Hitler started World War II in 1939 and when Italy invaded Greece in 1940, America's neutrality was rapidly dissolving.

On December 7, 1941, according to President Roosevelt "a day that will live in infamy," Japan attacked Hawaii, Guam, and the Philippines. Over twenty-three hundred people died and nearly twelve hundred more were injured in the attack on Pearl Harbor.[123] The following day, President Roosevelt declared war on Japan.

Eleanor Roosevelt's chapter continues with Women of World War II.

PART FOUR

WOMEN OF WORLD WAR II

INTRODUCTION

A DECADE MAY SOUND LIKE a long stretch, yet it only measures a period of ten years. To historians chronicling our nation's great struggle to evolve, followed by its astonishing progression from prosperity to the depths of despair, ten years is a relatively brief period.

Just ten years had passed since the Great Depression began, its devastation on everyday lives fresh in memory and ongoing. Furthermore, only two decades had elapsed since the destruction and great loss of lives in World War I, and now the United States was confronted with yet another terrorizing, injurious World War.

World War II is said to be the deadliest conflict in human history. It involved worldwide militaries which fought on land, in the air, and at sea, on reportedly over two-thirds of the world's surface. Global domination was at stake, with every major world power involved, and the result was over sixty million deaths (some estimate as high as seventy million). History's titanic war only came to an end after nuclear weapons were used, but not before most of Europe and sizeable areas of Asia were destroyed, and several countries teetered on the edge of collapse.

For a brief overview of the war, and to understand who the major players were, you have to go back as early as 1931. That is when Japan invaded Manchuria in its initial effort to conquer China and expand the Japanese Empire into Asia and eventually the South Pacific. Within two years Adolf Hitler, head of the Nazi Party, had become the dictatorial Chancellor of Germany, while Benito Mussolini was the residing dictator of Italy.

Both men had designed evil plans for global destruction. Mussolini sought an Italian Mediterranean Empire, whereas Hitler wrote his blueprint for Germany's world domination in the form of a book entitled *Mein Kampf*, beginning with the annihilation of all Jews. By 1935, German Jews were stripped of all rights and placed in concentration camps. Years later, the major concentration complexes and hundreds of subcamps holding thousands of prisoners, including young children, were discovered. Most notorious were Auschwitz (with some seven thousand individuals), Dachau, Buchenwald, and Mauthausen. Over six million civilian European Jews were killed in Hitler's Holocaust gas chambers.

Perpetuating the reign of terror, Japan launched its large-scale invasion on mainland China. Meanwhile Germany, the aggressor in Europe, invaded Poland (1939) with the cooperation of Joseph Stalin, General Secretary of the Communist Party in the Soviet Union. The two countries agreed to divide up Poland between themselves, and within one month, the country had been conquered. In Poland's defense, France and the United Kingdom declared war on Germany. In turn, Germany quickly seized Denmark and Norway before threatening Austria and then Czechoslovakia.

Within a year, the Nazis invaded France, Belgium, Luxembourg, and the Netherlands. True to the theory that there is no honor among thieves, Hitler's Germany then invaded the Soviet Union (1941), bringing the USSR into an alliance with France and Great Britain.

As with the First World War, America declared itself neutral and made every attempt to avoid getting involved in the conflict. Franklin D. Roosevelt, president of the United States, did increase economic sanctions on Japan when they invaded mainland China (1937), and even more so when Japan invaded French Indochina (1940). Prime Minister of Great Britain Winston Churchill also increased sanctions. Nevertheless, as the war progressed and increasingly aggressive foreign policies threatened more and more countries, neutrality became less and less feasible.

On December 7, 1941, Japan simultaneously attacked the United States (Pearl Harbor in Hawaii) and British assets in Southeast Asia (Guam and the Philippines). The United States declared war on Japan the very next day and three days later, Germany and Italy both declared war on the United States.

The majority of the world's nations were now split into two

opposing military alliances. Germany, Italy, and Japan formed the Axis coalition, while Allied forces consisted of Great Britain, France, Australia, New Zealand, Canada, South Africa, and the Soviet Union. When the United States joined the Allies, its armed forces and collaboration heavily tipped the balance of power.

In the end (1945), Soviet forces captured Berlin, forcing Germany to concede defeat. American forces captured the Japanese islands of Iwo Jima and Okinawa; however, the Japanese were unwilling to surrender. To finally stop the war and prevent additional U.S. causalities, the United States dropped the world's first atomic bomb on Hiroshima. Since Japan remained defiant, as many had predicted, three days later a second atomic bomb was released on Nagasaki. It was another five days before Japan agreed to an unconditional surrender.

Emerging from the Allied victory, the United States and the Soviet Union materialized as the world's two leading superpowers, setting the stage for yet another conflict which became known as the Cold War.

As in all previous wars, courageous women stood behind and alongside the heroic, honorable, and valiant men defending America. Eleanor Roosevelt's story continues from Part III, followed by Bess Truman and Mamie Eisenhower. Born and raised in three different parts of the country, with distinctly diverse personalities and natures, one woman was orphaned by the age of ten, while another lived with the shame of her father's suicide her entire life. The third had the good fortune of having both her parents approve of her marital choice and see his rise to fame.

Born before the turn of the century, all three grew up in families with means and were dedicated wives and mothers who lost at least one child. Eleanor will forever hold the designation of being First Lady longer than any of her previous or future sorority sisters. Bess, who lived into her late nineties, holds the sorority record for longevity. Married at the age of thirty-four, Bess lived her entire life in her mother's Missouri home and was seventy-one the first and only time she visited Europe.

Conversely, Mamie was a military bride at nineteen and moved over twenty-five times during her marriage. She lived down malicious rumors of alcoholism and maintained that the tales of her husband's infidelity were untrue, defending him even a decade after his death.

These forthright women and their unique stories follow.

7

First Lady to the World

ELEANOR ROOSEVELT

> In the long run, we shape our lives, and we shape ourselves. The process never ends until we die. And the choices we make are ultimately our own responsibility.
>
> —ELEANOR ROOSEVELT

EXACTLY THREE MONTHS TO THE DAY before the attack on Pearl Harbor, Sara Delano Roosevelt died. It was just two weeks shy of her eighty-seventh birthday. The "endless details," as Eleanor described the dismantling of a person's life, not surprisingly fell on her shoulders. In a letter to her friend Maude Gray, Eleanor wrote,

> I think Franklin will forget all the irritations & remember only pleasant things, which is just as well. What ironical things happen in life & how foolish it all seems. I looked at my mother-in-law's face after she was dead & understood so many things I'd never seen before. It is dreadful to have lived so close to someone for 36 years & feel no deep affection or sense of loss. It is hard on Franklin however.[1]

#32 Anna Eleanor Roosevelt Roosevelt

Born: October 11, 1884

Birthplace: New York, New York

Married: 1905 (Franklin Delano Roosevelt)

Children: 6

White House Years: 1933–1945

Died: November 7, 1962 (78 years old)

Fact: First Lady for 12 years; wrote newspaper column "My Day"

AKA: First Lady to the World

In her column, "My Day," Eleanor acknowledged,

> [Sara's] strongest trait was loyalty to her family...She was not just sweetness and light, for there was a streak of jealousy and posses-

siveness in her where her own were concerned. Grande dame was truly applicable to her.[2]

No sooner had she begun attending to the details of Sara's estate than she received a distressing phone call from Walter Reed Hospital in Washington. Her brother Hall was dying of liver disease brought on by years of excessive drinking. Eleanor immediately rushed to his bedside and refused to leave the hospital. For ten days, she slept in her clothes and watched her younger brother's laborious struggle to breathe and his attempts to speak prior to his passing. Before the First Lady accompanied his body back to Tivoli, New York, and the Hall family vault, she held a service for him in the East Room of the White House. Expressing her feelings in writing came naturally to Eleanor, and she wrote a tribute in her "My Day" column to commemorate her brother's life.

It was a very difficult two weeks, but there was no time to mourn or be depressed. Eleanor had already accepted her first official government position. The Office of Civilian Defense (OCD), not yet organized or fully developed, would be responsible for civilian protection, volunteer participation, and morale improvement in addition to coordinating community needs with federal agencies. With the United States' entrance into World War II, the country's needs were increasing. Fiorello LaGuardia, the mayor of New York, would head up the newly formed organization, while Eleanor would be in charge of the volunteer work. Her primary plan, which she stayed up all night drafting, included three goals.

1. Offer every person wishing to volunteer an opportunity to train.

2. Provide meaningful jobs that would benefit communities, such as work in nursery schools, housing projects, homes for the aged, and more.

3. Prepare citizens to meet emergency calls.

Before breakfast, her devoted and trusted assistant-secretary, Malvina (Tommy) Thompson, typed and prepared multiple copies of her proposal.* After breakfast and with no sleep, Eleanor walked over to the OCD headquarters on Connecticut Avenue to report for work on the first day of her new position as deputy director. She told the staff that she would be on the job every business day at 9:00 A.M. and stay as late as possible.

The president was delighted that Eleanor had a project she felt passionate about. In actuality, she worked tirelessly on numerous projects and addressed a dauntingly wide range of issues. More than likely the president was thrilled that his wife would now be consumed with something other than her overtly political activities.

Up until the attack on Pearl Harbor, night after night, Eleanor put material in the president's inbox for his review. Week after week, she raised important concerns that needed assessment. No one could possibly question the First Lady's well-intended aspirations or her desire to achieve immediate equality between the sexes and instantaneous justice for all Americans, regardless of race.

It was true that far too many people were destitute and in need of proper housing and nutrition. Countless citizens were still unemployed and a large number of those with jobs deserved better working conditions. Nor had the lengthy post-Depression crisis been limited to one occupation or a narrow region. Farmers, miners, steel workers, and dozens of others with various livelihoods all across the country had real problems that needed addressing. Nevertheless, with her boundless energy, it was hard for Eleanor to recognize the limitations of those mere mortals around her.

The First Lady would often say, "Franklin, I think you should or Franklin, surely you will not..."[3] If the president refused to see someone or listen to a particular cause, the First Lady would invite the spokesperson to lunch and seat him or her next to the president. For the vast majority—outsiders as well as those within the internal government bureaucracy—the First Lady provided access to the pres-

* Tommy worked with Eleanor as her key aide for twenty-five years. She became a dear friend, business traveling companion, and the First Lady's gatekeeper. When Eleanor remodeled her Val-Kill furniture factory, she designed an apartment for Tommy which included two bedrooms, a living room, a kitchen, and a screened-in porch. Tommy died eight years to the day after FDR and Eleanor noted in her book, *You Learn By Living*, "I learned for the first time what being alone was like."

ident. She forwarded ideas and proposals, gave him letters and articles to read, and shared her opinions. Known as FDR's nagging conscience, Eleanor was relentless when it came to the needs of others. The president jokingly advised Lorena Hickok,

> Never get into an argument with the Missus, you can't win...you think you have her pinned down here...but she bobs up right away over there somewhere! No use—you can't win![4]

Yet at the same time, Roosevelt respected his wife's opinion and appreciated her intelligence. He would bounce ideas off her and goad her into an argument to better clarify his own thoughts. She never knew if her arguments changed his mind because unfortunately, FDR rarely acknowledged his wife's influence. Nor did he express his admiration or appreciation of her; Eleanor recalled,

> Very often he would bait me into giving an opinion by stating as his own, a point of view with which he knew I would disagree. I remember one occasion I became extremely vehement and irritated.
>
> The next day to my complete surprise, he calmly stated as his own the arguments that I had given him the night before![5]

She may have been amused to hear her husband extol her point of view, but on some level, Eleanor resented his lack of acknowledgement, for she also admitted he would adopt her stance, "without giving me a glance or the satisfaction of batting an eyelash."[6] She never sought (nor would it have ever occurred to her that she might receive) public recognition from her spouse; but privately, his acknowledgement would have gone a long way toward improving their personal relationship.

Truly the only people Eleanor wanted and more importantly needed to be worthy of were her husband and children. Outside ridicule did not bother her; she expected it. Eldest son James, now one of his father's secretaries, admitted that neither FDR nor he and his brothers did much to promote Eleanor's emotional security. It was easy to make fun of her shrill voice and prudish manner. In truth, they discounted her value or merely dismissed her.

Within six months of accepting the OCD position, Eleanor felt compelled to resign. She strongly emphasized social services, while Mayor LaGuardia was far more concerned with matters of defense.[7] Her ultraliberal leanings fiercely angered the conservatives in Congress, and her husband's political enemies ruthlessly attacked her. Although Eleanor continually denied having any political power with the president, his rivals disagreed. At various press conferences she firmly asserted,

> I wouldn't dream of doing more than passing along requests or suggestions that come to me.[8]

> I never urged on him a specific course of action, no matter how strongly I felt, because I realized he knew of factors in the picture as a whole of which I might be ignorant.[9]

> I never tried to influence Franklin on anything he did, and I certainly have never known him to try to influence me.[10]

Irrefutably, Roosevelt was his own man who made his own decisions and had a firm grip on the presidency. While Eleanor did not see her prodding and debating as attempts to influence, they were still opportunities to present her one-sided point of view. The president received advice from several advisors (sadly, his chief advisor Louis Howe had passed away), but Eleanor's unrelenting persistence proved to be wearing. On occasion, when FDR needed some downtime from his presidential pressures, he would retreat into his office and make it clear that Eleanor was not welcome. Their daughter Anna later commented,

> Mother often miscalculated people's moods and tried to bring up serious matters when everyone wished to relax and be frivolous.[11]

In retrospect, Eleanor had this to say:

> [FDR] might have been happier, if he had always been perfectly sure that I would have agreed. He wasn't. And it was probably good for him that he wasn't. But there must have been times when he would have liked it if he didn't have to argue things. I acted as a spur, even though the spurring was not always wanted or welcome. I had this horrible sense of obligation, which was bred in me, I couldn't help it. It was nothing to be proud of, it was just something I couldn't help.[12]

When the United States entered World War II, all of Eleanor's sons were called to active military duty. James (thirty-four) went into the Marines while Elliott (thirty-one) joined the Army Air Corps; Frank Jr. (twenty-seven) and John (twenty-five) were in the Navy.* Author and friend Joseph Lash, who lived in the White House during the Roosevelt administration, wrote,

> Eleanor began to sob as she spoke of how difficult it had been to say good-by [to her sons leaving for war]. Simply by the laws of chance, not all four of her sons would return.[13]

A few months later, on June 7, 1942, Eleanor told a friend,

> Perhaps we have to learn that life was not meant to be lived in security but with adventurous courage.[14]

With her sons at war and her dear friend Louis Howe no longer around to soothe the uneasiness between her and Franklin, the wedge between the couple seemed to widen. In the past, when they disagreed, Roosevelt never tried to censor his wife. Just the opposite; he told her,

> You go right ahead and stand for whatever you feel is right. I have to stand on my own legs. Besides, I can always say I can't do a thing with you.[15]

* All four men became officers and were decorated for their bravery, and all four survived the war.

In other words, FDR used Eleanor when it was to his advantage and acted as if he couldn't control her when she espoused a conflicting opinion.

Roosevelt chose to share nothing of his international policies with his spouse. If his lack of disclosure were not a strong enough message, according to Blanch Wiesen Cook, Eleanor's biographer, FDR "demanded her silence" in that area.[16] With the OCD position no longer providing Eleanor with purpose and legitimate work, she once again found herself in the unbearable place of believing herself useless. But if she learned nothing else from her first eight years in the White House, Eleanor did learn that in order to survive in politics there were three vital lessons she had to understand. You cannot take anything personally, you cannot bear grudges, and you have to take defeat over and over again—then pick up and go on. To her credit, she never considered a political setback a permanent defeat.

Traveling around the country gathering information for her husband's New Deal programs no longer took precedent. She wanted to go to Europe and help the Red Cross with refugee relief efforts, but it was quickly determined that the risk of the president's wife being kidnapped was far too great. With the Red Cross efforts squashed, Eleanor immediately began work on advocating visitors' visas for British children seeking asylum in the United States. She wrote articles for *Liberty* magazine, denouncing anti-Semitism.

As the State Department was declining thousands of applicants, Eleanor was successful in getting a few hundred Jewish refugees admitted to the United States. Her attempt at getting a bill passed—one which would have admitted an additional twenty thousand children in excess of the German quota—failed, and Eleanor had lingering regrets that she was unable to do more.[17]

During this period, some of the couple's most intense arguments revolved around the president's cautiousness in advancing civil rights. Eleanor was angry at FDR's failure to do more to help European Jews. She voiced her compelling protests publicly and joined Jewish-American leaders on speaking tours to raise public awareness of the crisis. Additionally, she was vehemently opposed to the internment of Japanese-Americans and persuaded the attorney general to fight the policy.

But the public was fearful, and anti-Japanese sentiment was strong. Therefore, Eleanor did the next best thing. She insisted families stay together (there were ten camps in various Western states) and intervened with the War Relocation Authority to secure early releases. For those Japanese citizens who were denied American citizenship, she helped facilitate access to frozen bank accounts. She also visited a Japanese-American relocation camp in Arizona to express her regrets and show compassion.

As the war raged on, the president's health began deteriorating. During 1942, FDR had hoped that his partner of thirty-seven years would remain at home and be a more frequent White House hostess. He actually suggested they try to reclaim their marriage. But far too many years had passed since that door had closed and although Eleanor could forgive, she could never forget Franklin's disloyalty and her feelings of inadequacy. She too had hoped for a closer, more intimate marriage, whereby she was her husband's confidante in a full partnership of equals. Had that happened, it is possible the Lucy Mercer affair could have slowly died away beneath a stronger, more united marital bond. Unfortunately, Roosevelt's emotional makeup prevented him from doing that.

Though the outside world may have perceived both parties in the Roosevelt marriage as equals, the truth was they were not. Years later Eleanor acknowledged, with a slight bitterness, "I was one of those who served [FDR's] purposes."[18] She described her disappointment when she wrote,

> His was an innate kind of reticence...an older father and a very strong-willed mother, who constantly tried to exercise control over him in the early years...it became part of his nature not to talk to anyone of intimate matters.[19]

> Every woman wants to be *first* to someone sometimes in her life...if only men understood it![20]

In his book *Eleanor and Franklin*, Joseph Lash observed, "Everyone's interests were subordinated to his," and Eleanor's affection was more, “a labor of love by serving his work.”[21]

There was no going back for the couple or the country, only forward, and Eleanor’s search to be more useful in the war effort intensified. When she realized her plan to help U.S. citizens through her work at the OCD and her efforts to save thousands of European refugees were ineffective, she turned her attention to the needs and morale of military servicemen. After months of pleading to be once again her husband’s eyes and ears, she finally received Roosevelt’s approval.

The First Lady of the United States would soon become the First Lady to the world. She went on tours of American military bases abroad and both her appearances and detailed inspection reports proved beneficial to all. She met with thousands of soldiers and asked each one, “What do you need?” and “Can I take a message home for you?” Upon learning that the fighting men and women needed warmer socks, she made sure they received them. Dressed in her Red Cross uniform, Eleanor visited hospitals and personally stopped by the bed of every wounded soldier, with a warm smile and a message of appreciation for their service. In addition to walking countless miles, she signed thousands of autographs.

After returning to the States with dozens of notebooks filled with addresses and phone numbers, she immediately began writing notes and phoning loved ones. The White House switchboard was continuously lit up with operators calling homes all across the country with the same salutation: “The White House is calling.”[22]

Accompanied by her assistant Tommy, her first trip in 1942 was to Europe, making her the first incumbent First Lady to make a trip outside of the United States without the president. In addition to learning useful information regarding how various agencies and volunteer organizations operated, Eleanor cemented good relations with the King and Queen of England. At dinner, she met with some of the highest dignitaries, including Prime Minister and Mrs. Winston Churchill. The next day, she began her round of inspections, tours, speeches, and receptions. A British reporter wrote,

> She walked me off my feet!...fifty miles through factories, clubs, and hospitals.[23]

Her seven-day tour included the Midlands, Ulster, and Scotland. Just prior to her departure, Eleanor received a handwritten note. It was from Prime Minister Churchill who wrote, "You certainly have left golden footprints behind you."[24]

In 1943, the First Lady toured Australia, New Zealand, and the South Pacific. This time she went alone, because she felt the twenty thousand mile trip would be too strenuous for Tommy. Once there, she was eager to visit Guadalcanal, where some of the bloodiest battles occurred. Admiral William F. Halsey was extremely hesitant, as the Japanese were still bombing the island daily. Reluctantly he agreed to accompany her and said afterward,

> I marveled at her hardihood, both physical and mental. She walked for miles, and she saw patients who were grievously and gruesomely wounded. [The First Lady] alone, had accomplished more good than any other person, or any group of civilians, who had passed through my area.[25]

Telling jokes was not Eleanor's forte; nevertheless, when she met with large groups of soldiers, she enjoyed sharing one particular story. There were a few different versions, but the ending was always the same.

> A marine went to his sergeant depressed, because he hadn't killed any Japanese. The sergeant directed him to a hill and said just shout out To hell with Hirohito! The Japanese will jump up and you'll have an opportunity. The marine returned the next day despondent. Hadn't his shouts evoked a response? Oh yes, but they shouted back, To hell with Roosevelt! and I couldn't shoot fellow Republicans![26]

The joke received genuine laughter. It also expressed the First Lady's compassion and empathy.

Each trip was more successful than the last, and in 1944 Eleanor toured some thirteen thousand miles of the Caribbean, posts in Central America, and the Galapagos Islands. During all of her military travels, she kept this poem in her purse.

Dear Lord,
Lest I continue
My complacent way,
Help me to remember that somewhere,
Somehow out there
A man died for me today.
As long as there be war,
I then must
Ask and answer
Am I worth dying for?[27]

During the previous year, President Roosevelt, Prime Minister Winston Churchill, and Soviet Union General Secretary Joseph Stalin met at the first Big Three Conference. Held at the Soviet Embassy in Tehran, Iran, the three world powers designed a strategy to finalize the war against Nazi Germany. In February of 1945, the same parties met in Yalta, Russia, for their second conference, this time to discuss Europe's postwar reorganization.* Anna Roosevelt, who had moved into the White House to act as hostess and keep her father company during her mother's long absences, accompanied the president to Yalta as his confidential secretary. The First Lady wanted to attend; however, since no other wives were going, Roosevelt said no.

Two months after the conference, the president's health had noticeably deteriorated; his facial complexion was an ashen gray. The First Lady was concerned for her husband's health and was delighted when the president said he was going to Warm Springs, Georgia, for a much-needed rest. Two of his cousins, Margaret Suckley and Laura Delano, would join him. In her book, *This I Remember*, Eleanor wrote,

> I knew they [FDR's cousins] would not bother him as I should have by discussing questions of state; he would be allowed to get a real rest and yet would have companionship—and that was what I felt he most needed.[28]

* Five months later (July of 1945) the third and final Big Three Conference (to determine how to administer punishment to the defeated German Nazis, establish peace treaties, and create postwar order) took place in Potsdam, Germany.

On April 12, 1934, the First Lady was attending a charitable benefit in Washington when she received an urgent summons back to the White House. Upon her arrival, she learned that the president had suddenly died.* True to form, her first reaction was for others:

> I am more sorry for the people of this country and of the world than I am for ourselves.[29]

Vice President Truman rushed over from the Capitol as soon as he received the news. Concerned for the First Lady, he politely asked her, "Is there anything I can do for you?" Eleanor's now famous response was, "Is there anything *we* can do for *you*? For you are the one in trouble now."[30] Once the new president was sworn in to office, Eleanor sent a telegram to her sons, who were stationed in various parts of the world:

> Darlings: Father slept away this afternoon. He did his job to the end as he would want you to do.[31]

Later that evening she flew to Warm Springs, arriving just before midnight. The president's passing was a shock, but specifics surrounding his death were even more troubling for Eleanor. Grace Tully, the president's private secretary for seventeen years, was with him. Both the president and the First Lady had a handful of extraordinarily devoted friends and employees who would never consider sharing the Roosevelts' confidences. An excerpt from Tully's eyewitness report read,

> At 1 PM on April 12, Roosevelt sat in the living room of his cottage surrounded by friends and family. As he signed letters and documents, an artist stood painting his portrait at an easel nearby. The conversation was lively, the atmosphere congenial. Suddenly,

* President William Henry Harrison was the first Chief Executive to die in office of natural causes; Zachary Taylor was the second, Warren Harding the third, and FDR the fourth. Presidents Abraham Lincoln, James Garfield, and William McKinley were assassinated, as was future president John F. Kennedy.

> he grabbed his head complaining of a sharp pain. The president was suffering a massive cerebral hemorrhage that would end his life in minutes. I could feel a chill in my heart.[32]

Tully's report was accurate, but not specific enough. The family Tully referred to was the president's cousins. The friends were herself and Lucy Mercer Rutherfurd.

Laura Delano almost immediately disclosed these heartbreaking details to Eleanor. Defending her cruel action, Laura said too many people knew about it and Eleanor was bound to find out anyway. Lucy Rutherfurd, still very attractive and now a middle-aged widow, had commissioned her good friend Madame Shoumatoff to paint the president's portrait. Both women had been staying in the guest cottage for the past three days. Composed and expressionless, Eleanor later remarked,

> You build a façade for everyone to see and you live separately inside the façade. My grandmother brought me up to prepare for it, in a social way. I was trained to put personal things in the background.[33]

After spending about five minutes alone with her husband's body, Eleanor chose FDR's burial suit and had her husband's casket placed in the living room. The next morning, Eleanor accompanied his body back to Washington on a train. The president's casket was visible through a large window and hundreds of thousands of people lined the eight-hundred-mile track as the train slowly motored down the landscape. Lit up throughout the night, the presidential car could be seen from nearly a mile away. Not surprisingly, Eleanor could not sleep. As she remembered,

> I lay in my berth all night with the window shade up, looking out at the countryside he had loved and watching the faces of the people at stations, and even at the crossroads, who came to pay their last tribute all through the night.[34]

For a brief moment and only once did it appear that Eleanor might lose control. As tears welled up in her eyes, in a broken voice she asked Grace Tully if Franklin had given her any burial instructions. Fortunately, he had. On a memo in his bedroom safe were FDR's last wishes. He wanted to be buried in the rose garden at Hyde Park, with a plain white non-scrolled monument stating simply his dates of birth and death. He then added, "[I] hope my dear wife will on her death be buried there also."[35]

Anna, along with her brother Elliott and his wife, met Eleanor at Union Station in Washington. Sons Frank Jr. and John were both in the midst of battle and James had not yet arrived from California. As the funeral procession continued down Constitution Avenue, President Truman, his Cabinet, General Marshall, and members of Congress all followed the First Lady up Pennsylvania Avenue to the White House. A flag-draped caisson drawn by six white horses carried the president's coffin. The mourning crowds extended down the side streets, as far as the eye could see. As army bombers thundered overhead, the only other audible sounds were the sobs from thousands of mourners.

A service was held in the East Room of the White House before the president's body traveled to Hyde Park. Eleanor endured yet another sleepless train ride, watching again as crowds of people stood in respect and sorrow. After the president's burial she remained in the large estate at Hyde Park just long enough to greet personal friends and officials who had come in from Washington. Afterward, that same evening, Eleanor returned to Washington with President and Mrs. Truman who encouraged her to stay as long as she needed in the White House. But Eleanor was anxious to leave the Executive Mansion, and moved to her New York apartment only one week after her husband's death.

On her last full day in the White House, Eleanor hosted a tea for the Women's Press Corps in the State Dining Room. In traditional Eleanor fashion, she warmly greeted all fifty-seven newswomen at the front door, shaking each one's hand. When she saw a reporter's notebook, she immediately announced,

> This is a social thing not a press conference. If you want to say Mrs. Roosevelt said this or that in conversation, that is your privilege but I do not want to be quoted directly.[36]

In conversation, she mentioned that she hoped her children would agree to bequeath to the nation her late mother-in-law's large home at Hyde Park.* Now she only wanted to care for her cottage on the estate and her New York apartment. Upon arrival in New York the next day, yet another group of reporters met her. Completely exhausted, Eleanor said simply, "The story is over."

Before Eleanor could begin her new life, she had to come to terms with the one that just ended. It was not the first time in recent years that the president had seen Lucy Mercer Rutherfurd. She had been to the White House on several occasions, all arranged by Anna Roosevelt. In addition to Lucy's White House visits, the president often took a long drive down a dirt road in the Virginia countryside. Each time, the president's car would come upon the same woman walking alone. He always offered her a ride and the two shared a lovely, scenic drive together. The same Secret Service men followed behind in a separate car. On his fifth excursion, the president noticed one man in his security detail who was not the usual agent. Laughing aloud the president said, "I see it's your turn to find out what's going on!"[37] Mr. J. B. West (the White House usher) confirmed the woman was in fact Lucy.

Knowing that Anna arranged for those intimate White House dinners rubbed salt into Eleanor's already open wound. Enraged, she confronted her daughter, and Anna said she was afraid Eleanor would never speak to her again. From a daughter's point of view, Anna insisted she was simply trying to bring a little relaxation and cheerful distraction to an old man's very stressful life. She emphasized the point that there was always someone else around, including herself, and the visits were innocent in nature. Elliott defended his sister. What was Anna supposed to do? he asked. She truly wanted both of her

* Both Springwood, the large Roosevelt estate at Hyde Park, and Val-Kill Cottage, the only site dedicated to the memory of a First Lady, are open to the public and run by the National Park Service.

parents to enjoy a little happiness, and a daughter could no more be a spy for her father than for her mother.

Both Eleanor and FDR experienced deep suffering. The inherent responsibilities of any presidency are incredible. Add to that a nationwide financial crisis and a horrendous war, the daily burdens become inconceivable, maybe even insurmountable. Unlike Edith Wilson, who believed it was her duty to provide her husband with a stress-free zone, Eleanor was unable to create a relaxing, work-free environment. She unintentionally depleted the president's resources when he needed to be re-energized. There is little doubt the companionship Lucy provided FDR during this terrible time in history helped and sustained him.

The circumstances did strain relations between mother and daughter but not for long. Eleanor recognized that it was never Anna's intention to hurt her. She was an adult child, caught in the middle of her parents' personal issues. On reflection, Eleanor wrote in *This I Remember*,

> Franklin might have been happier, with a wife who was completely uncritical. That I was never able to be, and he had to find it in other people.[38]

> I decided to accept the fact that a man must be what he is, life must be lived as it is, circumstances force your children away from you, and you can not live at all if you do not learn to adapt yourself to your life as it happens.[39]

In reference to political issues and debates, a reporter commented that Eleanor never got angry. "Oh no," she responded, "You see I try to understand people."[40] When Eleanor had a better understanding of her family dynamics, she was ready to forgive Anna, and finally Franklin. Though she never mentioned Lucy in her biographies, she did say,

> All human begins have failings, all human beings have needs and temptations and stresses. Men and women who live together through long years get to know one another's failings; but they

> also come to know what is worthy of respect and admiration in those they live with and themselves.[41]

> My husband and I had come through years with an acceptance of each other's faults and foibles, warm affection and agreement on essential values. We depended on each other.[42]

According to historian Doris Kearns Goodwin, after Franklin's death, Eleanor found a small watercolor of her husband that Madame Shoumatoff had painted. Having come to terms with her husband's relationship, Eleanor instructed her secretary to send the painting to Lucy. In appreciation, Lucy wrote her former boss,

> Thank you so very much, you must know that it will be treasured always...I have wanted to write you for a long time to tell you that I had seen Franklin and of his great kindness about my husband when he was desperately ill in Washington, and of how helpful he was too, to his boys—and that I hoped very much that I might see you again...I think of your sorrow—you—whom I have always felt to be the most blessed and privileged of women must now feel immeasurable grief and pain and they must be almost unbearable...As always, Affectionately, Lucy Rutherfurd.*[43]

When Eleanor left the White House in 1945, she was sixty years old. She may have thought the story was over; however, for a woman of her vigor, political savvy, and interest in social justice, it would have been criminal for her to retire. Besides, she had already bemoaned the fact that she "did not want to cease feeling useful in some way." She was active in politics prior to her marriage, and with the removal of White House restraints she had greater political freedom than before.

Not surprisingly, Eleanor continued to have her critics. Racists despised her and there were those who still believed she was a communist. Booed for fifteen minutes during a speaking engagement, she continued to answer hostile questions cordially. The negative

* There is no record of Lucy ever seeing Eleanor again. Lucy Mercer Rutherfurd died in 1948.

reception was somewhat reminiscent of the 1940 campaign button that read, "We Don't Want Eleanor Either." Dr. George Gallup said of Eleanor,

> [She was probably the] target of more adverse criticism and the object of more praise than any other woman in American history. One Gallup poll reported that for every two persons who thought the First Lady talked too much...three approved of her courage and ability to speak out. It was rare to find a respondent who was neutral about her.[44]

On the other hand, President Truman saw a brilliant world leader in her. He wanted to appoint the former First Lady as a delegate to the first meeting of the United Nations General Assembly. Initially she was opposed to the idea, maintaining she knew nothing of parliamentary procedure and had very little experience with foreign affairs, but Truman insisted, "Your country needs you. Indeed, this troubled world needs you."[45] After receiving considerable opposition during her Senate confirmation hearings, Eleanor became the only woman of fifty-one delegations to attend the December 1945 meeting in London.

It was a new beginning for Eleanor, one in which she would display her wisdom, good judgment, and shrewdness. She believed her attendance was a tribute to FDR, and as she had always claimed, her work was on his behalf. Nevertheless, this final stage of Eleanor's life truly proved to be her greatest personal success. As one of her grandsons confirmed, "The condescension of the other male delegates was fairly obvious."

Soviet delegate Andrei Vishinsky was particularly challenging. No one wanted to stand up to him, so Eleanor did. She argued firmly,

> We here in the UN are trying to frame things which will consider first the rights of man and what makes men more free—not governments, but men.[46]

When Vishinsky's proposal was voted down, he told Eleanor, "I admire your fighting qualities." Her response was, "Why, thank you.

Perhaps next time you might try using *your* fighting abilities on the *right* side."[47]

With no personal aspiration or political ax to grind, Eleanor quickly won the other delegates over. Elected to chair the committee drafting a Universal Declaration of Human Rights (1946–1948), also referred to as the international Magna Carta of all mankind, one reporter described Eleanor's role as,

> A super mother, presiding over a large family of often noisy, sometimes unruly, but basically good-hearted boys who now and then needed firmly to be put in their places.[48]

Sometimes working eighteen-hour days, negotiating between delegates from differing cultures, philosophies, religions, government systems, and economic levels, somehow Eleanor forged a common standard among all the diversities. On December 10, 1948, the General Assembly unanimously passed the document and Eleanor received the honor of a standing ovation. Michigan senator Arthur Vandenberg conceded publicly what many others may have felt:

> I want to say that I take back everything I ever said about [Eleanor Roosevelt] and believe me, it's been plenty.[49]

The United Nations was a huge triumph for Eleanor and perhaps the most successful of all her careers. No longer under Franklin's overshadowing prominence, she now achieved recognition all on her own. In addition to her tenure as a U.N. delegate, Eleanor augmented her already grueling schedule to include writing her daily newspaper column, giving over one hundred annual lectures, and hosting a weekly TV program. She was also on the executive board of the NAACP and worked for the United Jewish Appeal, the Americans for Democratic Action, and the Citizens Committee for Children. She learned many lessons from her years at Allenswood, and perhaps the strongest of all was, thou shalt not ever have an idle minute.

Between 1948 and 1951, Eleanor produced radio shows for ABC and NBC. She refused proposals to run for the Senate and in 1952 halted a movement drafting her for the presidency, saying,

> No woman has, as yet, been able to build up and hold sufficient leadership to carry through a program. Besides if I do not run for office, I am not beholden to my Party…I am too old to want to be curtailed in any way in the expression of my own thinking.[50]

When President Eisenhower replaced Eleanor as a delegate to the United Nations in 1953, she immediately volunteered her services to the American Association for the United Nations, which entailed traveling around the country organizing chapters throughout the United States. In addition, she was an American representative to the World Federation of the United Nations Associations, and later became the chair of the Associations' board of directors. In 1954, Eleanor celebrated her seventieth birthday and was still circling the globe every year.

As one of the nation's most influential and admired figures of the twentieth century, Eleanor blazed paths for women everywhere and fought for social justice around the world. In 1957 she traveled to Russia to interview Nikita Khrushchev. By 1958, Eleanor's stance on civil rights had earned her an increased number of death threats, and the Ku Klux Klan had a $25,000 bounty on her. Yet she maintained her sense of humor. On a lighter note she joked,

> I had a rose named after me and I was very flattered. But I was not pleased to read the description in the catalog: No good in a bed, but fine against a wall.[51]

The year Eleanor turned seventy-five (1959) she began hosting a program on public television called *Prospects of Mankind*. Her first guest was Martin Luther King Jr., and the program ran for three years.* She continued to lecture at Brandeis University and served on its board of trustees. Several Phi Beta Kappa keys and honorary degrees, including one from Oxford in England, substituted for the college degree

* Eleanor interviewed President Kennedy for her PBS program just after his election regarding his hopes and his proposal for the newly established Peace Corps. A video clip of that interview can be seen at www.pbs.org/wgbh/amex/eleanor/sfeature/tv_large.html.

Eleanor yearned for. Additionally, over her lifetime, she authored sixteen books (which does not include those she coauthored).* Time healed her broken heart, and as her son Elliott recalled,

> Mother chose to remember only the lovely times they [the Roosevelts] shared, never the estrangement and pain.[52]

She survived her husband by seventeen years and had earned so much prestige and respect in the world of politics, many candidates believed her support meant the difference between victory and defeat. Reluctantly, Eleanor supported John Kennedy (she had always been an Adlai Stevenson supporter); in 1961, President Kennedy reappointed her as a delegate to the United Nations. Evidently, the president believed in the adage, if you want to get something done give it to a busy person, because he also appointed Eleanor as a member of the National Advisory Committee of the Peace Corps and chair of the President's Commission on the Status of Women.

In the fall of 1962, Eleanor struggled to complete her last book, *Tomorrow is Now*, in which she pleads for racial, political, and social justice. "Staying aloof is not a solution," she wrote, "but a cowardly evasion." A woman of true courage, she walked the walk and followed her own advice when she said, "Determine one's position, state it bravely, and then *act boldly*."

On November 7, 1962, Eleanor Roosevelt died from an incurable blood disease and was interred next to her husband in Hyde Park. She was seventy-eight. While former president Truman called her "The First Lady of the World," Adlai Stevenson, U.N. ambassador, said,

> The United States, the United Nations, the world, has lost one of its great citizens. Mrs. Eleanor Roosevelt is dead, and a cherished friend of all mankind is gone.[53]

* *It's Up to the Women, A Trip to Washington with Bobby and Betty, This Is My Story, This Troubled World, Christmas: A Story, The Moral Basis of Democracy, The Autobiography of Eleanor Roosevelt, This I Remember, Ladies of Courage, It Seems to Me, The United Nations, On My Own, You Learn By Living, The Wisdom of Eleanor Roosevelt, Eleanor Roosevelt's Book of Common Etiquette, Tomorrow is Now* (published posthumously in 1963).

Indeed, Eleanor is recognized as one of the most memorable First Ladies in history. Her metamorphosis from a shy, insecure, and intimidated young woman was enormous as she grew and developed into a woman of conviction.

For all her candor and outspokenness, including her multiple autobiographical books, Eleanor never wrote about her husband's infidelity or the pain it caused her. Considering her unwillingness to address an issue of such major significance, it is not surprising that she also declined to publicize her feelings on the topic of love.

As with so many other aspects of Eleanor's life, it seems nearly everyone has an opinion about her romantic interests. Some believe Eleanor was gay, others say bisexual, while still others claim she did not enjoy sex at all. Yet she was, in fact, a very passionate, loving being.

There are many who surmise, reason, theorize, and even presume to know the truths of Eleanor's heart. Of those who have commented publicly, some were family members, in particular her daughter Anna and son James; others include dear friends Esther Lape and Marion Dickerman, biographers Blanche Cook and Joseph Lash, and countless other authors. (According to Amazon.com, the number of books written on Eleanor is 1,375 and counting!) The truth is no one knows, nor should it matter when considering the totality of this remarkable woman's life and her incredible legacy, one which will no doubt survive for decades to come.

What was obvious and endearing about Eleanor's emotional makeup was her ability to love deeply. She was not a victim, but rather a woman of great strength and compassion, and she will be remembered as a remarkable person in American history for decades to come.

WHAT ELEANOR TAUGHT ME

When you consider Eleanor Roosevelt's energy for life, her various careers, her numerous achievements, and her repetitive circling of the globe, it is easy to understand why she was once described as "ubiquitous." In addition to her nonstop travels, Eleanor gave some 1,400 speeches and 700 lectures, and wrote 8,451 "My Day" columns. There was in fact a continual battle between Eleanor the individual and her more public persona. She once said,

> [I] had driven up in the capacity of Eleanor Roosevelt and only on arriving became FDR's wife.[54]

At some point, I believe the person and the persona merged. Starting out an insecure and frightened young girl, Eleanor Roosevelt struggled almost her entire life to find self-worth and an identity of her own. She demonstrated for me the importance of having "infinite patience and never-ending persistence." Although I am sometimes weak on the patience aspect, I have learned you cannot fail if you never give up.

Eleanor's human experiences offer so many significant and indispensable life lessons, it would be shortsighted to spotlight only one. She was a woman who gave her life to public service, and her hard-won wisdom could fill a book of quotations. Just a handful of what Eleanor ultimately learned includes:

> The life you live is your own.
>
> Never stop learning, never stop changing.
>
> Work is always an antidote to depression.
>
> It takes as much energy to wish as it does to plan.
>
> No one can make you feel inferior without your consent.
>
> There is no experience from which you can't learn something.
>
> You can often change your circumstances by changing your attitude.

And one that Eleanor especially liked to share with others was a quote credited to Samuel Levenson: "Learn from the mistakes of others. You can't live long enough to make them all yourself."[55]

8

Independent Lady from Independence

BESS (ELIZABETH) TRUMAN

Well, I'm pleased that I resemble Mrs. Roosevelt in at least one respect.
—BESS TRUMAN, WHEN TOLD SHE AND ELEANOR ROOSEVELT BOTH HAD MESSY CLOSETS

FILLING THE SHOES OF A FIRST LADY is challenging and arduous enough. When your occupancy of the White House follows that of an individual who is your antithesis, and you are succeeding to the Executive Mansion after a president's death, the experience is even more taxing.

#33 Bess (Elizabeth) Wallace Truman

Born: February 13, 1885

Birthplace: Independence, Missouri

Married: 1919 (Harry S. Truman)

Children: 1

White House Years: 1945–1953

Died: October 18, 1982 (97 years old)

Fact: The longest-living First Lady

AKA: The Boss

It was not the first time the United States would experience such circumstances, nor would it be the last. We saw the country's reaction to Elizabeth Monroe following on the heels of Dolley Madison, as well as Sarah Polk succeeding Julia Tyler and Edith Roosevelt subsequent to Ida McKinley. In two of those instances, it was a breath of fresh air for the country because both women met or exceeded public expectation.

While Eleanor Roosevelt did not enjoy universal approbation like some of her more popular predecessors, the country had grown accustomed to her style, activism, and weekly press conferences. Many younger people had no other point of reference, as Eleanor was the only First Lady ever to have resided in the White House for twelve years. No other president had run for a third, much less a fourth, consecutive term; moreover, the twenty-second amendment to the Constitution (passed in 1951) prevents a person from being elected to the presidency more than twice, so Eleanor will always be the longest-term First Lady.

With the country in shock over President Roosevelt's sudden death, many sought familiarity to lessen the trauma and hoped the new First Lady would be similar to her predecessor. That was certainly the consensus of the press. But Bess Truman, lovingly called the Boss by her husband, knew she was nothing like the previous First Lady, and that she could never hope to emulate Eleanor—nor would she honestly want to.

An incredibly private individual, Bess did *not* want to live in the White House. She was at odds with her husband when Truman acquiesced to Roosevelt's insistence, during his fourth election bid, that Truman run for vice president. (First John Garner and then Henry Wallace served as vice president during Roosevelt's three earlier terms. In fact Wallace missed being the thirty-third president of the United States by just eighty-two days!)

Some individuals in the president's inner circle knew that Roosevelt's health was extremely fragile. Bess certainly was not privy to any specific information but she suspected the truth. I think it is fair to say that, given her horror of the highly visible lifestyle of the country's top-ranking politician, the very thought of Roosevelt's potential demise while in office terrified Bess. Ironically, she hadn't even had a chance to adjust to the idea let alone the reality of being the wife of the newly elected vice president when, twelve weeks later, Roosevelt died. Bess was instantly thrown into the fishbowl known as the White House. Life as she knew it was over; she would be scrutinized as never before.

Like her predecessors Jane Pierce and Margaret Taylor, both of whom prayed vehemently that they would never have to live in the White House, Bess was aghast at the possibility. She had a more compelling reason than either Jane or Margaret, though: the public did not know that the new First Lady was hiding a dark and shameful secret. One so private, so suppressed, it had not been divulged in over forty years! An event so horrible and traumatizing it haunted Bess her entire life.

An exceptionally reticent woman, Bess would have much preferred to return to her Midwestern roots in Independence, Missouri, than reside in the White House. However, like so many of her sorority sisters before her, Bess soldiered forward. As she pointed out,

> We are not any one of us happy to be where we are but there's nothing to be done about it except to do our best—and forget about the sacrifices and many unpleasant things that bob up.[1]

Life had indeed taken many turns since Bess's childhood and young adulthood. Given the deep pain and shame of some of those years, Bess hoped she would never have to relive them.

The same year Elizabeth Virginia Wallace was born, the first modern bicycle was built, the Dictaphone and the electric transformer were invented, and Karl Benz assembled the world's first gasoline-powered vehicle. It had a traveling speed of nine miles per hour!

While the Washington Monument was being dedicated in the nation's capitol, the first commercially operated electrical streetcar began operation in Baltimore. The year was 1885 and Independence, Missouri, was a small country town of about thirty-five hundred people.* Elizabeth's birth on February 13 was a welcome Valentine's gift to David and Madge Gates Wallace. She was their first child and only daughter.

Madge (whose given name was Margaret) was the daughter of a wealthy businessman, the cofounder of the Waggoner-Gates Milling Company in Independence, which manufactured the flour used by millions of Midwestern housewives. The significance of social standing was inescapable during the nineteenth century, and Madge Gates was a very class-conscious woman from an affluent family. Described as a lady, Madge was also depicted as a "very, very difficult

* Within five years, the 1890 census listed the U.S. population at nearly sixty-three million. At that time, prior to child labor laws, almost twenty-three thousand children worked in factories in thirteen Southern states.

person...[T]here wasn't anybody in town she didn't look down on."[2]

David Wallace was a gregarious, handsome man whose father had been mayor of Independence at one time. But it was soon apparent that his salary as a customs officer would never be sufficient to cover his wife's expensive tastes and well-heeled lifestyle.

Young Bessie, as her family called her, was a vivacious, attractive girl with golden hair and bright blue eyes; she was the first grandchild and cherished niece in the extensive Gates family. Bess grew up just two blocks from the two-and-one-half story mansion in which her mother had been raised, built by maternal grandfather George Gates.

Bess's three younger brothers (Frank, George, and Fred) made up the balance of the Wallace household (there was also one daughter who died in infancy). As the family and corresponding financial obligations increased in size, so did David Wallace's drinking; before long, Bess's father, now a confirmed alcoholic, was in debt and unable to provide for his family.

Perhaps in part due to her husband's malady, Madge grew unreasonably dependent on her eldest child, Bess, who was more mature by far than the average teenager. Many years later, Bess's daughter Margaret Truman describes in her biography, *Bess W. Truman*, how her grandmother Madge took vacations with her sister and "left her fourteen-year-old daughter [Bess] in charge of the house. One letter, somewhat incongruously addressed to 'my dear little daughter' [instructs Bess] not to let her brother Frank out of the house after dark because he had a cold and make sure he took citrate of magnesia every night." The letter concludes, "Order what you need and want at the grocery and meat shop."[3]

In addition to assuming an adult level of responsibility for her younger brothers, Bess was a good student. She was also very much a tomboy as well as an accomplished athlete. A champion slugger on her brothers' baseball team, a demon ice skater, a smashing Ping-Pong player, an expert horseback rider, and a shot put winner, Bess was also allegedly the best tennis player in the state. One lesser-known accomplishment: she was the only girl in town who could whistle through her teeth.

Unbeknownst to Bess, there was a young lad in the neighborhood who was smitten from the day he first laid eyes on her. Harry Truman recalled meeting Bess in Sunday school at the First Presbyterian Church. She was five years old, he was six. Their paths crossed again at school; Harry later reminisced about Bess,

> She sat behind me in the sixth, seventh and high school grades, and I thought she was the most beautiful and the sweetest person on earth.[4]

Branded with the nickname Four Eyes because he wore coke-bottle glasses, Harry's poor eyesight caused him to be an inept athlete. He much preferred piano lessons to playing sports, which could explain why Bess paid little attention to him.

Bess was a popular and friendly girl who enjoyed a good laugh. Possibly as a counterbalance to her daughter's tomboy tendency, Madge insisted that Bess attend Miss Dunlap's dancing classes, which assured her attendance at the weekly hop or other dance reception. Bess graduated high school at sixteen; however, there was no hope of her attending college. The reality was that Bess's beloved father could not afford to send her.

Humiliated and depressed at his inability to support his family, Mr. Wallace (whose income could barely maintain his wife's lifestyle, let alone a growing family) was continually borrowing money from his father-in-law. In 1901, with his taxes two years in arrears, losing the family home was a frightening possibility. Once again Grandfather Gates assisted financially.

Like many women of her era, Madge lived in the insular realm of a woman's sphere; she believed a man's domain, which included finances and supporting the family, did not concern her. Unable or unwilling to share her husband's distress and worry or offer him much support, Madge had no idea of the depths of his despair and hopelessness.

In 1903, four days after their twentieth wedding anniversary, David Wallace left his wife sleeping and slipped out of their bedroom at dawn. He tiptoed down the hall to a bathroom in the rear of the home. Moments later, a shotgun blast and a crashing noise thundered through the house. Eighteen-year-old Bess "sat trembling in her bed" when she heard her brother Frank's cry of anguish, "Papa! Papa's shot himself!"[5] Wallace was only forty-three years old. Jolted out of bed, Bess fled outside where she paced back and forth behind the house and listened to her mother's shattering sobs echoing from inside.

Graphic details such as "The ball passed through his head and out at the right temple and fell into the bath tub" were published across the front page of the Jackson *Examiner*, the most widely read paper in the county outside Kansas City. The family's agony was only worsened by all the public attention. Suicide was considered an appalling and disgraceful act and stigmatized the whole family; it was once described as "mortifying beyond belief." Grief-stricken, Madge took her four children to Colorado Springs to be with other family members. They stayed there one year.

Upon their return to Independence, the clan moved in with Madge's wealthy parents. By now, Bess had become acting head of the Wallace family—she cared for her younger siblings as well as her mother, who found it impossible to resume a normal life. Madge lived as a recluse for the rest of her life, her name never again appearing in any social notices. To quote Margaret Truman, Madge was "the self-sentenced prisoner of shame at 219 North Delaware Street." Grandfather Gates, who had four other children and additional grandchildren, once more rescued the Wallaces by providing food, shelter, clothing, and servants.

Trying to recoup the pieces of her life, in 1905 twenty-year-old Bess enrolled in the Barstow School for young women in Kansas City. Barstow was both a finishing and academic prep school for girls going off to elite East Coast colleges like Radcliffe and Vassar. She excelled in sports, acting as the star forward for the basketball team and winning the shot put in the spring track meet. Bess was an excellent academic student as well, earning an A in Rhetoric, an A in French, and an A+ in Literature.

Instead of heading for college like many of her classmates, Bess returned home to be with her mother. It appears Madge had the same magnetic effect on her sons as well. When two of the boys married (which could only reinforce an old maid complex for their older sister), both men continued to live with their spouses in small homes on the Gates property. The small cluster of houses was sometimes referred to as the Wallace compound. Eldest son Frank went so far as to make a ritual of visiting with his mother for a half hour every day after work. Years later, when youngest son Fred married, he and his bride moved in with Madge in the Gates mansion.

Back in Independence, Bess resumed old friendships and made new ones, once again cultivating a social life. She played tennis in addition to bridge, went on twenty-five-mile hikes, and supported the Needlework Guild, which helped families in need of assistance.

Bess had various suitors, but it would always become obvious early on that Madge came as part of the package. Few men relished the thought of living with Madge for the remainder of her life...which could well have been the bulk of their life as well. Madge was now a hostile widow who believed every man was trying to steal her only daughter away from her. It is reasonable to believe that Bess had developed her own doubts and feelings of mistrust as well. Unable to escape the aftermath of her father's death, Bess surely felt men provided neither safety nor security, and the world in general must have seemed a harrowing place. The only man she trusted and felt safe with was Grandfather Gates.

It was 1910 when Harry Truman reentered her life. It had been nine years since their graduation from Independence High School, and Bess had not seen or heard from him since then. But one summer evening, Harry appeared at her front door, incongruously enough with an empty cake plate in hand. One of his cousins had been the recipient of a cake Madge had baked; while visiting his relative, Harry was innocently asked to return the clean plate to Mrs. Wallace. "With something approaching the speed of light," Harry eagerly accepted.

Harry was now a part-time soldier in the Missouri National Guard (due to his poor eyesight, Harry was told he could never get into the U.S. Military Academy), sporting self-confidence and a matured physical posture. Apparently he showed up at an opportune time, for the former classmates visited for nearly two hours. Harry was now living some four hours away, by buggy, working on his father's six-hundred-acre farm in Grandview.

It appears the gap between them had widened from merely social to geographical. The distance, however, did not stop Harry from asking Bess's permission to call on her again. He also wrote frequent, voluminous letters to his sweetheart. Over seventy years would go by and Bess would pass away before her astounded daughter would discover some sixteen hundred letters Bess had accumulated in the attic from the former Mr. Four Eyes. Many of them are contained in *Dear Bess, The Letters from Harry to Bess Truman, 1910–1959.* (Copied faithfully as originally written, it was apparent that Harry's literary skill was not his greatest asset.)

In addition to writing letters, Harry made the long trek to Bess's home as frequently as possible. When he could he used the train; however, it often failed to run and he would lose an entire night's sleep trying to get back home. In one letter he wrote Bess, "Papa says he's going to adopt a boy if I don't stay home on Sundays. I told him to go ahead."[6] Within a year, Harry proposed marriage...more or less. He wrote, "Would you wear a solitaire on your left hand should I get it?" Heartsick when his true love turned him down, Harry managed to find some solace when Bess indicated that she hoped "they could continue to be friends."[7]

Willing to accept any time he could spend with his adored sweetheart, Harry returned every Sunday. They took pleasure in marathon walks, and although Harry had no interest in fishing, he would bait a hook for Bess before reading or visiting with her while she enjoyed the sport.

Two and a half years would pass before Bess told Harry that her feelings for him had changed. She was now twenty-nine years old and "had begun to think that if she married anyone, he would be the man." Harry recorded,

> When it comes to the best girl in the world, in all the universe, caring for an ordinary gink like me—well, you'll have to let me get used to it.[8]

Unfortunately, Madge's feelings toward Harry *never* improved. Not only did she believe Harry was undeserving of Bess, Madge viewed him as a dirt-poor farmer who would never amount to anything...an opinion she held even after he became president! (It was a point of view Madge Wallace shared with Lemira Goodhue, Grace Coolidge's mother. An opinion not exclusive to mothers, as Florence Harding and Julia Grant both had fathers who never approved of their presidential sons-in-law.)

The next several years were financially difficult for Harry. It was one monetary setback after another. He jointly invested in his father's farm, which had repeatedly failed to produce. Then his father passed away and Harry assumed the business's $12,500 debt. He later borrowed $11,000 and invested it in a lead-and-zinc mine, whose stock descended to zero. The relative who talked Harry into the investment had made over $100,000 in one such venture. Extremely discouraged, Harry wrote Bess,

> I seem to have a grand and admirable ability for calling tails when heads come up. My luck should surely change...If I can't win straight, I'll continue to lose. I'm the luckiest guy in the world to have you to love and to know that when I've arrived at a sensible solution to these direful financial difficulties, I've gotten into, that I'll have the finest, best-looking and all the other adjectives in the superlative girl in the world to make the happiest home in the world with.[9]

Unofficially engaged, Harry worked hard at paying off his obligations. As much as he ached to have Bess as his wife, he was not about to get married knowing he was unable to support her. Bess believed in him; now deeply in love herself, she waited patiently for the solitaire Harry could not yet afford.

Finally, in March of 1917, the couple was talking about an official spring engagement with marriage in the fall. Just one month later, President Wilson (who had managed to avoid involvement with World War I for nearly three years) at long last sent a declaration of war to Congress. World events and life would once again impede the couple's hopes and dreams.

As Truman would recall years later, he was "stirred heart and soul" by the president's repeated plea for patriotism and courage.[10] Harry decided he could not marry Bess as planned. He told her,

> I don't think it would be right for me to ask you to tie yourself to a prospective cripple—or a sentiment...you may be sure that I'll be just as loyal to you as if you were my wife.[11]

Approaching thirty-three years old, Bess was more than ready to get married. Although she protested their wedding postponement, Bess learned early on that her affectionate designation as the Boss was in name only.

While Harry struggled to gain promotion to captain, Bess volunteered to sell war bonds and dealt with wartime shortages such as sugar, flour, and coal. Furthermore, she continued to be companion and comforter to her demanding mother. About a year into Truman's service, during the same time her adored Grandfather Gates was dying, Bess learned that Harry, now in France, had been ordered to the front.

It was a particularly troublesome time for Bess. Harry continued to write faithfully, sharing every detail of his horrifying ordeal. Commentary such as "I have just finished putting eighteen hundred shells over on the Germans in the last five hours" did nothing to assuage her worry and trepidation.[12]

As soon as the war ended, the standing joke was whether or not Captain Truman "might go AWOL and swim the Atlantic" in order to marry Bess.[13] Shortly after Harry's safe return home, and despite Madge's bitter disapproval, Bess's brother Frank escorted her down the aisle of Trinity Episcopal Church. It was a hot Missouri summer day; with a simple yet pretty gold band placed upon her finger, Bess became Mrs. Harry S. Truman on June 28, 1919.* She was thirty-four years old.

They had known one another for nearly thirty years—almost their entire lives—and Harry had courted the only woman in the entire world he ever loved romantically for nine of those years, so it was no

* The initial S is not an abbreviation for a name. Both Truman's paternal and maternal grandfathers' names began with an S, and the use of the initial alone avoided showing any favoritism between the gentlemen.

wonder a friend who attended their wedding wrote Bess saying, "Never did we see such a radiant *groom*."

The newlyweds went to Chicago for a honeymoon, but they were not allowed a guilt-free interlude. Within a week, Bess received a letter from her brother stating, "Mom says if she doesn't hear from you, she's going to telegraph the hotel."[14] Upon their return home, the couple took up residence at 219 North Delaware Street. Madge remained in the master bedroom in the front of the house, while Harry and Bess occupied the same bedroom Bess resided in before her marriage. Her youngest brother Fred and his wife had a bedroom down the hall. It was Madge who inherited the large residence (which remained hers until her death), and she was the one to set all of the house rules.

Within months of marrying, Harry opened a men's haberdashery in Kansas City in partnership with his good friend and former canteen sergeant Eddie Jacobson. He sold his equity in the family farm to his mother and his sister, Mary, in order to invest in Truman & Jacobson, Men's Furnishers. It was a grueling work schedule, as the store was open twelve hours a day, six days a week, and Harry was onsite for the majority of those hours. Bess often helped by working late into the night, managing the store's double-entry ledgers.

The first year of marriage was bittersweet for the Trumans. The business was doing well, in fact some say very well. But now, with money concerns apparently a thing of the past, personal tragedy struck: at thirty-five years of age, Bess suffered a miscarriage. She began to think she had waited too long to start a family, which both she and her husband dearly wanted.

Meanwhile, the country was experiencing its first postwar recession. It became more and more difficult for people to spend money on fine clothing, and the consequence was the decline and ultimate failure of Truman & Jacobson, Men's Furnishers. The business went bankrupt as did Eddie Jacobson; however, true to his core beliefs, Harry refused to file personal bankruptcy. Slowly but surely over the next two decades, Truman paid back all of the store's creditors, including the shop's extensive lease balance, which they never used.

Having learned a lesson from her parents' marriage, Bess made a point to remain involved in all aspects, positive and negative, of her husband's life. She would support his failures and share his successes, for they were a team. Bess undoubtedly had concerns when Harry expressed an interest in politics. He wanted to run for the eastern judgeship of Jackson County, which was an administrative (not judicial) job that controlled county funds and oversaw the condition of county roads.

Political boss Tom Pendergast supported Harry, which had both positive and negative aspects. He was the strongest political machine in Missouri and his endorsement brought considerable clout. So long as no strings were attached, Harry was happy to receive support anywhere he could find it. On the down side, Pendergast had connections to the mob; furthermore, he was later convicted of tax evasion. To some, Truman's reputation for honesty and integrity was tainted because of their relationship, but Harry considered his association with Pendergast the price to pay for being in politics.

Truman won his bid for election, but not before Bess endured her second miscarriage. Extremely distraught, she honestly believed she was going to have a breakdown. How much of her misfortune could be attributed to the turmoil and strain of the campaign—or her age—will never be known. Either way, she was now the wife of a politician who was responsible for the dispensation of over a thousand jobs.

In addition to his grueling day job, Harry enrolled in the Kansas City Law School and began to study in the evenings. After two years he determined a career in law was not for him. Bess, still her mother's primary companion, apprehensively found herself pregnant once again. This time she superstitiously refused to purchase any baby supplies or clothing, for fear of yet another disappointment.

While at home during a horrific snowstorm, four days after her thirty-ninth birthday, Bess at long last gave birth to a baby girl.* The new mother was certain her husband wanted a boy and immediately (and unnecessarily) began to cry, as Harry was euphoric with jubilation at the sight of his daughter. Grandmother Gates, who died later that same year, had the joyful experience of seeing her great-granddaughter's birth and holding the newest addition to the clan in her arms. Now four generations of the Gates family lived under the same

* Mary Margaret Truman [Daniel] (1924–2008).

roof. (Grandfather Gates had passed away six years earlier in 1918, while Harry was still overseas.)

With no baby provisions, a bassinet, or even a blanket to wrap the newborn in, Harry was immediately given a long list of necessary supplies. But he was unable to plow through the blizzard until the next day, so they created a makeshift baby bed for the child they so desperately wanted: she spent her first night in an open bureau drawer.

One would think that after delivering a child, particularly after two miscarriages, the most difficult part was over, but this was not so for the Trumans. It would be another *four years* before they would agree on their daughter's name, demonstrating their equal stubbornness. Not surprisingly, Bess wanted to name her Margaret Wallace Truman, after her mother. But her husband was insistent that the Truman family receive equal representation in the child's given name.

They finally agreed on Mary (after Harry's sister) Margaret. Bess, clearly the disciplinarian in the family (she was not above reaching for the hairbrush when her daughter misbehaved), called her offspring Marg, while Harry took on the role of chief spoiler and called his daughter Margie.*

During those early years, Harry made countless visits to various townships and political rallies, and continued to spend two weeks a year away with the Missouri National Guard. He and his lifelong sweetheart had already established the practice of exchanging daily letters whenever they were apart.

I found one particular pair of letters amusing. Around this time, a new hairstyle became quite the rage. Women all across the country were cutting their hair short into what was called a bob (this was the same fashionable hairstyle Calvin Coolidge forbade his wife Grace to wear). Bess wanted to try it; however, Harry preferred her dark blond hair long. They discussed it in their correspondence.

When may I do it? I never wanted to do anything as badly in my

* The Truman Presidential Library does not have a birth certificate for Mary Margaret (always known as Margaret), so we can only assume it read Baby Girl Truman. That was not unusual for children leaving the hospital prior to being named. The unusual part was how long it took the Trumans to agree on a name.

> life. Come on, be a sport. Ask all the married men in camp about their wives' heads & I'll bet anything I have there isn't one under sixty who has long hair.[15] (Bess)
>
> If you want your hair bobbed so badly, go on and get it done. I want you to be happy regardless of what I think about it. I am very sure you'll be just as beautiful with it off and I'll not say anything to make you sorry for doing it.*[16] (Harry)

Harry lost his reelection bid for the eastern judgeship and began selling memberships for the Kansas City Automobile Club. He was then elected to the post of presiding judge (also known as the chief executive) of Jackson County. Finances would once again become worrisome. The country had experienced a crippling depression, and Judge Truman halved the salaries of everyone on the county payroll—including his own—to sell the local bond issue to the public. In addition, Margaret recorded that her weekly allowance of fifty cents was "slashed to a quarter."[17]

After Harry served two four-year terms as presiding judge, he made the decision to run for the U.S. Senate in 1934. Bess was less than enthusiastic. A world-class worrier to begin with, Bess now found several reasons why Harry should not pursue the national post. Her mother's feeling of abandonment was only one reason...albeit a *very large* one.

Nonetheless, Bess held the deep conviction that her husband should make those types of decisions. Although Harry consulted her frequently and respected her views, she could not always change his mind, particularly since she was not one to nag, strong-arm, or browbeat him into her point of view. Because she only voiced her misgivings privately to Harry, no one else knew about her uneasiness with his decision to run for Senate.

When Truman won the Senate seat (which paid ten thousand dollars a year), Bess accepted her new responsibility with the stoicism

* There is no further correspondence regarding the subject, so it's anyone's guess if Bess ever did have her hair bobbed.

and apparent lack of emotion she had learned to exhibit over the years. Her ten-year-old daughter, however, burst into tears when she was told the family would be spending six months a year in Washington, D.C.

The thought of living somewhere else was painful and threatening to Bess largely because she would be so far away from her own needy mother. Yet she bluntly and unemotionally told her daughter "there was no point in crying about it." Bess had learned many years earlier that tears were futile in creating a different reality, regardless of how devastating the news might be.

No amount of time could repair the overwhelming anguish Bess felt as a result of her father's alcoholism and eventual suicide. Years of sleepless nights, feelings of guilt, confusing questions, and disbelief that her father had abandoned his family in such a horrific way—all this combined to create a harsh, callous aspect to Bess that she deeply repressed beneath her soft loving side.

It was Margaret who, as a vulnerable young girl, occasionally experienced what she perceived as coldhearted or even cruel interactions with her mother. Years would pass before Margaret could fully understand Bess's unsympathetic and at times insensitive remarks.

In the meantime, the family was headed to Washington, D.C., and Bess immediately set out to make arrangements for their new life. She found a four-room apartment on Connecticut Avenue, appalled that the rent, like everything else in Washington (especially compared to Missouri), was outrageously high: one hundred fifty dollars per month. She then enrolled Margaret in private school, joined the Congressional Club, and immediately made friends with other cabinet wives.

Just as she had back home, Bess visited her husband's office frequently, helped out with routine correspondence, and showed a warm interest in his staff's personal lives. She also enjoyed the cabinet wives' traditional Thursday afternoon tea and stayed well informed on legislative and Senate debates. In addition to writing her mother daily, including a special delivery letter on Sundays, Bess (with Margaret) returned home every summer for longer and longer periods of time. Shuttling between homes was demanding for her. Bess had a lifelong aversion to change and although she adapted well to her new lifestyle, she felt heartsick for her mother, knowing the anxiety her departures caused Madge.

To give one a glimpse of what she was up against, Bess was in Washington less than three months when Madge wrote asking when she was coming home. Comments such as "How much longer will it be before you are here? We are growing very impatient" tugged at Bess's heartstrings.[18]

It is difficult to fully comprehend the profound and complex relationship Bess shared with her mother. She must have pitied Madge, whose entire life had been shattered beyond repair; Bess also felt overly protective and accountable for her brothers, far beyond what most sisters would feel. No one can possibly know the intense grief or shared torment the Wallaces felt as a family or what they experienced during the year they spent with relatives in Colorado immediately after Mr. Wallace's suicide. It is easy, however, to see just how destructive and irreversible one event can be to so many lives.

Despite the difficulty of the dual-locale living arrangements, Harry proudly served in the Senate over the next ten years and made a good name for himself. He was respected as a man of integrity with principled morals and was known as one of the few workhorses in Congress. It was obvious from the couple's correspondence that Bess returned home frequently, and their months of separation were especially difficult on the senator. Bess inquired about the Fourth of July office picnic she missed; another letter expressed her guilt over her husband's lonely Thanksgiving.

A great many of Harry's letters indicated his loneliness and yearning to have his wife and daughter with him. The following series of comments (each one appeared in separate letters) gives an indication of Harry's frequent discontentment.

> I am somewhat disappointed that you don't look with favor on coming back.

> I just can't stand it without you. If we are poorer than church mice [referring to the expense of traveling back and forth], what differ-

ence does it make? There is only one thing on earth that counts with me and this is you and Margie.

I am terribly distressed that you are not here and getting more so all the time.

If you and Margie had just come on [to Washington] with me everything would be perfect.

I sure wish you were here but maybe you are happier where you are.[19]

Living apart definitely strained their marriage, and Bess had her intervals of longing as well. In one letter she shared, "It sure was lonesome last night," and in another she confessed, "I never did hate so to see you leave. It's a h--- of a way to live—the way we do."[20] Very much a lady, Bess was not one to use bad language. (Obviously she did not write it either.) On the other hand, her struggle to curb her husband's profanity or his sometimes inelegant speech was common knowledge. One small example is when a friend shared with Bess that she was unsuccessful in getting her husband to use the word "fertilizer" as opposed to "manure." Bess responded with, "Good Lord! It's taken me years to get Harry to use the word manure!"

Other common themes in their correspondence (which required a three cent stamp) included their lack of money, her worries in general, concerns for Harry's health, and of course politics. As their political partnership continued to deepen, Harry soon began to send his wife weekly copies of the *Congressional Record* so she could follow all of the issues in even greater detail.

Politics remained at the center of their lives, and their lengthy missives covered every detail of political happenings in Washington as well as Independence. The Truman correspondence shared some similarities with the letters Abigail and John Adams exchanged during another significant period in American history; as Harry told Bess, "I doubt if there was a woman in the country, including Eleanor Roosevelt, who was more intimately involved with this crisis [pertaining to the bitter battle of U.S. neutrality laws prior to the country's involvement in WWII]."*[21]

Even at a distance, Bess knew her husband's position on all matters. With respect to the neutrality laws, he inquired, "What would you do if you believed the plan is right but the approach is wrong?"[22] Bess had strong opinions, and one of them was how she saw her spousal responsibility. She believed it was her role as a wife to help her husband see all aspects of a situation and then support his judgment. Her frequent response to her husband's questions would be to in turn question him, forcing Harry to think through his positions and focus his capacity to articulate them clearly.

On Bess's fifty-second birthday in 1937, she received an interesting letter from her husband telling her to expect a small package:

> [In honor of] your seventy-second birthday or maybe it's your thirty-second—I haven't kept very close count on it. It would make no difference if it was your one hundred and fifty-second—to me you'd still be the prettiest, sweetest, best and all the other adjectives girl on earth—in heaven or in the waters under the earth.[23]

During that same time, Bess had taken up horseback riding again. "I feel more limber already," she wrote, and concluded with her attempt to teach their fourteen-year-old daughter to play tennis. "I tried to show M. how to serve but it was a washout." In her own defense Margaret recorded, "I think Chris Evert Lloyd [a number one world professional tennis player] might have had some trouble with Mother's serve."[24]

It appeared that Bess never lost her competitive spirit, and when it came time for her husband to seek a second term in 1941, Bess's diligent efforts to support her husband became more visible. In addition to laboring behind the scenes, Bess began to appear more frequently with her campaigning spouse; however, she always held the

* Abigail and John Adams exchanged over thirteen hundred letters during the course of their marriage. Some of their correspondence (shared in Volume I of *Loves, Lies, and Tears* gives historians incredible insight into the American Revolution and the nation's fight for independence.

belief that "a woman's place in public is to sit beside her husband, be silent, and be sure her hat is on straight."

Harry went so far as to put his wife on his Senate payroll for an annual salary of twenty-four hundred dollars. He declared Bess earned every penny of it, while she dismissed any criticism and pronounced frankly that they needed the extra income. (It should be noted that Senator Truman was neither the first nor the last to have a family member on the government payroll, nor is it illegal.)

Around this time, Harry determined it was necessary for the family to reside in Washington full time. Bess did her best to ignore her mother's sighs of disappointment and moans of dissatisfaction. As Margaret Truman later analyzed the situation,

> Her [Bess's] sense of responsibility for Madge Gates Wallace's happiness went deeper than either of them [her parents] could understand...a part of her soul that neither his love for her nor her love for him could touch—that dark, heartbreaking need to console Madge for the wound fate had inflicted on her.[25]

Bess worked hard to be a supportive and participatory Senate wife. As she grew more comfortable in her own right, she further adapted to the Washington social scene. She admired Eleanor Roosevelt's enormous energy and personally liked the First Lady very much, even if she did not particularly care for Eleanor's spouse, the sitting president. Unlike her own husband, who was candid and forthright (Truman prided himself on never using what he called forty dollar words), Roosevelt in Bess's opinion was more of a cunning politician.

In addition to her spousal and senatorial commitments, Bess worked several hours every Wednesday at the USO and remained very involved in her teenage daughter's life.* Together they would go to a movie, see a concert, or visit Washington monuments. Margaret believed it was the first time her mother would view her as a friend and not solely as a responsibility.

* United Service Organizations, Inc. (USO) is a private, nonprofit organization chartered by Congress and organized under the laws of the District of Columbia.

In 1944, Truman was voted one of the ten most useful politicians in Washington. The Democratic leaders, primarily the president, were putting intense pressure on Harry to accept the vice presidential nomination. Bess was not at all in favor of it and had no problem stating her opposition. Her misgivings were numerous.

To begin with, Bess had a long-running concern for Harry's health. She had already observed his series of severe headaches, physical and mental exhaustion, and problems with his heart, as well as an agonizing experience with gallstones. Her husband was now sixty years old; with the country embroiled in World War II, should he succeed to the presidency (which was a foreseeable outcome), Bess was apprehensive as to what inheriting a wartime presidency might do to his physical well-being.

External dangers had to be considered as well—there had been an assassination attempt on FDR's life in 1933, and Senator Truman received a death threat in 1937 that put the Trumans' unruffled public façade to the test. And Bess preferred that people saw only the façade; she thoroughly detested public scrutiny and did not want to subject Margaret to the cruel and nasty press Bess had witnessed so frequently. Perhaps worst of all was the terrifying possibility that journalists would uncover and reveal to the world her father's suicide.

Sacrifice had become second nature to Bess. She made countless ones her entire adult life in the service of her mother's mental serenity, her brothers' welfare, and her husband's career, as well as on behalf of her daughter. However, the consequences of suppressing her own personal wishes this time were almost more than she could bear.

Harry told the party bosses that he did not want to be vice president.

> The vice president simply presides over the Senate and sits around hoping for a funeral...the Madam doesn't want me to do it.[26]

Despite Harry's refusals, the president had made up his mind regarding who he wanted for his new running mate. Roosevelt responded sharply.

> If he [Truman] wants to break up the Democratic Party in the middle of the war, that's his responsibility.[27]

It was that particular accountability that caused Harry to finally accept the position. Bess was not pleased, to say the least!

Thankfully, during the presidential campaign of 1944, the only injurious issue involving Bess dealt with the fact she received wages as her husband's Senate secretary. Truman's response was simple.

> She's a clerk in my office...I need her there. I never make a report or deliver a speech without her editing it...there's nothing secret about it.[28]

Only eighty-two days after winning his fourth term in office, on April 12, 1945, FDR had a massive cerebral hemorrhage. Harry phoned his wife and told her,

> I'm at the White House. President Roosevelt died about two hours ago in Warm Springs. I'm sending a car for you and Margaret. I want you here when I'm sworn in.[29]

Overwhelmed, Bess broke down in tears.

Immediately upon her arrival at the White House, even before she saw her husband, Bess had enough composure and compassion to request a brief visit with Mrs. Roosevelt. In the midst of tragedy these two solid, no-nonsense women, who above all else were wives and mothers, reached out to comfort one another. Bess warmly and sincerely expressed her deep sympathy, while Mrs. Roosevelt replied,

> I just told Harry I am ready to do anything I can to help. That of course applies to you, too.[30]

In the Cabinet Room of the White House, her eyes red from crying, Bess Truman solemnly stood between her daughter and her husband as he was sworn in to office as the thirty-third president of the United States. The *Kansas City Star* reported on April 13, 1945,

"[President Truman said] Bess cried most of the night and it wasn't for joy, either." Once again, Bess relied on her ironclad self-control.

At her first press conference, the new First Lady informed reporters that it would be her last. Bess viewed press conferences as a visit with "a cage of cobras." Standing her ground, she told them, "I am not the chief executive, and I have nothing to say to the public." When a reporter inquired as to how they were ever going to get to know her, Bess responded,

> You don't need to know me. I'm only the president's wife and the mother of his daughter.[31]

Frankly, her attitude never changed. When a reporter inquired about what the First Lady would be wearing to a tea, Bess told her press aide, "Tell her it's none of her damn business."[32] Margaret Truman reported that after her assistant "picked herself up off the floor," the official response was, "Mrs. Truman hasn't quite made up her mind." On another occasion, Bess was asked to say something on tape. She replied, "I have no desire to have my voice recorded for posterity."

Eventually convinced she had to address the press on some level, Bess agreed to answer only written questions. The press was disappointed with her frequent response of "no comment"; occasionally the First Lady would clarify...well, almost. You can see how answers such as these would provide nothing but frustration to a hungry press:

> *Given a choice would you have gone into the White House?*
> "Most definitely would *not* have."
>
> *Would you want your daughter or son to be president?*
> "No."
>
> *Do you think we will ever have a woman president?*
> "No."

Regarding her wedding details, such as when, where, church name, attendance, best man, attire, reception, and honeymoon, "June 28, 1919," had to suffice.

When Mrs. Helm, the White House social secretary, told the First Lady that she was continually pestered for stories, Bess responded with, "Just keep on smiling and tell them nothing."

Only a handful of women experience the overwhelming invasion of privacy and unmitigated scrutiny a First Lady is subject to. Political differences aside, it is indeed a small sorority of mostly supportive women, who can truly understand the pressure and stress that come with living inside the White House. Republican First Lady Grace Coolidge wrote a considerate note of empathy when Democrat Bess Truman was thrust into the same undesirable position Grace had encountered. Both were married to the vice president when the sitting president unexpectedly died. Friendships develop, and as Dolley Madison had done nearly 120 years earlier for Julia Tyler and Sarah Polk, both Eleanor Roosevelt and Edith Wilson offered Bess their reinforcement.

Never abandoning or discarding their Midwestern roots, the Trumans had a pet name for anyone who got carried away or caught up in the Washington limelight. They called it "Potomac fever," and Bess wanted to make sure her staff did not acquire the fever as well. It was not long before a magazine writer wanted to do a profile on the First Lady's assistant. When she asked for permission, Bess answered with two unambiguous words: "Absolutely not!"

To demonstrate just how unaffected Bess was with her new living accommodations, after she moved into the Executive Mansion, she wrote "1600 Penn. Ave, Wash. D.C." for the return address on her correspondence.[33] The White House may have represented prestige or prominence to others, but as far as the Trumans were concerned, they candidly called it "the Great White Jail."

Truthfully, the Executive Mansion left a great deal to be desired in the late 1940s. The country had gone through one world war and a depression, and was still enmeshed in its second world war. To say the mansion had been neglected for many years was an understatement. It was in shambles. Twenty-one-year-old Margaret (now attending George Washington University and seriously considering a professional singing career) noted in her diary, "The White House upstairs is a mess…I was so depressed when I saw it." The private rooms were shabby, the furniture was in need of upholstering, dingy draperies hung lifeless, carpeting was worn, and the entire upstairs desperately required paint. To top it all off, it was infested with rats. It was a situation very similar to that which former First Lady Caroline Harrison had walked into some fifty-five years earlier.

Dismayed, Bess returned to Blair House, the couple's temporary residence across the street, while Mrs. Roosevelt was vacating the Executive Mansion. Bess ordered a major redecoration before ever moving her family into the residence. (Congress allotted fifty thousand dollars to paint and refurbish the interior.) Supervising the entire renovation, the First Lady determined the new color scheme, approved furnishings, and decided to add a bathroom to Margaret's private suite. Numerous carpenters, painters, and staff worked diligently to restore the president's home. Astonishingly, all the work was completed within *two weeks*!

The White House staff soon discovered that Bess was not at all like the cold, adversarial woman seen by the press. On the contrary, she was good-humored, approachable, and considerate. She established a schedule of work breaks for the staff during the week and firmly believed Sunday should be reserved for family. To that end, Bess had all housekeepers and maids take Sundays off to be with their relatives.

Maintaining an old Missouri tradition of study groups, Bess hosted a thirty-two-week Spanish class beginning in October of 1945. The classes, held on Mondays at 11:00 A.M. in the White House, attracted prominent Washingtonians such as Mamie Eisenhower. Wives of cabinet members and senators also joined the First Lady and Professor Ramon Ramos to study Spanish and promote good will with Latin American countries. Some of the ladies considered it a social gathering; Bess, however, studied hard and acquired a good working knowledge of the language.

The First Lady also hosted eight members of her Independence bridge club for a four-day visit to the White House. Acting as tour guide, Bess planned every activity and participated in sightseeing with her group at all the popular Washington monuments and attractions. The highlight of her friends' visit was the grand, formal dinner Bess arranged in the State Dining Room. Her old bridge club members discovered that Bess had not allowed the power, glory, and stature of the First Ladyship to change her in any way; she was just as down-to-earth and unpretentious in the Executive Mansion as she had been in Independence.

Alonzo Fields, head butler during Bess's tenure, wrote in his book, *My 21 Years in the White House*, "It was agreed upon by the staff she [the First Lady] would not stand for fakers, shirkers or flatterers." J. B. West, chief usher of the White House for twenty-eight years, described the First Lady's wit as "dry, laconic, incisive and very funny. She was at her funniest with a straight face, perfectly deadpan."[34]

Mr. West went on to share some insights regarding Bess's personal taste when it came to drinking old fashioneds. It seems the Trumans enjoyed a cocktail after work and before dinner most evenings; however, the First Lady had complained the drink was too sweet. After several attempts, the butler serving the drinks discovered just how "dry" they needed to be. In frustration he poured two big splashes of bourbon over ice, to which Bess finally replied, "Now that's the way we like our old fashioneds!"[35]

A stickler for cleanliness, Bess was not above pitching in to help. She knew what she wanted and established her high standards early on. According to historian Bill Harris, the family's dirty clothing was sent to Kansas City because the laundries in Washington did not measure up to her standards of perfection.

One longtime housekeeper learned firsthand of the First Lady's expectations. Henrietta Nesbitt had worked in the White House for over a dozen years. Although it was well known that former President Roosevelt frequently complained about the quality and quantity of meals served by Mrs. Nesbitt, she proceeded to run the kitchen as she pleased. It did not take long for Margaret to discover what President Roosevelt's son meant when he asked, "Has Mrs. Nesbitt begun starving you yet?" Before Margaret could answer, he said, "Don't worry, she will."[36]

It was the variety of food (or lack thereof) that ultimately pushed Bess over the top. The first public clue that something was awry in the White House kitchen had surfaced in a 1937 *New York Times* article which stated, "Any man [referring to Roosevelt] might rebel against being served salt fish for lunch four days in a row."

For President Truman, it was Brussels sprouts. The first night the president was served the vegetable in question he politely pushed them to the side. Bess was out of town at the time, so Margaret explained to Mrs. Nesbitt that her father did not like Brussels sprouts and would not eat them. The next night, the president was again served the same vegetable. Margaret once more reiterated her father's dislike. When Brussels sprouts appeared on the president's plate for the third night in a row, Margaret exploded. She had a long-distance telephone call put through to her mother. (Unlike today, long-distance calls were expensive and reserved for very important business.) No sooner had Bess returned to the White House than the staff learned that Mrs. Nesbitt was "retiring." Not all was lost for the defiant employee, as a few years later she published *White House Diary, Henrietta Nesbitt: FDR's Housekeeper.*

As it turned out, Bess's supervision of the preparation of meals, her diligence with cleaning, and the redecorating of the Executive Mansion could never be sufficient. The White House was literally crumbling, but no one knew it at the time. Sometime later, expert architects confirmed the ceiling was staying up solely out of habit. Luckily the old expression "ignorance is bliss" would be appropriate in this instance, as the president and First Lady had far greater dilemmas to deal with.

For Bess, Secret Service protection was one of them. She detested the idea of individuals following her everywhere. After all, outside of her home town, Bess was virtually unknown to the public and frequently went out unrecognized. Nonetheless, she couldn't avoid her Secret Service detail while in Washington. When she returned home to Independence on her frequent trips, though, she insisted on shopping and visiting friends *alone.*

Although the new First Lady remained totally unaffected, it was difficult for some individuals back home not to react with awe to her new status. Bess's first bridge club meeting with her hometown group was a good example: all the members stood up when she walked into the room. Her response was classic. "Now stop it, stop it this instant! Sit down, every darn one of you."[37] (Many years later, after the assassination of President Kennedy, Congress approved Secret Service protection for former presidents and their families. It was no surprise Bess rejected it. It took a personal phone call from then-president Lyndon Johnson to convince the former First Lady to accept the safety measure.)

The president's problems were significantly more critical. Former President Roosevelt had kept his vice president completely in the dark, and Truman had a great deal to catch up on. Sixteen hours a day, the president was dealing with several crucial problems, some of which were so top secret very few people, even in the president's innermost circle, knew about them. It was impossible for Truman to discuss every detail with his wife, as had been their habit over the years. Unhappily enough, Bess soon discovered she was no longer her husband's chief adviser, a disappointing and perhaps unanticipated turn of events.

The Truman partnership was going through very difficult, uncharted waters. Truman's preference was always to have his wife close by, and frankly, he wanted her to remain in Washington full time. Bess did not want to be there in the first place and found every reason to be absent.

One particular event became a bone of contention in their relationship. World events being what they were, several of the president's advisers had discussed with him the possibility of having to use an atomic bomb the United States had developed. Bess knew about the bomb; however, the president never discussed with her his decision to *use* it against Japan.

The United States had been entrenched in World War II for nearly three years when the leaders of the Allied forces called for a joint conference. In July of 1945 President Harry Truman, Communist Party General Secretary Joseph Stalin, and Prime Minister Winston Churchill agreed to meet in Potsdam, Germany, in accordance with Nazi Germany's earlier agreement of surrender. At Stalin's suggestion and with Churchill's agreement, it was decided Truman would be the presiding officer of the conference.

During the summit the president consistently wrote Bess, who was home in Independence, the most candid and forthright letters imaginable. Although Bess was some six thousand miles away, Harry wanted his wife to feel a part of the historic proceedings.

Japan continued to reject the Potsdam terms of "unconditional surrender" or, if they did not surrender, "prompt and utter destruction." The decision to release the bomb was prompted by Truman's desire to spare the lives of United States military personnel, but no matter the rationale, it must have been one of the hardest decisions made in the history of the world. On August 6, 1945, while the president was returning to Washington, the U.S. Air Force dropped the first atomic bomb on Hiroshima, Japan. As predicted, it was necessary to drop a second bomb three days later on Nagasaki. As agreed upon, the Soviets invaded Japanese-held Manchuria between the two bombings, and World War II finally ended. But not before tens of millions were killed during the course of the war. Estimates range anywhere from sixty to seventy million, the majority of whom were civilians. Six million civilian Jews alone lost their lives in the Holocaust. It was the deadliest military conflict in history.

Perhaps Margaret Truman said it best when she wrote,

> When he [Truman] made one of these rendezvous with history, he acted alone.[38]

Margaret strongly doubted that her mother would have tried to convince her father any differently. She knew that was not the main conflict, however:

> [Bess] had become a spectator rather than a partner in Harry Truman's presidency. That made her very, very angry.[39]

It would take a while before Bess could let go of her fury.

The president also struggled with redefining their partnership. A period of time had to elapse, mutual cooperation had to be sought, and a new understanding had to be forged before the couple could work through the difficulties and regain their marital closeness. Also, Truman had some understandable misgivings about the presidential role that had been thrust upon him. Years later he noted in his diary,

> When Franklin Roosevelt died, I felt there must be a million men

> better qualified than I to take up the presidential task. But the work was mine to do, and I had to do it. And I have tried to give it everything that was in me.[40]

Being wife, mother, and First Lady all at once is very difficult, demanding and exhausting at the best of times, and during wartime is anything but the best of times. Like other homemakers, Bess signed a housewife's pledge to voluntarily ration food in the White House. It set an example for other Americans to limit their consumption in order to provide food to the devastated populations of postwar Europe, desperately in need of basic provisions. She also continued Eleanor Roosevelt's fundraising efforts for the March of Dimes. Even Joseph McCarthy, a radical anti-Communist campaigner, praised Bess as the "only good thing about the White House."

Nonetheless, every First Lady is critiqued and disapproved of in some way, even the most popular. Edith Roosevelt was called a perfect First Lady, and it was said she never made a mistake. Perfect—no mistakes—and yet she too was ridiculed. Edith's offense was spending too little on her clothes.*

Bess was also rather thrifty and known for being a penny pincher, yet she was always impeccably groomed. Attired in tailored two-piece suits and simple dresses, Bess often accessorized with hats and gloves, while her evening gowns were accented with a single strand of pearls. She was a woman of medium height, somewhat stocky, with soft gray hair, and some referred to her as matronly. Predictably, her husband immediately came to her defense, saying his wife, at sixty, "looks exactly as a woman of her age should look."

In Bess's case, it was her defiance that some objected to. Her obstinacy prompted an uproar when she accepted an invitation from the Daughters of the American Revolution to a tea in her honor at Constitution Hall.† Congressman Adam Clayton Powell telegrammed the First Lady, urging her to withdraw her acceptance because his wife,

* A news article reported that the First Lady "dresses on $300 a year and looks it." To Edith's credit, the thrifty First Lady accepted the remark as a compliment and saved the article in her scrapbook.

† Constitution Hall was built by the DAR in 1929 to house its annual convention.

pianist Hazel Scott, had been refused permission to perform in the DAR's Constitution Hall because of her color. Powell wrote,

> No good will be accomplished by attending and much harm will be done. If you [Bess] believe in 100 percent Americanism, you will publicly denounce the DAR's action.[41]

A similar scenario had occurred years earlier, when black singer Marian Anderson was barred from performing in Constitution Hall in 1939. At that time, First Lady Eleanor Roosevelt resigned from the DAR in protest; however, the organization refused to change its biased policy.

Neither a segregationist nor a crusader, Bess dug in her heels. Still rejecting the idea that she too was now a public figure, Bess was determined not to let a congressman tell her where she could have a cup of tea. She wired back,

> The invitation...was extended prior to the unfortunate controversy which has arisen...In my opinion the acceptance of the hospitality is not related to the merits of the issue...I deplore any action which denies artistic talent an opportunity to express itself because of prejudice against race origin.[42]

After Bess attended the tea, Congressman Powell retaliated by calling her "the Last Lady." At the time, the president and First Lady were still dancing around her smoldering rage over her new notoriety and being shut out of her husband's inner circle, but Truman's loyalty to his Bess never wavered. Not one to quietly accept criticism directed toward his loved ones, the president immediately banned Mr. Powell from the White House.

The entire incident was an unfortunate clash of principles: Bess's determination to have autonomy, to not be dictated to, came up against both the Trumans' genuinely egalitarian way of life. It was not a matter of being politically correct, for the Trumans truly believed in equality for all races. J. B. West shared a behind-the-scenes personal look at the presidential couple in his book, *Upstairs At The White*

House. He affirmed that regardless of whom the Trumans were entertaining, when an individual entered the room (butler, doorman, or usher) they would introduce him by name to their guest, be it a family member or a prime minister. "They introduced all the staff to their visitors." Mr. West went on to say,

> They did not see the world as being composed of aristocratic leaders on the one hand and faceless servants on the other. They had a broad sense of humanity that bridged the divisions of job and status...Their humanity was sincere, albeit not learned or inherited from their mothers.[43]

Bess's mother was anti-Semitic and forbade Jews in her home. This included Eddie Jacobson, Harry's dear friend and partner in his haberdashery business. (Let us not forget the Wallace-Truman home on North Delaware Street was owned by Madge Wallace.) Yet eleven minutes after Israel was proclaimed a state, the president promptly recognized the new Jewish nation.

The president's mother had her prejudices as well. Martha Truman was only nine years old when the Civil War broke out. A Southerner to the core, she was anti-Union. When at ninety-two Martha learned that her son had been sworn in to the presidency, she calmly had two things to tell him. The mother in Mama Truman said, "Be good Harry, but be game too." Later when she went to visit the White House, the bias in Martha was quoted commenting, "You tell my son if he tries to put me in Lincoln's bed, I'll sleep on the floor."[44]

Still, it was Truman who created the Committee on Civil Rights, designed to deal with racial prejudice. Bess wholeheartedly supported it. (As she did the controversial decision to fire General Douglas MacArthur for insubordination because he publicly disagreed with Truman's Korean War policy.) Equality for all races was not only correct and moral, but long overdue. As Commander in Chief of the armed forces, Truman continued his support of civil rights and desegregated the army.

It is still hard to believe the United States' armed forces were segregated prior to 1948. Other firsts were also occurring around this same time. The Central Intelligence Agency was created (1947), the first union contract with a sliding wage scale was negotiated by General Motors and United Auto Workers (1948), and the minimum wage was raised to a whopping seventy-five cents an hour (1949). In 1948 the Republican Congress, like the majority of the press, inaccurately and ironically presumed the next president would be Republican. Hence they voted an annual salary increase from $75,000 to $100,000, plus a $50,000 tax-free expense allowance for the next Chief Executive.

There was considerable doubt as to whether Truman would even run for reelection. According to public opinion polls, only 36 percent approved of the job he was doing. Other Democratic leaders, including Elliott and Franklin Roosevelt Jr. (two of FDR's sons), urged the party to draft General Eisenhower (who had not yet affiliated himself with the Republican Party). Many within the party simply did not believe Truman could win.

What they did not know was that Truman wanted to be elected in his own right, as opposed to being president through the back door, as he called it. More of an optimist, perhaps, than a realist, and always a fighter, Truman was adamant.

> I want to say to you that for the next four years there will be a Democrat in the White House and you are looking at him.[45]

Bess too appreciated a good fight. She kept her combative side carefully concealed, but we must remember that it was the secret behind her youthful success as a champion tennis player.

By this time, the Trumans had regained and revitalized their working collaboration, and, we assume, put personal discord behind them as well. For a minimum of two hours every night in the president's upstairs study, the couple had long discussions about the issues and problems the president faced. Every speech included Bess's editing. According to J. B. West,

> Although it went unsuspected by nearly everybody in govern-

ment, Bess entered into nearly every decision the President made.[46]

They were all-embracing partners once again. Bess was now a full-fledged enthusiastic supporter and campaigner, even though she too was pessimistic about her husband's chances. According to Margaret, her father's poll ratings "had sunk so low you needed a wetsuit and a few tanks of oxygen to find them."

The Trumans campaigned tirelessly, even though all published reports indicated that things were heavily stacked against Harry. On a brighter note, female journalists finally had something to report regarding the First Lady:

> After shaking hands with 1,800 guests Tuesday afternoon, Mrs. Truman began another two weeks of luncheons, teas, [and] receptions.[47]

Both Bess and Margaret accompanied the president on his now famous whistle-stop train tour throughout the country. This was particularly significant because Madge Wallace, now eighty-six years old, was seriously ill, and normally Bess would have canceled every social and political commitment on the calendar to be at her mother's side. Throngs cheered at every campaign stop as, from the rear train platform, the president introduced Bess as "the Boss" and Margaret as "the one who bosses the Boss." Although Bess disliked her nickname, as Harry reminded her, it was always good for a laugh.

Newsweek magazine confirmed, "Fifty leading journalists predicted [the president] would be beaten so badly, the Democratic Party might disappear." When the Democrats held their 1948 convention in Philadelphia, it was a historic first as the proceedings could be seen on television. Not an auspicious beginning for this tradition: millions watched as the representatives argued, bickered, and squabbled endlessly before finally agreeing on a candidate. It was 2:00 A.M. before Truman could make his acceptance speech to the exhausted and drained delegates.

On election day, Truman remained faithful to his convictions. He had always been his own man and believed that once he made a decision on something, there was no sense in looking back or second guessing it. He was satisfied he was going to win, and even if he was wrong, it was too late to worry about it. The family had returned to Independence to vote and without the refuge of the White House, Truman knew he would not have a moment of peace away from the press. He made the decision to spend the evening alone in a hotel about forty miles outside of town. Bess and Margaret stayed behind in their home to track the polling by radio (they did not own a television) and cope with the hoards of reporters sure to converge on North Delaware Street, regardless of the outcome. Bess went to bed after midnight, as her husband remained ahead in the polls.

It was an excited Secret Service man who woke the well-rested president around 4:00 A.M. at his Excelsior Springs hideaway, telling him he was certain the president had won reelection. His opponent Thomas Dewey and other naysayers were still not convinced. Meanwhile, no official public announcement had been made.

Bess's and Margaret's first indication that Dewey had finally conceded defeat came at 10:14 A.M. when they heard "every whistle and car horn in Independence blowing." Margaret yelled joyfully, "It's nice to win." Her mother replied, "You bet it is!"

The *Chicago Tribune* had been so confident Dewey would emerge the victor, its November 3 headline read: DEWEY DEFEATS TRUMAN. The president gleefully had his picture taken holding the erroneous newspaper.

When Truman was inaugurated in 1949 he ensured that *all* minorities were welcome to stay in Washington hotels and attend all events. It was the first integrated presidential inauguration in the country's history. Also the first to be nationally televised; an estimated ten million Americans watched the proceedings…more than the combined total of all who viewed every previous presidential inauguration.

For the majority of Truman's second term, the family once again called Blair House home. It was still not known that the White House was in a state of almost complete disintegration, but the signs were grim. With its outdated plumbing and electrical systems, a sinking foundation, and floors on the verge of collapse, the mansion was determined unsafe for occupancy by the Secret Service (though it took a piano leg breaking through the upstairs ceiling to prompt this call).

In 1949, the Executive Mansion began undergoing a complete renovation. It was the First Lady who insisted the exterior remain as it was—for historical reasons—although the interior was completely gutted and rebuilt. Bess was far more comfortable in Blair House, so all the renovation-related turmoil which made the White House unavailable could have been a blessing in disguise. And there were other complications that caused even more anxiety. Madge was once again seriously ill; as Bess wrote a friend,

> We were afraid for a day or two [Mother] was not going to make it. But we got her back here [to Washington]...[where] she can have every attention and be under my eye too.[48]

In addition, Blair House came with its own set of restrictions. The main rooms only held a maximum of one hundred guests, so smaller dinners and receptions meant double and triple the amount of entertaining. (One typical two-week schedule listed thirteen major engagements for the First Lady.) Moreover, the building did not provide the same security afforded by the White House, as the front door opened directly onto the street where pedestrians were allowed to stroll by.

On November 1, 1950, the president and First Lady were scheduled to go to Arlington National Cemetery for a special dedication. It was a warm day and Bess had most of the windows and the front door of the house open, with only a lightly latched screen door facing the sidewalk. The president managed to take a nap before their scheduled commitment, while Bess visited with her mother upstairs. The First Lady had just left her mother's bedroom and gone to her own room to prepare for the engagement when suddenly several blasts of gunfire erupted. Within two minutes, twenty-seven explosions were heard.

By the time Bess hurried to the window, the entire area below was awash in blood. One guard, Leslie Coffelt, lay dead while another, Joseph E. Downs, was clutching his shattered leg. The two assailants were bleeding profusely. Crying, Bess rushed into her husband's bedroom and screamed, "Harry—someone's shooting our policemen!" As Truman dashed to the window, Bess could hear a man shouting "Get back, get back!" The president then went over to peek out his bedroom door, only to discover "a husky Secret Service man crouched at the head of the stairs with a submachine gun pointing at the front door."[49]

Two Puerto Rican nationalists (Oscar Collazo and Victor Torresola) had tried to shoot their way into the house. Torresola had gunned down the two guards. Mortally wounded, Coffelt managed to fatally shoot Torresola before passing out. Fortunately Collazo's gun jammed and "he was stopped on the steps by a hail of bullets from other policemen and Secret Service agents."[50] Although he was hit three times, none of Collazo's wounds were fatal.*

The Trumans' immediate reactions were characteristic of their personalities. The president calmed his wife down and advised her to finish dressing for their appearance at Arlington. He would find out the details and share them with her in the car. Not surprisingly, Bess was concerned for her mother and instructed the Blair House staff and her mother's companion to say *nothing* of the attack. Now eighty-eight years old, frail and hard of hearing, Madge seldom left her room. There was no reason for her to know about the incident. (Luckily, Margaret was in Portland, Maine, giving a vocal concert.)

Bess once again relied on her iron self-control. Within an hour of the shooting she and the president attended the ceremony at Arlington "as if nothing had happened." Truman's public comment was, "Presidents have to expect such things." Privately he wrote a cousin,

> I'm really a prisoner now. Everybody is much more worried and jittery than I am. I've been shot at by experts and unless your name's on the bullet you needn't be afraid—and that of course you can't find out, so why worry.[51]

* Originally condemned to die on August 1, 1952, Collazo's sentence was commuted to life imprisonment.

Shaken to her core, Bess found little comfort in her husband's point of view. All of her original anxiety regarding the presidency returned and intensified, creating a burden of fretfulness and concern throughout their final years in Washington.

Harry made a habit of writing his wife a memorable letter each year on their wedding anniversary. One cannot help but wonder if Bess had recently reread her husband's letter from the previous year.

> Thirty years ago I hoped to make you a happy wife and a happy mother. Did I? I don't know. All I can say [is] I've tried. There is no one in the world anyway who can look down on you or your daughter. That means much to me...that those dear to me were not made to suffer for my shortcomings...I'm very sure that if you'd been able to see into the future...you'd have very definitely turned your back on what was coming.[52]

There had been numerous other threats on Truman's life but the president had seen no need to mention them to his wife or daughter. In a confidential letter to another cousin, Truman explained why he could not attend his army reunion of the Thirty-fifth Division.

> The Secret Service have received more than the usual number of threats to rub me out at the reunion. You know I never worry about those things...But some good fellow who has three or four kids may be killed—to keep me from that fate.[53]

Security around Blair House tightened considerably. Not only was the number of guards increased, but the streetcar platform running down the avenue was removed and pedestrians were no longer permitted to walk in front of the building. Undeniably these were necessary precautions, yet the measures only reminded Bess of the terror she felt and the tragic loss of life she witnessed.

Nonetheless, Bess carried on and made an effort at normalcy. Family and friends continued to be the center of her life. Employees frequently commented on how extraordinarily close the Truman family was and how they genuinely enjoyed each other's company; staff nicknamed the family the Three Musketeers. In addition to dining together, the Trumans listened to the radio, played the piano, read, and simply conversed with one another.

Other than being surrounded by security, scrutinized on an uncomfortably personal level, and more often than not being held to higher standards, a White House family is like any other. They have disagreements, in-laws who sometimes live with them, children they adore and want to protect, and feelings they wish to share. One example was when Margaret gave a singing recital at Constitution Hall. Music editor Paul Hume wrote a less-than-enthusiastic review of her performance in the *Washington Post*. "With a pleasant voice of little size and fair quality, Miss Truman is flat a good deal of the time."

Margaret's father sent Mr. Hume a letter in his typical Truman-esque style. In addition to other things, he said the review was "poppy-cock" and Hume was "an eight ulcer man on a four ulcer job with all four ulcers at work." The letter ended with,

> Someday I hope to meet you. When that happens you'll need a new nose, a lot of beefsteak for black eyes, and perhaps a supporter below![54]

Highly criticized for his comments, the president insisted he had a "right to be two persons—the President of the U.S. and Harry S. Truman, father of Margaret."

Another example, on an even more personal note, revealed the husband in Harry Truman. J. B. West recalled that upon returning from a visit to Independence, the First Lady was "blushing like a young bride" when she asked him for help one morning.

> Mr. West, we have a little problem...it's the President's bed. Do you think you can get it fixed today? Two of the slats broke down during the night.[55]

A number of years later Bess affirmed,

> Harry and I have been sweethearts and married more than forty

> years—and no matter where I was, when I put out my hand Harry's was there to grasp it.[56]

In March of 1952, the White House restoration was complete, and it now included the ever-popular Truman balcony. In Independence, the family frequently gathered on the back porch to enjoy the outdoors. However, prior to the renovation, there was no private place outside the White House where the First Family could visit away from the curious view of the public. The Truman balcony has been enjoyed resoundingly by all subsequent White House denizens.

Furthermore, the Trumans brought back all the spectacle and splendor to the Executive Mansion. The majestic, elaborate state dinners began at eight o'clock and were always white tie. Bess was gracious and dignified, albeit reserved, as a hostess; the public did not see the First Lady's warm generosity or succinct wit. Privately she was friendly and jovial; however, in public, she would appear frigid or standoffish.

When the First Lady broke her own rule and courteously gave female reporters a tour of the new house, part of the interrogation went like this:

> *Would you like to spend four more years here?*
> "You're not going to get a yes or no out of me on that one."
>
> *Could you stand it if you had to?*
> "I stood it for seven years."[57]

During the final years of the Truman administration, North Korea and South Korea were engaged in what some called a civil war. The United States intervened on behalf of South Korea, while China intervened on behalf of North Korea. The span of the Korean War proved to be the most difficult period of the president's tenure at the helm of the country. Bess realized that if Truman won reelection, both she and her exhausted husband would be seventy-three by the time he finished another term in office. Unlike the consensus during his previous bid for reelection, the Democratic Party now believed that

Truman was the *only* man who could beat (Republican opponent) General Eisenhower.

Still considering the option, the president asked his appointment secretary, Matt Connelly, "Do you think the old man [referring to himself] will have to run again?" As Mr. Connelly pointed to a portrait of Bess, he raised the more important question: "Would you do that to her?"[58]

Bess was enormously relieved and visibly happy when Truman publicly announced his retirement from politics. There was only one event that overshadowed the First Lady's newfound joyfulness. Six weeks before they were ready to leave the White House, Madge Wallace suffered a stroke. Margaret Truman recalled how her mother "scarcely left her [Madge's] bedside." After five decades of devotion, love, and care, Bess could no longer sustain or protect her dying mother. With Bess and Harry both at her side, Madge died in the Executive Mansion on December 5, 1952. It was analogous to losing a part of her soul, as Madge had been so much a component of Bess's existence. While Madge never entirely accepted or approved of him, to President Truman's credit he noted in his diary,

> She was a grand lady. When I hear these mother-in-law jokes I don't laugh. They are not funny to me, because I've had a good one...[furthermore] my mother was a good mother-in-law.[59]

Before the Trumans returned to Independence, reporters and politicians alike gave the First Couple a rousing farewell. At a luncheon in her honor, the First Lady received from female reporters a particularly touching display of their esteem. They read a poem written for the woman who more often than not responded with "no comment" to their endless questions. The long poem began:

> We will think of you, rather as a friend,
> Whose kindnesses never seemed to end
> The appreciative little longhand note
> For something nice that somebody wrote,
> Or the flowers when somebody was sad or ill,

With a card that is surely treasured still.
And your wonderful way with a White House guest,
Who might be nervous at such a test,
And who probably never even knew
That the feeling of ease was due to you—
To your tact and kindness and savoir-faire
Which made hard things easy when you were there.

A multitude of individuals went to Washington's Union Station to say their goodbyes; however, the warmest, most heartfelt tribute came from the ten thousand people who met the Trumans at the Missouri Pacific depot and the fifteen hundred additional people who waited for them in the thoroughfares around 219 North Delaware Street in Independence.

There was no doubt that Bess was genuinely moved by the enormous reception. She felt rewarded at last for the trials, tribulations, and ups and downs of Harry's thirty years in elective office. As Truman noted in a letter to a friend:

> [Bess] remarked that our sendoff from Washington and our reception at home and along the [road] way made it all worthwhile.[60]

Undeniably, equally as gratifying was her feeling of relief. Bess had survived eight years in the White House without anyone discovering her humiliating family secret. Margaret was the only exception and she learned of it purely by accident at the age of twenty. When Truman accepted the vice presidential nomination, one of Margaret's aunts let it slip that the family skeleton would surely be out of the closet now. Margaret had always believed that Grandfather Wallace had died of a heart attack and asked her father to confirm the truth. Truman did and then *demanded* his daughter *never* speak to her mother about Wallace's suicide. Over the years, Margaret hoped the day would come when Bess could finally share this great secret with her, but that day never came. Thirty-seven more years would pass before the truth came out; Bess was unyielding in her determination to take the sordid story to her grave—and she did.

Returning to her quiet, anonymous Midwestern life proved to be both familiar as well as out of the ordinary for Bess. The latter because five thousand people now walked or drove past their home *daily* (reminiscent of Grace Coolidge's experience) and within the first two weeks alone, *seventy thousand* letters arrived. The experience was familiar in the sense that, like countless other private citizens, her husband did not receive any pension in recognition of his many years of work on the public's behalf.* Although a number of lucrative job offers were presented to him, Harry was adamant that "he was not going to sell the prestige of the presidency to anybody." Always true to his values, Truman decided he would write his memoirs and earn income from his own laborious efforts. Since that was going to take some time, one very familiar aspect of daily life reemerged. The homemaker in Bess instinctively began to focus on ways to economize.

Bess determined that one easy place to save would be to have Harry mow the lawn himself. Truman had to resort to political maneuvering to get around such a practical wife. He postponed the chore until the grass was so tall their front yard looked like an overgrown wheat field. One Sunday morning before church, Bess found Harry in the front yard pushing the lawn mower and happily visiting with neighbors on their way to services. Realizing Harry would not be joining her, Bess inquired, "What do you think you're doing?" With a fiendish grin, he replied, "What you asked me to do." Bess hired someone the next day to maintain the lawn.

The Truman partnership had gone full circle and their mutual love had survived the best and the worst of times. Harry soon commuted daily to an office in Kansas City where he worked on his memoirs (Volume I—*Year of Decisions*, Volume II—*Years of Trial and Hope*), made plans for the Truman Library in Independence, and dealt with an avalanche of correspondence. Bess rejoined her former bridge club, assisted with her husband's historical documents, and reviewed every word, of every draft, of Harry's memoirs.

Not surprisingly, the former president's memoirs were a huge

* Very possibly due to Truman's financial situation, Congress passed The Former Presidents Act in 1958, which provided a $25,000 yearly pension to all ex-presidents.

success. For all of his hard work, Truman received a flat payment of $670,000, of which he netted the grand sum of $37,000. Two-thirds of the gross payment went to taxes and the balance to his assistants for their clerical work, research, and organization. Bess was not included in that payout. Furthermore, his memoir-writing set a precedent for future presidents once out of office.* Luckily for the Truman finances, Harry and his siblings inherited property from their mother that proved to be a blessing; Truman was later quoted telling House Majority Leader John McCormack,

> I would practically be on relief, but with the sale of that property I am not financially embarrassed.† [61]

Three years after leaving the White House, in 1956, Margaret Truman married Clifton Daniel, an editor at the *New York Times*. The following year, Bess became a grandmother for the first time. She was seventy-two and delighted beyond words—literally. Her feelings of joy remained personal, and predictably she refused to say anything to reporters. An elated Grandpa Truman said enough for both of them.

Margaret ultimately gave birth to four sons, baffling Bess with her desire to have a large family. Although she remarked to her daughter, "Well, you're not a Catholic, so I can only conclude you're careless," Margaret confirmed "she [Bess] doted on all four boys" when they visited her. Margaret went on to say, "Gammy beamed while they fought mock battles in the living room, making twice as much noise as I ever dared to make at my most obstreperous." Bess also gave them a steady supply of brownies, with a cautionary "Don't tell your mother."

After so many years of caring for her mother, emotionally support-

* Former president Grant, who was dying of throat cancer in 1885, wrote his memoirs specifically to support his family, after leaving the White House. *Personal Memoirs of Ulysses S. Grant* (two volumes primarily focused on the American Civil War and available to this day) was published posthumously by Mark Twain and proved to be a critical, as well as financial, success for Grant's wife.

† When the Former President's Act was passed, Herbert Hoover was the only other living president. A wealthy and generous man, it is believed he only accepted the pension so as not to humiliate his good friend Harry Truman.

ing her siblings, and living in the White House fishbowl, retirement finally afforded Bess the opportunity to travel more and enjoy her enthusiasm for fishing. She and her husband drove to places like Illinois and Pennsylvania and vacationed in Hawaii, undeterred by being constantly surrounded by mobs of curious and admiring citizens. They also spent six weeks in Europe, pestered by hordes of newspaper reporters...Bess's favorite. Truman wrote a friend saying, "The jam at the Paris, Rome and Naples stations was like Washington in 1948 after the election."

Like former First Ladies Martha Washington and Florence Harding, Bess unfortunately destroyed a large quantity of personal correspondence. Truman recalled an evening around Christmastime when he found his wife sitting in the living room, going through a large stack of letters. After reading each one, Bess tossed it into the fireplace. When Harry inquired, "What are you doing?" Bess responded simply, "I'm burning our letters." "Think of history," he countered. "I have," Bess replied, as she watched the flaring fire.*

Forever the older, protective sister, it had to be difficult for Bess to endure the loss of her brothers. When Fred suffered a fatal heart attack in 1957, Bess rushed to his bedside. Despite the loving support and strength she tried to instill in him, Fred died a penniless alcoholic. Bess not only paid for his burial, she sent his wife and children a monthly check for living expenses. Within three years, her brother Frank also passed away.

Her later years brought additional heartbreak. In 1958, Bess discovered a lump in her left breast. Although she managed to ignore it for some time (certainly not one of her better decisions), by the time it finally reached the size of a small grapefruit, it had invaded the lymph nodes in both of her arms. Doctors determined a mastectomy was necessary, and her recovery from the operation was very slow. Not surprisingly, Bess demanded that all statements to the press omit any mention of the mastectomy. Bess, true to character, suffered privately; we can only imagine the physical and psychological anguish she underwent.

* Although Bess burned almost all of her letters to Harry, thankfully she spared the majority of his.

Nineteen sixty-three brought more painful and distressing news. Harry required a serious intestinal hernia operation at the beginning of the year, and his recovery was neither easy nor quick. Bess's sole surviving brother, George, died a slow and painful death from lung cancer that spring, and the shock of President Kennedy's assassination hit her hard in the fall. Bess had been enchanted with the young couple; just the year before, the Kennedys had invited the Trumans (including Margaret and her husband) to a most enjoyable weekend at the White House.

Despite these hardships, the warrior in Bess continued to battle forward through the years. In 1965 President Johnson paid a tribute to her husband when he signed the Medicare Bill into law at the Truman Library. Twelve years had passed since Truman left the presidency, and Johnson wanted to honor the former president's fight for government health care. Harry and Bess were the first two individuals to receive Medicare cards (numbers one and two). The timing was befitting, as Harry's health had been slowly deteriorating and it only continued to get worse. The frequency of Margaret's trips from New York, now her permanent residence, to Missouri, had increased considerably.

The golden years had begun to dim for the Trumans. Fifty-three years had passed since Bess agreed to love and honor the *only* man who truly worshiped, valued, and accepted her for the unique woman she was. Now, her husband lay mortally ill in Research Hospital for three weeks, and Bess scarcely left his side. On Christmas Day 1972 Margaret was as concerned about her exhausted mother as she was for her gravely ill father. The same courageous military captain who led his battery of men forward under fire, "with [German] shells falling on all sides of them" in a major battle during World War I, was now slipping away.

After Truman drifted into a coma, Margaret finally persuaded her mother to go home and get "some real sleep." Guilt haunted Margaret for some time thereafter, as her father passed away early the following morning. Margaret understood that although Bess could no longer *do* anything to help her husband, she wanted to *be* with him until the end.

An elaborate five-day state funeral was planned, whereby Truman's body would lie in state in the Capitol Rotunda before returning to Independence for burial. Somewhat frail herself, it was natural that Bess favored a simple service at home. Sprinkled among the many famous individuals on the limited guest list for the funeral were Harry's barber, the maid, the painter, and the gardener. Commonplace people just like Harry and Bess.

Margaret wanted her mother to move to New York so that Bess could be closer to her and the grandchildren. By now, though, Bess was embedded at 219 North Delaware Street. The fond memories of her husband and all of her other family members remained in that home...she was not about to leave now.

For the next ten years, Bess did not retreat from life or politics. Although she missed her husband acutely, she nourished her lifelong friendships and even endorsed a few senatorial candidates. She was once asked to be an honorary chairman for Senator Tom Eagleton's reelection campaign. Totally surprising her cochairman, Stan Musial, Bess carried on a lively and informed conversation with him about politics, as well as about her favorite baseball team (a passion she shared with former sorority sister Grace Coolidge). Musial commented,

> She [Bess] knew every player in the Kansas City Royals starting lineup and had very strong opinions of the plusses and minuses of each one.[62]

The baseball Hall of Fame great had no idea he was talking with an excellent ex–third basewoman, still very much in touch with the game at ninety-one years of age.

Major General Harry Vaughan, her husband's former campaign treasurer, Senate aide, and ultimately President Truman's military aide, stayed in written contact with Bess over the years and kept her in touch with the latest doings in Washington. Bess found an excerpt from one of his letters particularly witty. It was during the politically charged Watergate scandal.

My dear Lady,

As you may have gathered from the press, Mr. Nixon is a very worried man. He is not sleeping very well. One night he had a dream that he was talking to George Washington. President Nixon said, "I'm in a bit of trouble. What would you advise me to do?" President Washington answered, "Tell the truth." President Nixon replied, "I'm afraid it's too late for that. I'll have to think of something else." The next night, he had a similar conversation with Harry Truman and asked the same question. President Truman responded, "Tell 'em to go to hell." President Nixon replied, "I have tried that but it does no good." On the third night, he confronted Abe Lincoln with yet again the same question. President Lincoln advised, "Take a night off and go to the theater."[63]

The story is poignant when you realize that (then Senator) Nixon was President Truman's least favorite Republican politician. Bess had endured numerous political smears from Nixon, all directed toward the Truman administration. Though confident in his own judgment, Truman left office with an approval rating of only 25 percent. During the wake of Watergate, Truman's overall approval rating received an enthusiastic upsurge.* The public had high esteem for Bess as well. When she was listed in the "top twenty most admired women" in America, an indifferent and baffled Bess responded, "I don't know why," which ended any thoughts of a possible interview.

Times had surely changed, and Bess found herself discouraged with her political party in the 1970s. She was quoted as saying, "It's not the Democratic Party I knew." Even when the Democrats returned to power and occupied the White House in 1977, Bess was a little hurt by the way President and Rosalynn Carter ignored her.

Bess had reached a point in her life where reminiscing about the past—only the good times, never the bad—began to fill more and more of her days. "There are so many good times and fun things to remember," she would say.

* Today, historians consistently rank Truman among the top five of all presidents.

Her sister-in-law May (George's widow) lived nearby and visited frequently. Bess cherished her memories and would often reread her husband's annual anniversary letters. An avid reader, she enjoyed biographies and popular novels before she turned to mysteries.

Margaret routinely phoned her mother three to four times a week. In addition to conversations about the grandchildren, they shared a love of books and particularly those with intricate plots. Genuinely proud of her daughter, Bess was never one to gush or lavish praise on anyone. So when Margaret published her first novel, *Murder in the White House*, it was no surprise the only accolade she received from her mother was simply, "Good job."*

Old age and crippling arthritis soon constricted Bess's life considerably. She was forced to walk with a cane, then a walker, and finally required a wheelchair. As her eyesight worsened, books were eventually read to her. Bess celebrated her ninety-sixth birthday; however, a subsequent fall and debilitating stroke mercilessly took away her voice, preventing her from verbally communicating with those around her.

During the final year of her life, Bess's health continued to deteriorate and she made frequent trips to the hospital. Less than four months before her ninety-eighth birthday in 1982, Bess quietly passed away at home.

Margaret understood and respected her mother's decision to have a funeral with the greatest of simplicity. By then only a few friends from Independence had survived, yet history could not be totally ignored. Sitting First Lady Nancy Reagan and former sorority sister Betty Ford, whose direct honesty endeared her to Bess, were invited. Rosalynn Carter attended, uninvited. Initially adamant that no photographs be taken inside the church, for the sake of history, Margaret consented to one photo of the three women sitting beside one another.

Per Harry Truman's orders, in addition to Bess's name and other pertinent information, her tombstone includes: "First Lady of the United States of America, April 12, 1945–January 20, 1953." The former president also approved the burial location, which was within view of

* Margaret Truman became the renowned author of over two dozen mystery novels, all of which were set in Washington, D.C. Additionally, she wrote biographies of her parents, *Bess W. Truman* and *Harry S. Truman*, plus other works of nonfiction.

the office he so often used at the Truman Library. At the time, Truman told his wife,

> I like the idea [regarding their interment site] because I may just want to get up some day and stroll into my office. And I can hear you saying, Harry—you oughtn't![64]

Twenty-six more years would pass before the Three Musketeers were once again united. When Margaret died in 2008, her ashes and those of her husband were interred in her parents' burial plot.

WHAT BESS TAUGHT ME

Bess maintained friendships with Eleanor Roosevelt and Edith Wilson, yet when it came to her sorority sisters, she most admired Elizabeth Monroe, one of the Executive Mansion's earliest residents (1817). The reason she gave was Elizabeth's ability to "virtually disappear from the White House for most of her husband's two terms." As much as Bess tried to do the same, she is historically considered one of the hardest-working White House hostesses. Despite her personal wishes, like so many of her fellow First Ladies, Bess graciously and tirelessly performed as expected and fulfilled her White House responsibilities.

I believe strength of character best describes Bess Wallace Truman. Against subtle yet powerful opposition, she forged a partnership of love and support with her spouse. Years later Harry accepted the vice presidential nomination, forcing Bess into a nightmarish life of public scrutiny. The exposure was so unbearable she would cry herself to sleep at night. During her early White House years, there was no doubt about her unhappiness or how her initial exclusion from the marital partnership created an intense and serious strain on the marriage.

Bess's rediscovery that her husband's life was her life as well, compelling her to work through her personal and painful discomfort, is another lesson I draw from her life. She demonstrated the importance and necessity of sharing all aspects of your partner's life. Inclusion and participation build the bridge that surmounts the challenges in a marriage; withdrawal or removal reinforces only one half of the alliance and leaves the structure as a whole vulnerable to decay and dissolution.

9

First Lady—But Wife First

MAMIE EISENHOWER

I never knew what a woman would want to be liberated from.

—Mamie Eisenhower

Born during the Victorian era on November 14, 1896, Mamie Geneva Doud Eisenhower has the distinction of being the last woman to become an American president's wife who was born in the nineteenth century. A true product of her time, she held that a woman's appropriate sphere included only home, family, clothing, and social entertaining.

> **#34 Mamie Doud Eisenhower**
>
> **Born**: November 14, 1896
>
> **Birthplace**: Boone, Iowa
>
> **Married**: 1916 (Dwight Eisenhower)
>
> **Children**: 2
>
> **White House Years:** 1953–1961
>
> **Died**: November 1, 1979 (82 years old)
>
> **Fact**: Moved over 25 times during her marriage
>
> **AKA**: The General's Wife

Known for her love of the color pink and famous little-girl bangs, Mamie grew into the role of model military wife before she became the embodiment of the efficient 1950s housewife. This represented an unusual evolution from her pampered and coddled upbringing, but it was a testament to a woman who knew her own mind and lived life her way. Although Mamie was brought up with (and believed in) the Victorian values of her childhood, she still managed to be headstrong, confident, and straightforward.

Like her sorority sisters Martha Washington, Anna Harrison, Margaret Taylor, and Julia Grant, she married a military leader, but Mamie was the only one fortunate enough to have had a spoiled and indulged childhood. For a baby who weighed merely four pounds at birth (her uncle said she looked like "a little picked chicken"), Mamie's little body somehow developed a spine of steel. A tiny infant who grew to just over five feet tall, with sparkling brown eyes and wavy brown hair, Mamie matured into a no-nonsense woman who was unapologetic about who she was.

Married at nineteen, Mamie was ill prepared for the sacrifices, loneliness, and efficiency demanded by military life. She had never even made her own bed and knew nothing whatsoever about cooking, a philosophy attributed to her mother, who believed that "if you don't learn to cook, no one will ask you to do it."[1] Instead, Mamie learned how to run a household with servants, manage domestic finances, and take her rightful place in society (hers was a social circle where men always wore jackets outside the home).

So how exactly did a young debutante (otherwise known as Miss Doud) and David Dwight Eisenhower (who went by his middle name or his nickname, Ike), a military cadet who grew up on the wrong side of the tracks in a family on the brink of poverty, maintain a successful marriage for over fifty-two years? According to Susan Eisenhower, Mamie's granddaughter and biographer, "Mamie and Ike's very polarity would be the basis of their volatile but electric lifelong attraction."*

Born in Boone, Iowa, the second of four children, Mamie was eight years old when her wealthy businessman father, John Sheldon Doud, semi-retired to Colorado. The family first lived in Pueblo, then Colorado Springs, and finally settled down in Denver. He was only thirty-four and, courtesy of his meat-packing business, had already amassed a fortune amounting to more than one million dollars.

John had married Elvira Carlson when she was only sixteen. At the time they moved to Colorado, Elvira† was twenty-six and the mother

* Susan also confirmed that her grandmother was indeed christened "Mamie," not "Mary," contrary to some accounts.

† Sometimes spelled Elivera.

of four daughters between the ages of two and nine. A religious woman whose parents had emigrated from Sweden in 1868, Elvira adhered to the strict doctrines of the Swedish Evangelical Church her entire life. In addition to attending Sunday services, the family held daily Bible readings every morning and evening.

Mamie's maternal grandfather, Carl Carlson, was a successful businessman influential in Republican politics. Her paternal grandfather helped found the town of Guilford, Connecticut, which prompted Mamie's comment,

> I've never had any social ambitions, I didn't have to. I had my place in this world and I knew it. I came from a long family of Americans. I didn't have to prove anything.[2]

The Douds regularly spent their winters in San Antonio, Texas; the family lived a comfortable, privileged life, typical for their era and social circumstances. Though Mamie's formal education was sporadic, she did attend public schools in both Denver and Colorado Springs as well as high school in San Antonio. John Doud had no problem taking his girls out of school to accommodate their travel schedule. Besides, the two areas relevant to young women at that time were covered by Mamie's attendance at Miss Wolcott's School for girls, an elite finishing school, and Miss Hayden's Dance School.

What the Doud girls lacked was an abundance of good health. Eleanor, Mamie's older sister, suffered from a serious heart ailment. From the time she was eight years old she required round-the-clock nurses, and lived her short life as an invalid. Mamie herself developed a rheumatic heart before her tenth birthday and experienced other "debilitating bouts of sickness" her entire life.

Apparently Doud missed having a son around the house, since Mamie's younger sisters, Ida Mae and Mabel Frances, were incongruously nicknamed Buster and Mike. Reflecting on her youth, Mamie said, "Our whole life was centered around [our] family." Having fun was vital, and they latched onto any pretext to celebrate. Then in January of 1912, Eleanor died at the age of seventeen, leaving the family heartsick. Even worse, Eleanor's burial had to be delayed until spring because the winter weather was so severe that year.*

Every day prior to the burial, Elvira would take her daughters on a streetcar "just a half block away with one change," as Mamie recalled, to the cemetery. After Eleanor's interment they visited weekly, bringing fresh flowers for the grave. Years later, Mamie confessed that she thought it was "very wrong for parents to make young children focus on death so much."[3]

Over the next few years Mamie became one of Denver's most captivating belles. With a distinguished sense of style and absolute femininity she attracted several admiring beaus, and the *Denver Post* routinely ran photos and articles about the engaging Miss Doud. At age nineteen, Mamie made her debut in her family's San Antonio home. A short time later, during a visit with family friends at Fort Sam Houston, she met second lieutenant Dwight Eisenhower, a recent graduate of West Point. According to Mamie, he had broad shoulders and was "the handsomest man" she had ever met. A "far cry from the society boys" vying for her attention, Ike began courting her as well.

According to Ike, he was "intrigued by her appearance" and described Mamie as a "vivacious and attractive girl, smaller than average, saucy in the look about the face and in her whole attitude."[4] Taken with her charm, Ike phoned Mamie the next day. However, her social calendar was so full it was several weeks before the two finally went out. "What did he expect?" Mamie questioned in amazement. "I was booked solid. It was my debutante year!"[5] Repeatedly, Ike would visit with her parents on their veranda until Mamie returned from one of her many outings.

Soon thereafter, Mamie stopped accepting other invitations. Somewhat to everyone's surprise, her wealthy "all-girl family" somehow managed to complement rather than clash with the semi-impoverished "all-boy family" of the Eisenhower clan (Ike had six brothers). The Eisenhowers' motto was "Sink or swim, survive or perish."

There was something very special about the dashing twenty-four-year-old lieutenant who was still in debt to his father and earned only

* Her body was kept in a crypt at the Fairmount Cemetery until the ground thawed and she could be permanently interred.

$141.67 a month! According to historian Bill Harris, the couple's favorite dining spot was a local Mexican restaurant where the two could "feast on chili and enchiladas for $1.25."[6]

For Christmas in 1915, Ike gave Mamie a silver box with her initials engraved on it—a true sign of his affection. Ike was quick to point out that he would be unable to return the engraved present. Nevertheless, Mamie understood that her father's permission was required before accepting such a gift (which her father did allow her to keep).

Now steadily courting, Ike was still reserved in describing his relationship with Mamie. In a letter to a friend, he wrote,

> The girl I run around with is named Miss Doud...pretty nice—but awful strong for society—which often bores me. But we get along well together and I am at her house whenever I am off duty—whether it's morning—noon—night. Her mother and sisters are fine—and we have lots of fun together.[7]

As Mamie recalled there was no formal proposal; however, "We took it for granted that we'd marry." They decided to get officially engaged on Valentine's Day 1916, and in accordance with West Point tradition, Mamie was to be given a miniature of her fiancé's class ring. Per Susan Eisenhower, however, Mamie wanted "a miniature of nothing." Therefore, Ike gave and Mamie wore a huge copy of "the real thing." That only occurred after Mr. Doud returned home from a business trip the following month and gave his consent.

Unlike some other parents of future First Ladies (Jane Pierce, Julia Grant, Grace Coolidge, and Bess Truman, for example), the Douds liked Eisenhower. However, like Anna Harrison's father, Mr. Doud was very concerned about his future son-in-law's career. Mamie took her comfortable life for granted, whereas military life came with hardships she could have no way of foreseeing. Cramped living quarters and constant household moves, no permanent home, loneliness, and financial limitations would be part of the lifestyle she could expect.

Understanding that the young couple was "wild about each other" (to quote Mamie, "All I wanted was that man!"), her father agreed. However, he forewarned his daughter that she "would have to live within her husband's means," and he would not give her an allowance. Mr. Doud then conceded that "there was no reason why scrimping and saving would not lay a foundation for an enduring marriage."[8]

Looking ahead, Eisenhower applied for and was accepted into the army's aviation program, which would mean a fifty percent increase in his monthly earnings. Mr. Doud, however, was alarmed, regardless of the monetary advantage. Only thirty years had passed since the Wright Brothers' initial flight at Kitty Hawk, and he believed flying was a "dangerous and experimental endeavor." Doud said he would rescind his marriage approval if Ike became an aviator. Ike reassessed the matter and deferred his decision. Although aviation was his preference, he remained in the army corps. Doud later went on to say that the family was immensely relieved, as Mamie "raised quite a fuss" over her father's disapproval.

Incurring additional debt, Ike bought his fiancée a one-and-one-half-carat diamond set in platinum, and the couple set a November wedding date. Years later Ike reminisced about his financial sacrifice.

> I stopped smoking ready-made cigarettes, which were about $1.00 a carton, and went back to rolling my own.[9]

A good poker player, Ike managed to pay off the engagement ring and obligation to his father from his winnings.

During their engagement period, Mexico was enmeshed in a civil war. Mexican rebels began to raid U.S. border towns, including San Antonio, Texas, where Ike was stationed. In addition to the National Guard, the army's General Pershing was called in to deal with the dangerous situation. Mamie was naturally concerned for Ike's safety; as soon as she learned her sweetheart had managed to get a ten-day leave, Mamie immediately notified her parents that the wedding would be moved up.

Far more was involved than simply the planning and preparation for their daughter's wedding. Early in the twentieth century, when a socialite rushed into marriage, it usually meant she "had" to marry—in other words, she was pregnant. Concerned about the speculation and gossip a hurried wedding would generate, the Douds were flabbergasted. And so much would have to change. Instead of a church wedding, the ceremony would have to take place at home. As opposed to a custom-made gown, Mamie would have to purchase an off-the-rack dress, and her hope chest would remain unfinished. Defiantly, Mamie would not back down; luckily for her, the Douds adored Ike and at length acquiesced.

At twelve noon on July 1, 1916, Mamie married twenty-five-year-old, recently promoted second lieutenant Dwight Eisenhower. The newlyweds had something else to celebrate as well. Ike's promotion came with a twenty-dollar-a-month pay increase! After a few days in El Dorado Springs, a small resort near Denver, the couple traveled to Abilene, Kansas, to spend a few days with Ike's parents.

When Mamie recalled her first visit with her new in-laws, she said she thought it was "kind of strange" to meet her father-in-law in "shirtsleeves" at the train station. Mamie soon discovered other odd behaviors. Her mother-in-law, with the help of her young sons, did all the housecleaning and cooking for the family. After that shocking revelation, she learned that fried chicken was on the evening's menu. Chicken that was *fried*? Mamie exclaimed, "I'd never heard of such a thing!"[10] To her astonishment, the Eisenhowers went to bed early, got up very early, and eschewed alcohol and cards. With sublime understatement, she concluded, "They were completely different from my family."

Mamie's first encounter with army life followed soon thereafter when she and Ike settled into a two-room accommodation in San Antonio. Fortunately, Ike knew how to cook and even liked to do so. Although Ike was the family's culinary expert, Mamie did eventually learn enough to prepare a meal. As provost marshal of the post, Ike worked long into the night. Less than a month into her marriage, Mamie experienced the first of countless long and lonely evenings by herself. For a young woman who had *never* spent a night alone in a house, the experience must have been very unsettling. Ike soon told Mamie something she could never disregard or forget:

> Mamie, there is one thing you must understand—My duty will always come first. You come second.[11]

As Mamie put it years later, "I made my own bed," and she was resolved to make the best of it—which she did. It soon became obvious that Mamie was an immeasurable asset to both Ike's career and his well-being.

By the end of the year Mamie was pregnant; shortly thereafter, President Wilson urged Congress to declare war against Germany. World War I had been raging in Europe for nearly three years, and Ike's desire to serve on the front line was unequivocal. Instead, he was assigned to train officer candidates at Camp Oglethorpe, Georgia. While many fathers-to-be would have been relieved, Ike was disappointed. Meanwhile, Mamie stayed in San Antonio and prepared for the birth of her first child. Elvira Doud made the first of many trips to San Antonio to be with and assist her daughter.

When Mamie went into labor, she and her mother had to catch a ride on a "mule-drawn wooden wagon" to Fort Sam Houston's infirmary, a facility with no maternity provisions. Within hours she gave birth to a son who was immediately nicknamed Little Ike, which was soon shortened to Ikky.* Some say the name came from "diapers" while others claim it was Grandma Doud's description of the hospital surroundings in which the child was born. In any case, three days passed before Ikky's father, then on maneuvers, learned of his son's birth.

That Christmas Mamie caught a bad cold, which went into a severe case of pneumonia. It was before the discovery of antibiotics and as Mamie recollected, "You either came through or you didn't." Ike was given three days of emergency leave to visit his ailing wife and see his newborn son for the first time. After her husband's departure, a frail Mamie took Ikky and went to her parents' Denver home to recuperate.

Although Ike's repeated pleas to be sent to the front line in France were ignored, he continued to work hard and rarely saw his family. He was rewarded with a promotion to lieutenant colonel in recognition of his service. Amid rumors of an armistice, Ike finally received orders that he would embark for France on November 18, 1919. In the meantime, Mamie learned that her younger sister Buster had developed a kidney infection, which progressed rapidly and took her

* Dwight Doud Eisenhower (1917–1921); John Sheldon Doud Eisenhower (1922–present).

life on November 9. Duty prevented Ike from accompanying his wife to her sister's burial; after the funeral Mamie planned to stay with her parents while Ike was away. During the emotional family gathering, however, Mamie was gratified to hear some redeeming news. On November 11, an armistice had finally been signed.

With the war over, Mamie looked forward to living with both her baby son *and* absent husband. Ike had barely seen Ikky during the first seven months of his life, and the couple had spent less than half of their marriage together. Ordered to report to Camp Meade in Maryland (now known as Fort Meade), Ike found a small place to live. Actually the space consisted of a one-room walkup. Ikky temporarily went to live with Mamie's parents while Ike and Mamie searched for something more suitable—which they never located. Mamie found herself living in a tiny room, with no electricity from 6:00 A.M. to 6:00 P.M. due to power shortages. While Ike continued to work extraordinarily long hours, Mamie sat alone, completely isolated, waiting for him to return home. When he did, they would eat a late dinner at a local boarding house. Missing her son terribly and unable to cope with her dismal surroundings, at the end of one month, Mamie told Ike she "couldn't take it any longer" and returned to her parents' home. Mamie confessed years later that she felt remorse for (as she put it) "[having] given up and thrown in the sponge."

The separation was once again difficult on both of them and caused a great strain on the couple's marriage. Ike adored his in-laws; however, he wanted his wife with him and resented her frequent trips home. Months later, the army found some wartime barracks and Ike qualified for one, but he had to furnish it and make the necessary improvements with his own funds. Mamie returned to help remodel the dilapidated quarters. Eight hundred dollars later Ike and some friends had refinished the floors, partitioned the rooms, and installed a kitchen and bath.

Using necessity combined with ingenuity, Mamie made a dressing table with used orange crates, which she covered with thumbtacked upholstery fabric. Tattered old furniture from a Red Cross building helped populate their meager quarters. Sleeping on army cots concealed with "a Japanese print material," at long last the couple once again shared a home. Best of all, Ikky returned, and for the first time in more than eighteen months, Mamie had her family unit together.

One advantage of army post living was the many friendships that developed from common experiences. Wives helped one another out and understood firsthand the hardships they all experienced. During their stay at Camp Meade, Bea and George Patton (who ultimately became a four-star general) were next-door neighbors. Ike and George developed a camaraderie during their twice-weekly poker games.

Entertaining was expected in the service and came with high standards. Mamie entertained so frequently their quarters became known as Club Eisenhower. Ikky was declared Mascot of the Corps and given a Tank Corps uniform made expressly for him. The traditional Sunday open house buffets Mamie held were in addition to potluck dinners, card games, and songfests. As a young girl, Mamie took piano lessons and was known to have an excellent ear. A rented piano soon became a necessary piece of furniture.

Wherever Mamie lived, she created the gaiety and amusement she grew up with. Her friendliness, concern for others, and polished manner made her the consummate hostess—a high compliment, especially considering the Eisenhowers always struggled with finances. Responsible for the family budget, Mamie made a point of scrutinizing everything that dealt with her home. Sometimes she had only seventy-five cents until payday. She proudly admitted, "I would squeeze a dollar until the eagle screamed."

Social faux pas were rare for Mamie; however, she was young and still had some things to learn when several Washington dignitaries visited Camp Meade. Newton Baker, then secretary of war, asked Mamie what she thought her husband was good at. "My, he plays an awfully good game of poker," she replied. Reportedly, Ike was "furious." In an attempt to defend herself Mamie shouted at her husband, "But everybody knows you're a good soldier!"[12]

Although her experience at Camp Meade began on a sour note, Mamie and Ike eventually made it a home where together they enjoyed a full and rewarding family life. Then on January 2, 1921, a date Mamie later claimed she never remembered, her life at Camp Meade was overshadowed with a sadness that would never be erased.

Three-year-old Ikky became ill with a high temperature and was soon hospitalized and put in quarantine. Then meningitis set in. Devastated and helpless, Mamie was at home fighting a terrible cold which was approaching pneumonia. Ultimately, Ike was allowed into his son's hospital room to hold and comfort his child. Without warning, Ikky died in his father's arms; the cause was scarlet fever. He was buried in Colorado next to his aunts Eleanor and Buster Doud.

Looking back, Mamie recalled, "We never talked about it. I did not ask him [Ike], because it was something that hurt him so badly." Ike later acknowledged that he "never fully recovered from his son's death" and said of Mamie, "The loss was heartbreaking and her grief, in turn, would have broken the hardest heart."[13]

The Eisenhowers' anguish and sorrow were not diminished by either their silence or the passage of time. Up until his own death, regardless of where in the world he was (including in the midst of war), Ike sent Mamie yellow flowers (Ikky's favorite color) on the anniversary of his son's birth. Ike remarked, "No matter what activities and preoccupations there were we could never forget the death of the boy." They chose to remember his birth, not his passing.

Ten months later Mamie was again pregnant, and that fall (1921) Brigadier General Fox Conner asked Ike to be his executive officer for the infantry brigade in Panama. Mamie had traveled to Panama with her parents years earlier and was familiar with the insect-infested region. During the previous twenty years, thousands had died there from yellow fever and malaria—hardly a resounding endorsement. A move to Panama would test every fiber of Mamie's strength and resolve, as she was understandably anxious to ensure her second child's safe and healthy birth. Not wishing to repeat her perceived initial failure at Camp Meade, and possibly to prove her faith in her spouse, Mamie, despite her misgivings, agreed to transfer to Panama with Ike.

Upon their arrival, the Eisenhowers moved into a house that was built in the early 1900s and had not been occupied for nearly a decade. Not only was it infested with cockroaches, lizards, and snakes, the porch was collapsing from damp and mildew. Mamie vividly remembered their first night in Panama: "A rat gnawed on the leg of a nearby chair all night long."[14] In addition to fumigating their mattress weekly, they had to set the legs of their bed in cans of kerosene to kill bedbugs that infested their bed. Mildew on their clothing and furniture was somewhat reduced by the use of electric lightbulbs.

Because she was frightened by "the bats that crawled under the door at night and flew around the room" and "the huge cockroaches that jumped at you from the top of the door," Mamie reported that General Conner's wife "thought she [Mamie] was a namby-pamby." In her defense Mamie responded, "Anyway...I wasn't feeling my best." I would think not! To her credit, by late May, Mamie had "achieved an uneasy peace with her surroundings."[15]

There was no maternity facility available, and Mamie, along with other army wives, organized parties and picnics to raise private funds for a much-needed clinic to benefit enlisted men's expectant wives. In addition to raising the one thousand dollars needed to make the clinic a reality, the women sanitized a small building and converted it into a habitable venue. Although she was prepared to give birth in the local clinic she had helped establish, as soon as her parents arrived for a visit they insisted Mamie return to Denver for the delivery of their grandchild.

As Mamie described it, John Eisenhower—named in honor of his maternal grandfather—was "literally laughed into the world" on August 3, 1922. Ike arrived in the United States just prior to his son's birth. At his in-laws' home, the night before the baby was born, Ike read aloud to his wife and Mamie was frequently overcome with laughter at Ring Lardner's short story. Suddenly, her water broke and Mamie went into instantaneous labor. Elvira Doud, aka Nana, was so concerned the car engine would wake the Douds' neighbors, thus "alerting them to the event," Nana talked her son-in-law into "rolling the car out of the driveway before starting it." Ike pushed the car down the driveway then hurriedly jumped in and hit the gas. The car did not move. He pushed the gas pedal harder and harder, but to no avail. Once again engulfed in laughter, Mamie reminded her husband that "you have to start the ignition first."

When Mamie returned to Panama, now with an infant son and a nurse (paid for by her parents and at their insistence to help with the baby), life in the jungle proved more draining than ever before. Ike was either working away from home for weeks at a time or discussing work long into the night with his mentor, General Conner. Depressed, unable to sleep at night and suffering digestive problems, Mamie made the decision to return to her parents' home. Although Ike "begged her" to stay, Mamie argued,

> There was something about the tropics that got to me. I was down to skin and bones and hollow-eyed; so ill I'd have to walk all night long.[16]

During her recuperation, Mamie took a long hard look at her marriage and what it meant to be a good soldier's wife. Able to fully grasp her husband's perspective, Mamie at last came to terms with it.

> He was always dedicated, serious and purposeful about his job. *Nothing* came before his duty. I was forced to match his spirit of personal sacrifice as best I could.[17]

This proved to be a major turning point in Mamie's life. At the age of twenty-five, she made the decision to recommit herself to her husband and their marriage. She would have to unequivocally acquiesce to everything required by her husband's career, which she ultimately called "our career." That meant she would have to adapt to endless hours alone, complain even less than before, make a greater effort to share her husband's recreational interests, and make certain she was socially sophisticated. Basically she would have to be satisfied with every aspect of her husband's life that touched on hers.

Steadfast in her pledge to stay married and with a new sense of dedication to her spouse, Mamie recommitted herself to Ike and his lifestyle. She was determined to focus on the better parts of her life and celebrate her husband's accomplishments, which were destined to be many. At the end of his Panamanian tour, Ike was presented with the Distinguished Service Medal.

Over the next fifteen years, Mamie would make a home for her family in locations including Baltimore, Maryland; Fort Logan in Colorado; Fort Leavenworth in Kansas; Fort Benning in Georgia; the

Wyoming Apartments in Washington, D.C.; Paris, France; back to Washington, D.C.; the Philippines; the Presidio in San Francisco; Fort Lewis in Washington; Fort Sam Houston in Texas; Fort Meyer in Virginia; and the Wardman Park Hotel in Washington, D.C. More than once the family moved away from, and later moved back to, the same location, though not ever the same accommodations twice. "I've kept house in everything but an igloo," Mamie declared.

One historical account claims Mamie moved seven times in one year. Another alleges she relocated twenty-five to twenty-seven times before occupying the White House. In his book, *The First Ladies Fact Book*, historian Bill Harris made an effort to document all of the various residences the Eisenhowers called home over the years. Mamie had long since forgotten many of them. She did comment, however, that "I'd like to be a homebody, but I'm really just a movebody."[18]

Regardless of his assigned post or position, Ike continued to do an outstanding job and garnered glowing written commendations. He received a permanent rank of major, graduated from Infantry Tank School, and ranked first in his class of 275 from Command and General Staff School. At the same time Mamie, along with other wives of advanced army school graduates, received acknowledgement in the form of a PHT diploma (Pushing Hubby Through).

While the Eisenhowers were living in the United States, newspapers and other venues frequently published articles about them, particularly with respect to Mamie's hostess skills. For regular entertaining, Mamie had it down to a science. First she planned a menu and then calculated its entire cost. She did this repeatedly until she designed a collection of several set menus. Current cash flow would determine which menu Mamie would use.

Even while she was living in Paris, occasionally the *New York Herald* and other newspapers made note of Mamie's entertaining, including the following excerpt from an article in the *Chicago Tribune*:

> One of the largest parties...was given by Major and Mrs. Dwight D. Eisenhower...Major and Mrs. Dwight D. Eisenhower entertained a few friends [sixteen couples] yesterday evening commencing with a cocktail party at their home in the quai d'Auteuil.[19]

Travel and entertaining, interspersed with prolonged and painful separations, became the fabric of their lives. After Ike's discharge from Paris and before returning to Washington, D.C., the Eisenhowers enjoyed an exciting and interesting seventeen-day vacation that took them over eighteen hundred miles through four countries (Italy, Belgium, Germany, and Switzerland). It was not uncommon for them to dine with kings, queens, and heads of state. In June 1929, in reinforcement of her pledge to her marriage, Mamie wrote home,

> The weather is marvelous now and one forgets the long bad weather [of the past]. If we couldn't forget some of the bad things in this life, we wouldn't have the courage to continue, would we?[20]

Several months later the stock market crashed, devastating countless Americans.

Ike was assigned to a project for the War Department in Washington. Mamie was no doubt grateful her husband had the benefit of stable income; nonetheless, she was on a tight budget. Their rent at the Wyoming Apartments for a three-bedroom flat was $130 a month, plus utilities, telephone, and food (and don't forget Ike's $5 a week for incidentals). (Now converted to condominiums, a *one*-bedroom unit in the Wyoming rents for more than $1,900 a month.) Even so, Elvira's fundamental point of view about housekeeping still influenced her daughter's life, and John Doud once again paid for someone, this time a maid, to help Mamie.

As the Depression deepened, Ike was looking at a ten percent pay cut. As in every other city across the country, homeless individuals and families were forced to live on the streets of Washington. With twenty-eight vacancies (out of 105 units), the Wyoming Apartments went into receivership, though this did not immediately affect the Eisenhowers. The 1932 election was observed with great vigilance by most Americans, including Mamie. Her interest was unusual among "professional soldier families"; the army held that officers and their wives, in particular, did not "vote any political opinion."

When Franklin D. Roosevelt won the presidential election, he retained General Douglas MacArthur as his chief of staff. In turn, with no salary increase, Ike was appointed MacArthur's personal assistant and ultimately his chief of staff. Life in Washington remained pretty much the same for the Eisenhowers. Mamie continued to host card parties and evening get-togethers, albeit on a more reserved and economical basis. They maintained a close circle of friends and Ike continued to work endlessly long hours.

Respected for his work ethic and knowledge, Ike was offered a very enticing civilian position as military correspondent for a newspaper chain. Although the offer came with a monetary increase of *five times* his three thousand dollar annual salary, it was Mamie who best understood her husband's needs. She told him,

> I don't think you'd be happy. This is your life, and you know it...we have other personal things that make up for lack of currency.[21]

As the New Deal began to help alleviate the effects of the Depression, Mamie noted her appreciation. "We have a good, warm home and plenty to wear—and good friends...a lot to be thankful for." A little thing like sleeping in was an added pleasure. Both Eisenhowers liked to sleep late and on those Sundays when Ike and Mamie were not required to make formal protocol visits, John remembered,

> My parents had the most wonderful ways of spending Sunday. They wouldn't move a muscle until 5:00 in the afternoon.[22]

An even bigger pleasure was that the cook would have the day off and "Dad would do all the cooking."

Not long thereafter, Ike received a substantial pay increase and now had sufficient prominence to appoint his own personal staff officer. Becoming a lieutenant colonel may have sounded beneficial on the surface; however, it came with considerable anguish and grief. Ike was ordered to the Philippines to assist General MacArthur in his new position as chief military adviser to the Philippine government. With no limit on her husband's length of tour, one can only imagine Mamie's torment. To say she was terrified of once again living in the tropics was an understatement! Not only that, John was quickly approaching adolescence and both mother and, especially, son needed Ike's presence. Still, Mamie was adamant in her decision to remain in Washington.

For the next year, Mamie did her best to carry on and in fact made a life for herself. Friends frequently entertained her in their homes or escorted her to various events and parties. Ike, on the other hand, found the "forced separation from his family intolerable." Mamie confirmed his letters were "far from cheerful."

Twenty years had passed and Mamie was now well versed in the difficult and sometimes unacknowledged commitment to service that army families make to their country. Sacrifice and pain are often irrefutable consequences that stem from their duty, and although locations may change, little else does.

Living apart once again put Mamie face to face with her decision to stay married to her husband. After one year, it became apparent Ike would not be returning home. Therefore, after packing and putting her personal belongings in storage—yet again—in October of 1936 Mamie and John made the twenty-seven day journey to Manila via the army transport *Grant*. Years later she explained simply, "Ike was my career."

Home was now a two-room suite in the Manila Hotel. While John went to a boarding school in the mountains, Mamie and Ike dealt with the adjustments that both were required to continually make after their long separation. In a letter to her parents, Mamie acknowledged:

> You know I am pretty level-headed about what I know is right. I made a terrible mistake in not coming here with Ike. It's up to me to rectify lots of things...[I realize that] the only way I can get along with him is to give him his own way *constantly*.[23]

The choice was hers to make and for Mamie, it was more than simply getting reacquainted with her absent husband. She also had to contend with the tropical heat (their quarters were not air-conditioned), sleeping under mosquito nets (being claustrophobic did not help), typhoons and earthquakes ("the darn things scared [her] pink"), and the inconvenience of having to boil fresh vegetables before you could eat them.

Unfortunately Mamie's health was never robust and in 1938 it was determined that she needed surgery (some say for her gall bladder, others contend it was gynecological). Ike was granted a three-month leave and because of Mamie's fear of flying—she called herself a "sissy about airplanes"—the couple spent almost two-thirds of that time traveling by boat to and from the United States for her operation. Upon their return to the islands, their separate spheres of marital responsibility, home for Mamie and work for Ike, resumed.

Ike was not one to share the details of his work. Mamie confirmed,

> I never felt like I had to help Ike in any way, except in making as nice a family life as possible. I thought he was perfectly capable of paddling his own canoe. It just never occurred to me to give him any advice on his business. That was his.[24]

While Mamie returned to her primary job of maintaining the home, Ike found himself responsible for establishing the Philippine Air Corps, a position that gave him the opportunity to fulfill one of his earlier aspirations. He completed flight training instruction, received a pilot's license, and thereafter narrowly escaped two potentially fatal flying accidents.*

In common with most things in life, living in the Philippines had its pros and cons. John was doing well in a good school and Mamie admitted,

> We've been financially on easy street for the first time in our married life—having pretty near anything we wish.[25]

Yet they had been there for four years and Mamie yearned to return to the United States. Global events reinforced her wishes. With the potential of threatening the world's freedom and safety, another Great War (World War II) had already been launched in Europe. Japan had conquered Manchuria and was preparing to invade northern China. Meanwhile Mussolini and Hitler were preparing for their own

* Eisenhower was the first president to receive a pilot's license.

destructive and devastating crusade, the likes of which the world had never seen.

Hitler had his sympathizers, but Ike was not one of them. The Jewish community in Manila knew of Ike's intense opposition to the dictator. They offered him a job relocating Jewish refugees in the Philippines, Southeast Asia, and anywhere else they had been established. The offer came with an annual salary of sixty thousand dollars. To sweeten the offer even more, three hundred thousand dollars would be placed into escrow, and Ike could draw on it anytime.

Nevertheless, it was never about money for Ike. The army was his life, and service during war, which he believed would be inevitable for the United States, was his commitment. Years later, looking back on his decision, Ike shared with his son that the offer "had few temptations" for him. It was the army that "brought [him] into contact with men of ability, honor, and a sense of high dedication to their country." When it came to promotion or lack thereof, he "refused to bother [his] head" about it. Ike went on to say,

> The real satisfaction was for a man who did the best he could. My ambition in the Army was to make everybody regretful when I was ordered to other duty.[26]

Ike achieved his ambition time and time again. When he was summoned from the Philippines back to Fort Lewis, outside of Seattle, General MacArthur wrote to Ike commending his "superior professional ability, unswerving loyalty and unselfish devotion to duty... I cannot tell you how deeply I regret your leaving."

Devoid of accolades or acknowledgement for *her* devotion to duty, Mamie geared up for another transfer. She immersed herself in the familiar activities of packing the household and saying goodbye to dear friends, and prepared to readjust to the army's code of behavior. Although she was thrilled to be back in the States, it had been over ten years since Mamie had lived on an army post. She had almost forgotten how army wives typically seemed "more vested in their husbands' status" than women living outside of the military.

Heavy scrutiny, gossip, and petty rivalries existed among some of the women. As an example, instead of using a woman's first name, many referred to the wives of the top brass as Mrs. General. Never mindful of rank herself, Mamie took umbrage to this practice and reminded a friend,

> You know Janie [Howard], you don't have any rank, it is your husband [who does].[27]

During Mamie's short stay at Fort Lewis, she returned to her practice of entertaining large groups at the drop of a hat. Reportedly she had already invited some fifty people to their new home, with "only...about 90 more people to entertain," when Ike was ordered to San Antonio. This move included a promotion to colonel and made him responsible for all military installations in the northwestern United States.

The Eisenhowers arrived in San Antonio on their twenty-fifth wedding anniversary (July 1, 1941), the same day eighteen-year-old John reported for duty at West Point. Both Mamie and Ike had been steadfast in their opinion that John needed to make the decision for himself. Other colleges were open and available to him, and as Ike reminded his son, the army had a restrictive seniority system. Believing the rank of colonel would in fact be his own highest rank, Ike told his son, "We're talking about a career, not miracles."

It was not a miracle, but rather intense energy, technical competence, and focused drive that once again propelled Ike beyond his imagined limitations. In October, he achieved the rank of general. When her husband received his first star, Mamie described it as her "proudest moment."

Before Ike had an opportunity to bask in his new position, the Japanese bombed Guam, the Philippines, and Pearl Harbor. It was December 7, 1941, "a date which will live in infamy," as President Roosevelt proclaimed. The very next day, the United States declared war against Japan and General George Marshall wanted Ike to report immediately to the War Department back in Washington. Like all of her other brave military sisters, Mamie had no idea when she would once again share a dwelling with her husband.

Although Ike was unable to return home to San Antonio for Christmas, Mamie was grateful to learn that her husband's assignment in Washington, D.C., was now permanent—at least for the time being. Familiar with the routine of packing and the army's grueling policy requiring careful documentation of each item, Mamie confessed, "I feel like a football—kicked from place to place." While she organized and packed daily necessities in preparation for moving, Mamie put their valuable belongings and almost everything else in storage.

She was relocating from a spacious five-bedroom home in San Antonio to a small one-bedroom apartment in Washington's Wardman Tower, directly above a ballroom whose music penetrated their apartment. Mamie had no idea that the most difficult years of her married life were just beginning. One small part of the hardship was that over a decade would pass before she would see her stored personal belongings again.

To the complete astonishment of both Eisenhowers, Ike was awarded his second star at the end of May 1942. With his increased rank and salary, they moved into a beautiful brick home at Fort Myer, Virginia. One fleeting month later, Ike was promoted to commanding general of the European theater of operations, requiring his presence in Europe. Four short months after that, he was promoted to commander in chief of Allied forces in North Africa.

Once again Mamie had to say goodbye to her Europe-bound spouse for an undetermined amount of time. The country was at war, and on top of worrying about her husband's safety, Mamie was given one week to move! As she later recalled,

> They didn't care where I went. They ordered Ike away; and I was ordered off the [Fort Myer] post.[28]

Fortunately Mamie caught a break and had the opportunity to move back into the Wardman Tower. Only this time she shared an apartment with Ruth Butcher (whose husband, Harry, was a naval aide to Ike) and Ruth's elementary school–age daughter. Along with the other military wives, Mamie did her best to stay occupied. In addition to participating in potluck suppers, mah-jongg, and bridge games, Mamie volunteered at the Red Cross and was a waitress at the Soldiers, Sailors and Marines canteen. Being busy was not, however, a substitute for having a husband and family at home.

Washington's punishing heat was an added trial for Mamie (the apartment was not air-conditioned); she was already beset by lonesomeness and the ever-present concern about Ike in the war zone. To add insult to injury, she suffered from food allergies and digestive ailments. Looking back on those grueling times, Mamie recalled, "We [referring to other army wives] had one little ration card [each], and we never got a decent meal unless we all got together and everybody put her things in."[29]

Distance and separation once again added heavily to Ike's already fierce pressures and intense stress. His family was continually on his mind and in no way far from his heart. As a testament to Mamie's dutifulness and devotion, Ike wrote his wife,

> How I wish you were living here. You cannot imagine how much you added to my efficiency in the hard months in Washington. Even I didn't realize it then; at least not fully—but I do now, and I'm grateful to you.

In another letter, he goes on to say, "Well sweet—I miss you dreadfully. This job would be much easier if I had you to come home to. Don't forget me!" Ike also shared his feelings about his sons:

> I do get so lonesome and anxious to hear from you both [Mamie and John]...send him my deepest affection. I'm so tied up with him it hurts.

> Tomorrow, Sept. 24th, Ikky would have been 25 years old. Seems rather unbelievable doesn't it? We could well have been grandparents by this time. I'm sorry we're not![30]

During the United States' involvement in World War II from 1942 to 1945, Mamie saw her husband only once. It was impossible for either spouse to fully appreciate the other's situation, and it was a trying and disturbing time for them both. Ike was responsible for mounting the largest allied coalition invasion in military history, coordinating the United States' efforts with those of the United Kingdom, France, Poland, Czechoslovakia, South Africa, Australia, New Zealand, Greece, and India. Meantime, Mamie was approaching another birthday alone and, more importantly, hearing rumors of a romance between Ike and his pretty female driver, Kay Summersby.

It would have been naïve to deny that proximity affords opportunities for marital misbehavior, especially in circumstances that would foster camaraderie or even fraternization. Then add the harrowing reality of being surrounded by an overwhelming world war. How does one cope with the demanding decisions, the grueling maneuvers, the daily dangers, the horror of seeing your friends and fellow soldiers mutilated or dying? More specifically, how does a general endure his hardships? Regarding his circumstances Ike wrote Mamie,

> Loneliness is the inescapable lot of a man holding such a job. Subordinates can advise, urge, help and pray, but only one man, in his own mind and heart, can decide "Do we, or do we not?" The stakes are the highest and the penalties are expressed in terms of loss of life...No man can always be right. So the struggle is to do one's best; to keep the brain and the conscience clear...; never to be swayed by unworthy motives or inconsequential reasons, but to strive to unearth the basic factors involved and then...to do one's duty. It is not always easy.[31]

Mamie was denied the opportunity to alleviate Ike's burdens or provide him with the stress-free home environment she had so graciously managed over the years. He was living under harsh conditions and unimaginable pressure, witnessing carnage day after troublesome day. Still, Mamie believed in her principled spouse. The following excerpts from Ike's letters to his wife speak louder than any speculation about Kay Summersby and Ike penned by history's authors.

> You will understand why your [forty-sixth] birthday letter had to be written some time in advance. You will also realize that I have

been busy—very busy…I truly feel that what the U.S. and the world are facing today is so much bigger than any one of us can even comprehend, that personal sacrifice and loss must not be allowed to overwhelm any of us.

I will be thinking with the deepest gratitude of the many happy hours and years you've given me. I am quite aware of the fact that I'm not always easy to live with—that frequently I'm irascible and even mean—and my gratitude is all the greater when I realize how often you have put up with me in spite of such traits…I wish my powers of expression were such as to make you understand that thoroughly—clearly and for always. I've never wanted another wife— you're mine, and for that reason I've been luckier than any other man.

You must understand that a newspaper man always has to draw on his imagination freely in order to give his stories "color." Actually I don't know what they print—but I do know that whatever it is—much of it is exaggeration. I've never known what it was to miss anyone so much as I've missed you and John these last weeks.

I love you all the time—don't go bothering your pretty head about WACS—etc. etc.* You just hold the thought that…I'm on the run to you the day the victorious army marches into Berlin!…It is easy for rumors to get started without the slightest foundation in fact…So I want you to know you can smile at anything.

Algiers, December 30, 1942

Sometimes I get to missing you so that I simply don't know what to do. As pressure mounts and strain increases, everyone begins

* The Women's Army Corps (WAC) was the women's branch of the U.S. Army. As an auxiliary unit, its name was converted by Congress in 1943 from its original, the Women's Army Auxiliary Corps (WAAC).

> to show the weaknesses in his makeup. It is up to the Commander to conceal this; above all to conceal doubt, fear, and distrust, especially in any subordinate, and to try to overcome the defects he finds around him. When the strain is long continued the commander gets to feeling more and more alone and lonesome, and his mind instinctively turns to something or someone that could help. This, of course is not well explained—but I mean only to tell you that constantly I think of you as someone who could provide the counterbalance for me—. No one else in the world could ever fill your place with me—and that is the reason I need you. Maybe a simpler explanation is merely that I LOVE YOU!! which I do, always. Never forget that.[32]

Implications and gossip of an affair Ike allegedly had with Kay Summersby haunted Mamie for many years. Cruelly enough, rumors even resurfaced during the last years of her life, long after Ike had passed away. Until her dying day, Mamie never believed the speculation. Although she was terribly hurt and humiliated by the allegations, she always behaved with the quiet dignity expected of a lady from her social class, and acted as if the entire matter were a nonissue.

Ike was proud of his wife's demeanor and told her so, more than once. He wrote lovingly,

> I do have time to tell you again that I'm prouder of you every time someone brings me news of the way you handle yourself—of the serene way that you (my mother, too, God bless her) brush off the chance to indulge in cheap publicity. You are a thorobred [*sic*], and, merely incidently [*sic*], I love the hell out of you.[33]

On another occasion he reinforced his admiration.

> All through this publicity storm you've been tops—sensible, considerate and modest. You are all that any man could ask as a *partner* and a *sweetheart*. I realize that this whirlwind of newspaper notoriety places a heavy burden on you.[34]

Ike's admiration and praise meant a great deal to Mamie. She not only loved him, she respected his allegiance to his country and believed in his ethics. Certainly her heart ached (how could it not?), and she experienced bouts of depression, but she never strayed from her convictions. Years later, Mamie acknowledged her unwavering regard for Ike.

> Up to the day he died, I had utter respect for everything he thought, and I would never have done anything that would have in any way changed his opinion of the woman he married.[35]

Drawing on her pragmatic side, Mamie understood that gossip and publicity created a "two-edged sword that could cut both ways." Aware that her own behavior was also being scrutinized, Mamie had to cope with the reality that she had no more control over the rumors circulated about her than she did over those whispered about her husband.

Hearsay could come from anywhere and be directed toward anyone. Nobody was sheltered from nasty slander, and Mamie exercised caution, allowing only the very closest of friends into her inner circle. When Ike was first sent to Europe Mamie had moved in with fellow Army wife Ruth Butcher; now, unwilling to take the slightest risk of scandal, Mamie decided living alone was in her own best interest. It created tremendous hardship and unrelenting loneliness; with both her husband and son away, Mamie was utterly and entirely on her own.

To make matters worse, Mamie suffered from Meniere's disease, an inner ear disorder. In addition to ringing in her ears, headaches, dizziness, and vertigo, lack of equilibrium sometimes made her unsteady on her feet. Not surprisingly, individuals with no direct knowledge still speculated as to the cause. Malicious gossips put it about that Mamie had a problem with alcohol. In truth, there was *no* problem, but sensationalism sold newspapers regardless of veracity.

To avoid being observed drinking soda water (erroneously reported as liquor), Mamie declined invitations and avoided the social companionship which would have helped combat loneliness and provide some distraction from worry. More importantly, she was guided by higher principles. During a violent time of war, she would not allow herself to be seen participating in what might be described as carousing while her husband was obliged by duty to send young soldiers to their deaths.

Rumors then began to surface that Mamie's drinking problem was so severe she needed to be locked away. It was futile to try to combat patently false stories and assumptions. Instead, Mamie set an excellent example for other worried army wives when she reminded them of the realities of soldiers' lives in wartime:

> Nobody's safe...and Ike's got the whole burden on his shoulders. Never let me hear you complain about anything, because your husband is a professional soldier and we're the ones who have to hold up. We're the ones who can't complain. You can't do much to help your husband, but you can do a lot to hurt him.[36]

Looking back, Mamie said, "Not going out wasn't a sacrifice. I believed in it." At the same time, she described that period of her life as a "gloomy experience."

> I could not stand this absolute loneliness...[During prior intervals] I had a baby or I had John for company...The only time I ever got a good night's sleep was when [one of my female friends] would come over and stay all night.[37]

It had been a time of whirlwind change in the Eisenhowers' lives. Over a period of fifteen months Ike had been promoted from lieutenant colonel to four-star general.* Husbands of Mamie's closest friends were now Ike's subordinates and Mamie, like "The General," had to conceal any possible "doubts, fears or distrust." Exceeding all expectations, according to her good friend Janie Howard, Mamie "demonstrated remarkable self-control." Janie went so far as to say,

* Army ranks consist of Second Lieutenant (2LT), First Lieutenant (1LT), Captain (CPT), Major (MAJ), Lieutenant Colonel (LTC), Colonel (COL), Brigadier General (BG)/One Star, Major General (MG)/Two Star, Lieutenant General (LTG)/Three Star, General (Gen)/Four Star, General of the Army (GOA)/Five Star.

> If [Mamie] ever got depressed, she would never let you know it...she was always optimistic. Never, never did she have any sadness.[38]

Nonetheless, the dangers of war coupled with Ike's added responsibilities and burdens created mounting vulnerability for his wife.

Innuendos and suppositions regarding Kay Summersby were heard all around Washington. When Ike originally learned of these stories, he expressed great frustration. Overcome with annoyance, he once wrote his wife,

> So *Life* says that my old London driver came down [to North Africa]! So she did—but the big reason she wanted to serve in this theater is that she is terribly in love with a young American colonel [Dick Arnold] and is to be married to him come June—assuming both are alive. I doubt that *Life* told that![39]

Mamie remained steadfast in her position. When the subject of a romance regarding her husband came up, she simply replied, "I know Ike," and left it at that. Although correspondence confirms that Mamie confided in her parents over the years, there is no evidence she disclosed any concerns with them regarding this issue. She did, however, share what she referred to as the latest "not pretty" stories with her husband.

In excerpts from a letter written on June 11, 1943, Ike responded to the latest allegations.

> At the same moment that your letter arrived I received a report that [Dick Arnold] was killed—by a mine! I knew him quite well and I liked him—he was 32 and was a full colonel of engineers, commanding a regiment. In an active theater of war when death is an every day [*sic*] occurrence and one is constantly receiving notice of the death of valued subordinates—and sometimes close friends—I suppose that senses of values do change—but not as to fundamentals. Decency—generosity—cooperation—assistance in trouble—devotion to duty; these are the things that are of greater value than surface appearances and customs...here we considered him [Arnold] a valuable officer and a fine person. I'm saddened by his

> death. His name is added to a list that includes other senior officers and good friends of mine that are no more. War is often sad...
>
> Your letters often give me some hint of your loneliness, your bewilderment and your worries in carrying on your own part in this emergency. Don't think that I do not understand or that I am not truly sympathetic to the lost feeling you must so often have. Just please remember that no matter how short my notes I love you—I could never be in love with anyone else—and that you fill my thoughts and hopes for the future always. You never seem quite to comprehend how deeply I depend on you and need you. So when you're lonely, try to remember that I'd rather be by your side than anywhere else in the world.[40]

Days later Ike wrote his wife again.

> These days are so crowded I meet myself at the corners—but it's the best way in times of emergency. One shouldn't have too much opportunity to think about tragedies. My worst one—so far—is separation from you. That's something I never accept gracefully in my mind. If you could be here—or wherever I'm serving—this whole thing would be easier for me.[41]

Over the years, much has been said of Kay Summersby. Some of the remarks were generated because of Kay's frequent appearances with the general. Other commentary came from unnamed sources, in addition to reports from individuals who knew Kay very well. Adding to the confusion was the inconsistency in Kay's own oral and written accounts. She once said,

> [General Eisenhower] was like an older brother to me, kind, thoughtful and considerate...Yes, I was in love with Eisenhower, and so was everybody else who had anything to do with him...[Ike's] immediate staff, official family, frankly worshipped "The Boss." Most of our admiration stemmed from his natural thoughtfulness... [which was directed toward] all of us, at one time or another.[42]

In her first book, *Eisenhower Was My Boss* (1948), Kay wrote a memoir of her war years. It made no mention of any affair. Then nearly thirty years later, when Kay was dying of cancer and struggling financially with medical debts, she began another book. Ike had died six years earlier when her second book, *Past Forgetting: My Love Affair with Dwight D. Eisenhower*, was ghostwritten by Barbara Wyden and published posthumously under Kay's married name, Kay Summersby Morgan. She recounts a more flirtatious, intimate relationship which consisted of romantic kisses but no physical sex—because "Ike was impotent."

This juicy gossip appeared in several other written accounts. A particularly notorious one was *Plain Speaking* by Merle Miller. It was described as a brief "oral biography" of President Truman based on a series of taped interviews that Mr. Miller conducted in 1962 with the outspoken, highly respected former president. The author's original aspiration, which never came to fruition, was that a major network would purchase the interview rights from him. When that did not happen, the veteran journalist eventually turned the transcript into a best-selling book. Some of the material was apparently fictitious, and Truman allegedly threatened to file a lawsuit if Miller printed the "inaccuracies."

Miller did indeed publish *Plain Speaking*, but not until 1974—two years after Truman passed away. In it Miller claims Eisenhower wrote a letter to General George C. Marshall requesting a leave from the army for the purpose of obtaining a divorce and marrying Kay. (Kay asserted she "had no idea Ike planned to make her his wife." Indeed. Why would he not tell the woman he supposedly loved of his intention to marry her?) General Marshall, who by 1974 had also passed away, was said to have denied Ike's request and informed him in a letter that he would "destroy Eisenhower's career" and make his life a "living hell" if he divorced Mamie. To back up his claim, Miller said Truman stated that he had obtained these letters from the army archives and as his last official presidential act had destroyed them.

Over the years, many critics have questioned both the accuracy of some statements Miller attributed to Truman and the authenticity of those (conveniently destroyed) letters. Several historians, including Dr. Robert Ferrell, professor emeritus of History at Indiana University and Truman biographer, contend that Miller fabricated many items in the salacious *Plain Speaking*.

In yet another account, *Ike & Mamie, The Story of The General and His Lady*, author Lester David tells of an interview he had with Dr. Forrest C. Pogue, a United States Army historian during World War II and official Marshall biographer, who examined thousands of the general's documents and letters. According to Dr. Pogue, not only did he not find any such letters, but "the harsh or threatening tone" and "caustic warnings" in those purported letters to Eisenhower were not Marshall's "style at all" and did not appear in any other Marshall correspondence, of which there were volumes.

Friends and family alike disputed the planned divorce claim, as well. The Pittsburgh *Post-Gazette* (January 21, 1975) quoted Anthea Saxe, one of Summerby's closest friends: "[Kay] absolutely denied such a letter existed. [Kay] said she would have come to know of it, and she never had." A former roommate of Kay's during the war, Anthea was with her dear friend when she died.* Mrs. Saxe argued that Dick Arnold was Kay's true love. He very well could have been, as pictures of him and letters from Arnold were found among Kay's belongings after her death. She had kept them all those years. Anthea went on to say,

> After Dick died, Kay went into a deep depression...General Eisenhower did notice the change, and tried to help by keeping her busy so that she would have as little time to brood as possible. He gave her extra work to do, letters to write, filing, other secretarial duties. It is evident that Kay did play a part in his life. She was invaluable to the general, not as a lover, not as an object of romance, but because she was right there...He would use her as a sounding board for ideas, perhaps gripes he might have, to let off steam.[43]

John Eisenhower emphasized,

> Dad would have made a lousy philanderer because he was so damned Victorian and moral. Sure he was attracted to vital

* Kay was godmother to Anthea's son.

> women, like Marian Huff in the Philippines and Kay during the war, but these were friendships, not torrid affairs.[44]

No one, other than Ike and Kay, will ever really know the totality of that relationship. Ike did prove to be insensitive to appearances. Yet history has documented over three hundred love letters Ike sent to his wife during the war; also, the army repeatedly denied petitions requesting that Mamie be allowed to join him during those years.

When you consider that Ike did not continue a relationship with Kay after the war, nor did he ever divorce his wife, it appears the alleged romance was no more than shared wartime experiences between two officers who just happened to be male and female. Unfortunately, many people then and now would hold that, although the relationship certainly did not appear to be physical in nature, Eisenhower and Kay probably committed some form of *emotional* adultery.

To Mamie's credit she joked,

> If I had one thought that there was an iota of truth to the Kay Summersby affair, I would have gone after Monty [the handsome General Montgomery]. And believe you me, my friend, I could have gotten him![45]

Meanwhile the war raged on, and by Christmas of 1943 Ike was promoted to Supreme Allied Commander of the European front. Six months later, he directed the largest land, sea, and air invasion of all time—the D-Day Invasion. It was June 6, 1944, the very same day his son graduated from West Point. Like any other mother, Mamie was profoundly proud of her son, but at the same time she was in agony knowing that John would now join his fellow soldiers overseas.

Now a five-star general, Ike led one final assault. In May of 1945 he accepted Germany's unconditional surrender.* Ike would return to the United States a genuine war hero. Although she was delighted at the thought of once again *possibly* living with her spouse, being the seasoned army wife that she was, Mamie knew her life was still in a state

* The date is sometimes referred to as V-E Day for Victory over Europe. Japan surrendered in August, also known as V-J Day or Victory over Japan.

of uncertainty. With limited positions for her husband's high rank, where in the world would the army send him next? Mamie went on to acknowledge that Ike had "changed terrifically" and as she told a friend, "Neither of us really knew what the other [had been] through."

Both had grown more self-reliant, more autonomous than in the past, and getting reacquainted would not be easy, particularly for Mamie. John recalled that his father had grown "almost blind" when it came to the wishes of others, and showed a "resolute stubbornness" with respect to many issues. Ike wrote,

> Of course we've changed. How could two people go through what we have, each in his own way...and still believe they could be exactly as they were? [46]

When General George Marshall announced his retirement that November, Ike was ordered to take over as chief of staff of the army. *Life* magazine reported a humorous incident at a banquet honoring the retiring general. The toastmaster commented, "Marshall wanted nothing more than to retire to Leesburg with Mrs. Eisenhower." Embarrassed at the audience's laughter, he quickly added, "My apologies to the general." With that, Mamie inquired, "Which general?"

For the next three years, Mamie and Ike resided at Fort Myer. In addition to a cook and a personal maid for Mamie, the general retained a staff of two sergeants. All four stayed with the couple after Ike retired from active military duty in 1948. He wrote his wartime memoirs, *Crusade in Europe*, which became a best seller, and accepted employment as president of Columbia University in New York.

Now the wife of the president of one of the oldest and most distinguished universities in the country, life for Mamie was finally comfortable. Financial worries were a thing of the past, given her husband's new annual salary of twenty-five thousand dollars, which was in addition to his army retirement pay. Mamie now resided in a fully staffed four-story mansion in New York City, entertained frequently, and dined with corporate moguls when she was not doing volunteer work. To her great delight, John was now a teacher at West Point; married over a year, he had started his own family. As the younger

Eisenhower family lived less than fifty miles away, a limousine driver would take Mamie to visit her grandchildren on a regular basis.

Another exciting change was on the horizon. After thirty-four years of marriage, Mamie would at long last own her own home. Years earlier she had fallen in love with the Gettysburg area in nearby Pennsylvania, and planned to retire there. On a pre–Civil War farm, with a panoramic view of the mountains and large ash trees, stood a quaint old farmhouse that required total refurbishment. It would take a great deal of time and work to make it habitable; however, Mamie looked forward to the task.

Before she could even start the sizeable project, world events once again intervened. When the Korean War broke out in 1950, President Truman asked Ike to assume command of the North Atlantic Treaty Organization (NATO) in Europe.* Given that service to his country always came first, Eisenhower took an indefinite leave of absence from Columbia University. Mamie wrote her mother:

> It doesn't seem possible I am going again to a new place to live. It seems so crazy at our age that we can't seem to settle down.[47]

Mamie's new residence was a fourteen-room villa that had been used by both Napoleon and Louis Pasteur, ten miles west of Paris, which came with round-the-clock security. She would now be entertaining princesses, countesses, and other high-level dignitaries. There was one area in which she apparently was not quite up to French standards: although she did purchase some clothing in Paris, the local press criticized Mamie for her preference for American clothing. Astonished, she wrote,

> Imagine paying $800 or $900 for a dress! I'm perfectly happy with those little $17.95 numbers I order from New York newspaper ads.[48] [This may have been a slight exaggeration; it is highly doubtful Mamie wore gowns purchased through the mail!]

* An intergovernmental military alliance, the purpose of which is to defend against an external attack.

Ike had no intention of running for public office. Had President Truman not asked for his service to head up the NATO alliance in Europe, he would have remained a university president until retirement. However, back home, thousands of people participated in an "Ike for President" crusade (one estimate put the number at twenty-five to fifty thousand). According to Mamie, "He [Ike] was so overwhelmed and overcome with the public demonstration...he burst into tears."[49] Remarkably, even with his name not on the ballot, Ike received 108,692 write-in votes from Minnesota alone. It was not until after he involuntarily won the 1952 New Hampshire primary with fifty percent of the vote that Ike decided to return to the United States and officially run for the presidency.

Prior to his departure from Europe, Ike was given one of France's highest military honors, the Médaille militaire. Mamie too was acknowledged for her "unselfish service to mankind" and was presented with the Cross of Merit. She was quoted as saying,

> It was more wonderful than anything I expected or deserved; I came away from France with a new strength of purpose.[50]

Ike found politics to be a "really lousy business," especially in contrast to the somewhat sheltered army life he was accustomed to. The "lousy business" included various ludicrous allegations directed against him and his family. Not only was the Kay Summersby issue revisited, Ike was accused of being anti-Semitic while Mamie's purported alcoholism was discussed. When asked directly by reporter Barbara Walters, Mamie replied,

> It never bothered me if people thought that. I lived with myself, I know it wasn't so. And my friends knew I was not [an alcoholic].[51]

Besides, Mamie was far more concerned with her family's welfare than with misrepresentations generated by the political machine. As the Korean War continued, her son received orders to report to the front line. Now a presidential candidate, Ike had some blunt parting remarks for his son. John reported,

> Dad gave me the admonition. Never get captured. [If] I ever found myself surrounded by Chinese or North Koreans, I had every intention of keeping my promise and using my .45 pistol, taking I hope[d], some of them with me.[52]

Mamie was an active and enthusiastic campaigner, proving to be an asset to Ike's election run. She not only dictated seventy-five appreciative letters every day (eventually thousands of supporters were acknowledged), she kept her sense of humor about a rather personal critique: the Eisenhower headquarters received countless comments about Mamie's bangs. So many of them were unfavorable, a special form letter was used to respond. Unaffected, Mamie declared, "I like my bangs and I don't intend to change them for anyone."[53]

Throughout the country the popular slogan was "I Like Ike, But I LOVE MAMIE." The extremely popular war hero won a landslide victory over his divorced opponent, Democrat Adlai Stevenson, to become the nation's thirty-fourth president. "I love Mamie" was a reference to another enormously popular figure in the early 1950s. Comedian Lucille Ball had a number-one rated television show called *I Love Lucy.* An all-time classic program that ran for six seasons, it is still being shown regularly on TV to this day, nearly sixty years later.

Lucy was such an iconic figure, the episode depicting her in labor was coordinated to air on the actual day of her son's delivery. The news was of such magnitude that the inauguration of the president was bumped off the front page of newspapers. Not only that, more people tuned in to watch that *I Love Lucy* episode than to witness the swearing in of President Eisenhower.

That same year (1953), the Ford Motor Company celebrated its fiftieth anniversary and the Academy Awards were televised for the first time. Over the next two years, authors J. R. R. Tolkien and William Golding published *The Lord of the Rings* and *Lord of the Flies,* respectively, while Tennessee Williams released his ever-popular play, *Cat on a Hot Tin Roof,* to critical acclaim. Elsewhere in the world of entertainment, singing idols included Elvis Presley, Bill Haley & His Comets, and Chuck Berry, while the newest musical craze—rock and roll—was believed to contribute to juvenile delinquency and was roundly denounced as immoral. Teenagers purchased their first McDonald's hamburgers for fifteen cents, and baseball great Hank Aaron hit the first of 755 home runs.*

It was also during this period that the president signed legislation permitting the highest salaries ever paid to government officials. While the minimum wage was $1 an hour and the average annual income was around $4,000, congressmen would earn $22,000 a year and the vice president and the Speaker of the House earned $35,000. The president's salary was $100,000, plus a $50,000 nontaxable expense account. A typical large purchase in the United States at that time was a new car for $1,900; however, gasoline would eat up 23¢ a gallon.

The eight years Mamie lived in the White House was the longest period of time she had spent in any one residence. An old pro at running a large home with servants, Mamie managed the domestic staff of eighty, in the Executive Mansion's 132 rooms, as if *she* were the five-star general. It was said her orders were "staccato, crisp, detailed and final." One of the president's executive assistants remarked,

> Mrs. Ike was an easy person to get along with, as long as you did things right. If you didn't, she'd let you know, and fast.[54]

Very much a perfectionist, Mamie was in charge of everything and anything involved in the administration of the president's home. Division of labor in the Eisenhower marriage had long been established. The president was in total command of his work life, while his family life was entirely separate and remained under Mamie's capable authority.

Known as a stern, hands-on taskmistress, the First Lady would check stock in the White House pantry, search for grocery bargains, and perform "white glove" housekeeping inspections to ensure the staff's work met her meticulous standards. Furthermore, employees were banned from using the private family elevator...presumably because privacy was so difficult to come by. But she was hardly cold and

* At the time, Mr. Aaron earned five thousand dollars a year, which ultimately grew to an annual salary of two hundred and fifty thousand dollars when he retired from baseball in 1976.

distant; in fact, Mamie considered everyone in the household part of her extended family and inquired about their health, activities, and home life. She personally selected and wrapped both birthday and Christmas presents for all who worked for her, including Secret Service personnel, housekeepers, drivers, and aides.

As First Lady, Mamie was reserved and dignified. As a hostess, she was warm, welcoming, and amiable. She stated emphatically,

> In our entertaining, neither religion nor political party played any part…I never knew whether one was a Republican or a Democrat… I didn't want to know. I liked that person for what they were—my guest.[55]

Jacqueline Kennedy, recently married to Democratic senator John Kennedy, corroborated such in her note to the First Lady following a senate wives' luncheon:

> I think it is so wonderful the way you make everyone feel so much at home. Thank you so much for having made such a memorable occasion possible—I will never forget it.[56]

Congressman Gerald Ford's wife, Betty, commented, "Mamie was very friendly, very big on teas, and always had something personal to say to each guest."[57]

J. B. West, then deputy chief usher of the White House, said of Mamie,

> If there were a thousand people going through the line, she'd have a thousand little items of small talk for them. In fact, she could charm the socks off of anybody she met.[58]

Unfortunately, Mamie's father had died eighteen months earlier. Though he had proudly acknowledged his son-in-law's place in military history, he did not live to see his daughter's final destination of duty. However, like her predecessor Bess Truman, Mamie was fortunate enough to have her mother living with her at the White House.

And like her mother, who stayed in bed until late morning, Mamie spent the majority of her mornings in bed as well, which prompted the maids to nickname her Sleeping Beauty. This sensible schedule should not have been confused with incapacitation, but of course it was by her critics. Mamie deliberately chose this strategy to save energy and avoid being on her feet. Wearing her now famous bed-jackets, with a writing tray over her lap, the First Lady would meet with various administrative staff members and housekeepers as well as her personal secretary, and conduct all of her morning business from bed.

By the end of her tenure, the White House Social Office recorded half a million letters that Mamie sent out to members of the general public. During her first term alone, *Newsweek* reported the First Lady had "[shaken] hands with one hundred thousand persons and...launched as many as five charity drives a week."

Like the majority of her sorority sisters, Mamie performed her strenuous public duties cheerfully. Her pastor even commented,

> [Mamie's] entire forearm and hand, as well as her ankles and feet, were swollen, the result of shaking hands with hundreds of people at a White House ceremony the day before. But she had uncomplainingly carried on.[59]

Having lived abroad extensively proved advantageous for the cultured and polished hostess. In addition to welcoming "old friends" like Queen Elizabeth and her husband Prince Philip, Winston Churchill, and Charles de Gaulle, Mamie entertained seventy heads of state during her tenure, more than any previous First Lady. Her style of entertaining was lavish and formal (white tie and tails), while her fashion sense reflected personal taste rather than current trends. She loved the color pink and was not embarrassed to accentuate her waist or bustline and show off with strapless gowns. Now in her early sixties, Mamie remarked, "I hate old-lady clothes and I shall never wear them," prompting a designer to comment, "[Mamie's] making maturity glamorous."

Being glamorous and a grandmother was considered somewhat conflicting back in the early 1950s. Mamie had her grandchildren call her Mimi as opposed to grandma, and to preserve her youthful appearance she frequented health spas in Arizona. Although the president and First Lady commonly have separate bedrooms, it was widely known that Mamie and Ike shared the same bed. She admitted her desire to "pat Ike on his old bald head anytime I want to."

Although the White House had been completely renovated during her predecessor's administration, Mamie still managed to put her own personal touch on the Executive Mansion. After she received a valuable collection of gilded silver as a gift, Mamie created the Vermeil Room to house the exquisite assortment. She also had all of the White House china and tableware researched and cataloged by a Smithsonian Institution curator.

While Mamie tackled domestic and social issues, the president had his plate full with worrisome matters relating to communism, segregation of schools, and civil rights. A Baptist minister in Montgomery, Alabama, by the name of Martin Luther King Jr., was an early civil rights activist. He advocated passive resistance and gained national prominence as the leader of black Americans, encouraging them to boycott in public places. When Rosa Parks, a black woman, refused orders to give up her bus seat to make room for a white passenger, she was arrested. Parks' arrest provoked the legendary Montgomery Bus Boycott. But segregation was not limited to transportation. It took a federal court order to integrate public schools in Little Rock, Arkansas.

The president had concerns outside of the United States as well. Communist paranoia was fueled by Senator Joseph McCarthy, who led hearings and maintained blacklists of individuals suspected of supporting the Communist Party. (Mamie refused to have the senator on any White House invitation list.) Many Americans were convinced that Russia was spying on the country when they launched *Sputnik*, the first satellite. Then hysteria over the Cold War with Russia increased when Julius and Ethel Rosenberg were executed for giving atomic secrets to the Soviets.

The presidency imposes a heavy toll on those who occupy the Oval Office, and Mamie was rightly concerned about the state of her husband's health. Not only was he a very heavy smoker, Ike suffered from high blood pressure and Crohn's disease, a chronic inflammatory ailment of the intestines. After the president suffered a heart attack on what would have been his deceased son Ikky's thirty-fifth birthday, Mamie never left her husband's side during his nineteen-day hospitalization.

As a sign of his gratitude for Mamie's continuous loyalty and support, Ike designed a gold medallion for her. The inscription read,

> For never failing help, since 1916, in calm and in crisis, in dark days and in bright. Love, Ike.[60]

Even though the president's health was still somewhat below par, after his cardiologist declared him fully recovered, the American public in forty-one states overwhelmingly elected Ike to his second term in 1956.

Margaret Truman (author and presidential daughter) maintained that Mamie, one of the least politically inclined of presidential wives, entered the Oval Office only four times during her eight-year tenure. It has been said that Mamie loved being First Lady. Nevertheless, she loved her husband more, and had her doubts about spending four more years in Washington. Her trepidation was well-founded: Ike experienced a bowel obstruction which required surgery, and a bit later, only ten months into his second term, the president suffered a mild stroke. It was severe enough to prevent him from attending a White House state dinner. Vice President Nixon and his wife were asked to help Mamie host the affair. Richard Nixon commented,

> [The presidency] really is too much for any one man to bear...That night, a very troubled First Lady greeted her guests with superb poise and charm.[61]

During Mamie's second tenure, she too was hospitalized. The First Lady underwent a hysterectomy, which was vaguely reported as an operation "typical of women her age." Despite their respective medical problems, the presidential couple managed some lighter moments, too. Before leaving the Executive Mansion the president renamed the presidential retreat (then known as Shangri-La) Camp David in honor of his grandson.*

The emotional pendulum swung back to somber when, after having been bedridden for over a year, Mamie's eighty-two-year-old mother passed away in 1960. Understandably grieved, Mamie still continued her extensive charity work for the American Heart Association in addition to several other organizations, and also reinstated the White House Easter Egg Roll. The tradition had been established in 1878 by former First Lady Lucy Hayes, but it was suspended during World War II. Mamie made sure that, for the first time, the event was racially integrated. She also held the first-ever White House reception for the National Council of Negro Women.

The country was changing as well—and literally growing. Alaska and Hawaii were proclaimed the forty-ninth and fiftieth states. Across the globe Nikita Khrushchev became the first secretary of the Communist Party in the Soviet Union. In the world of pop culture the Barbie doll was introduced and Rodgers and Hammerstein composed the score for *The Sound of Music*. Folks all across America were too frightened to take showers after Alfred Hitchcock released the suspense thriller *Psycho*, and people everywhere were doing the Twist, an international dance craze from the eponymous song by Chubby Checker.

On their last evening in power, Ike and Mamie dined alone. Forty-six years of honorable duty and service to their country were coming to a close. For the umpteenth and final time, Mamie packed up their personal belongings, gratified to know that no further transfer orders would be forthcoming. The local residents of Gettysburg waited to welcome the former president and his lady. Finally unfettered by aides, assistants, or Secret Service men, Mamie would at last have her husband to herself. As an added bonus, Mamie was delighted when John and his family moved to a home adjacent to his parents' farm. She had built a strong and close relationship with her grandchildren, who had visited the White House often.

Now as the family matriarch, Mamie had earned her retirement

* Every president since FDR has used the former Naval Support Facility in Maryland as a mountain-based sanctuary to entertain heads of state and personal guests.

and time to relax with the things she valued most—family and her marriage. When a guest visited her Pennsylvania home, although they would still see Ike's handsome West Point photo sitting on her dressing table, absent were mementos of her White House years or pictures of famous people. Mamie always maintained,

> I am an army wife...the other things [spouse of Columbia University's president, First Lady to a nation] were interims.[62]

She continued to entertain friends and family, carried on with her charity work, played solitaire, and enjoyed her afternoon soap operas. Mamie was a devoted fan of *As the World Turns*. She began watching it in the White House and Mr. West said, "She wouldn't miss a program for anything!"

Ike was involved in the development of his presidential library and museum, which were established in Abilene, Kansas. He wrote extensively and eventually published three books. In addition to his beloved game of golf (in which he once made a hole in one, at the Seven Lakes Country Club in Palm Springs, California), he enjoyed playing bridge and creating beautiful oil paintings. Ike reportedly completed nearly three hundred paintings during the last twenty years of his life. Many were made into prints and given as Christmas gifts. His rank of five-star general was restored as well (it had been suspended during his presidential service, as was customary). However, Ike did not collect military retirement because he received a presidential annual pension of twenty-five thousand dollars, plus fifty thousand dollars for office staff and expenses.

Ten years after his first coronary, in 1965 former president Eisenhower suffered another heart attack. No doubt thinking of his own mortality, he later went to Denver, accompanied only by a Secret Service detail, to have Ikky's coffin removed and reinterred at the Eisenhower Museum in Abilene, Kansas.* Then in 1966, Mamie and

* Mamie was actually credited with the reestablishment of Secret Service protection for former presidential families. In a conversation with her friend and incumbent First Lady, Lady Bird Johnson, Mamie expressed her fears of one day living alone and unprotected as a presidential widow. Lady Bird shared her conversation with President Johnson, who made lifetime Secret Service protection available to former White House residents.

Ike celebrated their fiftieth wedding anniversary with a family reunion. It was said Mamie looked stunning in the strapless gold-and-white organdy gown she wore to the black-tie affair.

The next generation of Nixons and Eisenhowers continued to keep the families connected. After a childhood friendship where they played on the White House lawn together, eldest grandson David Eisenhower and Richard Nixon's daughter Julie became engaged. Mamie was delighted and immediately gave David her own mother's (Elvira's) engagement ring for Julie.

In support of his former vice president, Ike agreed to address the Republican National Convention when Nixon decided to run for the presidency in 1968. He had already survived a third heart attack; with his health deteriorating, Ike nonetheless gave a televised speech from his Walter Reed Hospital room. Ike's good deed, which was both emotional and draining, almost proved fatal. The following morning, he suffered yet another coronary that left him in serious condition. Family flew in from across the country to be with him. A doctor told them that two men, "independently of one another, volunteered to donate their hearts" to the esteemed former general for transplant!

Forever a warrior, Ike held on. One time when a doctor told visiting family members that it was time for them to leave so Ike could rest, Susan Eisenhower recalled her grandfather roaring, "And how many stars do you have?" "Three," the army doctor responded. "Well, I have five and I tell you they are going to stay," the general ordered.[63] From then on, Mamie carefully monitored how many visitors could stay, and for how long. A nurse would firmly relay the message: "On Mrs. Eisenhower's orders, time is up."

Ike spent the last year of his life at the Walter Reed Medical Center. Mamie rarely left her husband's side, regardless of what was happening in the outside world. When Nixon won the presidential election, David and Julie moved up their wedding date to ensure their privacy. (Obviously, not all brides want to be married in the White House.) Arrangements were made for Ike and Mamie to watch the ceremony on closed-circuit television. Three short months later, her son John and grandson David were with Mamie as she sat holding her husband's hand on March 28, 1969. Ike was heard saying,

> I have always loved my wife. I have always loved my children, I have always loved my grandchildren, and I have always loved my country.[64]

Then when he was ready, Ike insisted his son and grandson "lower the shades and pull him up." "I want to go. God take me," were his final words.[65] He was seventy-eight years old. Per the former president's instructions, he was buried in a sixty dollar G.I. coffin next to his son Ikky at the Eisenhower Museum in Abilene, Kansas.

At seventy-two, Mamie faced her most difficult challenge ever—she was forced to live life without her beloved Ike. To help with the transition, John suggested that his mother join him on his new assignment—he had recently been appointed ambassador to Belgium—thinking the trip would provide a nice distraction for his mother. John's wife stayed in the States, packing up the household, while Mamie accompanied John and acted as his hostess; the people of Belgium treated Mamie like a "queen." Nonetheless, she soon returned home to deal with her late husband's affairs and face life as a widow.

In addition to her annual trips to Kansas to visit the graves of her husband and son, Mamie also spent many of her winters in Palm Desert, California. There she dedicated a hospital wing to former president Eisenhower. She was also a strong supporter of Eisenhower College in Seneca Falls, New York. On a less uplifting note, the Watergate scandal consumed much of her thoughts during the early 1970s; Mamie forever remained a loyal friend to Pat Nixon and returned frequently to the White House and Camp David during the Nixon administration.

Never a supporter of the Women's Liberation movement, Mamie opposed the honorific "Ms." as a replacement for "Mrs." and "Miss." She also tried hard to understand why so many young people were getting divorced in these modern times. Somewhat preoccupied about living on a fixed income, Mamie was now less willing to spend money on herself than she had been in her younger years and often declined to attend family gatherings except at her own Gettysburg farm. She did not feel it was fair to take her Secret Service men away from their families.

In 1976, the same year that Mamie marked her eightieth birthday, the United States celebrated its 200th anniversary of independence.

President Gerald R. Ford and First Lady Betty Ford hosted a special state visit for England's Queen Elizabeth II and her husband Prince Philip, who were both attending Bicentennial festivities. New York City and Boston held festive nautical parades, where millions of observers witnessed a large international fleet of tall-masted sailing ships.

The Federal Reserve honored the occasion with newly designed coinage. The quarter, half dollar, and silver dollar all bore Bicentennial designs with the date 1776–1976. In addition, the two-dollar bill was reintroduced. The bill, which had been discontinued ten years earlier, now featured the Founding Fathers signing the Declaration of Independence.

It is inconceivable that America's early visionaries could have ever imagined the advancements in technology or the changes in daily life that would occur in the country's first two hundred years of existence. In 1976, it took just over thirteen hours for a Pan American airliner to fly 8,088 miles to complete the world's longest nonstop commercial flight. Further out in space, NASA's two Viking spacecrafts successfully landed on Mars and transmitted information about the planet's surface back to earth.

While the Apple I personal computer sold in stores for $666.66, actor Sylvester Stallone's movie *Rocky* won Oscar's Best Picture award.* Author and humorist Erma Bombeck published *Life Is Always Greener over the Septic Tank*, and Barbara Walters became the first female network television news anchor.

The Eisenhower family celebrated their matriarch's birthday with a book of remembrances. It was her grandson David's contribution that made Mamie "roar with laughter." In addition to "where else can [David] get consistently reliable fashion tips on the length of men's hair styles," he wrote,

> Today, she [Mamie] is every bit as much feminine, saucy, wise, sharp, loyal, vigilant and idealistic as she ever has been.[66]

* In November, 2010, an original Apple I computer handmade by Steve Wozniak and mailed from Steve Jobs' parents' house (the original packaging with the return address was included in the auction) sold at Christie's for $213,600, per *PC World*.

Though Mamie never lost any of the aforementioned characteristics, her body had begun to fail. Over the next two years, she experienced several minor strokes and the loss of close friends younger than herself. Being the perpetual organizer, Mamie not only kept a bag packed and ready for any possible hospital emergency, she also prepared a hanging bag with the dress she wanted to be buried in.

As fate would have it, in the spring of 1979, a television miniseries based on Kay Summersby's book *Past Forgetting* was aired. Merrill Mueller, who was hired as a technical adviser on the series, left the project specifying that "no technical advisory credit be listed." He emphasized that the story was "laughable, ridiculous," and lamented that history had been "kicked out of the window." Though Mamie watched every segment, including the "torrid love scenes," she never gave any indication that it upset her. According to her son, "The only thing that really disturbed her was receiving sympathy letters," which "flooded in from all over the country."

Six months later, one day after what would have been Ikky's sixty-second birthday, Mamie suffered a stroke that paralyzed half of her body and severely impaired her speech. After spending a month at the Walter Reed Medical Center, Mamie announced to her granddaughter Mary, "I'm going to die tomorrow," and in fact, she did. Prior to her passing, Mamie's son John and her sister, Mike, both visited her for the last time. As Susan Eisenhower, Mamie's biographer, noted, "Mamie died as she lived so many times of her life, peacefully but alone."[67] It was two weeks shy of her eighty-third birthday. Only then did her family discover that Mamie had had the presence of mind to bring a separate hanging bag with her to the hospital. In it, they found the ensemble she wore to her fiftieth wedding anniversary. After her final trip to Abilene, Mamie was laid to rest in her beautiful gold-and-white organdy gown, beside her husband and young son. Sitting First Lady Rosalynn Carter and former First Lady and family friend Pat Nixon attended her funeral. One journalist wrote of her passing:

> There are very few originals in this world and when one leaves it there is a void. Mamie Eisenhower was an original. She had the courage to define herself rather than have outsiders tell her what

> she was and what she should be...she wore her dignity like a mantle...she had the guts to be her classic self.[68]

The following year (1980) Mamie's birthplace in Boone, Iowa, was dedicated as a historic site; Abigail Adams is the only other First Lady to be so honored.

WHAT MAMIE TAUGHT ME

Mamie summed up her life when she said simply, "[I'm] thankful for the privilege of tagging along by Ike's side." Mamie Doud Eisenhower's journey included a wide variety of human experiences and sentiments. In addition to immense love, she experienced extensive loneliness. For all that people admired her, she also suffered deep public humiliation. Although she was blessed with devoted friendships, she suffered through devastating loss and tragedy.

Her philosophy and practice of making every effort "to minimize sadness" and always be present for friends while asking nothing in return are lessons well worth taking to heart. Mamie also illustrated for me the remarkable resilience of marriage: how a couple's relationship can develop, retreat, and then carry on and grow even stronger. Bonds can weaken, even decline, and still be rebuilt. Most importantly, Mamie proved relationships can heal and thrive.

PART FIVE

WOMAN OF DISTINCTION

INTRODUCTION

NORMAN MAILER, THE TWO-TIME PULITZER PRIZE–WINNING novelist, journalist, and playwright, said of Jacqueline Bouvier Kennedy Onassis,

> She wasn't merely a celebrity, but a legend; not a legend, but a myth—no, not just a myth, rather a historic archetype, virtually a demiurge.[1]

Senator Ted Kennedy said of his sister-in-law,

> No one else looked like her, spoke like her, wrote like her or was so original in the way she did things. No one we knew ever had a better sense of self.[2]

World-renowned fashion designer Valentino Garavani declared,

> Few women in history have captured the imagination the way she did, and it was Jackie's courage and grace that have made her image an enduring one. She was an original, an icon.[3]

And in the end, President Bill Clinton remembered this one-of-a-kind icon,

> With admiration, love and gratitude, for all the inspiration and the dreams she gave to all of us, we say goodbye to Jackie today.[4]

Jackie Kennedy was the thirty-fifth member to join the White House sorority of First Ladies, and everything about her demeanor set her apart from her fellow sisters—right down to her official First Lady picture (as shown on this book's cover). At thirty-one, Jackie was the third youngest presidential wife and the only one to step into the position in her thirties.*

Unlike her fellow First Ladies, who dutifully attended obligatory White House affairs, Jackie had no desire to take part in tedious female gatherings and shunned such events that did not include her husband. Always graceful yet headstrong, Jackie was her own woman and did things her own way. For a brief shining moment in history, she made Americans proud as the country's Ambassador of Goodwill.

For those who enjoy fictional stories, consider this one. There was a shy young princess who preferred to read Chekhov and Shaw as opposed to taking her afternoon naps. As the princess blossomed into a privileged, multilingual debutante, she entered society with cautious hopes and optimistic dreams.

Although already affianced, the princess accepted an introduction to an attractive, charismatic, and wealthy man who represented the cream of American aristocracy. Twelve years her senior, the good-looking Prince Charming had numerous opportunities to marry, yet up until their meeting, he had not found his ideal bride. With a hopeful heart, she ended her engagement and set out to captivate the man no other woman had managed to capture. Successful in her quest, she married her handsome prince and lived in the towering white castle, something only a handful of damsels will ever experience. With motherhood her greatest ambition, she suffered first a miscarriage and then a stillbirth as she concealed the pain and heartache of her husband's infidelity.

With the births of two healthy children, life would at last deliver happiness to her magical world. But before she could fully savor the blissfulness of her life, tragedy would not only take away her newborn son, it would obliterate her fairytale world. On a beautiful sunlit afternoon, in the midst of an adoring crowd, shots rang out, ending her

* The two younger First Ladies, Julia Tyler and Frances Cleveland, were both in their early twenties and both married a sitting president. John Tyler was thirty years older than Julia, while Grover Cleveland topped his young bride by twenty-eight years. The dreamlike, romantic, and legendary stories of the two youngest First Ladies can be found in Volume I of *Loves, Lies, and Tears*.

husband's life in a gory spectacle that would haunt both her and the nation for decades. She survived the unspeakable horror, but forever embedded in her memory would remain the inescapable pictures of what she had endured, leaving her with crippling guilt for years to come.

However, her spellbinding tale would not end there. Choosing life over despair, she would move forward and trade being perceived a heroine for the stigma and disgrace of looking like a gold digger with the basest of material motives. The utmost wealth in the world afforded her opulence and extravagance, but not yet happiness.

Like mercury, her shape and form would constantly change, from captivating highs to devastating, mind-numbing lows. Before Jackie became a first-class jetsetter, she lived the life of a stately queen. With the financial freedom to do anything she wanted, Jackie chose to embark on a vocation. When companionship, stability, serenity, and the joyful satisfaction of feeling passionate about her work were all finally achieved, her forever-impalpable life would take yet another unforeseen turn.

This is the true-life story of Jacqueline Kennedy Onassis.

10

Tragic Sophistication

JACQUELINE KENNEDY

If you bungle raising your children, I don't think whatever else you do well in life matters very much.

—JACQUELINE KENNEDY

NEARLY FIFTY BOOKS HAVE BEEN WRITTEN exclusively about Jacqueline Kennedy and over *one hundred ninety thousand* books include information about her. The reason for this is simple: Jackie represented glamour, affluence, resilience, and tragedy. It didn't hurt that she was undeniably attractive, sophisticated, intelligent, and charming. She created an aura of mystery and elusiveness; her picture alone sold books, magazines, and manuscripts.

#35 Jacqueline Bouvier Kennedy Onassis

Born: July 28, 1929

Birthplace: Southampton, New York

Married: 1953 (John Fitzgerald Kennedy; died)
1968 (Aristotle Onassis)

Children: 3 with Kennedy

White House Years: 1961–1963

Died: May 19, 1994 (64 years old)

Fact: Most photographed woman of her era

AKA: Jackie

Charlotte Curtis, a former classmate of Jackie's and a journalist at the *New York Times*, said, "Jackie wore so many masks, she was impossible to decipher...With her elevation to First Lady, she became even more elusive, more secretive, and more dramatic."[1] The *Evening Standard* said Jacqueline Kennedy "has given the American people...one thing they had always lacked—majesty."[2] She was truly America's aristocracy—a public person who wanted to live a private life.

The White House had been home to some First Ladies who were younger, some who were considered prettier, and others who were apparently smarter, but none of them embodied all three of those qualities quite the way Jackie did. Jackie herself once said "it was better to be a poor original than a good copy." She was undeniably a bona fide original and a very tough act to emulate. With a strong sense of who she was, Jackie demonstrated self-possession at a very early age. One story in particular is enlightening. When she was a young girl, she would often walk in Central Park with her nurse. One afternoon, their outing included Jackie's newborn sister as well. Soon Jackie wandered off and before long discovered she was alone. Impeccably dressed, sporting stylish white gloves and a bonnet, the poised four-year-old walked up to a police officer and stated firmly, "My nurse and baby sister seem to be lost."[3]

According to Helen Thomas, author and correspondent for the White House Press Corps, she and her colleagues were "insatiable for news about Jackie Kennedy."* They were "shameless" in their efforts to question her "hairdresser, her caterer, even the White House diaper supplier" as well as anyone else who might come in contact with her.

Jackie not only mesmerized Americans, she had the same effect on the people of Canada, France, Greece, India, Italy, Morocco, Pakistan, South America, and Turkey. Canadian Prime Minister John Diefenbaker said, "Her charm, vivacity, and grace of mind, have captured our hearts."[4] President General Charles de Gaulle of France was said to be reduced to the equivalent of Jell-O around her.[5] Astonishingly, Jackie persuaded him to allow the *Mona Lisa* to be exhibited in the United States. Similarly, Soviet Premier Nikita Khrushchev, who at the time was in the midst of tempestuous discussions with President Kennedy, was enamored with the First Lady.

To the delight of foreign-born citizens, Jackie would make short speeches in French, Spanish, and Italian, which prompted President Kennedy to remind the general public, "I assure you that my wife can also speak English." Thirty-three years earlier, First Lady Grace Coolidge was dubbed National Hugger and Public Female Favorite Number One. Reflecting all the positive enthusiasm Jackie stimulated, she was known as the Number One Ambassador of Goodwill.

* An experienced eyewitness, Ms. Thomas was a White House news correspondent for fifty-seven years!

Today the American public is still familiar with the names Martha Washington, Abigail Adams, Mary Todd Lincoln, and Eleanor Roosevelt. A hundred years from now, will people remember the name Jackie Kennedy? I mean no disrespect when I say that I would guess not; and regardless of how history judges her, it is undeniable that during her time in the spotlight, Jackie was one of the most famous, instantly recognizable women in the *world.*

In 1961 Jackie was such an international star she was named "Woman of the Year" in more than one hundred international periodicals. Jackie Kennedy and Pope John XXIII were selected as the two outstanding models "for the world."[6] Yet, putting aside all the accolades and attention, Jackie perennially focused on what mattered most to her—raising her children.

According to Mr. J. B. West, chief White House usher, "Jacqueline Kennedy devoted considerable time, energy, and concentrated attention to her children...She pleaded for a simple, unspoiled, normal life" for them. (Naturally, Jackie's idea of normal and simple meant a normal life for a very wealthy family, like the one she grew up in.) Her legendary life story of wealth, heartache, love, and devastation began and ended in New York City, with many years of notoriety and global travel in between.

Although she lived a fairytale existence, more than a few chapters in her life read more like horror stories. In response to the question, "What is your proudest accomplishment?" Jackie responded, "I went through some pretty difficult times, and I consider myself comparatively sane."[7] While Jackie lived only a brief sixty-four years, those years were filled with enough joy and misery, darkness and celebrity, disappointment and triumph, to last many, many decades.

Some of Jackie's "pretty difficult times" essentially began in 1936, when the *New York Daily News* published a particular photograph of her parents. Her father, John Vernou Bouvier III, was an exceptionally handsome man with thick black hair, beautiful blue eyes, a dark complexion, and a pencil-thin mustache. (Think Clark Gable in *Gone*

With The Wind.) Though Bouvier was not an actor, he certainly had star qualities. He was a stockbroker who was always immaculately groomed in perfectly tailored clothes and well-shined, stylish shoes. His nickname—Black Jack—came from his dark, exotic looks, which many women found attractive.

Bouvier's wife, Janet Lee, was a New York socialite sixteen years his junior. Rated one of the best women riders on the eastern seaboard, Janet was an accomplished horsewoman of medium height, with a slender well-toned body, sparkling dark eyes and auburn hair. This *Daily News* photo showed Janet in her stylish riding clothes, sitting on a fence looking into the camera. Behind her sat a pretty young woman next to Black Jack who stood leaning against the fence. The photograph captured Black Jack and the other woman openly holding hands. Not surprisingly, Janet was profoundly humiliated.

Up until that time, Jackie's life consisted only of privilege and good fortune (although the stock market had crashed barely three months after her arrival). It was fitting that in May of 1929 the first Oscars were awarded by the Academy of Motion Picture Arts and Sciences, because on July 28, 1929, in the affluent and exclusive area of Southampton, New York, a star was born! From then on, Jacqueline Lee Bouvier Kennedy Onassis captured the public's imagination for over five decades.

Her prosperous family had a longstanding membership in the Long Island horse and dog set. At the age of two, Jackie made her debut appearance on the society page, photographed leading her Scotty puppy up before the judges at the East Hampton Dog show. Her love of animals, particularly horses, was well established; at age five, she and her mother took third prize at an East Hampton family horse event.

The Bouviers made a practice of spending their summers in the Hamptons, where Jackie's paternal grandparents owned a comfortable home well-staffed with servants. Not far from the Bouvier clan's tennis court, her father stabled his seven horses on ten acres of land. Black Jack was known to tell his daughter,

> Jackie, you never have to worry about keeping up with the Joneses because we are the Joneses.[8]

Being well-off financially can guarantee abundance and provide for indulgences, but happiness itself cannot be purchased, and Janet Bouvier was far from happy. Black Jack was a compulsive womanizer and reckless spendthrift who ultimately became a heavy drinker as well. He and Janet argued constantly, and although the couple now had two daughters, Janet soon insisted on a separation. (Younger daughter Caroline, who went by her middle name of Lee, was nearly four years Jackie's junior.) A brief reconciliation ensued, but on January 26, 1940, the *New York Daily Mirror* headline announced Jackie's greatest heartache: "Society Broker Sued for Divorce."

Even more hurtful were the salacious details of the breakup the newspaper published, accompanied with dates and photographs—presumably provided by Janet's lawyer—of women allegedly involved with her husband. Soon the story and photos were reprinted in newspapers across the country. It was Jackie's first experience with public humiliation and she learned rather quickly how to develop a protective shield around herself.

Divorce is never easy on children; however, it can be horrific when both parents continually fight. Jackie at eleven was at a vulnerable age for a girl, particularly one who absolutely worshipped her father. Years later, her sister Lee shared some insight into their childhood.

> I think it [the divorce] was probably one of the very worst...There was such relentless bitterness on both sides, only myself and Jackie, one felt constantly pulled in the other one's direction, and then they [her parents] spoke of each other in such very unpleasant ways.[9]

Black Jack moved into a hotel, where he continued to live a life of self-indulgence. Janet lived with her daughters in an eleven-room duplex in one of New York's most prestigious Park Avenue apartment buildings; she paid no rent, as it was one of several buildings built and owned by her real estate mogul father, James T. Lee. No stranger to comfort or culture, Janet had the financial backing to provide the best of everything for her daughters, and she did.

In addition to painting, ballet, social dancing, and horseback riding lessons, the girls were afforded the best private education available, beginning with the elite Chapin School. Jackie then went on to attend Miss Porter's School in Farmington, Connecticut. She loved to read, write poetry, sketch, and listen to music. In fact, Jackie learned to read before attending kindergarten and her passion was fervent.

> I read a lot when I was little, much of which was too old for me. There were Chekhov and Shaw in the room where I had to take naps and I never slept but sat on the windowsill reading, then scrubbed the soles of my feet so the nurse would not see I had been out of bed. My heroes were Byron, Mowgli, Robin Hood, Little Lord Fauntleroy's grandfather, and Scarlett O'Hara.[10]

A very bright student and reportedly full of the devil, Jackie finished her lessons rather quickly. Then out of sheer boredom, she became a classroom nuisance, causing her teachers to call her a problem child.

Lee recalled their mother's demands for perfection, her awful criticisms, and her insistence that her daughters excel at whatever they do—no doubt misdirecting her pent-up anger and resentment regarding her husband to her daughters. Jackie remarked, "Lee was always the pretty one. I guess I was supposed to be the smart one."[11] The sisters shared an intense rivalry that lasted well into their adulthood. Mixed in with the jealousy and envy, though, was an overriding interdependence that proved crucial over the years for both women.

Meanwhile, saddened and distraught over the absence of her father, whom she now only saw on Sundays, Jackie resented her mother for keeping them apart. She also felt like her father had let her down. Experiencing considerable anguish over the separation, Jackie worked hard to bury her emotions. Exceedingly shy, she found it imperative to conceal her pain, particularly in public, becoming reserved and withdrawn around her teachers and school friends. Lee remembered feeling envy over her sister's ability "to press an internal button and tune out."[12]

It was a quality Jackie developed very young and perfected over the years, one that proved useful during her many visits with Miss Stringfellow, the headmistress at Chapin Elementary. When her mother inquired as to why Jackie had been sent to see the headmistress, she narrated the encounter for Janet.

> Miss Stringfellow says, Jacqueline, sit down. I've heard bad reports about you. Then Miss Stringfellow says a lot of things—but I don't listen.[13]

That approach proved vital for Jackie. Growing up she had a sense of being an outsider, different from others, and disconnected. I think it is fair to say that Jackie interpreted that as being unique rather than inferior. Lee described their younger years as "not having a very normal family." Today it would be called a blended family and is far more common.

In 1942, within two years of her divorce, Janet married Hugh D. Auchincloss Jr., a wealthy attorney, investment banker, and heir to Standard Oil Company. She was thirty-five and he was forty-five, twice divorced with three children. As the saying goes, money attracts money, and Janet knew exactly what she wanted. Not to be overlooked was his standing at the top of the social register, which was very important to her. Auchincloss's fortune was reportedly greater than that of the Lees and Bouviers put together! The couple had two more children after they married (making seven altogether).

The girls moved with their mother to Auchincloss's forty-six-acre Virginia estate, Merrywood. It was just across the Potomac from the Capitol in Washington. The house consisted of eight bedrooms, a kitchen large enough to serve three hundred guests, and additional public rooms that could hold several hundred more; the grounds had an Olympic-sized swimming pool. Their second home, Hammersmith Farm, was a seventy-five-acre estate in fashionable Newport, Rhode Island, where the extended family spent their summers. The main house purportedly had twenty-eight rooms and thirteen fireplaces. Of her two homes, Jackie said,

> I will never know which I love best—Hammersmith with its green fields and summer breezes, or Merrywood in the snow...I love them both, whichever I am at.[14]

Surrounded by maids, butlers, nurses, and chauffeurs, Jackie was undoubtedly denied very little in the way of material things. Still, both she and Lee had chores to do around the working farm, where prize Black Angus cattle were raised and separate stables were dedicated to workhorses and riding ponies. Jackie was responsible for feeding the chickens. By her teens, she had grown into an excellent horsewoman and, like her mother, loved foxhunting. She was also considered an expert swimmer and water skier, and she was a committed bookworm.

From all outside appearances, Janet's second marriage was successful. Jackie affectionately called Auchincloss "Uncle Hugh," and often said he was a wonderful stepfather. Nevertheless, Jackie's continued adoration of her father equaled Janet's never-ending resentment and bitterness toward him. Over the years, Jackie continued to see her father as often as she could. Neither woman's feelings toward Black Jack ever altered, and this caused a big wedge between mother and daughter.

At fifteen, Jackie was enrolled in Miss Porter's prominent college preparatory boarding school in Farmington, Connecticut, some five hundred miles from her Virginia home. It was the first time Jackie had lived away from her family, and she was soon terribly homesick. To console her, Jackie was permitted to have her favorite horse sent over to be boarded in the school stable.

To her great delight, Black Jack visited often. Evidently her friends were equally thrilled.

> All my Farmington friends loved Daddy. He'd take batches of us out to luncheon at the Elm Tree Inn. Everybody ordered steaks and two desserts. We must have eaten him broke.[15]

During the three years Jackie attended Miss Porter's, she maintained an A- average and her favorite subject was Latin. Dances with the prestigious boys' prep schools in the area were commonly arranged, which in no way detracted from Miss Porter's strict academic schedule and high standards. Oddly, Jackie found she had nothing in common with the prep school boys. Dismayed with her marital prospects, Jackie once wrote a friend,

> I just know that no one will ever marry me and I'll end up as a house mother at Farmington.[16]

Not that marriage appeared to be particularly high on her priority list. She wrote in her senior yearbook (June 1947) that her ambition in life was to "*not* be a housewife."[17]

Instead, Jackie would prepare for college. She passed her college-aptitude exams in the 90th percentile, an achievement earned by a very small number of students. Several colleges offered her admission, and not surprisingly, Jackie chose Vassar, her mother's alma mater.

Prior to leaving for school, Jackie enjoyed the high society custom of a young woman's social debut. First, an afternoon tea party was shared jointly with her five-month-old stepbrother's christening. Later, Jackie participated in a formal coming-out dinner dance with another young debutante at Newport's esteemed Clambake Club.

One nationally syndicated columnist for the widespread Hearst newspaper chain pronounced Jackie "Queen Deb of the Year." He described her as,

> A regal brunette who has classic features and the daintiness of Dresden porcelain. She has poise, is soft-spoken and intelligent, everything the leading debutante should be.[18]

The press coverage only added to Jackie's already captivating appeal. Young men in her hometown, as well as those already in college, wanted to meet the impressive beauty. The summer of 1947 was filled with festivities and celebration.

When Jackie settled into college life, she soon became one of the more popular undergraduates on the Vassar campus. She was witty, flirtatious, and extremely bright in a nonthreatening way. There were very few weekends she went unescorted by Ivy Leaguers from Harvard and Yale. Because she always preferred the company of men, Jackie made few close women friends. She was polite and well-mannered, yet some of her female peers found her withdrawn and distant.

In addition to her various social engagements, Jackie made time to visit her father regularly. She also repeatedly made the dean's list. She had a curious mind and was particularly interested in and appreciative of the performing arts. One area that held absolutely no appeal for her at all was politics.

The summer after her freshman year, Jackie had an opportunity to visit Europe with three other girls and a chaperone. Their voyage began on the *Queen Mary* in the summer of 1948. As luck would have it, one of Jackie's companions was related to the undersecretary of the treasury. It took some serious effort, but in the end arrangements were made for the girls to attend a garden party at Buckingham Palace. After the teenagers waited in a long receiving line to see King George VI and his mother, Queen Mary, the girls discovered that Prime Minister Winston Churchill was also in attendance. They waited in line a second time to shake the prime minister's hand as well.

Before returning home two months later, the elated travelers visited London, Paris, the French Riviera, Italy, and the Alps. At nineteen years of age, Jackie could never have imagined what the near future held for her. A mere thirteen years later, King George VI's eldest daughter, Elizabeth, would be sitting on the British throne, and Jackie would be living in the White House!

That trip was the beginning of Jackie's irrepressible love for Europe, and she yearned to return. By her junior year she was bored with Vassar and contemplated dropping out of college. Since she had participated in several fashion shows, Jackie actually considered becoming a photographer's model at one point. Then a stroke of luck (or destiny) provided an opportunity to study abroad through a program offered by Smith College. Because of her French heritage, Jackie wanted to study at the Sorbonne in Paris. Several things had to happen, though, before that could become a reality.

To begin with, she needed permission from the Vassar board, which was not easy to obtain. Then, in addition to her regular school curriculum, she had to take additional courses in French to perfect her conversational ability. All students were to live in a dormitory where English was spoken, but Jackie did so well with her French she was permitted to pay for boarding with a French-speaking family by the name of de Renty. Madam de Renty was a widow who had a small apartment with one bathroom, minimal hot running water, and no central heat. Seven people, including Jackie, lived there. It was said she did her homework wrapped in a sweater, bundled up in mittens, a scarf, and earmuffs.

It was a time of discovery and newfound independence. In reference to a trip she took with Claude de Renty, Mme de Renty's daughter, Jackie wrote,

> I had the most terrific vacation in Austria and Germany. We really saw what it was like with the Russians with Tommy guns in Vienna. We saw Vienna and Salzburg and Berchtesgaden where Hitler lived: Munich and the Dachau concentration camp...It's so much more fun traveling second and third class and sitting up all night in trains, as you really get to know people and hear their stories. When I traveled before it was all too luxurious and we didn't see anything.[19]

She told her stepbrother, Hugh Auchincloss III, that,

> I have to write Mummy a ream each week or she gets hysterical and thinks I'm dead or married to an Italian.[20]

Not only did Jackie enjoy going to the opera, the ballet, and the Louvre, she fell in love with the culture and every aspect of Parisian life. Later, she wrote:

> I loved it more than any year of my life. Being away from home gave me a chance to look at myself with a jaundiced eye. I learned not to be ashamed of a real hunger for knowledge, something I had always tried to hide, and I came home glad to start in here again but with a love for Europe that I am afraid will never leave me.[21]

Looking back, Jackie recalled the trip with great enthusiasm. She described the de Rentys as "the most wonderful family" and referred to the experience as a "high point of her life."

Upon her return to the United States in the summer of 1950, Jackie resumed her lavish life at Merrywood and spent her senior year at nearby George Washington University. During that time, Jackie entered a *Vogue* magazine Prix de Paris competition. Contestants had to supply virtually enough material for an entire issue of *Vogue*, including fashion articles, a personal profile, and an essay on "People I Wish I Had Known."

The winner of the contest would be awarded a one-year internship at *Vogue*, which included six months in their New York office and six months at their Paris location. Unlike a number of other applicants, Jackie did not write about political figures. Instead she chose Oscar Wilde, a British author; Sergei Diaghilev, a Russian ballet producer; and Charles Baudelaire, a French poet. In addition to her extensive research, Jackie also needed to take a course in typing, which up until that time she had no interest in learning. Out of the 1,280 contestants, Jackie won first prize! After all of her effort, her parents worked hard and persuaded Jackie not to accept the award. Her mother was convinced if Jackie went back to Paris, she would never return.

It was her stepfather, Uncle Hugh, who came up with an alternative. As graduation presents he would pay for Jackie and Lee to spend the summer in Europe. It took the girls nearly a year to obtain their mother's permission.

Then on June 7, 1951, after Jackie graduated from George Washington University with a degree in French Literature and Lee graduated high school from Miss Porter's, the two sisters departed for their European sojourn. It was a summer they would never forget. In addition to other adventures, the sisters drove around in a car with a stick shift and celebrated Jackie's twenty-second birthday in Florence.

When they returned home on September 15, as a thank-you for the extraordinary opportunity, Jackie and Lee presented their parents with a handmade book of their memorable voyage. *One Special Summer*, which also included photographs, was written and illustrated by Jacqueline and Lee Bouvier. Jackie contributed the drawings, the poetry, and the sections on Rome and Spain, while Lee described most of their adventures on the *Queen Elizabeth* and in London, Paris, Venice, and Florence. As Lee wrote in the introduction,

We did this book in a state of joy and laughter, which was our mood throughout the trip.[22]

Upon their return, Black Jack wanted Jackie to move in with him in New York. Janet was equally adamant that her daughter remain in Washington and promised to help Jackie get a job. Uncle Hugh suggested journalism as a career choice, and using his various contacts arranged an interview with the editor of the *Washington Times-Herald*. Jackie began as a receptionist and soon volunteered to be the "Inquiring Photographer" for the newspaper. She wrote a bylined column accompanied by a picture of the interviewee.

While working for the newspaper, Jackie began dating John Husted, a New York stockbroker and Yale University graduate, whose family was listed in the *Social Register*. It was a long-distance relationship with Jackie doing most of the commuting. The couple generally saw one another when Jackie stayed at her father's New York apartment on East Seventy-Fourth Street. In January of 1952, the *New York Times* announced their engagement. According to Husted, Janet sabotaged the relationship because he did not make enough money for her daughter, even though he earned seventeen thousand dollars a year.

Although Husted's interpretation may be perfectly correct, there was also another mitigating circumstance. Both Jackie and Husted were invited to the Washington home of Charles and Martha Bartlett. Husted was unable to attend because of business, but he encouraged Jackie to go anyway. It was there she first met John (also known as Jack) Kennedy, a congressman from Massachusetts and former war hero who had received both a Purple Heart and the Navy and Marine Corps medals. Soon thereafter Jackie called off her engagement, telling friends that Husted was immature and his work was too tame. She later explained that the Bartletts had been shamelessly matchmaking and also confided that "she was attracted to Kennedy because he was dangerous, just like Black Jack."[23]

Many years later Jackie's stepbrother, Hugh Auchincloss III, told television personality Larry King that Jackie "always looked for chivalry, grace, charm and courage in her men."[24] Both men quickly agreed Kennedy had all four qualities. On the other hand, displaying her trademark charm, Jackie said what was most important to her in a man was that "he weighed more [than she did] and have bigger feet than I do." At five feet seven and a half inches, Jackie wore a size ten women's shoe. She went on to say,

> I look at a male model and am bored in three minutes. I like men with funny noses, ears that protrude, irregular teeth, short men, skinny men, fat men. Above all, he must have a keen mind.[25]

Some time passed before the Bartletts again invited their single friends over for a dinner party.* By the end of the night, Jack had invited Jackie out for an evening of dinner and dancing. Many more dates ensued over the next several months. It was not long before Jackie found herself taken in by the Kennedy charm. They enjoyed one another's sense of humor and she respected the things Jack believed in.

It would be naïve, however, to say that Jack's ten-million-dollar trust fund was irrelevant. After all, Jackie had grown up believing that money was enormously important; it was also true that the men in her life held the purse strings. At the same time, Jack found a kindred spirit in Jackie. He appreciated her good looks, her refinement, and her stylishness.

Jackie was certainly cognizant of Jack's well-deserved reputation as a womanizer (or as Jackie put it, "Here was a man who did not want to marry"), and the real possibility of heartache in a future with Jack could easily be predicted. Yet, Jackie concluded that "such heartbreak would be worth the pain."[26] It took some conscious maneuvering on her part, but when Jackie put her mind to something, she usually succeeded. Convinced that "men are such a combination of good and evil" and "all men are unfaithful to their wives,"[27] she embarked on a course to set herself apart and make herself highly desirable to the man she had genuinely fallen in love with.

Bear in mind that Jack was some twelve years Jackie's senior. Con-

* The Bartletts remained very close friends of the Kennedys over the years. Jack Kennedy was godfather to the Bartletts' daughter and Martha Bartlett was godmother to John Kennedy Jr.

sidering that she was in her early twenties, it is certainly plausible that Jackie fondly believed that her presence in his life would cause Jack to change his ways. (There is no substitute for experience and maturity!)

Her plan was definitely working, because Jack invited her to his family's home in Hyannis Port on Cape Cod (an almost unheard-of occurrence when it came to his female friends) for the long Fourth of July weekend. Jackie was quickly swept up into the exuberance of the Kennedy clan.

> How can I explain these people, they are like carbonated water, and other families might be flat. Everybody would be talking about something. They had so much interest in life—it was so stimulating. Just watching them wore me out![28]

In truth, Jack's sisters wrote Jackie off as being too delicate, calling her "the deb" in reference to her debutant of the year status. She made her most favorable impression on Jack's father, Joe Kennedy Sr.

Several things impressed the senior Kennedy. Not only was Jackie's family on the social register, she was fashionable, pretty, well educated, and—earning major points—Roman Catholic. Joe understood the important role a supportive wife played in a politician's future. Jackie had the essentials covered and then some; she met or exceeded Joe's expectations for his son's future wife.

By now a great deal of Jack's time was spent campaigning for a seat in the United States Senate (which he won), and Jackie played her part in the courtship dance magnificently. She was not always available to take his phone calls, and even took off on weekend trips without telling him ahead of time. Her strategy was simple. If being out of sight means being out of mind, so be it. However, if being out of sight means the heart grows fonder, then her plan worked. Jack wanted her there and her absence brought the point home.

When Jack proposed marriage in the spring of 1953, Jackie sealed the deal when she left for London still contemplating his offer. She had received a last-minute invitation from a friend to join her at Queen Elizabeth's II coronation. In addition to her personal enjoyment,

Jackie made the trip professionally successful when she convinced her editor at the *Washington Times-Herald* that she would send back columns, interviews, and personal sketches of the event as human interest stories for the paper. Everyone, including Jack, was impressed with her excellent work.

Before returning home the young women spent an extra week of fun in Paris. This had an unexpected downside for Jackie, though, as she was charged over a hundred dollars for the considerable extra weight in her suitcases on the flight home. As it turned out, she had made several stops at numerous bookstores during her trip. As a present to Jack, she purchased volumes of information on history and legislation, his favorite subjects.

By the time she returned from Europe, Jack was eagerly waiting for her at the airport. He was a man unaccustomed to being ignored, and Jackie was the one prize he could possibly squander away. Ending any further speculation, Jackie immediately accepted his proposal, quit her newspaper job, and began her preparation to become Mrs. John F. Kennedy. Though their families knew of her decision, the couple held back on a public announcement. As it happened, the *Saturday Evening Post* was scheduled to run a feature story entitled "Jack Kennedy—the Senate's Gay Young Bachelor." Among other engaging bits of information, the article concluded with, "During the campaign every woman who met Kennedy wanted to mother him or to marry him."[29] Obviously, Jackie was no exception. Later, when Jack confessed he had decided to marry her the first night they met, Jackie swiftly responded with, "How *big* of you!"[30]

Janet fully expected to orchestrate her daughter's wedding. But so did Joe Kennedy. The bride's mother envisioned a quiet, dignified affair, while the groom's father foresaw and expected a social event to top the greatest of all jamborees. When the families got together to make plans, the disparate arrangements each proposed made for a rather difficult discussion. Jack was amused when his future mother-in-law stood up to all of his father's stipulations, while Jackie was delighted to see that "Mummy was terrified of Jack because she can't push him around at all."[31]

In the end, though Janet thought the final plans were gauche, she had to accept the fact that her daughter was marrying a political figure. The size and scope of the wedding, including significant press coverage, were inevitable. Attendees beyond its capacity crowded into Newport's Saint Mary's Catholic Church on September 12, 1953, to see Archbishop Richard Cushing officiate over the largest political and social event of the decade. Four priests assisted the archbishop, and before the mass, a special blessing from Pope Paul XII was read.[32] The radiant twenty-four-year-old bride, with her ten bridesmaids, and the handsome thirty-six-year-old groom, with his fourteen ushers, stood poised before their six hundred–plus guests.

The event was followed by a reception for more than seventeen hundred people at Hammersmith Farm. A great many of Boston's Irish Democrats, as well as New York and Washington Republicans, joined the entire membership of the United States Senate and most of Newport society to celebrate the Bouvier-Kennedy marriage.

The day would have been perfect except for the ongoing feud between Janet and her ex-husband. Jackie, who was still very close to her father, wanted Black Jack to walk her down the aisle. But Janet would not hear of it! She insisted that Black Jack was intoxicated that morning and unable to perform the duty. (Purportedly Janet sent someone to Black Jack's hotel room, perhaps with the intention of getting him drunk—which would not have been terribly difficult considering his heavy drinking habit.) Uncle Hugh stepped in and gave the bride away, just as Janet had masterminded.

The truth was that although Jackie's father's name was never mentioned anywhere (the wedding invitation read "Mr. and Mrs. Hugh Dudley Auchincloss request...of Mrs. Auchincloss's daughter...") and he had been banned from attending the ceremony, Black Jack was in town for the wedding. But whether or not he was tipsy in his hotel room was irrelevant; he was not welcome at the church and had never really been part of any of the wedding plans. Nor had he been welcome to participate in any of the pre-wedding festivities.

The entire bridal party was invited to the Kennedy compound in Hyannis Port where additional houses were rented to accommodate the large group. Tennis, touch football, swimming, sailing, and picnicking were scheduled for the afternoons, while a scavenger hunt and charades were planned for the evenings. Other activities included a bachelor party for the groom and a separate bridal dinner, both in Newport.

The couple honeymooned in Acapulco, Mexico, in a pink stucco villa overlooking the Pacific. After making a few additional stops, like the San Ysidro Ranch in Montecito, California, they returned to a rented house in Georgetown and a hectic life of public service. Though she occasionally accompanied her husband on speaking trips and immersed herself in the various cocktail parties and dinners, Jackie found politicians boring. The youngest wife of any senator, Jackie commented, "Being married to a Senator, you have to adjust to the fact that the only routine is no routine."[33] To please her husband, she enrolled in an American history course at the Georgetown School of Foreign Service and even went to cooking school.

Like all young brides, Jackie had her share of cooking disasters, and soon thereafter hired a cook. With good humor, she wrote of one incident:

> Suddenly, I don't know what went wrong, you couldn't see the place for smoke. When I tried to pull the chops out of the oven, the door seemed to collapse. The pan slid out and the fat spattered. One of the chops fell on the floor but I put it on the plate anyway. The chocolate sauce was burning and then exploding. What a smell!!! The coffee had all boiled away. I burned my arm and it turned purple. It looked horrible. Then Jack came home and took me out to dinner.[34]

Despite her lack of culinary skills, Jackie did bring stability to her husband's life. Using her training from Miss Porter's and Vassar College, she helped Jack slow down his speech and ensured that he no longer left for work with "one black shoe and one brown." Instead of the haphazard meals associated with a bachelor pad, they now ate good food on a regular basis; Jackie also educated herself on fine wines and in turn educated her husband. The appearance of her home and making it feel warm and comfortable were important to the new bride, and she spent countless hours decorating and redecorating. Constant "improvement" in his surroundings was not as necessary to her spouse. "Dammit Jackie," Jack once exclaimed, "Why can't I come home and find the same house I left?"[35]

Being young, good-looking, and financially comfortable did not insulate the couple from commonplace problems. The Kennedys would revisit four painful issues throughout their entire marriage: on his part, Jack's poor health and womanizing were upsetting, while Jackie's problems with having children and with finances—specifically her spending habits—were bothersome.

Jack's health, primarily related to spinal problems, was troublesome for his entire adult life. Originally injured playing football at Harvard and then again when his PT boat was wrecked during World War II by a Japanese destroyer, Jack continually suffered with back pain. He frequently used crutches to help alleviate his discomfort; however, by the summer of 1954 his pain was so severe he agreed to have a double spinal fusion. Jack was seriously ill for eight months—undergoing two surgeries—and *twice* was so close to death a priest was called in to give him the last rites.

During his lengthy recuperation, Jackie seldom left his side. She made it her business to monitor her husband's medication and diet, and later supervised a strict exercise schedule. There was an unlikely silver lining to all this misery. Jackie found a project that helped channel her husband's energies away from his pain, and gave her an opportunity to assist her spouse in achieving—of all things—a Pulitzer Prize. While Jack was rehabilitating from the multiple surgeries, Jackie did research, organized material, and helped him draft his award-winning book, *Profiles in Courage*. In the preface, Jack conceded he "could not adequately acknowledge his wife's assistance."

The following year, the couple experienced their second upsetting ordeal—a miscarriage. The fact that her sister-in-law, Ethel Kennedy, had already given birth to four healthy children only exacerbated Jackie's sadness. She once commented, "Ethel drops kids like the rabbits," adding that her in-law was a "baby-making machine—wind her up and she becomes pregnant."[36]

Jackie turned to the reliable distraction of redecorating their new Georgian estate, Hickory Hill, situated on six acres of land in McLean, Virginia. She used her considerable intelligence and design savvy to ensure the estate would accommodate Jack's special physical needs—employing what we would now call universal design—particularly when it came to having to bend down to reach things. A nursery was included; clearly they planned to raise a large family in the enormous home, which contained thirteen bedrooms and thirteen bathrooms. Sadly, eight months into her second pregnancy, Jackie gave birth to a stillborn child. She was overwhelmed with despair and worried that she might *never* have children.

While Jackie was dealing with her anxiety over childbearing, Jack talked about running for president, a direction Jackie had not yet embraced. Then at the 1956 Democratic National Convention, Jack was considered as a vice-presidential nominee. He believed it would be a good stepping stone to the presidency. Joe Kennedy, on the other hand, was opposed to the idea because second place would never be an acceptable option. In the end Jack lost the nomination to another senator, which in turn put in motion his run for the presidency in 1960.

Looking ahead and with the intention of living in the White House, Jack sold the Hickory Hill home to his brother Bobby. In reality it made good sense, as Bobby and Ethel Kennedy eventually had eleven children. Years later, their mother Rose Kennedy jokingly commented to Bobby, "If I had known it was a competition, I would not have stopped after having only nine [children]." Being part of such a large family unit only increased Jackie's desire for her own family.

Jack's painful back and Jackie's inability to have children were only the beginning of their ongoing sorrows. Two other major issues existed, and they were never satisfactorily resolved for the couple. Money and sex are frequently listed at the top of marital problems. In the Kennedy marriage, it was her over-the-top spending habits and his perpetual flirtatiousness and pursuit of women that caused the most harmful damage to their partnership. Some suggested that there was a point at which Jackie considered leaving her philandering spouse.

Time magazine went so far as to report that Joe Kennedy offered his daughter-in-law a million dollars to stay married to Jack; there was, however, no evidence of the bribe. When she heard this outrageous rumor, Jackie immediately phoned Joe to ask, "Why only one million dollars, why not ten million?"[37] Jackie's relationship with her in-laws mirrored the one she had with her own parents: she adored her father-in-law and maintained a close and loving connection to him, while her relationships with her mother and mother-in-law were polite yet more formal and obligatory.

When Jackie describes the early years of her marriage, it is easy to understand why planting roots meant so much to her.

> We were like gypsies living in and out of a suitcase. It was turbulent. Jack made speeches all over the country and was never home more than two nights at a time. To make matters ever more restless, we had rented a house in Georgetown for six months, and when the lease ran out, we moved to a hotel.[38]

After the sale of their Hickory Hill home, the couple purchased another house—not nearly as sizeable—in Georgetown. Having a stable home of her own was understandably very important to Jackie; it ranked right up there with having children. She remarked,

> The thing that gives me the greatest satisfaction is making the house run absolutely smoothly so that Jack can come home early or late and bring as many unexpected guests as he likes. Frankly, this takes quite a bit of planning.[39]

While looking forward to some stabilization and the decoration of her own residence, Jackie found out she was once again pregnant. Extremely excited, somewhat fearful, and entirely hopeful, she cautiously waited. Then in August of 1957 her beloved father, Black Jack, passed away. The two had maintained a very close relationship and saw one another often. It was Jackie who planned every detail of her father's funeral.

Finally, in November 1957, a blessing followed the day after Thanksgiving with the birth of Caroline Bouvier Kennedy.* At long last, Jackie had a home and a child!

The only thing missing now was a husband. "I was alone almost

* Caroline Bouvier Kennedy [Schlossberg] (1957–present); John Fitzgerald Kennedy Jr. (1960–1999); Patrick Bouvier Kennedy (1963–1963).

every weekend." It was all wrong, Jackie complained, "politics was sort of my enemy, and we had no home life whatsoever."[40] As Caroline's nanny recalled, "The Senator was not often to be seen."[41] Instead, the senator had been crisscrossing the country giving numerous speeches. Kennedy had not yet announced his presidential candidacy; however, he was laying down all of the groundwork.

When he did return home, it was with a clear-cut vision. Get reelected (in 1958) to the Senate, and then immediately put his entire campaign strategy and supporters together for a run at the 1960 presidential election. The entire family (including Jackie) began a highly developed and well-defined campaign to support their candidate. As historian Bill Harris put it, "The Kennedys were establishing themselves as a kind of American royal family."[42]

Soon Jackie was drawing larger crowds than the candidate himself. However, when Kennedy won his party's presidential nomination in Los Angeles in July of 1960, Jackie was spending the summer in Hyannis Port. She had dropped out of the campaign for the one reason that was acceptable to everyone—she was again pregnant. She was missing out on a campaign that was hard fought on various levels. The slightly younger, somewhat less experienced senator from Massachusetts was running against his former colleague, Republican Richard Nixon.

Both men began their political careers in 1946 when they were elected to the House of Representatives. Both won reelection and were then elected to the Senate in 1950. From 1952 to 1960, while Kennedy had remained in the Senate, Nixon had gone on to serve as vice president under President Eisenhower. Ironically enough, years earlier, when Jackie was working as the "Inquiring Camera Girl," she interviewed both Richard and Pat Nixon for her column.

Aside from the political differences between Nixon and Kennedy, Kennedy was Catholic and his religion came into play with some voters. Jackie once commented,

> I think it's so unfair of people to be against Jack because he's a Catholic. He's such a poor Catholic. Now, if it were Bobby, I could understand.[43]

Former President Truman, who was not a Kennedy supporter, said bluntly, "I am not against the Pope. I'm against the Pop." His comment was in reference to Joe Kennedy, who had been working painstakingly and nonstop behind the scenes. Many believed Joe had rigged the election, and Rose Kennedy made the unfortunate mistake of once saying,

> It's our money, and we're free to spend it any way we please.[44]

To keep matters jovial, Jack himself deadpanned,

> I got a wire from my father—it reads, Dear Jack: Don't buy one more vote than necessary. I'll be damned if I'll pay for a landslide.[45]

It was no secret that the aggressive multimillionaire and former United States ambassador to England wanted his son to become the first Catholic president. Jack openly admitted,

> My father wanted his eldest son in politics. "Wanted" isn't the right word. He demanded it.[46]

When Joe Jr., the eldest Kennedy son, was killed during World War I, Paul "Red" Fay remembered that his good friend John Kennedy said at that time,

> Now the burden falls on me. I'm going to have to be—carry the ball for my father.[47]

Neither death nor the passage of time ever altered Joe Sr.'s political ambitions for his sons. After the war John became a senator and again reiterated his father's expectations.

> Just as I went into politics because Joe died, if anything happened to me tomorrow, my brother Bobby would run for my seat...And if Bobby died, Teddy would take over for him.[48]

The game of politics never interested Jackie, and she had little patience for glad-handing and small talk. She clearly lived in two different realities—her public persona and her personal life. Over several months during the campaign, Jackie shared her point of view, one which never changed throughout the years.

> I separate politics from my private life, maybe that's why I treasure my life at home so much. In this business there're always going to be flare-ups about something. And you must somehow get so it doesn't upset you. I think I was always good at it. I do drop this curtain in my mind.[49]

> Nothing disturbs me as much as interviews and journalists. That's the trouble with a life in the public eye. I've always hated gossip-column publicity about the private lives of public men. But if you make your living in public office, you're the property of every taxpaying citizen. Your whole life is an open book.[50]

Yet at the same time she also asserted,

> My life revolves around my husband. His life is my life. I think every woman wants to be needed, and in politics, you are.[51]

With a voice no louder than a breathy whisper, Jackie often hid her intelligence behind a mask of childlike innocence. She established early on,

> I certainly would not express any views that were not my husband's, I get all my views from him. Not because I can't make up my mind on my own, but because he would not be where he is unless he was one of the most able men in his party.[52]

Jonathan Isharm, a gentleman who had once dated Jackie and knew her well, recalled this about her:

> She was so much smarter than most of the people around her that

> she sublimated it. Therefore, she sometimes comes across as the wide-eyed, sappy type. It's pure defense.[53]

When it came to the mainstream voter, Jack viewed his wife as being too aristocratic, having "too much status and not enough quo." He told her,

> The American people just aren't ready for someone like you, I guess we'll just have to run you through subliminally in one of those quick flash TV spots so no one will notice.[54]

The comment reduced Jackie to tears. She disliked the idea that people only thought of her as a socialite, particularly when that person was her husband, whom she greatly admired. She wanted to be respected for her opinions and intellect, qualities she had surely demonstrated to her spouse, if not to the general public. In an attempt to explain her demeanor, Jackie said,

> People of a private nature are often misunderstood because they are too shy and too proud to explain themselves. The truth of the matter is that I am a *very* shy person.[55]

One of Jack's closest friends, Lem Billings, saw it a little differently. He believed,

> They were so much alike, even the names—Jack and Jackie: two halves of a single whole. They were both actors and I think they appreciated each other's performances.[56]

As the election drew closer someone jokingly said, "It would be just like Jackie to have the baby on the eve of the election, to sway the voters." Only half mockingly she responded, "Oh, I hope not. I'd have to get up the next day to go and vote."[57] Later, when asked what she would do if the baby were born on Inauguration Day, she responded naively, "When's Inauguration Day?" You could hear laughter from reporters in the background and see confusion on her face. But that was genuine Jackie. She never attempted to answer a question if she did not know the answer.

Today the press would have made mincemeat out of such an inexperienced response from any candidate's wife. Yet Jackie had such a mesmerizing and captivating effect on people, men in particular wanted to protect her vulnerability. With wide, innocent eyes and a magnetic smile, Jackie's persona was just what the country wanted.

Nevertheless, she was not without her critics. *Women's Wear Daily* said she spent $45,000 a year on clothes. (As a point of reference, the nation's vice president earned an annual salary of $35,000, plus a $10,000 taxable expense account.) "I couldn't spend that much, unless I wore sable underwear!" Jackie shot back.[58]

To a handful of individuals, she appeared haughty or arrogant. It was the beginning of a new decade, and some found it difficult to imagine Jackie doing the Twist. In Chicago, Hugh Hefner opened his first Playboy Club; medical science produced its first birth control pill. *To Kill a Mockingbird* was the current Pulitzer Prize–winning novel. In the world of digital equipment, technology had just reached a staggeringly new realm. The PDP-1, the first commercial computer equipped with a keyboard and monitor, sold for $120,000![59]

Along that same line, television played a large role in the 1960 election. It was a new and unique tool to connect with the American people. Kennedy understood this and used it wisely. When the candidates participated in the first of four televised presidential election debates, the results were revealing. People who heard the first debate on radio designated Nixon the victor. Those who saw the debate on television selected Kennedy as the champion. Personality, appearance, and charisma made the winning difference and proved to be a factor in all future presidential campaigns.*

When the country went to bed on election night, results were still too close to call a winner. Jackie divulged to Arthur Schlesinger, historian and special assistant to her husband,

* Kennedy also held the first live presidential news conference carried on radio and television.

> I cast only one vote—for Jack. It is a rare thing to be able to vote for one's husband as president of the United States, and I didn't want to dilute it by voting for anyone else.[60]

Schlesinger later discovered that it was the first time Jackie had ever voted. Prior to meeting Jack, she was apolitical—in fact, she remained so throughout her life. Her husband once said of her, "She breathes all the political gases that flow around us, but she never seems to inhale them."[61] Ironically, both the Bouvier and Auchincloss families were Republican.

The next morning brought exciting news: by the very narrow margin of less than one hundred twenty thousand popular votes and just eighty-four Electoral College votes, Kennedy was elected the country's thirty-fifth president. It was the fifth time in history the country had elected a Harvard graduate. Former presidents John Adams, John Quincy Adams, Theodore Roosevelt, and Franklin D. Roosevelt had all graduated from the prestigious Ivy League college. To date, however, John F. Kennedy is the only Catholic, and at forty-three years old, the youngest elected Chief Executive the United States has ever had.*

Celebration at the Kennedy compound in Hyannis Port was exuberant. The large Kennedy clan had all gathered together to rejoice and participate in the making of history. While the entire family reveled inside, a photographer managed to catch Jackie walking alone along the cold, desolate beach. Now eight and a half months pregnant, she was contemplating her future. To say the prospect was daunting is an understatement. Jackie articulated her feelings when she protested,

> It's as though I had just turned into a piece of public property. It's really frightening to lose your anonymity at thirty-one. I'll be a wife and mother first, then first lady.[62]

* Teddy Roosevelt, later elected in his own right, was forty-two when he succeeded to the presidency in 1901.

The nation had grown accustomed to Mamie Eisenhower, Bess Truman, and Eleanor Roosevelt. Jackie's youth, glamour, and star quality all set her apart from the crowd, and the country was enthralled. Less than three weeks after her husband was elected president, the First Lady–elect became a mother for the second time. John F. Kennedy Jr., quickly known as John-John, was delivered prematurely by Caesarean surgery. While still in the hospital, a female patient happened to notice the young mother. "You're Mrs. Kennedy, aren't you? I recognize you from your pictures." "I know," Jackie grumbled, "that's my problem now."[63]

A mere two weeks after surgery, Jackie made the traditional introductory visit to the White House. It can be a little awkward when the outgoing and incoming residents are from opposing parties, and neither she nor the departing First Lady, Mamie Eisenhower, looked forward to the meeting and tour. Still, both women were cordial toward one another. Almost two hours later, totally fatigued and apparently in physical pain, Jackie departed.

Her first impression of the Executive Mansion left her far from impressed. She told her social secretary, Letitia Baldrige, the mansion looked like "a hotel that had been decorated by a wholesale furniture store during a January clearance."[64] Mamie's comments about Jackie to Chief White House Usher J. B. West were not exactly uplifting:

> Well, she's awfully young...there certainly are going to be some changes made around here...she's planning to redo every room in this house. You've got *quite* a project ahead of you.[65]

Within two months, Mr. West was able to fully comprehend her remarks. The entire White House would be turned inside out and upside down.

Before tackling the Executive Mansion, Jackie launched a makeover of sorts for herself by arranging for designer Oleg Cassini to become her personal couturier. He was an old friend of Jackie's, and she appreciated his European fashion sense. She requested he dress her as if "Jack were President of France" and immediately followed up with,

> Make sure no one has exactly the same dress as I do. I want all mine to be original and no fat little women hopping around in the same gown.[66]

Luckily for public relation purposes, Mr. Cassini was an American citizen. With some of Jackie's hand-drawn sketches, he created the "Jackie Look." Her gowns featured bare shoulders, and her monochromatic dress suits sported large-buttoned jackets set off by matching pillbox hats.

The style was so classic and popular it not only swept the entire nation, it was copied literally around the world by fashion-consciouss women. Even her headscarves, white gloves, and large-framed sunglasses became favorite accessories. One of Hollywood's finest designers, Edith Head, considered Jackie the "greatest single influence in fashion history."[67]

Before ever entering the White House, Jackie was clear on her priorities. During one exchange with reporters, she gave them a glimpse of her attitude. One reporter stated,

> *When you are first lady, you won't be able to jump into your car and rush down to Orange Country to go foxhunting.*
> "You couldn't be more wrong. That is one thing I won't ever give up."
>
> *But you'll have to make some concessions to the role, won't you?*
> "Oh I will. I'll wear hats."[68]

The Kennedy inauguration was attended by several former and future First Ladies. Previous sorority sisters Edith Wilson, Eleanor Roosevelt, Bess Truman, and Mamie Eisenhower were in attendance along with Lady Bird Johnson, wife of the new vice president; Pat Nixon, wife of the outgoing vice president; and Betty Ford, wife of Congressman Gerald R. Ford.

Jackie was still recuperating somewhat from her recent delivery, and all of the pre-inaugural celebrations left her exhausted. Nonetheless, looking absolutely radiant, she managed to attend a few inaugural balls before she would retire at midnight. The president, who was frequently referred to as JFK, remained energetic and high-spirited until nearly four thirty in the morning as he attended the remainder of the festivities alone.*

The demands and expectations on every First Lady are substantial. However, Jackie learned rather quickly how to maneuver through all of the various burdens and obligations, and in the process created her own unique First Ladyship. Years later she boasted that she was told of at least ninety-nine things she *had* to do as First Lady and yet she had "not done one of them."[69] To begin with, she did not want to be called the First Lady, because, as she explained, "It sounds like a saddle horse." The White House staff was instructed to refer to her simply as Mrs. Kennedy.

The president's spouse is obliged to entertain a number of semi-official visitors and those paying formal calls. "I can't stand those silly women," Jackie reported, and her staff quickly became familiar with the "PBO," otherwise known as the polite brush-off.[70] She even refused to attend the Congressional Wives Prayer Breakfast. When it came to organizations such as the March of Dimes, the American Heart Association, the Girl Scouts, and dozens of others, Jackie said freely, "Give them to Lady Bird."[71]

Lady Bird Johnson, the vice president's wife, was an exceedingly gracious, hard worker who rapidly became Jackie's obliging fill-in hostess. She did so countless times, as did Jackie's mother, Janet. After an apologetic excuse was given for the First Lady's absence, sometimes the administration was embarrassed when photos later appeared showing Jackie doing something recreational or more to her liking. Rose Kennedy, Jackie's mother-in-law, infrequently visited the White House, mostly when the First Lady was away. Although the women were courteous and respected one another, they did have very different views. "You want Caroline to be like you," Jackie told her very religious mother-in-law, and "I want her to be like me."[72]

Above all else, Jackie detested the hordes of reporters that intruded

* Some presidents were commonly identified by their initials. Examples include TR for Teddy Roosevelt, FDR for Franklin Delano Roosevelt, JFK for John Fitzgerald Kennedy, and LBJ for Lyndon Baines Johnson.

into her personal life, particularly those who hounded her children. Pamela Turnaure, Jackie's press secretary, knew the rules: "Press relations will be minimum information given with maximum politeness."[73] The First Lady did not wish to give interviews, press conferences, or photo sessions. Her insistence regarding her family's privacy led Jackie to have an attorney draw up a pledge statement. Her entire staff was required to agree in writing to never talk or write about their experiences with the First Family.

Ostensibly the pledge had no legal basis; however, when the press heard about it, they were outraged. How could the White House muzzle its employees? The backlash was so intense, President Kennedy personally asked Chief Usher West to accept total responsibility for the pledge. If it were Mr. West's request, solely for protection of the First Lady's privacy, at least the president would not be blamed for what was considered a grave injustice and blow to free speech. Being the professional he was, Mr. West replied, "[Well] I did ask the staff to sign it, Mr. President."[74]

J. B. West had worked in the White House since 1941. He had already interacted with three prior presidential families and understood the seriousness, responsibility, and scope of his position. His experience and proficiency were indisputable. The first time Mr. West met Mrs. Kennedy, he was "struck by how young she appeared." Initially he thought she whispered, but then realized her speech was deliberately soft. It forced you to listen intently, focus attention on her face, and respond while looking into her persuasive deep brown eyes—eyes that at some times had the appearance of determination and other times, vulnerability.

Not long after they began working together, the following dialogue occurred between Jackie and her new majordomo.

> "Mr. West, did you know that my doctor ordered a wheelchair the day I first went around the White House?"
>
> "Yes, I did."
>
> "Then why didn't you have it for me? I was so exhausted after

> marching around this house for two hours that I had to go back to bed for two whole weeks!"
>
> "Well, it was certainly there...we were waiting for you to request it."[75]

What he politely did not tell her was that Mrs. Eisenhower had not wanted Jackie to use the chair and had no intention of pushing the new First Lady around in it. To West's surprise, Jackie "giggled" as she confessed, "I was too scared of Mrs. Eisenhower to ask!" From that moment on, Mr. West confirmed he "never saw Jacqueline Kennedy uncertain again."

What he did see was a highly organized woman who was a master at details. Like her predecessor, Jackie was thoroughly prepared to run a large mansion with domestic help. Because of her privileged background, she had been surrounded by servants all her life and knew exactly how she wanted things done. She personally preferred spontaneity, so a formerly regimented and finely tuned household would now need to operate on an impromptu basis, with a head mistress who kept no schedule. Jackie told J. B. West,

> I want you to run this place just like you'd run it for the chinchiest President who ever got elected. We [the Kennedys] don't have nearly as much money as you read in the papers![76]

Perhaps not, yet JFK, like former President Hoover, donated his entire government salary to charity.

It is not uncommon for a new First Family to immediately redo the upstairs private living quarters. After all, the White House is in fact their primary residence, and each family has different needs and tastes. Immediately following Kennedy's inaugural parade—even before the start of the evening inaugural balls—Jackie informed Mr. West, "We've got a lot of work ahead. I want to make this into a grand house!" Little did he realize the new First Lady had a vision to transform the entire mansion, changing it from a historic house into a bona fide national monument. "Do you think" or "Could you please" were as much of a command from Jackie as Mamie's "Do this ASAP" order.

Jackie moved into the Queens' Bedroom while JFK was placed in the Lincoln Bedroom, where they remained until all of the upstairs family quarters were completely redone to the First Lady's precise decorating specifications. Within two weeks, Mamie's favorite color, pink, had entirely disappeared, as did the fifty-thousand-dollar appropriation budget which had been approved by Congress. It was said the same room was painted two or three times before it suited her, generating some claims of reckless expenditures.

When Jackie declared, "We'll need a kitchen [upstairs]," she was immediately asked if she wanted to see some designs.

> Oh heavens no. I couldn't care less about the kitchen! Just make it white and ask Rene [her new French chef] what he wants in there.[77]

The dusty-rose colored bedroom Mamie's mother previously occupied quickly became a stainless steel kitchen with commercial-size appliances. While Jackie didn't care about kitchens, flowers were very important to her; she announced, "I couldn't stand the arrangements around here!" and made sure new ones were brought in that were more to her liking.

In her various decorating notes, Jackie concluded the bedroom curtains looked like a "tired Christmas tree" in "seasick green." The East Room floor looked like a "roller skating rink," and the ground-floor hall resembled a "dentist's office bomb shelter." Despite these acerbic comments, Mr. West referred to the First Lady as a "daily delight"; according to him, "Every day, she said something that was just plain funny."[78]

In addition to the numerous paintings, watercolors, and original works of art Jackie brought with her, she also borrowed some twenty portraits from the Smithsonian to hang upstairs. One day by chance, Jackie popped into Mr. West's office; to her astonishment and great delight, she discovered he had a Grandma Moses oil painting hanging on his wall. President Eisenhower disliked it so much he had exiled it out of sight. Mr. West explained the painting was actually hers, as it belonged to the White House. In her whispered breathy voice, she requested, "Would you mind terribly, Mr. West, I'd love it for Caroline's room," which naturally became its new location.

Her love for and commitment to the arts were clearly established. Within the first week of her tenure, Jackie met with members of the National Gallery, experts from the Commission of Fine Arts, and the head choreographer for the New York City Ballet. These individuals, along with others, became known as Mrs. Kennedy's Cabinet.

It was during those initial early weeks that Mr. West observed the private Jackie. He described her as "casual, impish, and with an irrepressible humor." He found her very informal. When in residence the First Lady wore only comfortable, casual pants outfits, while skirts and high fashions were worn solely in the presence of company. The First Lady had a wonderful wit, liked to tease people, and poked fun at nearly everything, including herself. Reportedly, she did "wicked impersonations of everyone," including the Queen of England. She mimicked her husband's Massachusetts accent together with his chopping hand motions. Yet her informality was never to be confused with or construed as familiarity or closeness. Regarding the public Jackie, West portrayed her exactly as the populace saw her: "Elegant, aloof, dignified and regal."[79]

Before turning her attention to the ground floor of the White House, Jackie saw to it that her children's needs were vigilantly taken care of. She created a kindergarten class for Caroline (with ten other pupils), and part of the White House lawn was turned into a playground with a sandbox, swing set, trampoline, and tree house, all obscured from public view. Still, Caroline and John-John were the most photographed children since Shirley Temple. What the general public did not realize was that, like Edith Roosevelt before her, Jackie stage-managed her children's publicity. In addition to the little stories she dreamt up, certain photographs were agreed upon for magazine, newspaper, and television news reports.

But Jackie could not control everything. It was common knowledge that the president enjoyed the positive publicity his children garnered; particularly when his wife was away from the White House, he was far more indulgent with reporters. A picture of five-year-old

Caroline riding her pony Macaroni, unaccompanied, brought back tender memories of little five-year-old Quentin (Teddy Roosevelt's youngest child) sneaking his pony Algonquin into the White House elevator in order to cheer up his brother Archie, who was upstairs sick in bed.

When it came to entertaining, the press was only included when the First Lady determined the event was of national interest. The intimate parties held on the second floor and the dinner dances that lasted until dawn were strictly off limits.

It did not take long before invitations to Jackie's White House receptions and dinners were more sought after than any invitations in the history of the presidency. The *Boston Globe* announced that prior presidential hostesses held the title of "Washington's most popular hostess" in name, but "Jacqueline Kennedy now holds it in fact, and there are no two ways about it."[80]

With the exception of state dinners, she put an end to the annoying and convoluted reception line. By doing so, she created a more relaxed and casual intermingling of her guests. Black tie attire replaced the more formal white tie and tails. Cocktails were served before dinner, and round tables seating no more than ten guests each replaced the long U- or E-shaped tables that made conversation so difficult.

Several memorable events were carefully orchestrated. For the emperor of Ethiopia, the ballet was performed, while a passage from Shakespeare was recited for the grand duchess of Luxembourg. At eighty-five years of age, Pablo Casals, the world's greatest cellist, performed for the Puerto Rican governor. Casals' first performance at the White House had occurred in 1904 for then-president Teddy Roosevelt. Violinist Isaac Stern, cellist Leonard Rose, and pianist Eugene Istomin entertained a gathering of all living Western Hemisphere recipients of the Nobel Prize. President Kennedy toasted his guests:

> I think this is the most extraordinary collection of talent, of human knowledge, ever gathered at the White House, with the possible exception of when Thomas Jefferson dined alone.[81]

One particular dinner stands alone in its magnificence. Jackie decided she wanted to host one hundred and fifty guests at a state dinner for the president of Pakistan. The White House had successfully produced many triumphant state affairs. However, the First Lady was acutely aware of all the complications and obstacles involved in this particular event. She wanted a candlelight dinner held outside on the lawn at Mount Vernon, George Washington's plantation home overlooking the Potomac.

The innumerable details, planning, and logistics would be daunting. Transportation of all the guests and food alone required extensive maneuvering. Everyone and everything had to be ferried up the river. To see exactly what needed to happen and how it would work, Jackie took copious notes as she and some members of her staff made a few dry runs. Marines needed to be stationed on the other side of the Potomac, waiting in limousines, ready to drive guests to the estate. Tents had to be erected, flowers and other decor required attention, and the proper acoustics were needed for the National Symphony Orchestra to perform. Furthermore, the weather had to cooperate and a backup plan had to be prepared, just in case. Not to be overlooked was the need for discreetly concealed portable lavatories.

After the First Lady recounted her entire proposal to Mr. West, she said cautiously, "I suppose you're going to jump off the White House roof tomorrow." "No," he replied, "not until the day after the dinner"—which was executed flawlessly.[82] Around Washington, people lightheartedly joked that,

> Many people would have committed at least one cardinal sin for an invitation to the Kennedy White House.[83]

Jackie made it crystal clear that she believed the president's home should have the *best* of everything. The entertainment, the furnishings, the food, nothing was overlooked. Jackie, in addition to recognizing quality, appreciating beauty, and respecting history, demanded excellence—sometimes even at the expense of others. Instead of paying for an item directly with cash, at times Jackie tried to convince the seller to accept a signed picture of herself or something similar, claiming its value would be worth much more in the future.

Her expensive tastes and expectations sometimes exceeded even the Kennedys' means. In 1961 her personal expenses alone for clothing, paintings, posh foods, and antiques were purportedly over $105,000. (Keep in mind that was fifty-some years ago!) The president reprimanded his wife for her extravagant spending, which remained a constant sore spot between them and was never resolved. The following year (when Jackie was supposedly economizing), her private expenses rose to $121,000.[84] Getting Jackie to curtail her expenditures reminds me of the old expression, "It's like fighting city hall." In other words, you can never win.

When it came to his wife's spending, Jack fought a perpetual Battle of the Budget. The reality was that had she not been such a political asset, the president might have chosen to fight a bit harder, but the end results she achieved were simply too remarkable. Jackie charmed everyone she met, and thousands more wanted to meet her.

Clothing does not make a woman, but it sure does make an impression and get attention. When the couple went on a goodwill tour, the First Lady never wore an outfit more than once. Furthermore, it was not unusual for her to change clothing two to three times a day in preparation for her various outings and appearances. Extensive planning and logistical maneuvering went into caring for Jackie's wardrobe—coordinating all the necessary accessories, keeping a ledger and documentation for each outfit, and, when traveling, managing the voluminous luggage needed to properly care for the exquisite designer creations. It was a project unto itself.

Her sartorial efforts did not go unnoticed, and I do not say that to take anything away from her charm and intelligence. Jackie was admired and lauded around the globe for her personal and intellectual attributes, but there's no denying the wardrobe contributed enormously to her international cachet. Communist students in Caracas waved a sign that said: "Kennedy—No, Jacqueline—Yes." In Vienna crowds shouted "Jac-kie," and in Paris the Parisians screamed "Jacquii." All the attention prompted President Kennedy to tell an audience,

> I do not think it altogether inappropriate to introduce myself. I am the man who accompanied Jacqueline Kennedy to Paris, and enjoyed it.[85]

The positive accolades only gave the First Lady encouragement to proceed with her original intent with respect to redoing the White House. Not that she really needed the additional support, for her mind had been made up at the very beginning of her tenure. Her primary objective had always been to renovate the Executive Mansion into a historical museum, a venerable edifice that would make everyone proud. Money and other obstacles stood in her path, not the least of which was her husband's forceful opposition.

I think it is fair to say that no one in the White House supported her overhaul of the mansion. She was "warned, begged and practically threatened" not to do it.[86] Many arguments were put forth, none of which persuaded Jackie to back down. She had a will of iron, and in the end, the only thing her frustrated husband could say was,

> The trouble with you, Jackie, is that you don't care enough about what people think of you.

Jackie responded,

> The trouble with you, Jack, is that you care too much what people think of you.[87]

With the tenacity of a mother bear protecting her cub, the First Lady forged ahead. She did her homework admirably by studying blueprints and photographs of every room of the White House as it looked before she arrived. Once she settled in, she roamed every inch of the mansion, including the warehouse, which contained an inventory extensive enough to fill a massive bound book. She made it her business to personally see every last item, and soon discovered that a great many of the White House historic furnishings had been sold or given away. (Many years earlier, former presidents James Buchanan and Chester A. Arthur held public auctions to dispose of numerous wagonloads of unwanted furniture.) These were antiques, long gone astray, that the First Lady desperately wanted restored and returned to the White House.

A Fine Arts Committee of fourteen handpicked advisors was formed. Henry Francis du Pont, the distinguished authority on American furnishings, was appointed chairman by the First Lady. At their first meeting, Jackie announced her plan. "My main project here will be to make this a truly historic house," she declared. It was the committee's job to scour the country, locate antiques, artwork, and anything of value that had come from the mansion, and then persuade the owners to donate the items to the White House. The goal was to locate authentic furnishings that were historically accurate and of museum quality. Much easier said than done, but not impossible. "Mrs. Kennedy was in command at every step of the restoration, and involved in every decision," confirmed Mr. West.[88] Every lampshade, every vase, every chandelier came under her scrutiny.

Contributions began to flood in—some ridiculous, others priceless. Museums, antique dealers, third and fourth generations of presidential families, all were sought out. On occasion actual pieces used by a president were found. Sometimes it was necessary to make exact copies, such as reweaving antique rugs that could never hold up under heavy traffic. One thing was very clear: no government funds would be made available to finance the project. Therefore, wealthy benefactors were needed, and the First Lady wanted it understood that the endeavor was a restoration and not merely a redecoration of the White House!

Some individuals were gracious with their donations, others were not. Handwritten memos from the First Lady to her staff were very common. At times she expressed how "ENRAGED" she was at people trying "to gyp the White House." One memo read, "Tell him if he gives it, he can get a tax donation and photo in our book—if not—goodbye!"[89] Her willpower, energy, and drive amazed many people. One of her advisers commented,

> When the First Lady gets on the trail of something, she never gives up. If you have a bed that used to be in the White House, she'll have you sleeping on the floor before you know what happened.[90]

While the First Lady tackled her priorities, the president proposed some of his own. He had already set the tone of his presidency when he incorporated into his inaugural address this memorable appeal: "My fellow Americans, ask not what your country can do for you—ask what you can do for your country." The newly elected president immediately signed an Executive Order that officially launched the Peace Corps. Sargent Shriver, the president's brother-in-law, was named the program's first director. It was a volunteer organization of goodwill ambassadors whose mandate was to train workers and give technical assistance in underdeveloped nations.

As with the First Lady and her restoration project, the president had his skeptics. During the campaign, his opponent claimed the program would be nothing more than a haven for draft dodgers. Others had doubts as to whether college-aged volunteers had the skills needed to do the job. The program ultimately proved viable, as nearly two hundred thousand Americans (of all ages) have joined the Peace Corps and served in 139 countries since its inception.

Shortly thereafter, with Vice President Johnson as its chairman, the president established a Committee on Equal Employment Opportunity. Two months later, the minimum wage was raised from a dollar an hour to a dollar and a quarter over a two-year period.

The president than challenged the nation to send Americans to the moon prior to the end of the decade. Just twenty-three days after a Soviet cosmonaut became the first person to orbit the earth (1961), Alan Shepard became the first American to travel in space. The National Aero Space Training and Research Center (NASTAR Center) not only met the challenge, they exceeded it. Within five years, American Neil Armstrong was the first person to set foot on the moon.

Alongside success inevitably comes failure. With the objective to overthrow Fidel Castro's communist government, fifteen hundred Cuban exiles, trained by the Central Intelligence Agency and supported by United States government armed forces, invaded Cuba. The plan was unsuccessful; only three months into his administration, the president accepted total responsibility for the failed plot former President Eisenhower initiated. Known as the Bay of Pigs, the incident caused a break in diplomatic ties between Cuba and the United States.

Wary of future intervention by the United States, Castro pursued closer relations with the Soviet Union, which paved the way for the Cuban Missile Crisis nearly eighteen months later.

That crisis could well have turned into a major catastrophe. For years the United States and the Soviet Union (USSR) had been locked into a continual state of military tension, political conflict, and economic competition known as the Cold War. The United States and the USSR were the only two superpowers remaining after World War II, and they vehemently disagreed on the structure of the postwar world. The establishment of universal democracy versus Communism was the root of their contention.

The Cuban Missile Crisis developed when the Cuban and Soviet governments placed nuclear missiles in Cuba. Those missiles could well have destroyed large areas of the United States. When American military intelligence discovered the weapons, the president sought every possible measure to ensure their removal. While the Cold War had offered periods of both relative tranquility and extreme international tension, during the two-week missile crisis, the world came closer to nuclear war than ever before or since.

Meanwhile, on a more positive note, Jackie's project had progressed to fruition. On Valentine's Day, 1962, the First Lady gave a one-hour nationally televised tour of her newly completed project in a program entitled *A Tour of the White House with Mrs. John F. Kennedy*. A book by the same name soon followed. According to its author, Perry Wolff, the CBS program was viewed by some eighty million people, watching enthralled as Mrs. Kennedy described the significance and origin of each room's furnishings. Not only did the *New York Times* pronounce the First Lady an "extremely able historian, art critic, and narrator," the program received an Emmy and nationwide acclaim. It would not be long before the White House acquired a full-time curator.

To help with the millions of dollars in expenditures, it was Jackie's idea to set up the White House Historical Association, a nonprofit organization whose purpose was to research and publish an official guidebook for the president's home. The Executive Mansion quickly became the number one tourist attraction, and multitudes of people purchased *The White House: An Historic Guide* for one dollar a copy. Ultimately, the brochure's massive popularity financed the First Lady's immense restoration project.*

Before the close of 1962, the Cuban Missile Crisis had ended and the country once again turned its attention to more lighthearted subjects. Pictures of the First Lady and Elizabeth Taylor, the country's hottest movie actress, adorned the cover of *Photoplay*, a top movie magazine. In bold letters its caption read, "AMERICA'S 2 QUEENS."[91] Other stars of the year included Jackie Robinson, the first African American inducted into the Baseball Hall of Fame; basketball great Wilt Chamberlain, who scored a hundred points in a single game for a National Basketball Association record; and John Glenn, who circled the earth three times to become the first American to orbit the planet.

For the newly crowned queen, renovation of the White House was only the beginning. Blair House, Lafayette Square, and other buildings that front the president's home along Pennsylvania Avenue were also refurbished. Supporters of the First Lady respected her sense of history, praised her dedication, and admired her impeccable taste. Her detractors claimed that her personal indulgences and lack of responsibility regarding money dimmed the glow of her star.

Sometimes referred to as "Cleopatra of the Potomac," Jackie was not above using the government helicopter for her frequent four-day weekend trips to Glen Ora, their Virginia estate, or sending Air Force One to retrieve items left behind at their Palm Beach, Florida, home. She frequently traveled to exotic locations with her sister, who was now called Princess Radziwill, as Lee had married a deposed Polish noble.

During this time Jimmy Durante, a singer, actor, and comedian, hosted a popular radio show. Durante, nicknamed "Schnozzola" for his rather large nose, typically ended his programs with, "Good Night, Mrs. Calabash—wherever you are." In reference to the First Lady's extended vacations in Italy, India, Greece, Turkey, Morocco and yacht-

* *The White House: An Historic Guide* is now updated for every administration. Currently at one hundred and sixty pages, the book can be purchased for around seven dollars at the White House or online.

ing in the Mediterranean, all without her spouse, "Good Night, Mrs. Kennedy, wherever you are," became a familiar phrase.

Married only seven years when the couple moved into the Executive Mansion, the Kennedy marriage was still relatively in its infancy. Although she was youthful and contemporary in many ways, Jackie told an interviewer, "I'm an old-fashioned wife." She went on:

> We never talked of serious things. I guess because Jack has always told me the one thing a busy man doesn't want to talk about at the end of the day is whether the Geneva Convention will be successful...He wanted me as a wife and seldom brought home his working problems...The most important thing for a successful marriage is for a husband to do what he likes best and does well. The wife's satisfaction will follow.[92]

Despite her comments, the First Lady more often than not found satisfaction in doing exactly what she pleased, whenever she wished. If spending money was Jackie's Achilles' heel, then women and infidelity were the president's. The First Lady was aware of her husband's betrayals, but she pragmatically believed that all men were unfaithful. After all, her father and father-in-law, both of whom Jackie adored, were living proof of this truism. Once, in an attempt to console her sister-in-law Joan (who at the time was married to her husband's younger brother, Teddy), Jackie said straightforwardly, "Kennedy men are like that. They'll go after anything in skirts. It doesn't mean a thing."[93]

Her philosophy may have helped her attitude, but it did not entirely hide Jackie's deeply hurt feelings. Unlike the long-term affair Franklin Roosevelt had with Lucy Mercer or those Warren Harding had with Carrie Phillips and Nan Britton, Kennedy's indiscretions could fill an entire book, let alone a chapter.* The president's aides predicted, "This Administration is going to do for sex what the last one did for golf," in reference to Eisenhower's love of the sport.

* Women mentioned most frequently are Judith Campbell (Exner) (also mistress to Chicago mafia boss Sam Giancana), Mary Meyer, Blaze Starr, a number of Hollywood's acknowledged sex symbols—Marilyn Monroe, Angie Dickinson, Jayne Mansfield, Kim Novak—and countless other starlets that famed singer/actor Frank Sinatra set him up with.

Characteristically dignified in her silence, Jackie seldom showed any cracks in her armor. Occasionally, however, it was impossible for her to remain silent. As she handed her husband a pair of women's underwear, she was heard saying, "Here, would you find who these belong to? They're not my size."[94] Then once, when she was passing through the White House with a visitor, she introduced her press secretary, Pamela Turnure, as "the woman my husband is supposedly sleeping with."[95] In addition, "Fiddle and Faddle," two blond White House secretaries known to have kept company with the president, were referred to as "the White House dogs" by Mrs. Kennedy.

The president and First Lady, both very private individuals, showed little affection while in public and interacted almost formally with one another. The discreet White House staffers, however, were more attuned to the presidential couple's intimacy. In the afternoon when their children were down for naps, the two went behind closed doors and gave strict orders for "uninterrupted privacy." Employees could hear quiet music, often tunes from the musical *Camelot,* from the stereo the First Lady had installed in the West Hall passageway between her and the president's bedrooms. Regardless of anything else she was doing, the First Lady stopped to spend time alone with her spouse. Although President and Mrs. Kennedy had separate rooms, George Thomas, the valet who was in charge of waking the president every morning, often found him asleep in his wife's bed.

Chuck Spalding, a good family friend, insisted,

> Jack appreciated her. He really brightened when she appeared. You could see it in his eyes; he'd follow her around the room watching to see what she'd do next. Jackie interested him, which was not true of many women.[96]

Intrigue and allure were qualities Jackie came by naturally, and she made the most of them. Very early in their relationship, for instance, Jack asked a pensive Jackie, "A penny for your thoughts?" Jackie's atypical response was, "If I told them to you, they wouldn't be mine, would they, Jack?"[97]

According to former Florida senator George Smathers,

> Jack developed enormous respect for his wife's political judgment. His pride in her achievements grew stronger the longer he remained in office.[98]

Oleg Cassini said,

> JFK...fell in love with his wife a second time when they reached the White House and she was able to demonstrate her gifts and abilities.[99]

Nineteen sixty-three was a big year at the movies. Sean Connery was James Bond, Agent 007. Elizabeth Taylor and Richard Burton starred in *Cleopatra,* the movie that ended their marriages to other people. (The Taylor-Burton marriages did not last either. They were married and divorced twice.) Paul Newman gave a dynamic performance in *Hud,* and Sidney Poitier was the first black actor to win an Academy Award for his outstanding acting in *Lilies of the Field. The Twilight Zone* and *Perry Mason* were enormously successful television shows, while *The Ed Sullivan Show* became a Sunday night ritual. You could also purchase a McDonald's hamburger for fifteen cents.[100]

Treated like a movie star herself, Jackie graced practically every magazine published in 1963, and she was also pregnant again. While Jackie was vacationing on Cape Cod in August, Patrick Bouvier Kennedy arrived five weeks early, delivered by emergency caesarean section. The president, who was still working in the White House when he received the news, rushed to his wife's side and was with his infant son when he died two days later. Patrick's parents were engulfed in devastating grief, and Jackie was still too weak to leave the hospital. A funeral was conducted in Cardinal Cushing's private chapel in Boston. According to the cardinal, the president cried "copious tears." He then placed a silver St. Christopher's medal, given to him by his wife as a wedding present, in his son's tiny coffin.[101]

Visibly bonded closer together in their mutual sorrow, the following month the Kennedys celebrated their tenth wedding anniversary.

Jackie gave her husband a gold St. Christopher's medal to replace her original wedding gift. Shortly thereafter, Jackie accepted an invitation to join her sister on a Mediterranean cruise. Lee had befriended Aristotle Onassis, the notorious Greek shipping magnate with a somewhat shady business reputation. The billionaire hosted the Bouvier sisters on his 325-foot yacht, the *Christina,* along with Lee's husband, Stas Radziwill; Mr. and Mrs. Franklin Roosevelt Jr. (he was then undersecretary of commerce and a good personal friend of the president); and one of Onassis' sisters, Artemis. The timing of the cruise, its infamous host, and a photograph of the First Lady sunbathing in a bikini, sparked a great deal of juicy gossip. Nor did it help quiet the wagging tongues when the First Lady spent six weeks in Greece recuperating.

Prior to Jackie's return to the White House, the president had already made plans to visit Texas in preparation for his 1964 presidential campaign. Before the events of that summer, the First Lady would most likely not have joined him on this trip. However, much had changed in their relationship since their son's death, and Jackie was excited to accompany her spouse and even help campaign for him. Furthermore, it could only help mend her public reputation.

At their first two stops (San Antonio and Houston), the Kennedys were greeted with great enthusiasm. On Friday, November 22, again thousands lined the street to see the presidential motorcade ride into Dallas. Jackie sat smiling next to her husband in the open limousine's back seat as they traveled down Main Street at ten to fifteen miles an hour. To maximize exposure, the First Lady was instructed to wave to the crowds on her left, as the president looked to his right. Texas Governor John Connally and his wife were seated in front of the presidential couple. Vice President and Lady Bird Johnson rode behind the Kennedys in another limousine.

"You sure can't say Dallas doesn't love you, Mr. President," Mrs. Connally yelled out over the cheering crowd.

"No, you sure can't," the president responded, smiling broadly.

Literally just seconds later, three shots rang out. The first hit the president in his neck, causing him to lose all facial expression. Without a sound, he slumped down into his wife's lap. The second bullet hit Governor Connally, and the final, fatal shot hit the president in the back of his head which exploded in blood. The First Lady cried out in horror, "Oh, my God, they killed my husband! Jack! Jack!"

Three cars back in the motorcade, the vice president and his wife were instantly buried beneath Secret Service men. The presidential car then broke out of procession and sped off to Parkland Hospital at seventy miles an hour. Fifteen doctors had assembled in the emergency room, but little could be done. A breathing tube was put down the president's throat, and another was inserted into his chest to prevent his lung from collapsing. Blood was pumped into the president's left arm and left leg.

For ten minutes, Dr. Malcolm Perry continued to compress the president's chest in a futile attempt to restart his heart, but to no avail. The First Lady remained standing in the doorway of the trauma unit—watching, waiting, until finally another surgeon covered the president's entire body with a clean white sheet. Courageous in her conduct, Jackie held her husband's hand as Father Huber gave him the rite of absolution. She then removed her bloodstained wedding ring and kissed her husband as she placed it on one of his fingers.

A Secret Service agent rushed to a phone and called the Oneal Funeral Home. In an urgent voice he said,

> Load a coffin into your hearse, get a police escort, and get over to Parkland as fast as humanly possible. It's for the President of the United States.

When asked what type of casket he wanted, the agent replied, "The best you have."[102]

Just across the hall, doctors skillfully worked on Governor Connally's severe wounds. He survived the bullet that passed through his back, struck his right wrist, and lodged in his thigh.[103] Both Vice President Johnson and his wife were also rushed to the hospital, although, fortunately, neither was hurt. In her book, *Lady Bird Johnson, A White House Diary,* Mrs. Johnson recalled:

> Suddenly I found myself face to face with Jackie in a small hallway. I believe it was right outside the operating room. You always

> think of someone like her as being insulated, protected. She was quite alone. I don't think I ever saw anyone so much alone in my life. I went up to her, put my arms around her, and said something like "God help us all," because my feelings for her were too tumultuous to put into words.
>
> One leg [of hers] was almost entirely covered with [blood] and her right glove was caked, it was caked with her husband's blood.[104]

The Secret Service insisted the vice president and First Lady return to the security of Air Force One. Still in her bloodstained pink wool suit, Jackie stood dazed and in shock next to Lyndon Johnson as he was sworn in to the presidency. Jackie refused to change her clothes and said emphatically,

> I want them to see what they have done to Jack. It's my husband, his blood, his brains, are all over me.[105]

Professional journalists throughout the country choked back tears as they reported the news in strained and cracked voices. Even the highly respected and seasoned evening news anchorman, Walter Cronkite, was forced to remove his glasses and wipe away tears on national television. In her state of shock, the First Lady still had the presence of mind to think of history, and sent word to the White House that she wanted things to be handled "just like it was when Lincoln lay in state."

Meanwhile, a priest waited in the East Room for the president's body, which did not arrive until four thirty Saturday morning. His casket was accompanied by the First Lady and Attorney General Robert Kennedy, the president's brother, who stayed in the White House for the next week and immediately became Jackie's savior. The First Lady's mother and stepfather spent that first night in the Executive Mansion as well. In order to be with her sister, Lee also temporarily moved in along with her husband.

For the next several days, every television station suspended regular programming in order to maintain twenty-four-hour news coverage of the proceedings. Keep in mind that around-the-clock news was unheard of in the 1960s; CNN would not be launched for another seventeen years. Consequently, to watch history unfold minute-by-minute over the television set was an astonishing experience.

No facet of the event was too insignificant or irrelevant to be reported. And every detail was reported over and over and over again. It was impossible to escape the hourly happenings, and moreover the greater majority of the American population wanted it that way. It was as if everything else in day-to-day life came to a screeching halt, and the entire nation seemed paralyzed. Suddenly there were no political differences, no opposing positions. The country's president had been slain, and the nation, in fact the world, was respectfully in mourning.

While history was being broadcast live from the nation's capital, equally somber and momentous events were unfolding back in Dallas. Within two hours of the president's shooting, a man by the name of Lee Harvey Oswald was arrested on suspicion of killing J. D. Tippit, a Dallas police officer. Shortly thereafter, Oswald was connected to the president's assassination as well. No sooner had the country absorbed this bittersweet news than shockingly (just under forty-eight hours later), as Oswald was being transferred to the Dallas County Jail and handcuffed to a detective, he was fatally shot on live television in the basement of the Dallas police headquarters. The shooter was Jack Ruby.*

Throughout the entire ordeal, Jacqueline Kennedy demonstrated remarkable bravery, strength, and composure. It was said repeatedly that the First Lady became a symbol for all to follow. The president's body remained in the East Room, now draped in black crepe, for

* Almost immediately, speculation began about the president's assassination. Because of their tense political differences, Castro was implicated in the president's death, and several other conspiracy theories were put forth. Both the FBI and the Dallas police department concluded the murder was done "single-handedly," yet the question has been debated for years. In 1964, President Johnson established the President's Commission on the Assassination of President Kennedy with Chief Justice Earl Warren as its chairman. The Warren Commission, as it was known, concluded in its eight-hundred-eighty-eight-page final report that Lee Harvey Oswald acted alone in President Kennedy's assassination and the wounding of Texas Governor Connally. (It should be noted that the Warren Commission was controversial and later challenged, with no further definitive answers forthcoming. Some people are still of the opinion that Oswald killed the president as part of a conspiracy.) Jack Ruby, a Dallas nightclub owner, was convicted in 1964 of Oswald's murder. Ruby appealed his death sentence conviction; however, he died in prison of lung cancer in 1967.

twenty-four hours. President Abraham Lincoln had been lying in state, in that very same room with the same decor, ninety-eight years earlier.

On Sunday, three hundred thousand spectators watched as the president's flag-covered casket was transferred to the Capitol Rotunda to lie in repose. For the next eighteen hours, two hundred and fifty thousand people went there to pay their respects. It was extremely cold, but the line of mourners stretched for some forty blocks. Some waited up to ten hours just to walk past the president's closed coffin. Unexpectedly, around 9:00 P.M., masses of people were surprised when Jackie and Bobby returned to the Rotunda to revisit their loved one.

Monday, November 25 (the day President Kennedy was laid to rest), was declared a national day of mourning by President Johnson. As the entire nation remained at home to watch the proceedings on television, only essential emergency workers remained on duty. Images from that day remain impossible to erase from memory. Under Jackie's black mourning veil, you could see her solemn and drawn face, etched with tears. She stood tall and erect with her two precious young children, one on each hand, dressed in matching light blue coats. Caroline kneeled before her father's coffin and then slipped her tiny white gloved hand just beneath the American flag, as if to get closer to her daddy inside the casket. Little John-John dropped his mother's hand so he could salute his fallen father. It was his third birthday. Some had assumed John Jr.'s birthday celebration would be cancelled, but Jackie did not want her son to miss his party, so it took place later that same day.

First, however, the recently widowed thirty-four-year-old mother of two needed to lead the nation through a tragic and excruciating funeral. Mr. West recounted the process.

> We had lined up all the guests in the White House: All the visiting Heads of State were in the East Room; the Kennedy relatives in the Green Room; White House staff in the State Dining Room; and Congress in the Blue Room...all those waiting inside joined the procession behind her [Jackie] by order of rank, and walked behind the body to St. Matthew's Cathedral.[106]

Six horses pulled the caisson that carried the president's casket. In the military tradition of mourning for a fallen warrior, a single saddled horse with no rider displayed reversed boots in its stirrups. Uniformed pallbearers from every branch of the service walked alongside the casket as it left the Capitol Rotunda to pick up the funeral party waiting at the White House and then continue on to St. Matthew's Cathedral. On foot, Jackie headed up the lengthy procession of mourners with Bobby and Ted Kennedy at her side. Some members of the large extended Kennedy family (like the president's mother, who was then seventy-three) waited at the church, while others walked, as did the new president and First Lady. President and Mrs. Johnson were entirely surrounded by Secret Service members, who were completely opposed to the new president's participation during the outdoor activities.

Kings, prime ministers, foreign presidents, heads of state, members of royal families and dignitaries—two hundred and twenty individuals from ninety-two nations—all followed as everyone marched for over a mile down the middle of Connecticut Avenue. Every branch of government followed suit. Members of Congress, the Senate, Cabinet secretaries, Supreme Court justices, former United States presidents, and clergy fell into sequence.* A group of advisers, White House staff, and some close friends could be seen at the rear of the massive gathering. Reportedly over one million people lined the procession route, and the sound of a muffled drum roll echoed throughout the gloomy silence.

Cardinal Cushing, who had officiated at the Kennedys' wedding, baptized their children, and presided over their infant son's recent funeral, now blessed the president's coffin with holy water. At the end of the Mass, limousines transported the lengthy procession to its final destination at Arlington National Cemetery, three miles away.† There were so many vehicles that the last cars were still leaving the Catholic cathedral as the first cars arrived at the cemetery. Four and one half

* Police officials confirmed it was the biggest security nightmare they had ever faced.

† President Kennedy is the second president to be buried in Arlington National Cemetery. President William Howard Taft was the first in 1930. Helen Taft was the first First Lady to be buried there in 1943.

hours after it had begun, the lengthy and complicated service concluded with the lighting of an eternal flame. A twenty-one-gun salute was performed, three cannons blasted in sequence, fifty jets accompanied Air Force One as it soared overhead, and the sound of taps could be heard.[107]

Drained and beyond exhaustion, the First Lady then returned to the White House to begin receiving the various visiting heads of state, which included the president of France, the prince of England, the emperor of Ethiopia, the president of Ireland, and numerous others, far too many to list.

It was said by many that Americans *needed* Jackie's example to survive and heal. The country could not have asked for a better role model to guide them through this significant period. History was being recorded with Jackie in the leading role, and she performed flawlessly. It was only afterward, behind closed doors, that Jackie had the chance to experience her personal loss. Yet there was still so very much to do in so little time. Jackie found herself traumatized and lost, confessing later,

> Jack was the love of my life. No one will ever know a big part of me died with him.[108]

Still with remarkable dignity, a model of self-control, Jackie proceeded forward. She invited the new First Lady to the White House for the traditional upstairs tour. For two hours, Jackie discussed the mansion, its rooms, and its staff as she escorted Mrs. Johnson around, all the while repeating to her successor,

> Don't be frightened of this house—some of the happiest years of my marriage have been spent here—you will be happy here.[109]

No longer the inexperienced young woman who was once too scared to ask Mrs. Eisenhower for a wheelchair, Jackie was still very much terrified of her future. With her children's welfare always at the forefront of her mind, Jackie asked Lady Bird if Caroline and her fellow students could continue the kindergarten class that had been established on the third floor of the mansion. New arrangements would be made after Christmas, but for now, Jackie hoped to keep some continuity in her daughter's daily life. Graciously, Lady Bird said of course.

On her last night in the White House, Jackie wrote letters until four thirty in the morning. She had already written to Nikita Khrushchev. In part she said,

> The danger which troubled my husband was that war might be started not so much by big men as by the little ones. While big men know the needs for self-control and restraint—little men are sometimes moved more by fear and pride. If only in the future the big men can continue to make the little ones sit down and talk, before they start to fight.[110]

That letter was followed by a note to Mrs. Tippit, the widow of the Dallas police officer who was also killed by her husband's assassin. Finally, she wrote letters to the White House domestic staff.

Unlike Mary Todd Lincoln, who remained immobilized in the White House for five weeks after her husband's assassination, Jackie moved out just a few weeks later, on December 6, 1963. An hour before she quietly slipped out into the Rose Garden through a side door, the exiting First Lady stood for group pictures with electricians, plumbers, and other staff members as she said her final goodbyes.

As the last of the Kennedy belongings were shipped to Averel Harriman's house in Georgetown, Jackie made two final requests of Mr. West.* She wanted a plaque made for her bedroom mantel that read:

> In this room lived John Fitzgerald Kennedy with his wife, Jacqueline—during the two years ten months and two days he was President of the United States—January 20, 1961—November 22, 1963.[111]

* Jackie temporarily moved into the Harrimans' home, while they magnanimously moved into a hotel, until she was able to purchase her own house directly across the street.

She asked that it be placed near an existing brass marker that stated Abraham Lincoln had slept in the room. She then wanted another small bronze plaque to read: "In Memory of President John F. Kennedy by his family."[112] It was to be placed on a Monet painting the Kennedy family had donated to the White House. She wondered if the beautiful waterscape *Morning on the Seine* could be hung in the Green Room, as it was her husband's favorite room. Mr. West assured her that neither request would be a problem. Finally, Jackie left ten pages of handwritten notes pertaining to the operation of the White House, on her familiar legal-sized yellow notepad, for Lady Bird. When the new First Lady received the additional comments, she was taken aback by Jackie's consideration and remarked, "How can she be so thoughtful of me at a time like this?"[113]

Other loose ends still existed. The volume of sympathy mail was overwhelming. Reportedly, over eight hundred thousand letters were received in the first seven weeks alone. In return, the public received a printed form letter acknowledging their sympathy. (Postage had already jumped from four cents to five cents a letter. Though that might sound inexpensive today, it still cost over forty thousand dollars just to send the responses.) The majority of the condolence mail was ultimately destroyed; several hundred thousand pages, however, eventually found their way to the JKF Library in Boston. Only recently, nearly fifty years later, historian Ellen Fitzpatrick published *Letters to Jackie: Condolences from a Grieving Nation*.

As with any widow, Jackie found the first year difficult and lonely. She appeared distracted and lost in her thoughts—predominately because she was. Caroline told her schoolteacher that her mother cried a lot. For a woman who learned to maintain a façade and preferred a life of detachment, feeling deep emotion was foreign and most unpleasant for Jackie. She once said of her husband and herself, "We're a couple of icebergs, with most of who we are submerged beneath the surface."[114] Only now, her surface was severely fractured and nothing would ever be like it once was.

Enraged at the unfairness of life, Jackie was particularly incensed at the meaninglessness of her husband's death. "If it had at least been for his civil rights stand," she said despondently. Then, perhaps because of her sadness and internal pain over her husband's infidelity, Jackie was quoted as saying in January of 1964,

> I know my husband was devoted to me. I know he was proud of me. It took a very long time for us to work everything out, but we did, and we were about to have a real life together [in reference to after Patrick's death]...I know I held a very special place for him—a unique place.[115]

Like all First Ladies, Jackie wanted history to assess her husband in a positive light. But even long before historians would write history, it was important to her that people not forget the hero she believed Jack Kennedy to be. Heroes are not forgotten by history and she wanted others to see and always remember him that way, as well. During an interview with Theodore White, who was doing an article for *Life* magazine, Jackie deliberately coined a phrase that would come to define the early nineteen sixties and her husband's administration. She told Mr. White that she had come to think of her White House years in terms of the mythical kingdom of Camelot.* President Kennedy's favorite music came from the Broadway musical of the same name. Jackie then quoted part of the title song:

> "Don't let it be forgot, that once there was a spot, for one brief shining moment, that was known as Camelot..." There'll never be another Camelot again...I should have guessed it could not last. I should have known that it was asking too much to dream that I might have grown old with him and see our children grow up together. So now he is a legend when he would have preferred to be a man.[116]

Consequently, the Kennedy administration is identified with and often referred to as Camelot.

Life, however, inevitably continues to move on, and Jackie found it more and more difficult to break away from her past. Previously,

* The most famous castle and court associated with the legendary King Arthur of England.

distractions like decorating had provided some therapeutic comfort, but things were different this time around. As had happened for the Coolidges and Trumans after they left the White House, curious individuals and busloads of tourists swarmed the block where Jackie now lived. Secret Service and local police had to carve paths just so Jackie and her children could walk outdoors. A fleeting glimpse or quick photo of her kids soon became intolerable. Jackie protested,

> The world is pouring terrible adoration at the feet of my children and I fear for them, for this awful exposure. How can I bring them up normally? We would never even have named John after his father had we known.[117]

> Can anyone understand how it is to have lived in the White House and then suddenly, to be living alone as the President's widow?[118]

It was a rhetorical question.

In an attempt to escape the circus she found herself living in, Jackie moved to New York. There she purchased a fifteen-room co-op apartment on Fifth Avenue, across from Central Park, from which she commented,

> It was so awful living in Washington...[Photographers and reporters would] follow me everywhere and sit out there in front of the house all day and eat their lunch and throw papers on the lawn.[119]

Over the next few years, Jackie worked hard to cement the Kennedy legend. She was involved in establishing the John F. Kennedy Memorial Library and Museum in Boston and persuaded President Johnson to change the name of Cape Canaveral in Florida to Cape Kennedy. (The name was changed back in 1973; however, there is a Kennedy Space Center nearby.)

Over time, Jackie returned to a fairly normal life. In addition to attending the opera and ballet, she became an active member of the Essex Fox Hounds Hunt Club in New Jersey. She and her children also continued to spend weekends and holidays at one of her sanctuary estates. Although Jackie generally stayed away from politics, she did attend the 1964 Democratic National Convention to support both President Johnson's reelection campaign and her brother-in-law Bobby Kennedy's senatorial bid.

It was important to Jackie to maintain her independence, yet her extravagant lifestyle was getting more problematical to support on her $50,000 government widow's pension and the $200,000 she received annually from the Kennedy trust fund. Even more challenging and demanding were the never-ending memorials and reminders of President Kennedy's assassination; in 1965, for instance, Jackie joined Queen Elizabeth II in jointly dedicating Great Britain's official memorial to her late husband.

Not surprisingly, November proved to be a particularly stressful month. At one point Jackie "broke down and sobbed" to her longstanding hairdresser at Kenneth's Salon.

> Oh, Rosemary, I thought that moving to New York would make it easier for me. If God had only let my baby [Patrick] live. I walk down the street and see his [Jack's] picture in every window. I can't stand it. Why do they remember the assassination? Why can't they celebrate his birthday?[120]

She also confided in a relative that no matter what she did, she felt overshadowed by death.

> I can't escape it. Whether I'm helping with the Kennedy Memorial at Harvard or taking a plane from Kennedy Airport or seeing a Kennedy-in-law. I always think of Jack and what they did to him.[121]

During this time the country experienced its most active involvement in the civil rights movement, which produced the Civil Rights Acts of 1964 and 1968, dealing with racial discrimination and segregation. The leader of the civil rights movement, Dr. Martin Luther King Jr., was adamant in his position of nonviolent protests and acts of civil disobedience, which included boycotts, sit-ins, and marches. Activity occurred predominately in the South; however, young people of all ages and races across the country were inspired to participate.

Demonstrators focused on public places such as lunch counters, libraries, theaters, parks, and museums. Students made a "jail-no-bail" pledge, causing havoc with local authorities and creating crisis situations between activists and government. Sometimes brute force was required as authorities escorted demonstrators away.

In opposition to the mainstream Civil Rights Movement was the Black Power Movement, which emphasized racial pride and freedom from oppression by white Americans. Black Power advocates supported Black Nationalism and black separatism, and they were not opposed to using militant and sometimes violent means to achieve their political goals. Involved in the Black Power Movement, as well as politics, was the Black Panther Party. By the late 1960s, the Black Panthers had expanded into several large cities throughout the United States. Their membership had reached five thousand and their newspaper had grown to a circulation of two hundred and fifty thousand readers.

It was indeed a turbulent time for the country. In April of 1968 Martin Luther King Jr. was assassinated—he was only thirty-nine years old. Riots broke out in more than one hundred cities, including Boston, Chicago, Detroit, and Washington.* Prior to attending King's funeral, Jackie sent a note to his widow, Coretta Scott King.

> Your husband was one of the greatest and most inspiring leaders that any of us has known. I share your grief in this hour of sorrow but his death will help to free us from the violence and tragedy which hate often produces. He will always be remembered as one of our nation's martyred greats.[122]

Robert Kennedy, known for being a prominent civil rights activist, had already begun his campaign for the upcoming presidential election in November 1968. He had just won the June 4 California primary and delivered a brief victory speech at the Ambassador Hotel in Los Angeles when the unthinkable occurred. Before he could even go

* In order to avoid the death penalty, which a trial and conviction could have produced, James Earl Ray pleaded guilty to King's murder and received a ninety-nine year prison term. He died in prison in 1998.

upstairs to celebrate, Bobby was shot and fatally wounded by Sirhan Sirhan.* For nearly twenty-six hours, Jackie, along with the entire Kennedy family, prayed in vain for Bobby's survival. He had become a second father to Jackie's children, and to say she was distraught over her brother-in-law's death would be putting it mildly. Another knight in shining armor had been cruelly taken away from her.

Within a short five-year period, three of the country's foremost leaders were brutally and violently murdered. Jackie's initial fear turned to resentment; as she reported to a friend,

> I despise America and I don't want my children to live here anymore. If they're killing Kennedys, my kids are number one targets... I want to get out of this country.[123]

Very soon thereafter, rumors of Jackie's possible engagement caused many to feel betrayed, but not because anyone wanted to deny her happiness. It was her eventual choice of spouse that caused consternation. She was still a very young woman who had been photographed with a number of escorts; however, they were predominately male friends and colleagues of her late husband. One such escort was Roswell Gilpatric, a prominent New York lawyer, who had served as deputy secretary of defense in the Kennedy administration. Many in the press defined their relationship as romantic, making Gilpatric a logical choice for a spouse. But this was not the case, and Jackie's selection of a husband generated an unfair backlash of public disdain.

Jackie had become rather close to Aristotle Onassis, one of (if not the) richest men in the world in the late 1960s, a divorced Greek Orthodox Catholic who was twenty-three years her senior. The Kennedy family knew of the relationship and was greatly concerned how it might affect Bobby's bid for the presidency. Anticipating some repercussions, Bobby had asked Jackie to hold off on any plans she might have until after the election. Naturally, she agreed. Only now Bobby's White House ambition had been shattered forever, and with

* Sirhan Sirhan was sentenced to life in prison for the murder of Robert Kennedy.

his death, the press rumor mill went into overdrive regarding the future of America's queen.

Leaving love out of the equation, a Kennedy-Onassis marriage would provide advantages to both parties, at least initially. For Onassis, marrying Jackie was like winning the ultimate first-place prize—there was no greater trophy wife! It gave him status and entry into the elite social registry, which he never could have obtained on his own merits. For Jackie, it meant securing the well-padded financial lifestyle she had long grown accustomed to and insisted on maintaining. It also offered her some measure of privacy, impossible to find in any other way. In addition to his palatial yacht, Onassis owned Skorpios, a private island maintained by a staff of seventy, off the western coast of Greece.

Over the previous five years Jackie had come as close to sainthood as conceivably possible, yet she still loathed the intrusion of photographers, reporters, and a curious public into her private life. Once an idol, she was now on the brink of falling from grace. A friend warned her, "You're going to fall off your pedestal," to which Jackie replied, "That's better than freezing there...I can't very well marry a dentist from New Jersey."[124]

Ari, as he was commonly called, was crude around the edges, short, overweight, and not particularly good-looking. In fact many said he looked like a toad, and his appearance was often equated to that of a gangster—or as some believed, basically the antithesis of JFK. On the plus side, Onassis was a good storyteller, had tremendous energy, spoke several languages, and was a financial genius, known to be a workaholic who slept no more than four or five hours a night. The three commonalities Ari and Jackie shared, to varying degrees, were intelligence, wealth, and power. Qualities each found admirable, if not compatible, in one another.

Four months after Bobby's assassination, Jackie was ready to proceed with wedding plans. Although Ari had given her a forty-carat diamond engagement ring, he was reluctant to rush into marriage. But when the *Boston Herald-Traveler* made a front-page announcement of their upcoming nuptials, Jackie pressed the issue. She was not one to seek approval; however, in this instance she had already contacted Rose

Kennedy and Cardinal Cushing for their blessings. Although both admitted to having had initial misgivings, Cardinal Cushing agreed that Jackie deserved happiness "even if the Vatican refused to recognize it."

Regarding her mother-in-law, Jackie fondly remembered, "She of all people was the one who encouraged me" to marry Onassis, adding that the elder Mrs. Kennedy had said, "He's a good man. Don't worry, dear." Jackie went on to comment on "how extraordinarily generous that woman [Rose] is in spirit." Though Jackie might not have had the warmest relationship with her former in-law, predominately because she found her somewhat overbearing, nonetheless, she did admire Rose's strength of character. Jackie admitted,

> If I ever feel sorry for myself, which is a most fatal thing, I think of her. I've seen her [Rose] cry just twice, a little bit. Once...her husband was ill, and Jack was gone, and Bobby had been killed...[Later] after her husband died...something that reminded her...and her voice began to sort of break and she had to stop [talking]. Then she took my hand and squeezed it and said, "Nobody's ever going to have to feel sorry for me. Nobody's ever going to feel sorry for me," and she put her chin up. And I thought, God, what a thoroughbred.[125]

Just prior to their wedding on October 20, 1968, Onassis and Jackie made a press statement to the *New York Times*.

> We know you understand that even though people may be well known they still hold in their hearts the emotions of a simple person for the moments that are the most important of those we know on earth—birth, marriage, death. We wish our wedding to be a private moment in the little chapel among the cypresses of Skorpios with only members of the family present. If you will give us these moments, we will gladly give you all the cooperation possible for you to take the pictures you need.[126]

A lavish reception followed aboard the *Christina*. The bride was thirty-nine and the groom was sixty-two.

There has been a great deal of speculation about a prenuptial agreement between the couple and its content. In addition to various sums of money earmarked for a variety of purposes, such an agreement was rumored to include over 170 separate clauses—including sleeping arrangements and conjugal visits—none of which has ever been proven to be true. Keep in mind that actual facts or even partial truths are not as significant to some individuals (and publishers) as are salacious or scandalous particulars. In other words, don't believe everything you read!

With that said, a number of reputable authors did go to great lengths to uncover accurate details. Logic, reason, and practicality should be measured as well. It would not be logical, reasonable, or practical for these wealthy and somewhat notorious people to consider marriage without some form of an agreement before the fact. Would a divorced billionaire enter into a marriage contract (or any transaction, for that matter) where a great deal of his assets would be at stake, and not arrange for some form of protection? Or upon remarriage, would a wealthy, intelligent widow give up a large amount of income from a trust, with no promise of future security? It is highly doubtful in either case.

Depending on whom you ask, a purported prenuptial agreement assigned different dollar amounts for various purposes. The informed consensus was that Jackie received from Onassis three million dollars outright, plus large trust funds for her two children until they reached twenty-one; she also received an annual personal income in addition to a thirty thousand dollar monthly spending allowance. Terms were also spelled out in the event of divorce or death.

Public outcry was quick and critical. A variety of newspaper headlines around the world read "America Has Lost a Saint," "The Reaction Here Is Anger, Shock and Dismay," "Jack Kennedy Dies Today for a Second Time," and "Jackie Weds Blank Check." One said simply, "JACKIE—HOW COULD YOU?"[127] Looking back, Jackie later remarked,

> Nobody could understand why I married Ari. But I just couldn't live anymore as the Kennedy widow. It was a release, freedom from the oppressive obsession the world had with me.[128]

Like most newlyweds, the couple had their challenges. To begin with, Ari's two grown children resented Jackie and vehemently opposed the marriage. Twenty-year-old Alexander Onassis said plainly, "My father needs a wife, but I don't need a stepmother." He called Jackie "the widow" and did not come around very often. His eighteen-year-old sister, Christina, believed Jackie was simply after her father's money. At best, their relationship was strained and frankly never improved.

Besides the family issues, the pair had very different taste. Ari was thoroughly Greek Orthodox, and while Jackie had pride in her French background, she was completely American. He enjoyed the nightlife, international clubs, Greek belly dancing, and a circle of friends that Jackie found boring. In fact, their disparate social circles had little in common; Jackie loved the ballet, the theater, art galleries, and horseback riding, activities which held no interest whatsoever for her new husband. To top it off, Jackie didn't care much for Greek food.

Their primary residence was on the relatively isolated island of Skorpios. Both did maintain separate residences in New York (Jackie found every excuse to prevent Ari from sharing her apartment when both happened to be in the city), and the two traveled frequently around the world. As expected, Jackie completely redecorated Ari's home and made attempts to improve his clothing choices and manners as well. She had very little success, if any, with the latter. As the saying goes, "You can't teach an old dog new tricks," and in the end Jackie finally refused to eat with Onassis, as she found his table manners revolting.

Back in the States, Jackie endured a long-running hostile relationship with persistent photographer Ron Galella, who was ruthless in his quest to obtain pictures of Jackie and her children. After Galella jumped out from behind some shrubbery, causing John Jr. to nearly crash his bicycle, Jackie had had enough and sued him. Initially he was prohibited from coming within twenty-five feet of her and thirty feet of her children. Eventually he was forbidden from ever taking another photograph of her, but only after two highly publicized and lengthy trials. In one, Galella counterclaimed and sought an excess of one million dollars for "malicious persecution, and interference with his livelihood as a photographer." Though he lost, after all the time, aggravation, and cost involved, Jackie's victory was bittersweet.

It would not be long before Jackie discovered that even a private island with its own security force could not ensure her privacy. The international paparazzi were beyond brutal—wearing diving suits, with underwater cameras and sophisticated telescopic lenses—Jackie did not have the seclusion she had hoped to find on Skorpios. Photographs of her and Ari sunbathing nude were published. Shrugging it off, Jackie said something like, "I guess I should be flattered," but some say she was considerably upset with the indignity of it and again wanted to sue. Ari felt differently; he believed that "Publicity is like rain, when you're soaking wet, what difference do a few drops more make?"[129] His only comment was, "Sometimes I take my pants off to put on a bathing suit. Anything's possible."[130]

Meanwhile Ari renewed his long-term affair with Maria Callas, one of the most renowned opera singers of the twentieth century. Their relationship had begun when both were still married to their first spouses. Onassis pointed out, "There [was] just a natural curiosity; after all, we were the most famous Greeks alive in the world." Ms. Callas left her husband, and the following year, when Ari's wife discovered her husband's affair, she divorced him. Nine years later, when Ari decided to marry Jackie, he temporarily ended his relationship with Maria. True to Jackie's philosophy that all men were unfaithful to their wives, she appeared indifferent when Ari renewed the affair, and simply continued to live her life as she pleased.

Forever the consummate shopper and buyer, it was said that "Mrs. O. [also known as Jackie O.] spent Greek drachmas, French francs, and American dollars that staggered even a tycoon like Onassis." In the beginning Ari did not seem to mind; in fact, he would frequently buy his new wife jewelry as well. He reportedly spent five million dollars on numerous trinkets and gems for her. Yet for all of his wealth, Onassis was basically a man with very simple tastes. Eventually Jackie's lavish and extravagant spending habits not only irritated but infuriated him.

Arguments over money became common. Equally disturbing to Onassis was her continual jet-setting. As important as privacy was to Jackie, she grew bored with the island and seldom stayed home. Then tragedy would again interfere with their soap opera lives. This time the suffering landed squarely on Onassis. His only son, Alexander, was killed in a plane crash at the age of twenty-five. Ravaged by grief, Ari's zest for life diminished and his physical health soon deteriorated. He and Jackie quarreled more often, and when Onassis finally had enough, he talked about ending the marriage. He said of Jackie,

> I cannot understand her. All she does is spend, spend, spend—and she's never in the same place I am. If I'm in Paris, she's in New York. If I go to Skorpios, she goes to London.[131]

In preparation for a divorce, Ari rewrote his will. He left Jackie $200,000 a year for life, the minimum amount originally set out in their prenuptial. As it happened, however, a divorce would never take place. Onassis had been diagnosed with myasthenia gravis, a neuromuscular disease that leads to muscle weakness. The first sign of it appeared when Ari could no longer keep his eyes open. In order to see, he had to tape his eyelids to his forehead. Then in early February of 1975, while in Athens, he collapsed with chest pains.

On his doctor's orders Ari was flown to Paris, as his physician determined he would receive the best possible care at the American Hospital in France. Ari was convinced he would never see his home again, and he was correct. While in Paris Jackie went to visit her husband daily, but it was Christina (who flew in from Switzerland) and Ari's sister who took full charge of his care.* After several weeks in Paris, while her husband was still gravely ill, Jackie decided to fly home to New York for a few days. She needed some personal refueling and the doctors had concluded that Ari's condition was stable. But it was not stable enough, because on March 15, while Jackie was still in the States, Ari died. She returned to Paris the following day with her mother, her brother-in-law Ted Kennedy, and her children. The family then accompanied Onassis back to his final resting place.

With the world watching, Jackie gave a carefully prepared statement to the press. Unlike after President Kennedy's death, Jackie showed no signs of grief or mourning.

* In addition to his massive business holdings, Ari owned Olympic Airways. He and his family summoned airplanes like a New Yorker would hail a taxicab to ride downtown.

> Aristotle Onassis rescued me at a time when my life was engulfed in shadows. He meant a lot to me. He brought me into a world where one could find both happiness and love. We lived through many beautiful experiences together which cannot be forgotten, and for which I will be eternally grateful.[132]

She then attended her husband's funeral and returned to New York. It was her last visit to Skorpios; the strained relationship Jackie shared with her stepdaughter soon turned ice cold. Christina had already made arrangements to have all of Jackie's personal belongings removed from her father's home and yacht (which bore Christina's name).

For the next eighteen months, the two women were embroiled in a bitter legal battle over Onassis's estate. However, before all ties were severed between them, for some odd reason, they felt it was necessary to show some sort of family harmony. Clearly, there was no fondness between them. Nevertheless, Jackie was invited to and attended Christina's second wedding, just three months after Ari's death. After all was said and done, Jackie settled with Christina for $26 million and relinquished all further claims to her late husband's estate.*

It can be said that Jackie lived in and walked down the halls of both power (with her first husband) and money (with her second). Widowed twice and still only forty-six years old, she entered the third phase of her remarkable and extraordinary life. Once again Jackie turned all of her attention to what mattered most to her—raising her children. She was quoted as saying,

> I've seen the worst of everything, I've seen the best of everything. But I can't replace my family.[133]

* Christina lived the short remainder of her life insecure and unhappy. She married two more times and all four of her marriages ended in divorce. One month prior to her thirty-eighth birthday, Christina died of pulmonary edema, survived only by Athina, her three-year-old daughter. Athina would grow up and inherit an estate estimated between six hundred million and two billion dollars from her grandparents (Aristotle Onassis and his ex-wife Athina Onassis Niarchos).

Settled in New York, Jackie set out to establish a private life on her own. She said, "I have always lived through men. Now I realize I can't do that anymore."[134] Not surprisingly, Americans welcomed her back with open arms. Gloria Steinem, an active feminist and cofounder of the iconic feminist journal *Ms. Magazine*, said of Jackie at that time that the former First Lady was "almost overly discreet and delicate."

> She approved the movement [referring to the Equal Rights Amendment] and even supported it, but would not march. She did donate a large sum of money to the Ms. Foundation.[135]

No longer defined as the wife of anyone, and financially secure with no one to answer to, Jackie would at last come into her own.

> Learning to accept what was unthinkable...changes you. I don't think there is any consolation. What was lost cannot be replaced.[136]

Always mindful of the Kennedy name (though she never personally dropped the last name of Onassis), Jackie wanted her children to know their heritage. She often invited her late husband's friends and colleagues over to share memories and stories of Jack with her children. She wanted them to understand not only the man, but the Kennedy legacy as well, and that they too were Kennedys.

Never lacking for male escorts, Jackie remained involved in the arts and attended ballets and the theater. She was also interested in architecture and particularly the preservation of landmarks. No longer the frequent jet-setter she once was (not to imply that she did not travel or take vacations), Jackie built a Cape Cod–style mansion on Martha's Vineyard. It had nineteen rooms with an adjoining guest house on 375 acres of oceanfront property.[137] One escort in particular, Maurice Tempelsman, was a frequent visitor.

With her children now teenagers (Caroline was eighteen and John Jr. fifteen), Jackie became an employed working mother. As a part-time consulting editor for Viking Press (1975–1977) she earned a salary of ten thousand dollars a year. It is doubtful that her earnings even covered her beauty expenses, but that of course was not why she went to work.

> What has been sad for many women of my generation is that they weren't supposed to work if they had families...What were they going to do when the children were grown—watch the raindrops coming down the windowpane?[138]

Later in *Ms. Magazine,* Jackie was quoted as saying,

> Of course women should work if they want to. You have to be doing something you enjoy.[139]

Well aware of the fact that she would have to earn respect in the publishing world, Jackie took her job seriously. In the spring of 1978, she went to work for Doubleday as a book editor. She worked three days a week and edited twelve books a year. It took some time, however, for her coworkers to get accustomed to seeing the former First Lady in the elevator, even more so to hear her on the phone with a prospective client saying, "Hello, this is Jackie Onassis with Doubleday."

Nevertheless, after their initial astonishment, her coworkers found her "conscientious, perceptive, and shrewd."[140] It was the throngs of individuals who collected in the lobby—waiting to get just a glimpse of Jackie—that caused some congestion. Staffers would go downstairs on Mondays and Fridays to tell loiterers that Jackie did not work those days, but most did not believe it and waited anyway. Employed at Doubleday for over thirteen years, Jackie earned her colleagues' respect. Insiders said her annual salary increased to $45,000 by the time she ended her tenure with the publisher, only weeks prior to her death.

In addition to her professional insight, Bruce Tracy, another editor at Doubleday, once sought Jackie's personal advice. While working with her on a project, he had on opportunity to go to Europe, but it would mean missing some events regarding the book's publication. He was torn and asked her opinion, to which Jackie said simply, "Life comes first."[141] Her attitude never changed.

There is little doubt that Doubleday had hoped Jackie would one day write her memoirs. In fact, Bill Barry, Doubleday's deputy publisher, suggested as much. Her response was,

> Life is too precious: I want to savor it. I'd rather spend my time feeling a galloping horse, or the mist of the ocean up at Martha's Vineyard.[142]

Jackie never even kept a journal; as she put it, "I want to live my life, not record it." Then later in an interview with *Publishers Weekly*, Jackie said,

> One of the things I like about publishing is that you don't promote the editor; you promote the book and author.[143]

By 1980, Jackie discovered a loving companion she would spend the rest of her life with. Financier and diamond merchant Maurice Tempelsman was initially a friend who became a financial advisor and then devoted partner. A business leader and Democratic political supporter, he had met the Kennedys in the 1950s and was a guest in their White House as well as that of other administrations. As a financial advisor, Maurice helped Jackie turn her multimillion dollar inheritance from Onassis into hundreds of millions of dollars. Even more importantly, Maurice was able to provide her with support, stability, and serenity when it mattered most. Regarding their friendship, Jackie said,

> I admire Maurice's strength and his success. I truly hope my notoriety doesn't force him out of my life.[144]

Viviana Crespi, a longtime friend of Jackie's, said of Tempelsman,

> I had never seen her [Jackie] that happy or relaxed with anyone... they were equals...Maurice worshiped the ground she walked on.[145]

Like Jackie, Maurice was a deeply private person who had savoir faire. Both loved the arts, including opera; read extensively; spoke multiple languages; took pleasure in travel; and were fond of the sea. They frequently enjoyed outings on his seventy-foot yacht, the *Relemar*. (The name is an amalgamation of the first few letters of the names of his three children.) Charming, worldly, and effervescent were words often used to describe Tempelsman. Maurice, who was the same age as Jackie, was also the man with whom she shared the healthiest and most long-lasting, ongoing male relationship of her adult life.

Many believed Jackie would marry for a third time, but that was not to be as Maurice was already married. He was raised in a Jewish Orthodox family and his Orthodox wife refused to give him a legal divorce. She did agree to a "get," otherwise known as a Jewish divorce, and though the two were separated they remained on amiable terms. Meanwhile, Jackie had grown comfortable with her independence and recognized, "You don't have to be married to be together." With shared interests and an allegiance greater than either of Jackie's two husbands ever demonstrated, Maurice moved into her New York apartment.

In 1986 Caroline married Edwin Schlossberg, also of Jewish decent. She went on to earn a law degree from Columbia Law School and eventually made Jackie a three-time grandmother. As an adult, John Jr. made the cover of *People* magazine as their "Sexiest Man Alive" in 1988. Jackie remained the primary influence in her children's lives as she continued to guide them through life's landmines. With almost clairvoyant foresight, she insisted that her athletic and audacious son promise to give up his desire for a pilot's license. In addition, Jackie opposed John's career interest in acting. He too would earn a law degree and later worked in the Manhattan district attorney's office for four years before branching out on his own as founder of *George* magazine.

The end of the decade brought anniversaries and momentous events. In May of 1989, the Kennedy Library commemorated what would have been JFK's seventy-second birthday. Just two months later, and only one week shy of Jackie's sixtieth birthday, her mother Janet died after a long battle with Alzheimer's disease.*

* Coincidentally, Janet's death occurred on Rose Kennedy's ninety-ninth birthday. Rose lived to be one hundred and four years old and remained in touch with her famous daughter-in-law over the years. She visited Jackie on Skorpios a few times, and Caroline and John made biannual visits to their grandmother's home in Hyannis Port.

Now, for the third time in her life, Jackie successfully reinvented herself. In her twenties she was an educated and youthful socialite. By her thirties, she had grown into one of the country's youngest and most popular First Ladies.* After being a jet-set wife of a billionaire in her forties, Jackie became a serious and conscientious advocate for the arts in her fifties. Not only was she the lead force behind the creation of the National Endowment for the Arts, she raised funds and fought to preserve old buildings like the Grand Central Terminal in New York City. She adopted President Kennedy's philosophy:

> One man can make a difference and every man should try...We should all do something to right the wrongs that we see and not just complain about them.[146]

Now middle-aged and somewhat of a health enthusiast, Jackie watched her weight, exercised, and took private yoga lessons in her apartment. She remained beautiful, vibrant, and involved. It was probably the most satisfying and private time of her very public life.

Around 1992 in the *Reader's Guide to Periodical Literature*, there were more article entries under Jackie Kennedy's name than for any other living American woman. Amazed, she commented to her friend Jayne Wrightsman,

> I've been in the public eye for more than thirty years. I can't believe that anybody still cares about me or is still interested in what I do.[147]

Yet the country's fascination with Jackie *never* ended. When asked how she managed to deal with all of the tabloid gossip, she said,

> The river of sludge will go on and on. It isn't about me. When you get written about a lot, you just think of it as a little cartoon that runs along at the bottom of your life—but one that doesn't have much to do with your life.[148]

* The incredible fairytale life story of America's youngest First Lady, Frances Cleveland, is detailed in Volume I of *Loves, Lies, and Tears.*

Then in January of 1994, Jackie was diagnosed with non-Hodgkin's lymphoma. Two of her greatest strengths—determination and courage—were immediately apparent. Without any delay, she started chemotherapy, making no changes in her regular routine. She continued her work at Doubleday on Tuesdays, Wednesdays, and Thursdays, and pronounced clearly, "I refuse to believe that I am going to die."[149] Positive and cheerful, Jackie dropped the imaginary curtain in her mind and blocked out any possible unpleasantness.

She did surrender on one particular point, at her daughter's request. Caroline tearfully asked her mother to stop smoking, "if only for the sake of [her grandchildren] Rose, Tatiana and Jack."[150] Most people never even knew that Jackie had been a heavy smoker for forty years.* She regularly smoked Pall Malls and managed to hide it in view of photographers. (Of the many thousands of pictures taken of her over the years, there are only two or three photos of her with a cigarette.) Jackie agreed to her daughter's plea and quit.

In early February, the *New York Times* broke the story of Jackie's chemotherapy. In an interview, Nancy Tuckerman, her longtime friend and spokeswoman, gave a very optimistic assessment of Jackie's condition. However, Jackie's particular form of cancer was aggressive and highly malignant. By the middle of March it had already metastasized and she was forced to acknowledge the seriousness and inevitability of her circumstances. She went in and out of the hospital several times after that.

As her physical condition began to deteriorate, Jackie lost her hair from the treatments and began wearing a wig. One touching aspect of this final battle: with a heart full of gratitude, Jackie discovered that she had truly found a knight in shining armor who would remain at her side no matter what. To provide his beloved sweetheart with the last bit of anonymity she would ever have, Maurice booked all of her doctor and chemotherapy appointments under an assumed name.

* Reminiscing about her transition into adulthood, Jackie confirmed, "It happened gradually over the three years I spent at boarding school trying to imitate girls who had callers every Saturday. I passed the finish line when I learned to smoke, in the balcony of the Normandie Theater in New York." Led from the theater by the usher, Jackie was told, "Other people could not hear the film with so much coughing going on." (*The Eloquent Jacqueline Kennedy Onassis*, 11; *Jackie, Her Life in Pictures*, 8.)

The appointments were booked before regular office hours and Maurice would check the reception area before he escorted her inside. On the good days, she continued her daily walks (which at one time had been daily jogs) in Central Park, now holding onto Maurice's arm. Photographers captured her frail appearance and her picture was distributed around the world, as she knew it would be.

Clearly her once strong and healthy body was failing her, and she was too weak to continue her private yoga lessons. A habitual fingernail biter, Jackie was also forced to give up her weekly in-home manicure and pedicure. Still in command of what life she had left, Jackie reviewed her will and made it clear to her doctors that she wanted no "extraordinary measures to keep her alive." She seriously considered cremation but then conceded there was "a responsibility she could not escape." In the end, she would be laid to rest next to her husband and two small children in Arlington National Cemetery.* As Jackie explained, "I was the president's wife and the country would expect me to be buried there."[151]

Like two other very private First Ladies, Martha Washington and Bess Truman, Jackie consciously chose to destroy some of her personal correspondence. In doing so, she ensured that the contents of private letters from family and lovers would remain for her eyes and her memories alone.

On May 16 Jackie was again readmitted to the hospital, this time for pneumonia. Her children pleaded with her to try another round of chemotherapy, or an experimental medication, or at least more powerful antibiotics, anything—anything to keep fighting! But the cancer had spread to her liver and Jackie said, no more. "I want to go home to die."[152]

Against everyone's wishes, on May 18, she discharged herself from the hospital and returned home in an ambulance accompanied by a nurse, with Maurice holding her hand.

As her family and friends came to pay their last respects, several hundred people began to assemble near her apartment. Her dear

* The bodies of Patrick Bouvier Kennedy and Jackie's stillborn daughter were reinterred next to their father.

friends Bunny Mellon and Carly Simon arrived, as did Senator Ted Kennedy and numerous members of the large Kennedy family. Soon both sides of Fifth Avenue were flooded with people, and traffic came to a frozen standstill. Television cameras transmitted news and photos of the event. Across the entire country, those who could not go to pay their respects watched and listened by their televisions and radios.

With her children and Maurice at her bedside, America's Queen passed away on the evening of May 19, 1994. She was sixty-four years old. The family mourned in private until the next morning, when John finally came out to speak with reporters. Immaculately groomed, with microphones in his face and flashbulbs exploding, John stood poised as he politely announced,

> Last night, at around ten-fifteen, my mother passed on. She was surrounded by her friends and family and her books and the people and things that she loved. And she did it in her own way, and on her own terms, and we all feel lucky for that, and now she's in God's hands.[153]

By some estimates, thousands had gathered to quietly cry, remember, and leave flowers. An outpouring of grief covered the nation. The woman who captured the world's awe and wonderment was gone from sight, but not from our minds or hearts! Jackie undeniably touched a nerve, and her impact would live on for some time to come, particularly for those of us who experienced her presence.

On the morning of May 24, a service was held at St. Ignatius Loyola Church on Park Avenue. The street was closed off to traffic and barricades held spectators back. Per Jackie's wishes, television cameras were banned from inside the church; however, the audio portion of the service could be heard on loudspeakers outside the building, as well as on radio and television.

Afterward, family members escorted Jackie's body to Washington aboard a chartered jet. At Arlington National Cemetery, a retired Roman Catholic archbishop conducted a simple service attended by many distinguished mourners. Among them were friend and sitting First Lady Hillary Clinton and President Bill Clinton, who spoke briefly and said in part,

> God gave her very great gifts and imposed upon her great burdens. She bore them all with dignity and grace and uncommon common sense. May the flame she lit so long ago burn ever brighter here and always brighter in our hearts. God bless you, friend, and farewell.[154]

Both Caroline, now thirty-six, and John Jr., thirty-three, read their mother's favorite poems and knelt down to kiss her coffin. John also bent down and touched his father's gravestone. Maurice read from notes,

> And now the journey is over. Too short, alas, too short. It was filled with adventure and wisdom, laughter and love, gallantry and grace.[155]

Looking back on Jackie's philosophy regarding the importance of raising children, she did a remarkable job. Not only did she accomplish the arduous task alone, she achieved it against all odds! Both Caroline and John Jr. grew up to be well-adjusted, stable, and admirable adults who would have made any parent proud.

The fantasy had ended, but the legend lived on. Interest in and curiosity about Jackie's life remained high throughout the years. In 1996, Sotheby's in New York conducted a four-day estate sale of some five thousand personally selected possessions of Jacqueline Kennedy Onassis. The sale yielded thirty-four and a half million dollars—several times greater than the value of the objects—no doubt simply because of the original owner.[156]

Not included in that total price was a 584-page auction catalog, with color photographs and descriptions of each item auctioned. For the thousands of individuals who could only dream of owning something of Jackie's, they had the opportunity to purchase a hardcover copy of the catalog for ninety dollars, or a softcover version for merely forty-five dollars.

Tragedy still hounded the Kennedy family, even after Jackie's premature death. Five short years later, it was impossible to make any sense of the tragic loss of John Jr., who perished when he was just thirty-eight. He had been married nearly three years and had an understandably bright future ahead of him; John, his wife Carolyn, and his sister-in-law, Lauren Bassette, were killed when a plane John was piloting crashed off of Martha's Vineyard. The only saving grace, if there is any at all, is that Jackie's untimely death prevented her from having to survive her beloved son. Still others believe that if Jackie had lived, John would not have pursued his private pilot's license. The National Transportation Safety Board determined that the probable cause of the crash was pilot error.

WHAT JACKIE TAUGHT ME

It takes a unique and exceptional personality to capture and sustain the imagination of millions. On the rare occasions it does occur, the individual's life can offer several lessons. Such is the case with Jacqueline Bouvier Kennedy Onassis. Jackie not only held onto her dreams, she did not rely on others to validate them. She also embodied the truth that it is essential to remain focused and create a plan as well as discover your individuality and embrace it.

For Jackie, this was not complicated. She said of herself, "I wouldn't put on a mask and pretend to be anything that I wasn't."[157] Undeniably, she had a better sense of self than most. But when it came to her ability to cope, Jackie relied on the law of action, which is, "When you act as if…the feeling will follow!" She understood that when you looked fear in the face and refused to run away, your inner strength would materialize.

Certainly there is an advantage when you can blindly believe in something. Being optimistic opens the mind to possibilities that create opportunities. Yet even more advantageous and effective than simply believing something to be true is the trick of acting as if, indeed, it *were* true. The reality is, the more you act courageously or lovingly, the more you become those things.

The fact that Jackie suffered depression and sometimes despair is indisputable, yet she believed, "It's up to you to take what happiness you can find…you have to soldier on, whether you like it or not," and "One must not let oneself be overwhelmed by sadness."[158]

Everyone has blessings and no one is without challenges or adversity. Not the affluent, not royalty, not the most talented or celebrated, not even the most religious! As Jackie so wisely put it,

> We must give to life at least as much as we receive from it. Every moment one lives is different from the next. The good, the bad, the hardship, the joy, the tragedy, love and happiness are all interwoven into one single indescribable whole that is called life. You cannot separate the good from the bad. And, perhaps there is no need to do so either.[159]

Jackie modeled what to me is the most significant principle of life, and that is that life is meant to be *lived*, even if those we cherished are no longer with us in the flesh. Life goes on and so should we.

Notes

Part One: Women of World War I

Introduction

1. *The White House: An Illustrated Tour*, 26.
2. *The Complete Book of U.S. Presidents*, 411.

Chapter 1: Advocate for the Impoverished: Ellen Wilson

1. *First Ladies, A Biographical Dictionary*, 186.
2. *America's First Families*, 311.
3. *Profiles & Portraits of American Presidents & Their Wives*, 275.
4. *The First Ladies Fact Book*, 391; *First Ladies, A Biographical Dictionary*, 184.
5. *Presidential Wives*, 221.
6. *Profiles & Portraits of American Presidents & Their Wives*, 278.
7. *First Ladies, A Biographical Dictionary*, 186.
8. Ibid., 186.
9. Ibid., 187.
10. *First Ladies, An Intimate Group Portrait of White House Wives*, 53.
11. *American First Ladies*, 195.
12. *First Ladies, A Biographical Dictionary*, 188.
13. *American First Ladies*, 195.
14. *First Ladies Quotations Book*, 161.
15. Ibid., 161.
16. Ibid., 151.
17. Ibid., 162.
18. Ibid., 170.
19. *The First Ladies Fact Book*, 395.
20. Ibid., 394.
21. Ibid., 394.

Chapter 2: First Woman Co-President: Edith Wilson

1. *My Memoir*, 56.
2. *National First Ladies' Library*, website (www.firstladies.org).
3. *My Memoir*, 18.
4. Ibid., 34.
5. Ibid., 36.
6. Ibid., 38.
7. *Presidential Wives, An Anecdotal History*, 223; *The First Ladies Fact Book*, 412.
8. *Presidential Wives, An Anecdotal History*, 223; *Profiles & Portraits of American Presidents & Their Wives*, 284; *My Memoir*, 61.
9. *My Memoir*, 61–62.
10. *First Ladies, A Biographical Dictionary*, 192; *First Ladies, An Intimate Group Portrait of White House Wives*, 120.
11. *My Memoir*, 71.

12. Ibid., 75.
13. *First Ladies, A Biographical Dictionary*, 192.
14. *My Memoir*, 21.
15. *Profiles & Portraits of American Presidents & Their Wives*, 285.
16. *First Ladies, An Intimate Group Portrait of White House Wives*, 122.
17. *Profiles & Portraits of American Presidents & Their Wives*, 286.
18. *The President Speaks*, 108.
19. *My Memoir*, 274.
20. Ibid., 284.
21. Ibid., 284.
22. Ibid., 285.
23. Ibid., 289.
24. Ibid., 290.
25. Ibid., 289.
26. Ibid., 289.
27. Ibid., 297.
28. Ibid., 297.
29. Ibid., 299.
30. *The American President*, 326.

Part Two: Women of the Roaring Twenties

Introduction

1. www.wikipedia.org/wiki/Chrysler_Building.

Chapter 3: The Duchess: Florence Harding

1. *Florence Harding, The First Lady, The Jazz Age, and the Death of America's Most Scandalous President*, 22.
2. *The First Ladies Fact Book*, 437.
3. *Florence Harding, The First Lady, The Jazz Age, and the Death of America's Most Scandalous President*, 18.
4. Ibid., 22.
5. *Florence Harding, The First Lady, The Jazz Age, and the Death of America's Most Scandalous President*, 27; *The First Ladies Fact Book*, 429; *First Ladies, A Biographical Dictionary*, 202.
6. *Florence Harding, The First Lady, The Jazz Age, and the Death of America's Most Scandalous President*, 30.
7. Ibid., 31.
8. *The Complete Book of U.S. Presidents*, 432; *Incredible Era: The Life and Times of Warren Gamaliel Harding*, 8.
9. *The First Ladies Fact Book*, 437; *Florence Harding, The First Lady, The Jazz Age, and the Death of America's Most Scandalous President*, 103.
10. *The First Ladies Fact Book*, 430.
11. *The First Ladies Fact Book*, 431; *Florence Harding, The First Lady, The Jazz Age, and the Death of America's Most Scandalous President*, 45, 55.
12. *Florence Harding, The First Lady, The Jazz Age, and the Death of America's Most Scandalous President*, 55.
13. *The First Ladies Fact Book*, 433.
14. *Florence Harding, The First Lady, The Jazz Age, and the Death of America's Most Scandalous President*, 62; *The First Ladies Fact Book*, 433.

15. *Florence Harding, The First Lady, The Jazz Age, and the Death of America's Most Scandalous President*, 79.
16. Ibid., 99.
17. Ibid., 96.
18. Ibid., 98.
19. Ibid., 107.
20. Ibid., 112.
21. Ibid., 119.
22. *The First Ladies Fact Book*, 437.
23. *Florence Harding, The First Lady, The Jazz Age, and the Death of America's Most Scandalous President*, 144.
24. Ibid., 129.
25. *Florence Harding, The First Lady, The Jazz Age, and the Death of America's Most Scandalous President*, 156; *First Ladies, A Biographical Dictionary*, 205.
26. *Florence Harding, The First Lady, The Jazz Age, and the Death of America's Most Scandalous President*, 162; *The First Ladies Fact Book*, 439.
27. *Florence Harding, The First Lady, The Jazz Age, and the Death of America's Most Scandalous President*, 181.
28. Ibid., 181–184.
29. Ibid., 210.
30. *The First Ladies Fact Book*, 436.
31. *First Ladies, A Biographical Dictionary*, 205–206.
32. *First Ladies, A Biographical Dictionary*, 206; *The First Ladies Fact Book*, 441.
33. *America's First Ladies, Private Lives of the Presidential Wives*, 162.
34. Ibid., 162.
35. *First Ladies, A Biographical Dictionary*, 207.
36. Ibid., 207.
37. *Florence Harding, The First Lady, The Jazz Age, and the Death of America's Most Scandalous President*, 400.
38. *America's First Ladies, Private Lives of the Presidential Wives*, 163.
39. *Crowded Hours*, 325.
40. *The First Ladies Fact Book*, 435.
41. *Florence Harding, The First Lady, The Jazz Age, and the Death of America's Most Scandalous President, 374.*
42. Ibid., 377.
43. Ibid., 275.
44. Ibid., 379.
45. Ibid., 380.
46. Ibid., 380.
47. Ibid., 380.
48. Ibid., 381.
49. Ibid., 381.
50. Ibid., 285.
51. *The Complete Book of U.S. Presidents*, 443.
52. *Florence Harding, The First Lady, The Jazz Age, and the Death of America's Most Scandalous President*, 416.
53. *The Complete Book of U.S. Presidents*, 442.
54. *Florence Harding, The First Lady, The Jazz Age, and the Death of America's Most Scandalous President*, 466.
55. *Florence Harding, The First Lady, The Jazz Age, and the Death of America's Most Scandalous President*, 463; *New World Encyclopedia*, Warren Harding www.newworldencyclopedia.org/entry/Warren_G._Harding.

56. *Florence Harding, The First Lady, The Jazz Age, and the Death of America's Most Scandalous President*, 522.
57. Ibid., 285.
58. Ibid., 31–32.

Chapter 4: Teacher to the Deaf, Not the Mute: Grace Coolidge

1. *Alice, The Life and Times of Alice Roosevelt Longworth*, 125.
2. *American First Ladies*, 213.
3. *The Autobiography of Calvin Coolidge*, 93.
4. *Grace Coolidge and Her Era*, 17.
5. Ibid., 135.
6. *The First Ladies Fact Book*, 453.
7. *Grace Coolidge and Her Era*, 24.
8. *American First Ladies*, 214.
9. *The Autobiography of Calvin Coolidge*, 95.
10 Ibid., 95.
11. *First Ladies, A Biographical Dictionary*, 213.
12. *Crowded Hours*, 325.
13. *Grace Coolidge and Her Era*, 98.
14. Ibid., 25.
15. Ibid., 19.
16. *The Complete Book of U.S. Presidents*, 460.
17. *First Ladies Quotations Book*, 53.
18. *Grace Coolidge and Her Era*, 32.
19. *Grace Coolidge and Her Era, 27; The First Ladies*, 200.
20. *Grace Coolidge and Her Era, 136; The First Ladies*, 200.
21. *The First Ladies*, 203–204; *The Autobiography of Calvin Coolidge*, 190.
22. *The Autobiography of Calvin Coolidge*, 190.
23. Ibid., 190.
24. Ibid., 191.
25. Ibid., 191–192.
26. *Grace Coolidge and Her Era*, 177.
27. *The First Ladies*, 202.
28. *Presidential Wives, An Anecdotal History*, 262.
29. *Grace Coolidge and Her Era*, 87.
30. Ibid., 156.
31. Ibid., 155.
32. Ibid., 29.
33. Ibid., 335.
34. *The First Ladies Fact Book*, 464.
35. *Grace Coolidge and Her Era*, 337.
36. Ibid., 19.
37. Ibid., 27.
38. Ibid., 262.

Part Three: Women of the Great Depression

Introduction

1. *The Complete Book of U.S. Presidents*, 461.
2. *Calvin Coolidge—The Man from Vermont*, 71.

Chapter 5: Humanitarian Linguist: Lou Hoover

1. *The First Ladies*, 206.
2. *The First Ladies Fact Book*, 475.
3. Ibid., 471.
4. Ibid., 471.
5. *The Complete Book of U.S. Presidents*, 467.
6. *Wit and Wisdom of the American Presidents*, 49; Hoover Archives website, http://hoover.archives.gov/info.
7. *American Magazine* (June 1933), 115.
8. *Profiles & Portraits of American Presidents & Their Wives*, 329.
9. *My 21 Years In The White House*, 18.
10. *First Ladies, An Intimate Group Portrait of White House Wives*, 266.
11. *Forty-two Years in the White House*, 183.
12. Ibid., 183.
13. *The First Ladies*, 215.
14. Ibid., 216.
15. *Presidential Wives: An Anecdotal History*, 279.
16. *The First Ladies*, 213.
17. *The First Ladies Fact Book*, 472.
18. *Presidential Fact Book*, 195.
19. *First Ladies Quotations Book*, 4.

Chapter 6: Devoted Business Partner: Anna Eleanor Roosevelt

1. *Eleanor Roosevelt, Volume One, 1884–1933*, 1.
2. *First Ladies Quotations Book*, 222.
3. Ibid., 222.
4. *Betty: A Glad Awakening*, 131; *First Ladies Quotations Book*, 222.
5. *First Ladies Quotations Book*, 222.
6. *Eleanor Roosevelt, Volume One, 1884–1933*, 49.
7. Ibid., 44.
8. *First Ladies, An Intimate Group Portrait of White House Wives*, 58.
9. *Eleanor Roosevelt, Volume One, 1884–1933*, 62.
10. Ibid., 67.
11. *American First Ladies*, 225; *Eleanor Roosevelt, Volume One, 1884–1933*, 70.
12. *Eleanor Roosevelt, Volume One, 1884–1933*, 72.
13. Ibid., 82.
14. Ibid., 80.
15. Ibid., 58.
16. Ibid., 85.
17. Ibid., 81.
18. Ibid., 84.
19. Ibid., 87–88.
20. Ibid., 92.
21. *The Roosevelt Women*, 245.
22. *This I Remember*, 300.
23. *First Ladies, A Biographical Dictionary*, 231.
24. *Eleanor Roosevelt, Volume One, 1884–1933*, 115.
25. Ibid., 100.
26. Ibid., 131; *The First Ladies Fact Book*, 482.
27. Ibid., 131.
28. *First Ladies, A Biographical Dictionary*, 231.

29. *The Autobiography of Eleanor Roosevelt,* 104.
30. The Eleanor Roosevelt Papers Project, www.gwu.edu/~erpapers/abouteleanor/erbiography.
31. *Eleanor Roosevelt, Volume One, 1884–1933,* 130.
32. Ibid., 133.
33. Ibid., 146.
34. Ibid., 150.
35. Ibid., 157.
36. Ibid., 163.
37. Ibid., 141.
38. Ibid., 141.
39. Ibid., 184.
40. *The Autobiography of Eleanor Roosevelt,* 41.
41. *Eleanor Roosevelt, Volume One, 1884–1933,* 156.
42. Ibid., 9, 2.
43. Ibid., 166.
44. Ibid., 166.
45. *Princess Alice: The Life and Times of Alice Roosevelt Longworth,* 105.
46. National First Ladies Library website, www.firstladies.org.
47. *Eleanor Roosevelt, Volume One, 1884–1933,* 183.
48. *First Ladies, A Biographical Dictionary,* 232.
49. *The First Ladies Fact Book,* 486.
50. *Eleanor Roosevelt, Volume One, 1884–1933,* 305.
51. Ibid., 1.
52. Ibid., 161.
53. The Eleanor Roosevelt Papers Project, www.gwu.edu/~erpapers/abouteleanor/erbiography.
54. *Eleanor Roosevelt, Volume One, 1884–1933,* 156.
55. *The First Ladies Fact Book,* 486–487.
56. *Eleanor Roosevelt, Volume One, 1884–1933,* 193.
57. Ibid., 195.
58. Ibid., 198.
59. Ibid., 196.
60. Ibid., 197.
61. Ibid., 206.
62. *First Ladies, A Biographical Dictionary,* 233.
63. *Eleanor Roosevelt, Volume One, 1884–1933,* 218; *Franklin & Lucy,* 99.
64. *Eleanor Roosevelt, Volume One, 1884–1933,* 219; *Franklin & Lucy,* 99.
65. Ibid., 219.
66. *Alice, The Life And Times Of Alice Roosevelt Longworth,* 238.
67. *First Ladies, An Intimate Group Portrait of White House Wives,* 57–58.
68. *Upstairs At The White House,* 22.
69. *The Autobiography of Eleanor Roosevelt,* 62.
70. *Eleanor Roosevelt, Volume One, 1884–1933,* 264.
71. Ibid., 274.
72. Ibid., 276.
73. Ibid., 278.
74. Ibid., 313.
75. Ibid., 314.
76. *The First Ladies Fact Book,* 493.
77. National Park Service, www.nps.gov/elro/index.htm.
78. *Leadership, The Eleanor Roosevelt Way,* 95.

79. *American First Ladies, Their Lives and Their Legacy*, 291.
80. *Eleanor Roosevelt, Volume One, 1884–1933*, 464.
81. Ibid., 436.
82. Ibid., 437.
83. Ibid., 420.
84. Ibid., 420.
85. Ibid., 423.
86. Ibid., 424.
87. *The Complete Book of U.S. Presidents*, 476.
88. *Eleanor Roosevelt, Volume One, 1884–1933*, 457.
89. Ibid., 456.
90. Ibid., 446.
91. Ibid., 451.
92. Ibid., 461.
93. Ibid., 471.
94. *First Ladies, A Biographical Dictionary*, 239.
95. *First Ladies, The Saga of the Presidents' Wives and Their Power 1789–1961*, 452.
96. *Eleanor Roosevelt: A Life of Discovery*, 95.
97. *American First Ladies: Their Lives and Their Legacy*, 293, *Eleanor Roosevelt: Reluctant First Lady*, 85.
98. *American First Ladies: Their Lives and Their Legacy*, 293.
99. *Eleanor Roosevelt, Volume One 1884–1933*, 472.
100. *Eleanor Roosevelt: Reluctant First Lady*, 83.
101. Ibid., 80.
102. Ibid., 81.
103. Ibid., 82–83.
104. *Eleanor Roosevelt, Volume One 1884–1933*, 491.
105. *American First Ladies, Their Lives and Their Legacy*, 294. *First Ladies, A Biographical Dictionary*, 241.
106. *Upstairs At The White House*, 17.
107. Ibid., 11.
108. *Eleanor Roosevelt, Volume One 1884–1933*, 180.
109. Ibid., 493.
110. *First Ladies, An Intimate Group Portrait Of White House Wives*, 60.
111. Ibid., 60.
112. National First Ladies Library website, www.firstladies.org.
113. *Upstairs At the White House*, 19.
114. *Eleanor Roosevelt: Reluctant First Lady*, 71.
115. Ibid., 107.
116. *No Ordinary Time*, 126.
117. Ibid., 127.
118. Ibid., 133; American Ladies, 233.
119. Ibid., 135.
120. *Four Freedoms*, http://en.wikipedia.org/wiki/Four_Freedoms.
121. *First Ladies, An Intimate Group Portrait Of White House Wives*, 62.
122. Ibid., 59.
123. www.nps.gov/valr/historyculture/people.htm.

Part Four: Women of World War II

Chapter 7: First Lady to the World: Eleanor Roosevelt

1. *Eleanor and Franklin*, 642–643.
2. Ibid., 643.
3. *Presidential Wives, An Anecdotal History*, 298.
4. Ibid., 297.
5. *American First Ladies*, 231.
6. Presidential Wives, An Anecdotal History, 297.
7. *First Ladies, A Biographical Dictionary*, 243.
8. *The First Ladies*, 228.
9. *Presidential Wives, An Anecdotal History*, 297.
10. *First Ladies, An Intimate Group Portrait of White House Wives*, 62; *The First Ladies*, 227.
11. *The First Ladies*, 228.
12. *Eleanor and Franklin*, 457.
13. Ibid., 654.
14. Ibid., 654.
15. Ibid., 457.
16. *Eleanor Roosevelt, Volume Two, 1933–1938*, 5.
17. *First Ladies, A Biographical Dictionary*, 243.
18. *This I Remember*, 349.
19. *Eleanor and Franklin*, 344.
20. Ibid., 345.
21. Ibid., 344.
22. *First Ladies, A Biographical Dictionary*, 244.
23. *Eleanor and Franklin*, 661.
24. Ibid., 668.
25. *Presidential Wives, An Anecdotal History*, 299.
26. *First Ladies, A Biographical Dictionary*, 244.
27. *Eleanor and Franklin*, 654.
28. *This I Remember*, 343; *Eleanor and Franklin*, 718.
29. *Presidential Wives, An Anecdotal History*, 300.
30. *Memoirs: Year of Decisions*, 5.
31. *Presidential Wives, An Anecdotal History*, 300.
32. www.eyewitnesstohistory.com/fdrdeath.htm.
33. *No Ordinary Time*, 612.
34. *This I Remember*, 345.
35. *No Ordinary Time*, 613.
36. Ibid., 618.
37. *Upstairs At The White House*, 26.
38. *This I Remember*, 349.
39. Ibid., 349.
40. *Presidential Wives, An Anecdotal History*, 306.
41. *This I Remember*, 349.
42. *American First Ladies*, 234; *Profiles & Portraits of American Presidents & Their Wives*, 351.
43. *No Ordinary Time*, 631.
44. *Eleanor and Franklin*, 664.
45. *The First Ladies Fact Book*, 497.
46. Ibid., 498.
47. Ibid., 498.
48. Ibid., 498.

49. *The First Ladies*, 234.
50. *First Ladies, A Biographical Dictionary*, 247.
51. www.brainyquote.com/quotes/authors/e/eleanor_roosevelt.html.
52. *No Ordinary Time*, 633.
53. http://en.wikipedia.org/wiki/Eleanor_Roosevelt#United_Nations.
54. *The First Ladies*, 225.
55. www.brainyquote.com/quotes/authors/s/sam_levenson_2.html.

Chapter 8: Independent Lady from Independence: Bess Truman

1. *Bess W. Truman*, 258; *First Ladies, A Biographical Dictionary*, 255.
2. *First Ladies, A Biographical Dictionary*, 251.
3. *Bess W. Truman*, 7.
4. Ibid., 10.
5. Ibid., 17.
6. Ibid., 44.
7. Ibid., 39.
8. Ibid., 56.
9. Ibid., 59–60.
10. Ibid., 60.
11. Ibid., 63.
12. Ibid., 72.
13. Ibid., 74.
14. Ibid., 81.
15. Ibid., 96.
16. Ibid., 97.
17. Ibid., 16.
18. Ibid., 152.
19. Ibid., 145–157.
20. Ibid., 168; *First Ladies, A Biographical Dictionary*, 254.
21. Ibid., 185.
22. Ibid., 159.
23. Ibid., 160.
24. Ibid., 179.
25. Ibid., 141.
26. *American First Ladies*, 239.
27. *American First Ladies*, 239.
28. *The First Ladies*, 237.
29. *Bess W. Truman*, 249.
30. Ibid., 251.
31. *American First Ladies*, 240.
32. Ibid., 256; *Bess W. Truman*, 276.
33. *Bess W. Truman*, 272.
34. *Upstairs At The White House*, 68.
35. Ibid., 70.
36. *Bess W. Truman*, 284.
37. Ibid., 265.
38. Ibid., 146.
39. Ibid., 271.
40. *American First Ladies*, 238.
41. *Bess W. Truman*, 278.
42. Ibid., 278.
43. *Upstairs At The White House*, 71.

44. Ibid., 70.
45. *Bess W. Truman*, 318.
46. *First Ladies: The Saga of the Presidents' Wives and Their Power 1789–1961, 529; Upstairs At The White House*, 71.
47. *Bess W. Truman*, 318.
48. Ibid., 338.
49. Ibid., 360.
50. Ibid., 360–361.
51. Ibid., 362.
52. Ibid., 345.
53. Ibid., 418.
54. *Truman, 989; Upstairs At The White House*, 118.
55. *Upstairs At The White House*, 111.
56. *The First Ladies Fact Book*, 513.
57. *Bess W. Truman*, 382.
58. Ibid., 381.
59. Ibid., 392.
60. Ibid., 396.
61. *Truman*, 1139.
62. *Bess W. Truman*, 427.
63. Ibid., 428.
64. Ibid., 497.

Chapter 9: First Lady—But Wife First: Mamie Eisenhower

1. *Mrs. Ike, Memories and Reflections on the Life of Mamie Eisenhower*, 45.
2. Ibid., 6.
3. Ibid.,18.
4. Ibid., 34; *The First Ladies Fact Book*, 522.
5. Ibid., 34.
6. *The First Ladies Fact Book*, 522.
7. *Mrs. Ike, Memories and Reflections on the Life of Mamie Eisenhower*, 7.
8. Ibid., 8.
9. Ibid., 40.
10. Ibid., 42.
11. Ibid., 47; *First Ladies, An Intimate Group Portrait of White House Wives*, 213.
12. *Mrs. Ike, Memories and Reflections on the Life of Mamie Eisenhower*, 64.
13. Ibid., 72.
14. Ibid., 76–77.
15. Ibid., 77.
16. Ibid., 83.
17. Ibid., 85.
18. *The First Ladies Fact Book*, 528.
19. *Mrs. Ike, Memories and Reflections on the Life of Mamie Eisenhower*, 98.
20. Ibid., 98.
21. Ibid., 130.
22. Ibid., 129.
23. Ibid., 151.
24. Ibid., 64.
25. Ibid., 150.
26. Ibid., 165.
27. Ibid., 163.
28. Ibid., 184.

29. Ibid., 186.
30. Ibid., 185–186.
31. Ibid., 198; *Eisenhower, A Soldier's Life, 419–420.*
32. Ibid., 189–194.
33. Ibid., 194.
34. Ibid., 202.
35. Ibid., 197.
36. Ibid., 199.
37. Ibid., 198–199.
38. Ibid., 206.
39. Ibid., 194.
40. Ibid., 207.
41. Ibid., 208.
42. Ibid., 209.
43. Ibid., 208.
44. Ibid., 206.
45. *First Ladies, The Saga of the Presidents' Wives and Their Power 1789–1961*, 543.
46. Ibid., 233.
47. Ibid., 256.
48. Ibid., 259.
49. Ibid., 265.
50. Ibid., 268.
51. Ibid., 270.
52. Ibid., 271.
53. Ibid., 253.
54. Ibid., 170.
55. Ibid., 280.
56. Ibid., 280.
57. *Times of My Life*, 56.
58. *Upstairs At The White House*, 135.
59. *Mrs. Ike, Memories and Reflections on the Life of Mamie Eisenhower*, 280.
60. Ibid., 291.
61. Ibid., 297.
62. Ibid., 251.
63. Ibid., 312.
64. Ibid., 314.
65. Ibid., 314; *The First Ladies Fact Book*, 537.
66. *Mrs. Ike, Memories and Reflections on the Life of Mamie Eisenhower*, 322.
67 Ibid., 332.
68. Ibid., 332.

Part Five: Woman of Distinction

Introduction

1. *The First Ladies Fact Book*, 566.
2. *Remembering Jackie*, 114.
3. www.famous-women-and-beauty.com/jackie-kennedy-quotes.html.
4. *Remembering Jackie*, 124.

Chapter 10: Tragic Sophistication: Jackie Kennedy

1. *First Ladies, An intimate Group Portrait of White House Wives*, 31.
2. Ibid., 38; *Presidential Wives, An Anecdotal History*, 364.
3. *The Eloquent Jacqueline Kennedy Onassis*, 7; *Jacqueline Bouvier Kennedy*, 14–16.
4. *Presidential Wives, An Anecdotal History*, 364.
5. *First Ladies, An Intimate Group Portrait of White House Wives*, 38.
6. *The First Ladies*, 257.
7. *First Ladies Quotations Book*, 5; *The Eloquent Jacqueline Kennedy Onassis*, 5.
8. *Presidential Wives, An Anecdotal History*, 354.
9. *America's Queen*, 19.
10. John F. Kennedy Library website; *The Eloquent Jacqueline Kennedy Onassis*, 8.
11. Ibid., 19.
12. *America's Queen*, 20.
13. *The Eloquent Jacqueline Kennedy Onassis*, 9; *Presidential Wives, An Anecdotal History*, 371.
14. *The First Ladies Fact Book*, 543; *Presidential Wives, An Anecdotal History*, 60.
15. *The Eloquent Jacqueline Kennedy Onassis*, 18.
16. *The First Ladies Fact Book*, 543.
17. *The Eloquent Jacqueline Kennedy Onassis*, 10; *First Ladies Quotations Book*, 122.
18. *American First Ladies*, 251; *Presidential Wives, An Anecdotal History*, 355.
19. *Jacqueline Bouvier Kennedy, 81; The Eloquent Jacqueline Kennedy Onassis*, 13, 15.
20. Ibid., 17.
21. Ibid., 13.
22. *One Special Summer*, Introduction, no page number.
23. *The Eloquent Jacqueline Kennedy Onassis*, 30.
24. Larry King Live, CNN, September 23, 2003.
25. *The Eloquent Jacqueline Kennedy Onassis*, 25.
26. *The First Ladies Fact Book*, 547; *Jacqueline Bouvier Kennedy*, 95.
27. *Presidential Wives, An Anecdotal History*, 358.
28. *The Eloquent Jacqueline Kennedy Onassis*, 42.
29. *Jacqueline Bouvier Kennedy*, 95.
30. Ibid., 95; *Presidential Wives*, 358.
31. *The Eloquent Jacqueline Kennedy Onassis*, 29.
32. John F. Kennedy Library website.
33. *New York Times*, September 15, 1960.
34. *The First Ladies Fact Book*, 550.
35. *First Ladies, An Intimate Group Portrait of White House Wives*, 38.
36. *The Eloquent Jacqueline Kennedy Onassis*, 51.
37. Ibid., 47.
38. Ibid., 35–36.
39. Ibid., 35.
40. Ibid., 53.
41. *The First Ladies Fact Book*, 553.
42. Ibid., 553.
43. Ibid., 554.
44. *Rose, A Biography of Rose Fitzgerald Kennedy*, 214.
45. *America's First Families*, 122.
46. Ibid., 122.
47. Larry King Live, September 23, 2003.
48. *Life in Camelot*, 30.
49. *The Eloquent Jacqueline Kennedy Onassis*, 60.
50. Ibid., 59.

51. Ibid., 60–61.
52. Ibid., 60–70.
53. *Time,* Jan. 20, 1961.
54. *Presidential Wives, An Anecdotal History,* 361; *A Hero For Our Time, An Intimate Story of the Kennedy Years,* 144.
55. *The Eloquent Jacqueline Kennedy Onassis,* 50; *Kaybam International,* May 25, 1972.
56. *Presidential Wives, An Anecdotal History,* 359.
57. Ibid., 362; *The Eloquent Jacqueline Kennedy Onassis,* 81.
58. *First Ladies, An Intimate Group Portrait of White House Wives,* 31.
59. The National First Ladies Library website, timeline.
60. *The Eloquent Jacqueline Kennedy Onassis,* 81.
61. *Presidential Wives, An Anecdotal History,* 359; *The First Ladies Fact Book,* 554.
62. *Presidential Wives, An Anecdotal History,* 353; *The Eloquent Jacqueline Kennedy Onassis,* 3; *The First Ladies Fact Book,* 555; *First Ladies Quotations Book,* 211.
63. *The Eloquent Jacqueline Kennedy Onassis,* 83.
64. *The Eloquent Jacqueline Kennedy Onassis,* 107; *First Ladies, A Biographical Dictionary,* 274; *The First Ladies Fact Book,* 556.
65. *Upstairs At The White House,* 225.
66. *First Ladies, An Intimate Group Portrait of White House Wives,* 33; *The Eloquent Jacqueline Kennedy Onassis,* 101; *The First Ladies Fact Book,* 556.
67. *America's First Ladies, Private Lives of the Presidential Wives,* 212.
68. *The Eloquent Jacqueline Kennedy Onassis,* 87.
69. *American First Ladies, 256; First Ladies, An Intimate Group Portrait of White House Wives,* 39; *A Hero For Our Time, An Intimate Story of the Kennedy Years,* 293.
70. *Presidential Wives, An Anecdotal History,* 365.
71. *First Ladies, An Intimate Group Portrait of White House Wives,* 39.
72. *America's First Families,* 124.
73. *America's First Ladies, Private Lives of the Presidential Wives,* 208; *The Eloquent Jacqueline Kennedy Onassis,* 113.
74. *Upstairs At The White House,* 248.
75. Ibid., 225.
76. Ibid., 239–240.
77. Ibid., 230.
78. Ibid., 232.
79. Ibid., 226–232.
80. *Presidential Wives, An Anecdotal History,* 363; *Jacqueline Kennedy, A Biography,* 230.
81. *America's First Ladies, Private Lives of the Presidential Wives,* 211; *Turbulent Years, The 60s, Our American Century,* 51.
82. *The Eloquent Jacqueline Kennedy Onassis,* 114.
83. *America's First Ladies, Private Lives of the Presidential Wives,* 209.
84. *Presidential Wives, An Anecdotal History,* 365; *First Ladies, An Intimate Group Portrait of White House Wives,* 38.
85. *Profiles & Portraits of American Presidents & Their Wives,* 397; *My Life with Jacqueline Kennedy,* 177; *Presidential Wives, An Anecdotal History,* 367.
86. *First Ladies, An Intimate Group Portrait of White House Wives,* 33.
87. *The Eloquent Jacqueline Kennedy Onassis,* 37; *Presidential Wives, An Anecdotal History,* 372.
88. *Upstairs At The White House,* 271–274.
89. Ibid., 276.
90. *Presidential Wives, An Anecdotal History,* 363.
91. *American First Ladies,* 253.
92. *The Eloquent Jacqueline Kennedy Onassis,* 40, 91.

93. Ibid., 104.
94. *Presidential Wives, An Anecdotal History*, 366.
95. *First Ladies, An Intimate Group Portrait of White House Wives*, 41.
96. *Presidential Wives, An Anecdotal History*, 365; *Pat Nixon, The Untold Story*, 189.
97. *Presidential Wives, An Anecdotal History*, 372.
98. *First Ladies, An Intimate Group Portrait of White House Wives*, 42.
99. Ibid., 43.
100. Various websites.
101. *First Ladies, An Intimate Group Portrait of White House Wives*, 43.
102. *The Torch is Passed*, 15.
103. Ibid., 13–15.
104. *A White House Diary*, 4–6.
105. Ibid., 6; *American First Ladies*, 257.
106. *Upstairs At The White House*, 312–313.
107. *The Torch is Passed*, 92–96.
108. *The Eloquent Jacqueline Kennedy Onassis*, 4.
109. *First Ladies Quotations Book*, 260.
110. Ibid., 250.
111. *Upstairs At The White House*, 321.
112. Ibid., 321.
113. Ibid., 319.
114. *Hidden Power*, 107–108.
115. Ibid., 104.
116. *Look* magazine, Nov. 1964; *First Ladies Quotations Book*, 139; *Presidential Wives, An Anecdotal History*, 368.
117. *The Eloquent Jacqueline Kennedy Onassis*, 165–166.
118. *The First Ladies Fact Book*, 562.
119. *The Eloquent Jacqueline Kennedy Onassis*, 171.
120. Ibid., 171.
121. Ibid., 171.
122. *Jackie, Her Life in Pictures*, 109.
123. Ibid., 111; *The Eloquent Jacqueline Kennedy Onassis*, 177.
124. *The Eloquent Jacqueline Kennedy Onassis*, 196; *A Woman Named Jackie*, 498.
125. Ibid., 48; *Times to Remember*, 484.
126. *The Eloquent Jacqueline Kennedy Onassis*, 197; *Jackie, Her Life in Pictures*, 116; *A Woman Named Jackie*, 496.
127. *A Woman Named Jackie*, 497; *First Ladies Quotations Book*, 370.
128. *The Eloquent Jacqueline Kennedy Onassis*, 197.
129. *A Woman Named Jackie*, 526.
130. *The First Ladies Fact Book*, 564.
131. *The First Ladies Fact Book*, 565; *A Woman Named Jackie*, 560.
132. *The Eloquent Jacqueline Kennedy Onassis*, 203; *Jackie, Her Life in Pictures*, 133; *Presidential Wives, An Anecdotal History*, 370.
133. *A Woman Named Jackie*, 602.
134. *The Eloquent Jacqueline Kennedy Onassis*, 205.
135. *A Woman Named Jackie*, 579.
136. *The Eloquent Jacqueline Kennedy Onassis*, 160.
137. *A Woman Named Jackie*, 600.
138. *The Eloquent Jacqueline Kennedy Onassis*, 6.
139. Ibid., 210.
140. *Presidential Wives, An Anecdotal History*, 370.

141. *The Eloquent Jacqueline Kennedy Onassis*, 236.
142. Ibid., 232–233.
143. *Jackie, Her Life in Pictures*, 157.
144. *The Eloquent Jacqueline Kennedy Onassis*, 240.
145. *Jackie, Her Life in Pictures*, 153.
146. *The Eloquent Jacqueline Kennedy Onassis*, 139.
147. Ibid., 235.
148. Ibid., 233–234.
149. *Farewell, Jackie, A Portrait of her Final Days*, 117.
150. Ibid., 87.
151. Ibid., 170.
152. Ibid., 167.
153. Ibid., 179.
154. *Jackie, Her Life in Pictures*, 169.
155. Wikipedia Internet encyclopedia, Maurice Tempelsman. http://en.wikipedia.org/wiki/Maurice_Tempelsman.
156. *The Estate of Jacqueline Kennedy Onassis*, home page.
157. *First Ladies Quotations Book*, 19.
158. *The Eloquent Jacqueline Kennedy Onassis*, 164.
159. *What Jackie Taught Us*, back cover.

Bibliography

Adler, Bill. *The Eloquent Jacqueline Kennedy Onassis*. New York: Harper Collins Publishers, 2004.

———. *First Mom: The Wit and Wisdom of Barbara Bush*. New York: Rugged Land LLC, 2004.

Adams, Cindy, and Crimp, Susan. *Iron Rose: A Biography of Rose Fitzgerald Kennedy*. New York: NewStar Media, Inc., 1995.

Adams, Samuel. *Incredible Era: The Life and Times of Warren Gamaliel Harding*. New York: Octagon Books, 1979.

Anthony, Carl Sferrazza. *Florence Harding: The First Lady, The Jazz Age, and The Death of America's Most Scandalous President*. New York: William Morrow, 1998.

———. *First Ladies: The Saga of the Presidential Wives and Their Power, 1789–1961*. New York: William Morrow, 1990.

———. *First Ladies: The Saga of the Presidential Wives and Their Power, 1961–1990*. New York: William Morrow, 1991.

———. *America's First Families: An Inside View of 200 Years of Private Life in the White House*. New York: Touchstone Books, 2000.

Bassett, Margaret. *Profiles and Portraits of American Presidents & Their Wives*. New York: Grosset & Dunlap, 1969.

Berger, Jacqueline. *Loves, Lies, and Tears: An Intimate Look at America's First Ladies, Volume I, Martha Washington to Helen Taft, 1789–1913*. Thousand Oaks, CA: Roserita Books, Inc., 2008.

Black, Allida M. *Casting Her Own Shadow: Eleanor Roosevelt and the Shaping of Postwar Liberalism*. New York: Columbia University Press, 1996.

Boller, Paul F. Jr. *Presidential Wives: An Anecdotal History*. New York: Oxford University Press, 1988.

Bradford, Sarah. *America's Queen: The Life of Jacqueline Kennedy Onassis*. New York: Penguin Books, 2000.

Bouvier, Lee. *One Special Summer*. New York: Delacorte Press, 1974.

Caroli, Betty Boyd. *The First Ladies: Martha Washington to Laura Bush*. New York: Oxford University Press, 1987.

———. *America's First Ladies.* New York: Abbeville Press, 1992.

Cook, Blanche Wisen. *Eleanor Roosevelt, Volume 1: 1884–1933.* New York: Penguin Books, 1993.

———. *Eleanor Roosevelt, Volume 2: 1933–1938.* New York: Penguin Books, 1999.

Coolidge, Calvin. *The Autobiography of Calvin Coolidge.* New York: Cosmopolitan Books, 1929.

David, Lester and Irene. *Ike & Mamie: The Story of The General and His Lady.* New York: G. P. Putnam's Sons, 1981.

D'Este, Carlo. *Eisenhower: A Soldier's Life.* New York: Henry Holt & Company, 2002.

DeGregorio, William A. *The Complete Book of U.S. Presidents.* New York: Gramercy Books, 2001.

Eisenhower, Julie Nixon. *Pat Nixon: The Untold Story.* New York: Simon & Schuster, 1986.

Eisenhower, Susan. *Mrs. Ike: Memories and Reflections on the Life of Mamie Eisenhower.* New York: Farrar, Straus & Giroux, 1996.

Fields, Alonzo. *My 21 Years at the White House.* New York: Coward-McCann Inc., 1961.

Ford, Betty. *The Times of My Life.* New York: Harper & Row, 1978.

Foss, William O. *First Ladies Quotations Book.* New York: Barricade Books, Inc., 1999.

Fuess, Charles M. *Calvin Coolidge—The Man from Vermont.* Boston: Little, Brown, and Company, 1939.

Gaton, Leo. *The President Speaks.* Indiana: Airleaf, 2004.

Goodwin, Doris Kearns. *No Ordinary Time.* New York: Simon & Schuster, 1994.

Gould, Lewis J. *American First Ladies: Their Lives and Their Legacy.* New York: Garland, 1996.

Harris, Bill. *The First Ladies Fact Book: The Stories of the Women of the White House from Martha Washington to Laura Bush.* New York: Black Dog and Leventhal Publishers, 2005.

Healy, Diana D. *America's First Ladies: Private Lives of the Presidential Wives.* New York: Macmillan Publishing Company, 1988.

Heymann, C. David. *A Woman Named Jackie.* New York: Carol Communications, 1989.

Hickock, Lorena A. *Eleanor Roosevelt: Reluctant First Lady.* New York: Dodd Mead, 1962.

Hoover, Irwin. *Forty-two Years in the White House.* New York: Houghton Mifflin Company, 1934.

Johnson, Lady Bird. *A White House Diary.* New York, Holt, Rinehart and Winston, 1970.

Klapthor, Margaret B. *The First Ladies.* Washington: White House Historical Association, 1995.

Kane, Joseph N. *Presidential Fact Book.* New York: Random House, 6th Ed., 1998.

Kunhardt, Philip. *Life in Camelot: The Kennedy Years.* Boston: Little, Brown, & Company, 1988.

Lash, John P. *Eleanor and Franklin: The Story of Their Relationship, based on Eleanor Roosevelt's Private Papers.* New York: W. W. Norton & Company, 1971.

Longworth, Alice Roosevelt. *Crowded Hours.* New York: Charles Scribner's Sons, 1933.

MacNeil, Robert. *The Way We Were: 1963, The Year Kennedy Was Shot.* New York: Carroll & Graf Publishers Inc., 1988.

Martin, Ralph G. *A Hero For Our Time: An Intimate Story of the Kennedy Years.* New York: Fawcett Crest, 1983.

Marton, Kati. *Hidden Power: Presidential Marriages That Shaped Our History.* New York: Random House, 2001.

Matuz, Roger. *The Presidents Fact Book: A Comprehensive Handbook to the Achievements, Events, People, Triumphs, and Tragedies of Every President from George Washington to George W. Bush.* New York: Black Dog & Leventhal, 2004.

McCullough, David. *Truman.* New York: Simon & Schuster, 1992.

Persico, Joseph E. *Franklin & Lucy: President Roosevelt, Mrs. Rutherfurd, and the Other Remarkable Women in His Life.* New York: Random House, 2008.

Pottker, Jan. *Janet and Jackie.* New York: St. Martin's Press, 2001.

Roosevelt, Eleanor. *This I Remember.* New York: Harper & Brothers, 1949.

———. *This Is My Story.* New York: Harper & Brothers, 1949.

Roosevelt, Elliott, and Brough, James. *Mother R.: Eleanor Roosevelt's Untold Story.* New York: G. P. Putnam's Sons. 1977.

Ross, Ishbel. *Grace Coolidge and Her Era: The Story of a President's Wife.* New York: Dodd, Mead, and Company, 1962.

Sadler, Christine. *America's First Ladies.* New York: MacFadden, 1963.

Schlesinger, Jr., Arthur M., and Sobel, David. *A Thousand Days: John F. Kennedy in the White House.* New York: Black Dog & Leventhal, 1965.

Schneider, Dorothy and Carl J. *First Ladies: A Biographical Dictionary.* New York: Checkmark Books, 2001.

Spada, James. *Jackie: Her Life in Pictures.* New York: St. Martin's Press, 2000.

Teichmann, Howard. *Alice: The Life and Times of Alice Roosevelt Longworth.* New Jeresy: Prentice-Hall Inc., 1979.

Truman, Harry S. *1945: Year of Decisions: Memoirs, Volume I.* New York: Signet Books, 1955.

Truman, Margaret. *Bess W. Truman.* New York: Random House Inc., 1995.

———. *First Ladies: An Intimate Group Portrait of White House Wives.* New York: Macmillan Publishing Company, 1986.

Stolley, Richard B. *Our American Century: Turbulent Years, The 60s.* Virginia: Time-Life Books, 1998.

Van Rensselaer Thayer, Mary. *Jacqueline Bouvier Kennedy.* New York: Doubleday & Company, Inc., 1961.

Watson, Robert P. *American First Ladies.* Pasadena: Salem Press, Inc., 2002.

West, J. B. *Upstairs at the White House: My Life with the First Ladies.* New York: Coward, McCann & Geoghegan, 1973.

Wetherington, Roy. *The Wit & Wisdom of Our American Presidents.* Lombard, IL: Successories Publishing, 1994.

Wilson, Edith. *My Memoir.* New York: The Bobbs-Merrill Company, 1939.

Index

G

H

I

J

Y

Z